Monograph 47

T0126246

ARCHAEOLOGY IN THE BORDERLANDS

INVESTIGATIONS IN CAUCASIA AND BEYOND

EDITED BY

ADAM T. SMITH & KAREN S. RUBINSON

COTSEN INSTITUTE OF ARCHAEOLOGY
UNIVERSITY OF CALIFORNIA, LOS ANGELES
2003

EDITORIAL BOARD OF THE COTSEN INSTITUTE OF ARCHAEOLOGY AT UCLA
Jeanne E. Arnold, Marilyn Beaudry-Corbett, Ernestine S. Elster, Lothar von Falkenhausen, Richard M. Leventhal, Julia L. J. Sanchez, and Charles Stanish

THE COTSEN INSTITUTE OF ARCHAEOLOGY AT UCLA
    Charles Stanish, Director
    Julia L. J. Sanchez, Assistant Director, Director of Publications

Edited by Kathy Talley-Jones
Designed by William Morosi

Library of Congress Cataloging-in-Publication Data

    Archaeology in the borderlands: investigations in Caucasia and beyond/
    edited by Adam T. Smith, Karen S. Rubinson.
    p. cm. – (Monograph series ; 47)
    Includes bibliographical references and index.
    ISBN 1-931745-01-3
    1. Caucasus—Antiquities. 2. Excavations (Archaeology)—Caucasus.
    3. Bronze age—Caucasus. I. Smith, Adam T. II. Rubinson, Karen Sydney, 1943-
    III. Monograph (Cotsen Institute of Archaeology at UCLA) ; 47.

    DK509 .A693 2003 947.5—dc21
    2002012655

Copyright © 2003 Regents of the University of California
All rights reserved. Printed in the USA.

CONTENTS

Acknowledgments

We thank the American Anthropological Association and the Archaeological Institute of America for their sponsorship of the scholarly conference symposia that formed the basis of this volume. We also want to thank the discussants for those symposia, Fredrik T. Hiebert at the AAA and David Stronach and Christopher Edens at the AIA, whose cogent comments helped shape the revised papers and the editors' perspective. Additional useful insights were provided by the anonymous reviewers of the original manuscript submitted to the Cotsen Institute of Archaeology at UCLA. We are grateful also to Brian Horne for assistance in tracking down incomplete references in highly obscure places and to the Samuel H. Kress Foundation for its support of overseas participants at the AIA symposium.

INTRODUCTION

Archaeology in the Borderlands

KAREN S. RUBINSON & ADAM T. SMITH

Detailing their observations for King Louis XIV, two eighteenth-century travelers independently recorded impressions of contemporary Caucasia, that region nestled between the Black and Caspian Seas.[1] Their views could not have been more strikingly different:

> Everything there is ruined, deserted, or uncivilized. Every one there breathes only of tyranny and slavery in the civil state, and self-interest, superstition and ignorance in religion (Lucas 1714: 246).

> Our learned men may judge as they please; but as I have never seen a more beautiful Country than the neighborhood of Three-Churches [Echmiadzin], I am strongly persuaded that Adam and Eve were created there (de Tournefort and Bartlett 1717: II, 325).

A crossing place of continents and a hostile, impenetrable country, Edenic paradise and postlapsarian wasteland, Caucasia and the highlands of eastern Anatolia (its inseparable neighbor), have historically been rendered in conflicting terms as observers have noted contrasting elements of a complex landscape.

One particularly enduring geographical trope describes the region as a borderland separating, and threatening, competing Great Powers:

> The summit of Little Ararat is the meeting point of the Russian, Persian, and Turkish empires, and everyone knows that borderlands have been from time immemorial the haunts of dangerous and turbulent characters.... (Bryce 1896: 204).

Bryce's description highlights the creation of Caucasia as a borderland on the margins of the geopolitical forces of Europe and southwest Asia. For Bryce, the term referred not simply to geographic position but to a larger set of cultural associations that reflected a failure of the region to stabilize under the hegemony of a single national power—a failure that his imperial arrogance allowed him to read as a substantive reflection of local character.

Given the rather brutish genealogy of the term *borderland* as it has been applied to Caucasia and eastern

Anatolia, it is perhaps surprising that we reiterate it here in the title to a collection of essays on the contemporary archaeology of the region in what might fairly be termed an emergent postcolonial era. We employ the term *borderlands* in our title for two primary reasons. The first is steadfastly ironic in that the following studies highlight the problematic understanding implicit in a geography that has placed Caucasia and eastern Anatolia at the margins of an archaeological world centered in competing ancient Great Powers (Assyria, Babylonia, the Hittite Empire, Persia, Greece) and other powerful political and cultural forces (such as the Scythians and Cimmerians). It is not coincidental that the "great power" focus of traditional archaeological scholarship in southwest Asia, dependent as it is upon the blank margins for lending coherence to the centers, is exceedingly faithful in recreating Bryce's vision. In this sense, scholars have recreated the cartography of ancient southwest Asia in a familiar image with a handful of fully coherent hegemonic polities separated by turbulent (that is, underexplored and unexplained) borderlands. For example, during the fourth and third millennia BC, the Kura-Araxes (or Early Transcaucasian) ceramic horizon, which centered in the "borderlands," extended southwest as far as the Euphrates headwaters (and arguably into the northern Levant where it manifested in the Khirbet-Kerak tradition), southeast to the central Zagros (Godin Tepe), and north to the intersection of the Caucasus and Eurasian steppe. The Kura-Araxes was by far the most geographically dispersed horizon style in pre-Achaemenid southwest Asia. Yet the region's perceived peripheral status to Mesopotamia continues to condition the production of general historical theory in the region (for example, World Systems theory). This same perspective is reflected in the very literature in which curious scholars with access across these many political boundaries in the twentieth century made some of this information widely available. Among these works are the exhaustive compilation of Schaeffer (1948), the most recent comprehensive review in a western language of the archaeological history of the area, where one author characterizes himself as a "student of the ancient Near East" (Burney and Lang 1972: 1), and dedicated efforts to collate and translate important field data (Alekseev et al. 1968: x). As Henry Field wrote in his introduction to the Alekseev volume:

> Transcaucasia has long been of especial interest because of racial and cultural contacts with Southwestern Asia. Up to now little has been published in Western sources

regarding the archaeology of Soviet Armenia. Hence this [volume] should prove of great reference and comparative value (Alekseev et al. 1968).

The second sense in which we employ our titular term is more productive and anthropological. Within anthropology, the term *borderlands* has been used to critique the rigid mosaic of cultural geographies, defined in the shadow of Durkheim, that had long dominated the field:

> Our historical understanding of culture...has mostly made us see the world as a cultural mosaic, of separate pieces with hard, well-defined edges....There is, moreover, a strong sense of place. Cultures are understood to be territorial; they belong to nations, regions, or localities (Hannerz 1989: 201).

The term *borderlands* is employed in this sense as a critique of the assumed homogeneity of cultural spaces. In this sense, we employ the term as a corrective for the ingrained geographies of the east Anatolian and southern Caucasian highlands within which anthropologists and archaeologists traditionally work. That is, by examining areas such as Caucasia, by noting the dynamism that follows from sustained and profound cultural flows, we come to realize that no place is the homogenous "center" that we once believed. In this sense, Mesopotamia, Persia, and the other centers of southwest Asian ancient history are also borderlands, cosmopolitan locales of complex interactions amongst variously empowered cultural groups. Thus the general anthropological point of this collection of studies of the borderlands of Caucasia and eastern Anatolia is not to centralize the region and thus redraw a new take on old mosaics. Rather, these studies highlight the heterogeneous forces of cultural production that simultaneously marginalize centers and centralize margins in various archaeological places. The changing picture through time in this one geographical area clearly demonstrates such shifts.

THE GEOGRAPHY OF THE BORDERLANDS

The borderlands of Caucasia and highland eastern Anatolia cover approximately 425,000 km² (an area comparable to the modern nation of Iraq [434,000 km²]) extending across six nations—Armenia, Azerbaijan, Georgia, Iran, Russia, and Turkey. Caucasia is ecologically diverse, ranging from the subtropical Colchidian depression in the west to the high

The Borderlands:
Caucasia and Its Surroundings

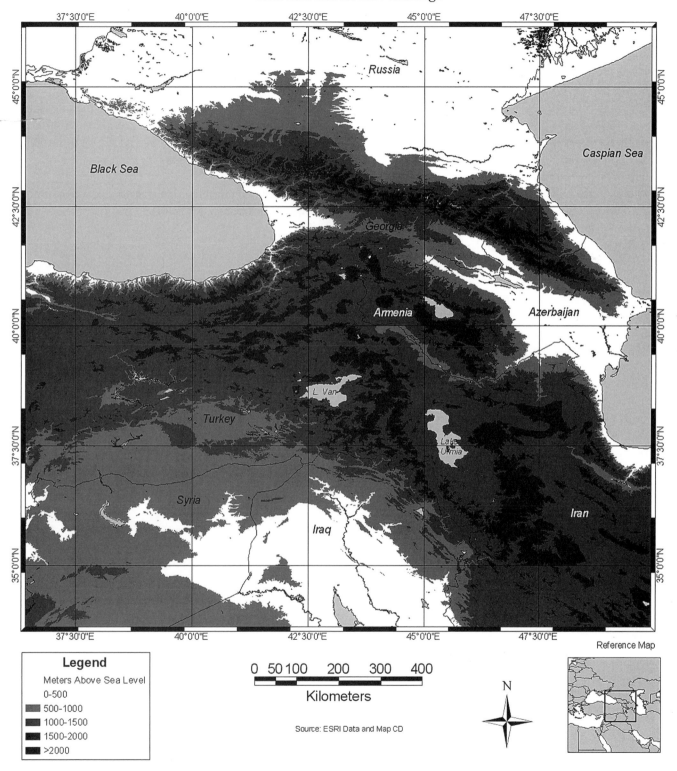

Reference Map

Legend

Meters Above Sea Level

0-500
500-1000
1000-1500
1500-2000
>2000

0 50 100 200 300 400

Kilometers

Source: ESRI Data and Map CD

N

mountains in the south to the arid steppes in the east. Climate is similarly variable, with average annual rainfall varying from around 2500 mm on the Black Sea coast near the modern city of Batumi to less than 200 mm on the Apsheron Peninsula of eastern Azerbaijan (Berg 1950; Cole and German 1961; Glumac and Anthony 1992; Plashchev and Chekmarev 1978). The period of heaviest precipitation is between March and mid-May and, while summers tend to be dry, heavy snows can fall during the winter.

Caucasia, also referred to as Transcaucasia, generally describes the isthmus set between the Caspian and Black Seas. In general, we use the term *Caucasia* here, as opposed to Transcaucasia, as the latter tends to emphasize a Russo-centric view of the region (the region is "across the Caucasus" only from a northern perspective). Eastern Anatolia is a less precise term that designates the highland regions east of the Euphrates and north of the Mesopotamian foothills. But the eastern extent of Anatolia is less clear. For the sake of simplicity, we will include the highlands of northwest Iran and the Urmia basin under the term *eastern Anatolia* as there is no compelling geographic feature that separates the two regions.

The borderlands are characterized by dramatic variability in elevation, ranging from Mt. Elbrus, the highest point in Europe (5633 m) to the sea-level lowlands of the Mughan steppe and the Caspian littoral. This variability contributes to an unusually diversified physical landscape and varied climatic regimes. It is generally customary to divide the Caucasus into seven geographic provinces based on elevation, hydrography, and climate (see Grossgeym 1948; Gvozdeskyi 1954); however, archaeologically it is more traditional to focus on five major areas to which we will add an additional four in eastern Anatolia. Southern Caucasia is most readily defined as the Middle Araxes River and its drainages—a region of rugged upland mountains and high plateaus. Average elevation is between 1200 and 1800 m above sea level dipping below 1000 m only in the Ararat plain. In contrast, the highlands of northern Caucasia are defined by the Upper and Middle Kura River and its drainages. Western Caucasia (the Colchidian depression, drained by the westward flowing Rioni and Inguri Rivers) and eastern Caucasia (the steppes of Azerbaijan, crossed by the lower Araxes and Kura as they flow to the Caspian) are both low-lying areas: while the former is dominated by a subtropical climate, the latter is typified by a drier continental regime. North Caucasia is dominated by the Great Caucasus range, with peaks that climb over 5000 m, which traverses over 1100 km from the Black Sea to the Caspian Sea along the northern end of the Caucasian isthmus.

To these Caucasian provinces we might add four more in eastern Anatolia (which subsumes northwestern Iran). The Çoroh River drainage links the interior of the Pontic range to the Black Sea and constitutes an archaeologically distinct province. The Tigris-Euphrates headwaters constitute a second major east Anatolian province, one that links the highlands to the lower lying regions of northern Syria. Lastly, the Lake Van and Lake Urmia drainages constitute two final distinct geographic provinces within the borderlands.

The region continues to be shaped by the tectonic action of the Arabian and Eurasian plates, a collision that has thrown up the Caucasus, folding the underlying bedrock and creating high volcanic peaks. The volcanic activity that raised Mt. Ararat and Mt. Aragats, to name only two, covered Caucasia and eastern Anatolia with a sea of lava, leaving behind vast deposits of basalt, tuff, and obsidian. The devastating December 1988 earthquake centered near Spitak in north central Armenia underscores the fact that Caucasia remains a land in formation.

The rivers of the highlands, with a few important exceptions, are located at the bottom of steep gorges for much of their flow. The Araxes is poetically described in Virgil's *Aeneid* as "the river that will not suffer bridges." Beyond the highlands, in the low-lying areas of western and eastern Caucasia, the lower Kura and Araxes Rivers flow through a virtually flat valley that is partly below sea level.

In addition to sharing geographic contiguity and a similar terrain, Caucasia and the highlands of eastern Anatolia share a similar climate. Ancient accounts of the highlands repeatedly emphasized the severity of the winter weather:

> ...while they were spending the night here [at the royal city of the Armenian satrap] there was a tremendous fall of snow, so much that it covered over both the arms and the men lying on the ground (Xenophon 1972: 193).

> Contrary to expectations, winter weather came on as early as the autumnal equinox, with storms and frequent snows, and, even in the most clear days, hoar frost and ice, which made the waters scarcely passable through the ice-breaking and cutting the horse sinews... (Plutarch 1914: XXXII).

While the ancients undoubtedly indulge in some hyperbole, the area's climate can be bitterly cold in winter, yet still reach over 40° C in some places during summer.

Regretfully, little systematic environmental reconstruction has yet been attempted for the borderlands, and a clear picture of the ancient climate remains to be developed. It has often been suggested that the shift at the end of the Early Bronze Age in northern Caucasia from large settled sites of the Kura-Araxes to cultures such as the Trialeti Culture where settlements are ephemeral reflects a period of aridity or other climatic change (Areshian 1990; Kushnareva 1997:208). Possible indirect evidence for such aridity is that Middle Bronze Age burials from Lchashen were revealed as the level of Lake Sevan was lowered some 13 to 14 m in 1956 in the course of a hydroelectric project (Khanzadian 1962; Piggott 1968:278). Whether varve data from Lake Van can be used to shed light on this question is problematic (Bryson and Bryson 1999:2), but there are indications of a significant drop in precipitation and increasing aridity in the region of Kars in Turkey in the mid to late third millennium BC (Bryson and Bryson 1999: 6 and Fig. 5).

Rivers and mountain ranges constrain much of the travel into, out of, and between adjacent provinces of the borderlands. While the topography of the region certainly limits the routes available for regular travel, it does not cut off communication. Indeed, by forcing travelers into a few pathways, the topography may encourage greater communication than a broad open plain. It is a prominent fallacy in the archaeological literature that limited routes of communication conspire to isolate a region culturally or economically; even landscapes without dramatic relief to impede movement tend to develop and maintain only a handful of well-traveled pathways (for example, caravan routes into Mesopotamia from the west). We must also distinguish between long-distance movements and local travel. Discussions with local villagers on the slopes of Mt. Aragats, for example, revealed that shepherds and their flocks travel great distances across the mountain landscape with little difficulty.

There are few passes through the Greater Caucasus mountains from the north into Caucasia. The three principal ones were, in Soviet times, the routes of the main military highways: the Klukhorskii pass on the Sukhumi military highway (Cherkessk-Sukhumi); the Mamisonskii pass on the Ossetian military highway (Beslan-Kutaisi); and the Krestovyi (Dar'yal) pass on the Georgian military highway (Ordahonikidze now Valdikavkaz-Tbilisi). This latter road was for centuries the only road through the Caucasus (Field 1953: 18) and was not passable all year round (Field 1953:19, citing Reclus; Haxthausen 1854: 12; Martel ND.: 14–15). Three other north-south passes are less accessible and remained unpaved well into the twentieth century: the Marukhskii pass between Karachaevo-Cherkesskaya and the region of Abkahzia, the Donguz-Orun pass between Kabardion-Balkarskaya and Georgia, and the Koborskii pass between Dagestan and Georgia. Of course the easiest way through the Caucasus range was to simply bypass the mountains to either the east, along the flat Caspian littoral that the fortifications of Derbent were constructed to defend, or to the west, along the scenic Black Sea coastline. Indeed, maritime traffic across the Black and Caspian Seas was likely one important route into, out of, and across the borderlands, although the intensity of this traffic has yet to be thoroughly studied.

Routes into the borderlands from the west and south, from central Anatolia and northern Mesopotamia, generally follow the major river courses: along the Euphrates and Araxes headwaters to the Kars plateau and Ararat plain, up the Tigris and Murat Rivers into the highlands west of Lake Van, or the somewhat more difficult route up the Great Zab from northern Mesopotamia into the mountains dividing the Van and Urmia basins. In 844 BC the Assyrian King Shalmaneser led an expeditionary force "against Nairi" up the Tigris, memorialized in an inscription on the stone at source of the river (Barnett 1982: 356). In the case of Sargon's eighth campaign, Assyrian forces moved against Urartu by entering the borderlands from the south of Lake Urmia via routes in the vicinity of Kirkuk and Sulamaniyah and returning to Assyria via the Great Zab.[2] From the southeast, the two primary routes into and out of the borderlands are either up the coast of the Caspian to the Mughan steppe or via the area around modern Tabriz north to Zangezur and Nakhichevan or west to Ararat.

While the papers collected in this volume represent a strong challenge to traditional macrogeographic representations of the region as a landscape too often defined in terms of marginality, a number of the papers do develop an understanding of borderlands at a micro level by attending to the social relations organized between elevated plains and mountain slopes. Several papers in the volume productively explore the social, economic, political, and cultural practices that arise out of these geographic links.

ARCHAEOLOGY IN THE BORDERLANDS: A SHORT HISTORY

The history of archaeological research in the borderlands is both historically deep and internationally varied. Austen Henry Layard incorporated part of the region into his investigations of Assyrian monuments when he visited Van Kale during the summer of 1880. Layard focused his investigations on making copies of the display inscriptions on the site but he did leave his associate Hormuzd Rassam to conduct excavations in the mound at Toprakkale (Barnett 1950). Van also became the centerpiece of investigations conducted by Nikolai Marr and a Russian team in 1915-16, during the brief occupation of the region by Russian forces in the midst of World War I (Marr and Orbelli 1922).

Regions to the north and east were studied by French researchers (Jacques and Henri de Morgan and Ernest Chantre in the 1880s onward; see, for example, de Morgan 1889), who excavated parts of cemeteries especially of the Late Bronze and Early Iron Ages and collected archaeological artifacts from local people. Contemporary German and Austrian projects followed similar patterns, with Austrian F. Bayern excavating the first materials deposited in the Museum of the Caucasus in Tiflis (now Tbilisi) in 1852. At the same time, the Georgian archaeologist Dimitri Megvinetukhutsesishvili began excavations at Uplistsikhe. In general, Russian archaeologists in the nineteenth century focused more on the northern Caucasus (see, for example, the many volumes of *MAK*, Krupnov 1960: 14, and Nagler 1996: 8–15), but, after the establishment of the museum in Tbilisi, also worked in Georgia and Azerbaijan (Lordkipanidze 1989: 33-34; Lordkipanidze 1991b: 17-18).

It is during the early twentieth century that we also see the full florescence of local archaeological research programs. Perhaps the most influential were the far-ranging architectural surveys conducted by Toros Toramanyan (1942) across the Armenian highlands. Not only did Toramanyan provide the first documentation of major sites that would later host major archaeological investigations in eastern Turkey and Armenia, including the sites of Horom (Badaljan et al. 1997) and Tsakahovit (Badalyan, et al., chapter 7), but his work also sparked sustained interest in regional surveys (such as those conducted by Kalantar (1994) in the 1920s, Piotrovskii (and Gyuzal'yan 1933; Adzhan et al. 1932) in the 1930s, and many others through to the present (Areshian et al. 1977; Avetisyan et al. 2000; Biscione, chapter 8; Esaian 1976; Mikayelyan 1968; Smith 1999).

The development of local archaeological research programs was further supported within the institutional settings of the Soviet Academy of Sciences, as well as through laws requiring salvage archaeology before most construction. By the 1920s and 1930s, European and local archaeologists were working and publishing steadily on many periods in both the northern and southern Caucasus. The local archaeologists were often publishing in their native languages, even in the time of the Soviet Union (Miron and Orthmann 1995: 19–22). Thus, western scholars who were examining already published material relied on summaries in familiar languages, although scholars such as F. Hançar (1937) worked to provide overviews of this otherwise linguistically hard-to-access work.

The excavation of the first Trialeti kurgans by B. A. Kuftin and their rapid publication incited further interest in the archaeology of Caucasia, as the Middle Bronze Age material was shown, from its initial publication, to have apparent connections with material from Turkey, Mesopotamia, and the Aegean (Kuftin 1941; Kuftin and Field 1946; Minns 1942, 1943; Schaeffer 1943, 1944a, 1944b).[3]

The history of the study of Eastern Anatolia (pre-Urartu) and Iranian Azerbaijan followed a similar pattern. The publication of surveys done by Europeans in the early years of the twentieth century (Lehmann-Haupt 1910-31; Stein 1940) stimulated archaeological interest, which earlier on had been limited to occasional excavation by gentlemen scholars (see, for example, Crawford 1975). More scientific archaeology began in these regions in mid-century (for example, Burton Brown 1951) and the history of those excavations can be found in the bibliographies of recent researches in the area (see Avetisyan et al. 2000; Edwards 1983; Kiguradze and Sagona. Chapter 3; Muscarella 1994; Özfirat 2001; Rubinson 1991b, 1994).

CURRENT INVESTIGATIONS IN THE BORDERLANDS

The papers drawn together in this volume represent a segment of contemporary research in the borderlands that has developed in the decade since the collapse of the Soviet Union. The papers were originally part of two separate conference symposia, one at the 1998 American Anthropological Association meetings in Philadelphia and one at the 1998 Archaeological Institute of America meetings in Washington DC. We would like to thank all of the members of those sessions who contributed papers, with special thanks to Fred Hiebert who served as discussant on the AAA panel and David Stronach and Christopher Edens who were discussants for the AIA panel, and thus provided some of the initial constructive commentary to the papers published here. This core group of papers was augmented as we moved to remake the conference papers into the present volume by the addition of chapters by Peterson, Puturidze, and Tsetskhladze.

A number of critical themes run through the papers collected here. Perhaps the most prominent is a debate over the issue of the proper scale at which we should theorize various dimensions of social, political, and economic life in the region. The geographic position of Caucasia and eastern Anatolia between what Peake and Fleure (1928) referred to as "the steppe and the sown" has long promoted a concern with the interplay of "global" forces across the isthmus. Indeed, the dynamism of populations documented at various times in the region's history and prehistory as well as the steady stream of materials established between the borderlands and other areas of western Asia both to the north and to the south certainly mitigates against any attempts to decouple the area from its neighbors. This perspective is strongly represented here in the discussions by Kohl on the tin trade in the ancient Near East as seen from the vantage point of Velikent in Dagestan and is an underlying theme of Rubinson's work. It is also the issue that Rothman explores and interprets in a new way. However, there is also a contrasting position that argues for more localized understandings of cultural transformations. The papers by Peterson, Tsetskhladze, Puturidze, and Badalyan, Smith, and Avetisyan argue from varying perspectives that the global perspective on the region has come at the cost of both fair assessments of local elements structuring the global flow of goods and an understanding of how imported goods were incorporated into unique cultural settings.

A second theme that occupies a number of the chapters centers on relationships among contemporaneous social groups within the borderlands. These relationships are variously sited in this volume as ethnopolitical (Stone and Zimansky) ethnosocial (Puturidze, Kiguradze and Sagona), or more straightforwardly geographic (Biscione). What is particularly important is that in none of the papers detailing such interactions are the units of interaction described as entirely unproblematic or historically enduring. That is, what these papers go to some pains to consider is the constitution of social groups within specific historical, geographic, and

political contexts. This is an important change—one might even posit, a radical departure—from traditional formulations of the implications of lines of social difference within a milieu that has been recently produced in the current media as one of enduring, rather than situational, ethnic conflict.

A final orienting concern that draws together a number of papers is the reporting of results from ongoing research projects. Given the dispersal of research results in numerous languages from Turkish and Russian to Georgian and Armenian to English, French, and German, opportunities to convey results of ongoing projects within a multinational forum such as this are rare and thus to be seized. Indeed much of the motivation for the present volume arose from the very simple desire to establish multilateral lines of communication for sharing both orientations to theoretical and historical problems and results of recent research. The reports of Kiguradze and Sagona; Stone and Zimansky; Badalyan, Smith, and Avetisyan; and Sevin, Çilingiroğlu, Biscione, and Rothman constitute communications from several of the most significant programs dedicated to exploring the region's prehistory, which will ultimately provide critical sources of information for exploring the anthropological and historical/chronological problems posed in many of the other contributions.

We have chosen to arrange the chapters of this book in roughly chronological order (from the Early Bronze Age to the first millennium BC) to juxtapose chapters that provide complementary discussions on overlapping times and places. Thus, the reader interested in gaining access to archaeological information about the area at any given time will find the organization straightforward. However, this choice also yields a challenging interdigitation of diverse research strategies and theoretical visions that provide, in toto, a melding of a range of intellectual positions and traditions. Along a geographic axis, the chapters represent an important intermingling of western and local traditions both in the methodologies employed in research and in the interpretive priorities of each chapter. Along a more disciplinary axis, the papers collected here arise from a range of different intellectual approaches, including anthropology, art history, archaeology, and classics. Rather than trying to force these into a singular vision, the goal of this book is to represent the vibrancy that arises from this pluralism. While the divisions that make communication between researchers difficult can often seem insurmountable, what we think shines through in all of the collected papers is that this diversity can be a strength of regional research, forcing constant thinking and rethinking of traditional positions. If problems in communication can be overcome, and we are optimistic that they can (this volume in itself provides testimony), the intellectual eclecticism of archaeologists working in the region can only promote a truly productive dialogue.

NOTES

1. We understand the term *Caucasia* to refer to the entire isthmus dividing the Black and Caspian Seas, while the term *Caucasus* refers more specifically to the mountain range at Caucasia's northern frontier. *Transcaucasia* and *Ciscaucasia* are perspectival designations referring to the areas immediately south and north of the Caucasus range respectively.

2. For discussions of Assyrian campaigning in Urartu, especially Sargon's eighth campaign, see Levine 1977, Thureau-Dangin 1912, and Zimansky 1990.

3. See Sagona 1984:15-21 for a discussion of the Kura-Araks culture that clearly lays out the interaction of local archaeologists and western scholars over almost a century in the study of Caucasian material.

CHAPTER 1

Integrated Interaction at the Beginning of the Bronze Age:

New Evidence from the Northeastern Caucasus and the Advent of Tin Bronzes in the Third Millennium BC

PHILIP L. KOHL

This chapter presents recently excavated materials from the site of Velikent in southeastern Dagestan, Russia. It focuses on the bronzes found at the site and evidence for metalworking at Velikent and at neighboring Kabaz Kutan to the west. It then relates this substantial corpus to broader problems concerned with the development of metallurgy in the Old World, particularly with the always-vexing problem of the advent of tin bronzes. The paper raises the theoretical issue of how best to conceptualize interregional interconnections in the Early Bronze period and attempts to make some general observations on developments in the Caucasus during Late Chalcolithic and Early Bronze times.

MODELING WORLD SYSTEMS IN ANTIQUITY: A FUTILE OR REWARDING EXERCISE?

Attempts to apply world systems terms, as defined initially by I. Wallerstein (1974), to prehistoric evidence have foundered on the lack of correspondence between structural components of the so-called modern world system (cores, semiperipheries, and peripheries) and their presumed counterparts in the late prehistoric world. Difficulties emerge as to the degree of integration of an ancient world system, the extent of structured inequality within it, the existence or nonexistence of economic dependencies based on long-distance trade or the so-called development of underdevelopment in antiquity, and the significance of areas beyond the postulated system's stretch—the ever-decreasing "margins," in Andrew Sherratt's terminology (1993). How do we best conceptualize the Caucasus during the Early Bronze Age? Was the area a periphery developing into a semi-periphery within an ancient Near Eastern world system? Did it at the same time function more as a "core" area to developments that took place farther north on the vast, interconnected world of the Eurasian steppes? Concepts such as "core" and "periphery" seem imprecise, if not misleading and dangerously anachronistic. Wherein lies their attraction or utility?

One point is obvious: a world systems model should not just represent a fashionable substitute for

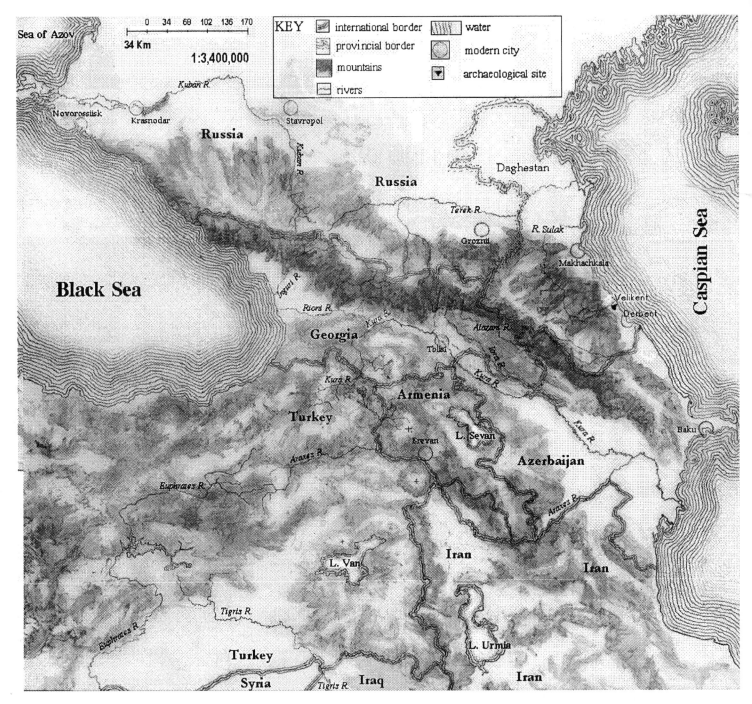

Figure 1.1 Map of the Caucasus.

documenting interregional interaction or connections on a broad scale. The model implies a much greater degree of integration and systemic interconnection than simple long-distance contact. I quote from Gil Stein's excellent critique (1998a: 225-226) of the world systems model as applied to the Uruk expansion from Mesopotamia into Anatolia during the mid- to late fourth millennium BC:

> The world systems model rests on three fundamental, but problematic, assumptions. First it assumes a fundamental power asymmetry between the different parts of the system, so that the core politically dominated the periphery either through direct colonial administration or through a combination of economic and

cultural hegemony. Second, the model assumes that as a result of these asymmetries the core was able to control the exchange system. Third, the model assumes that long-distance exchange relations structure all other aspects of political economy in peripheral societies. (Stein 1998a: 225-226)

Based upon materials for an Uruk presence at the Anatolian site of Hacınebi, Stein tests these assumptions of the world systems model and finds them wanting. His analysis focuses particularly on what he terms the "leveling effects of distance" during the Bronze Age. Methods of transportation were ultimately so constrained that long-distance exchange in bulk necessities was limited, if not impossible, after a certain distance threshold was reached. The less substantial interregional trade of luxuries, while important, never could play the critical role demanded by the world systems model. Moreover, cores did not dominate distant peripheral areas technologically or militarily at least over the long term, and there is no justification a priori to consider long-distance trade as the prime mover of change, while ignoring "the less visible, but, in the long run, far more important endogenous changes in domestic production, investment, and consumption" (Stein 1998a: 228).

This critique is highly persuasive, but does its acceptance necessarily imply an abandonment of the world systems model for all times and places during the Bronze Age or later prehistory? As I have suggested elsewhere (Kohl 1989), models that fail also can instruct in that the reasons for their failure may be quite interesting. I would argue that possibly the most basic assumption of the world systems model—even more fundamental than the three identified by Gil Stein—is that the "world" (whatever its spatial parameters may be at a particular time) under consideration is *systemically* integrated to the extent that what happens in one part of the system has serious consequences throughout the entire system. Can one still conceptualize a functioning world system without dominant cores and submissive peripheries? Are the asymmetries and dependencies fundamental to the model or can they be replaced by more balanced systems of long-distance exchange and structured interdependencies? Are we forever doomed to employing amorphous concepts for a discussion of broad interconnections, such as interaction spheres, which attract or repel us precisely because of their vagueness? Or can we detect this feature of systemic or structural integration during the Bronze Age? If so, when and where?

Stein's forcefully argued alternative, the "distance-parity" model (1999b:62-64), emphasizes parity and the limits to political and economic domination, a bias that potentially underestimates the complexity and sophistication of ancient exchange and other interaction networks. Symmetric exchange, peoples interacting with each other on an equal basis, undoubtedly occurred and continues to occur today even in our modern world system, and the reasons for such nonexploitative interaction often can be related to factors such as distance, overland and maritime transportation costs, and the like. But it is also true that peoples often do try to obtain a competitive advantage, get the upper hand, and exploit their neighbors politically and/or economically. One of the fascinating aspects of trying to model prehistoric trade networks is precisely to determine the balance of the trade, who may be benefiting and who, in some cases, suffering from participation in the exchange network. By emphasizing only parity and symmetric exchange, one risks missing the competitive tension inherent in an exchange network, ignoring the intentions of the trading partners—which constitute, of course, a form of human agency. Ancient cores may have been limited in their ability to exploit peripheries in the manner postulated by world systems theory, but the development of a highly differentiated, state-structured urban society in southern Mesopotamia had consequences that rippled far beyond the confines of the Mesopotamian alluvium. These consequences may not be adequately analyzed by world systems theory, but I also doubt that the distance-parity model will satisfactorily account for them either. This paper considers these problems by presenting some recently excavated archaeological materials from the northeastern Caucasus and their relation to the advent of the tin Bronze Age in this part of the world.

THE CHALCOLITHIC PRELUDE: THE BALKANS AND THE PONTIC STEPPES COMPARED TO THE CAUCASUS

The Copper Age of the Caucasus—or, more precisely, the immediately pre-Maikop and pre-Kura-Araxes horizons of, respectively, the northern and southern Caucasus—appears remarkably impoverished relative to the spectacular Chalcolithic developments that occurred initially in the Balkans and culminated in the famous Cucuteni-Tripol'ye culture with its gigantic proto-urban settlements in western Ukraine (Videjko 1995). Nothing comparable existed in the Caucasus

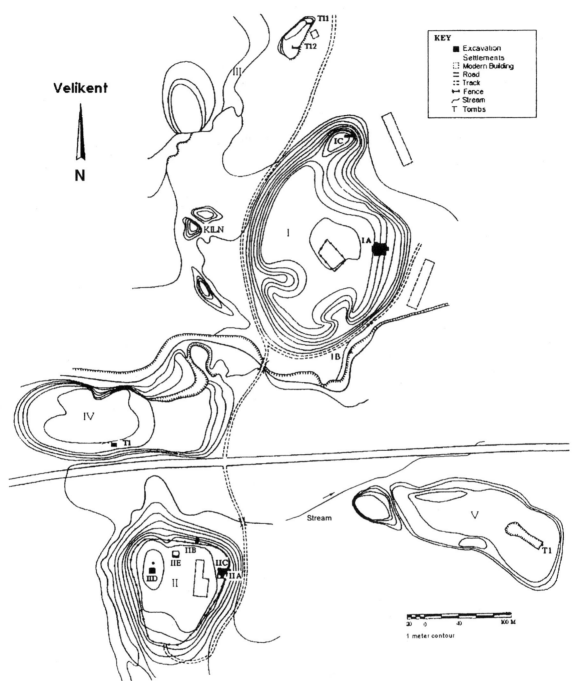

Figure 1.2 Plan of Velikent.

during the fifth and first half of the fourth millennia BC; even more striking is the underdevelopment of the northern Caucasus before the emergence of the famous Maikop culture, which most specialists (Munchaev 1994, 169–170) now date as beginning at least during the second half of the fourth millennium. Such under-development, of course, contrasts sharply with what occurs during the Early Bronze Age when the Caucasus becomes one of the main suppliers of arsenical bronzes

to the peoples of the steppes, particularly to the pit and catacomb grave communities. As E. N. Chernykh (1992:159–162) has so strikingly demonstrated, the northern Caucasus from Maikop times through the Middle Bronze period functioned as *the* critical inter-mediary for receiving metals that originated in Transcaucasia and producing and shipping bronze artifacts to the steppes. Clearly a major shift in inter-connections occurred initially sometime during the middle of the fourth millennium BC that brought the Caucasus onto the main stage of developments encompassing both the steppes to the north and the settled agricultural regions of the ancient Near East to the south.

Specialists differ in their assessments of which regions contributed to the formation of the Maikop culture, some emphasizing its steppe components (Nechitailo 1991; Rezepkin 1991) and others (Andreeva 1977; Trifonov 1994) its links with northern Mesopotamia. It is also well established that Mesopotamian elements, such as Halafian and Ubaid pottery, have occasionally been found on Chalcolithic sites in the southern Caucasus, such as Kyul-tepe and Leila-depe (Narimanov 1985), that push back some form of contact between the Caucasus and northern Mesopotamia at least into the fifth millennium BC. Nevertheless, the redating of both well-established Caucasian Early Bronze horizons—the Maikop and Kura-Araxes formations, which are based now not only on typological considerations, but also on calibrated radiocarbon determinations (for Transcaucasia, see Kavtaradze 1983)—suggest that both began to emerge toward the middle of the fourth millennium. This was, perhaps not coincidentally, at roughly the same time that the so-called Uruk colonies were documented in Anatolia on the middle to upper reaches of the Euphrates (for example, at Hacinebi, Stein et al. 1996). Similarly, the initial settlement at Velikent in southeastern Dagestan exhibits clear relations with Kura-Araxes sites to the south and also begins around the middle of the fourth millennium BC.

THE DAGESTAN AMERICAN VELIKENT (DAV) EXPEDITION

The Early Bronze Age site of Velikent was occupied from around 3600 to 1900 BC, as based on a series of twenty-one calibrated radiocarbon determinations (for previously published dates see Gadzhiev et al. 1997:218–219). This site is located around 25 km northwest of the town of Derbent on the Caspian plain of southeastern Dagestan along the southern edge of the contemporary village of Velikent (figure 1.1). Its cultural remains, which consist of three separate burial areas (mounds III, IV, and V) and two settlement areas (mounds I and II), sit on the top of natural clay terraces that extend over 28 ha (figure 1.2). Since the northwestern Caucasus mountains form a formidably high barrier that begins almost directly on the Black

Sea, the Caspian littoral plain represents the only natural unbroken corridor on the western side of the Caspian linking the south Russian steppes to the north with Transcaucasia and the eastern Anatolian and northwest Iranian plateaus to the south. This coastal corridor actually consists of a series of plains or bays successively interrupted by rivers and streams flowing down from the mountains and by the mountains themselves extending eastward to pinch the plain at several narrow critical points. The section of the plain on which Velikent sits forms a natural physiographic unit extending from where the mountains encroach on the plain at Izberbash in the north to where they nearly reach the Caspian at Derbent in the south. It is at Derbent the Sasanian ruler Khosrow I erected a fortress and a long fortification wall in the early sixth century AD that stretches along the ridge of mountains directly west of the town, attempting unsuccessfully to stop the periodic incursions from nomads from the steppes to the north. One of the main goals of the excavations at Velikent has been to document the nature of sedentary life on this plain and to record evidence for the initial stages of contact with the steppe cultures to the north.

The 1997–1998 investigations began to examine the settlement history of the Caspian plain and briefly conducted reconnaissances west of Velikent along the Ulluchai valley into the beginnings of the piedmont near the town of Madzhalis and also south of Derbent nearly to the Azeri border. A cluster of seven mounds was located immediately southeast of the village of Rodnikova and south of the Ulluchai at the edge of the plain and the beginning of the piedmont, around 7 km west of Velikent. From their surface remains, some of the mounds appeared to represent separate settlement areas, dating to the Early Bronze period and also to much later Medieval times; others, lacking surface cultural materials, may represent, like at Velikent, distinct burial or cemetery areas. A small sounding (2.5 x 2 m) was placed along the southern slope of the mound of Kabaz Kutan, around 1.6 m beneath the mound's summit. Cultural materials retrieved from this sounding closely resembled those from the earlier settlement mound II at Velikent, and two radiocarbon determinations (3015–2703 BC, 2 sigma, sample AA 27354; 2884–2500 BC, 2 sigma, sample AA 31774) from this sounding confirmed that this site was occupied at the end of the fourth and into the first half of the third millennium BC. Kura-Araxes-like wares—including fragments with characteristic Nakhichevan lug handles, and the highly fired, wheel-turned "high-quality

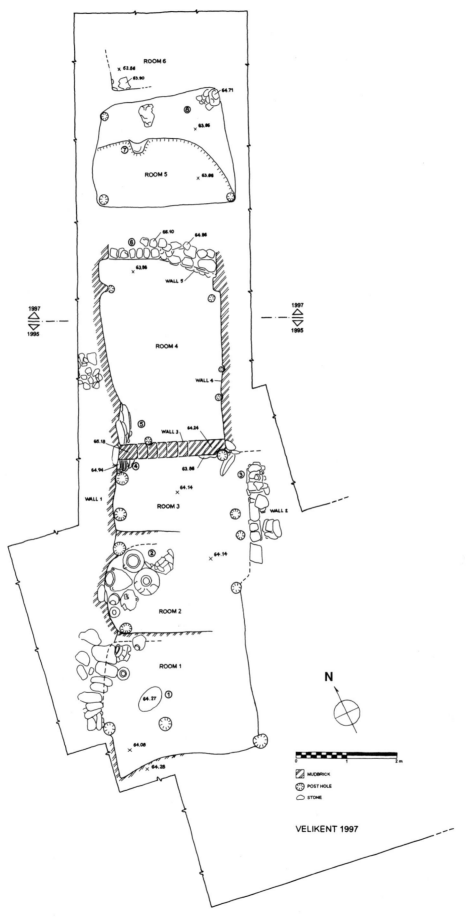

Figure 1.3 Mound I, multiroomed structure from second level.

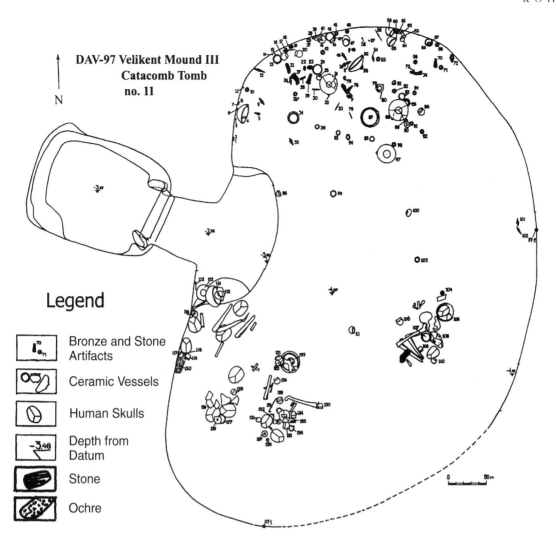

**DAV-97 Velikent Mound III
Catacomb Tomb
no. 11**

N

Legend

Bronze and Stone Artifacts

Ceramic Vessels

Human Skulls

Depth from Datum

Stone

Ochre

Figure 1.4 Velikent mound III, catacomb tomb 11.

wares," which have also been found in the earliest levels at Velikent mound II (below)—were recovered, as well as bone points, terra-cotta figurines, and grooved hammerstones and shaft-hole ground-stone axes. In addition, fragments of a fired ceramic crucible and of a mold for casting metal objects were recovered from this small sounding, suggesting metal-working activities took place directly on the site. Nine stratigraphic levels were recorded, and the total cultural deposit at Kabaz-Kutan was nearly 5 m or greater than at Velikent mound II. The materials recovered from this tiny sounding clearly suggest that this cluster of settlements at the very edge of the plain and beginning of the piedmont deserve more extensive investigation, and large-scale excavations at Kabaz-Kutan are planned for future seasons.

Returning to Velikent, excavations on the earlier settlement mound II have uncovered the remains of one circular mudbrick structure (around 6.3 m in diameter), presumably a dwelling, and numerous storage and refuse pits dug deep into this building and into the natural clay terrace. Occasional bronze artifacts have been encountered in these excavations, and a mold for casting a shaft-hole axe similar to those found in 1997 (see below and figure 1.5) was recovered in 1999 from the newly opened excavation (IIE) on the earlier settlement mound.

A distinctive form of ceramic found in the very earliest levels of the occupation at Velikent indicates the sophisticated ceramic and pyrotechnological skills already possessed by the initial settlers at the site. Many of the ceramics from Velikent such as lids, flat frying

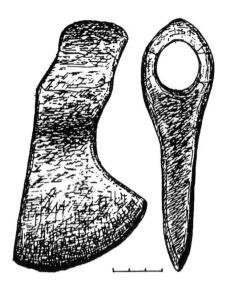

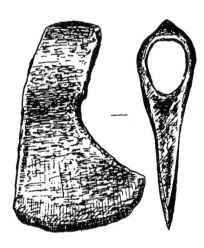

Figure 1.5 Shaft-hole axes from catacomb tomb 11, mound III.

of sand and highly fired, possessing an almost metallic hardness and resonance. They appeared to be wheel-thrown, and many were decorated with impressed or stamped zigzags, wavy lines, and herringbone and tiny wedge-shaped or nail-like impressions that sometimes encircled the body of the vessel beneath the neck.

In terms of their decoration, but not in terms of their manufacture, these wares recall the designs on steppe wares found in the northern Pontic area and illustrate the mixed character of the Velikent remains. First recognized during the 1995 season and compared with sherds also found on Kura-Araxes-related sites, such as Serzhen Yurt, in Chechnya to the northwest (Munchaev 1975, 337–344, Fig. 76), these "high-quality wares" were present throughout the prehistoric occupational sequence on mound II; that is, they occur in the very earliest building level. In fact, high-quality decorated fragments were found resting near a burnt hearth in trench IID to the west, a hearth that yielded the earliest C14 determination (3693–3380 BC, 2 sigma, sample AA 27351) currently available for the beginnings of the occupation at Velikent. The earliest settlers at Velikent arrived already possessing an unexpectedly sophisticated ceramic technology, reflective of a high level of craft specialization, which had been previously known only for sites dating to the mid-fourth millennium that were located much farther to the south. During summer 2001 identical high-quality wares were collected on Bronze Age settlements in northeastern Azerbaijan, such as Dashly-tepe and Serker-tepe. The Late Chalcolithic/Early Bronze materials from northeastern Azerbaijan are closely related to those from southeastern Dagestan and form a united culture area, however one wishes to designate it.

During the course of the third millennium BC the settlement seems then to have shifted to the north or to what is now our mound I. Two basic building levels have been documented in the excavations on this mound: an initial level where people seem to have lived in deeply sunk, oval pit houses and a subsequent horizon, overlying these pit houses, where we have partially excavated a multiroomed structure (figure 1.3), which had burned down in an intense fire, and which contained numerous large ceramic vessels that may have been produced near this special-purpose structure. Several of the metals excavated in this burned building closely resemble those found in the collective catacomb tombs excavated on mounds III through V, suggesting their basic contemporaneity. Thus, for example, a bronze medallion, which was

pans, braziers, pots of various shapes with distinctive so-called Nakhicevan lug handles, and variously shaped ceramic hearth supports or andirons are obviously related to the Kura-Araxes cultural tradition of the southern Caucasus. The relations between Velikent and Transcaucasia have long been recognized and have led to the classification of its early culture there as representative of the northeastern or Dagestani "variant" of the Kura-Araxes culture; such a designation, however, may be misleading because of the distinctive, syncretic character of the materials from the site. Surprisingly, more than 10% of the sherds recovered in one excavation unit on mound II had a much finer quality than the remainder of Kura-Araxes-related and local wares; the former were tempered with small inclusions

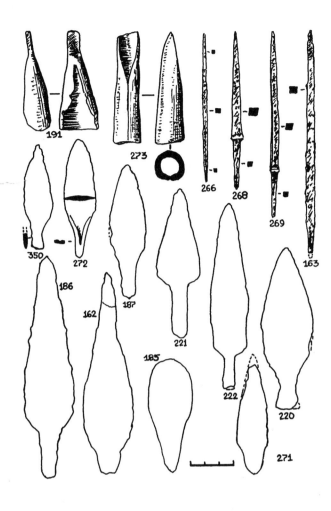

Figure 1.6 Metal weapons and tools from catacomb tomb 11, mound III.

has salvaged four more collective tombs: one each on mounds IV and V and two more—tombs 11 and 12—on mound III during the 1997 season. Unfortunately, the natural clay terraces into which the tombs had been dug are constantly being destroyed by local villagers using large mechanized excavators to procure the rich clay for construction purposes. The collective tomb 11 had been accidentally discovered and partially destroyed by local villagers just prior to the beginning of the 1997 season.

The burial chamber of tomb 11 was distinguished by its kidney-shaped form oriented northeast to southwest along its long axis and by its considerable size (4.3 x 6.2 m, figure 1.4). The chamber was connected to the entrance pit set to the northwest by a short T-shaped corridor or dromos, which took the form of a sharply descending ramp or incline from the large stone door slab blocking the entrance to the floor of the chamber. The stone entry door was found in situ, but the roof or vault of the burial chamber had collapsed in antiquity, and the chamber had been secondarily utilized and filled with alternating soft ashy and compact yellow clay levels containing bits of ceramics and human and animal bones. A nearly complete skeleton of a 7 or 8 year old child with its head unnaturally twisted back on itself, as if it had been bound or set within a sack, was encountered in the loose fill of a sounding placed above the entry pit and to the side of the burial chamber. A radiocarbon date taken from the phalanges of this skeleton yielded a date of 2194–1780 BC (two sigma, sample AA 27348) which provides a *terminus ante quem* for the initial utilization of tomb 11 (that is, prior to the collapse of its roof).

The metal and ground-stone tools and weapons found in tomb 11 can be paralleled to similar Early and Middle Bronze weapons from the northwestern Caucasus and the Eurasian steppes in general. The metal ornaments from Velikent, such as the anchor-shaped pendants (see figure 1.7), are more distinctively Velikent or found across a smaller North Caucasian area, suggesting that they did not diffuse as widely as the tools and weapons. The circular bronze medallions, some of which were elaborately decorated with a characteristic flap or loop bent back for suspension, on the other hand, have been found repeatedly on the steppes, suggesting contact with that area (see Nechitailo 1991, cover illustration and 86–87). Twisted ringlets, presumably worn in the hair, exhibit an even broader distribution both to the north and south; more than 80 complete and around 135 fragments of ringlets, twisted

found in the northwestern corner of room 6 just above its floor, was identical to an ornament excavated from tomb 11 on mound III to the west. Similarly, a flat axe found just above the floor of room 4 closely resembled an axe collected by the local school children from tomb 11 after this tomb had been initially exposed by the local villagers. A bronze awl was also found on the floor of room 4.

Ten collective catacomb tombs had previously been excavated on mound III at Velikent during the initial 1979, 1982-1984 field seasons. Some of these were remarkably rich containing numerous burial goods, including in one instance more than 1,500 bronze artifacts (for their analysis, see Gadzhiev and Korenevskii 1984). Since 1994 the Dagestan-American expedition

1.5 times, were recovered from tomb 11, including a single ringlet made of gold.

The numerous tools and weapons found in tomb 11 included four extremely well-ground and polished shaft-hole stone axe-hammers, made of marbled limestone (?), and more than 30 circular and pear-shaped mace heads, some of which had a slightly raised lip encircling their drilled hole. One mace head had four raised knobs, so far the only example from Velikent of this later, broadly distributed type. Metal weapons included two shaft-hole axes with their blades extended downward (figure 1.5), two flat axes or adzes, and twenty-two dagger or knife blades with simple tangs (figure 1.6). Bronze tools included awls (figure 1.6, nos. 163, 266, 268, 269) and chisels (figure 1.6, no. 273) of the well-known, standardized types of the Circumpontic metallurgical province.

Presently, the DAV has only obtained two C14 dates from the collective catacomb tombs, but both of these are congruent and suggest that the tombs should be dated earlier than previously thought. Part of the wooden handle of one of the shaft-hole axes from tomb 11, mound III was preserved and yielded a calibrated radiocarbon date of 2851–2367 BC (2 sigma, sample AA 27353), which closely resembled another date obtained from the skeletal remains in another collective tomb (tomb 1, mound V) excavated during the 1994 season: 2879–2474 BC (2 sigma, sample AA 15104; see Gadzhiev et al. 1995, 147). Although we do not know how long either of these tombs were utilized, the two closely matching radiocarbon dates indicate that the tombs date primarily to the early to middle third millennium and not to the end of the third or beginning of the second millennium BC, as proposed in the earlier literature. If correct, such an early dating may suggest the diffusion of metal tools and weapons or even a population movement from the northeastern Caucasus onto the steppes in the third millennium, rather than the reverse. Far-ranging stylistic parallels not only to the bronzes but also to the elaborately ground stone weapons, such as mace-heads and shaft-hole axes and hammers, can be traced both to the south and to the far north and northwest. What is the significance of the flourishing third millennium BC bronze industry at Velikent?

THE VELIKENT BRONZES AND THE ADVENT OF TIN BRONZES IN THE OLD WORLD

195 artifacts from the earlier excavated catacomb tomb 1, mound III at Velikent that contained around 1,500 metal artifacts were subjected to compositional analyses, and 15 of them or around 8%—one toggle pin, five rings, and nine bracelets—proved to be deliberately alloyed tin bronzes (Gadzhiev and Korenevskii 1984:24). The vast majority of the analyzed metal artifacts were arsenical bronzes, apparently utilizing known local metal sources in the northeastern Caucasus. It is interesting that none of the analyzed tools and weapons were tin bronzes, but just some of the ornaments, particularly the bracelets, leading the investigators to comment that "possibly the ancient inhabitants of Velikent were attracted to the golden color of the copper-tin alloy (ibid)." Moreover, the source of the copper for the tin bronzes seems to have been distinctive from those used for the production of the other bronzes, suggesting possibly that the tin bronzes were not alloyed at Velikent but imported in the already alloyed state. While more dates need to be processed, the two consistent, already cited early to mid-third millennium BC dates for the collective catacomb tombs at Velikent would make these tin bronzes among the earliest recorded for the Caucasus.

In general, tin bronzes begin to appear in very small quantities in post-Kura-Araxes culture times or towards the second half of the third millennium and then gradually increase in proportion to arsenical bronzes until Late Bronze times or the second half of the second millennium BC when tin bronzes become dominant. During the Late Bronze and Early Iron periods, the Caucasus—both Transcaucasia and Ciscaucasia—is one of the richest metal-working areas of the Old World with tens of thousands of bronze artifacts having been unearthed in clandestine and controlled excavations dating back to the last century. E. N. Chernykh's discussion (1992: 275–295) of this later "Caucasian Metallurgical Province" which takes shape around the middle of the second millennium BC refers extensively to the highly distinctive and isolated character of the bronzes produced in the Caucasus at this later time and contrasts its paradoxically isolated character first with the range of metal products distributed across the contemporaneous vast "Eurasian Metallurgical Province" centered far to the northeast (Chernykh 1992: 192) and then with the earlier role of Caucasian metallurgy in the late third and early second millennium for supplying metals over much of the western Eurasian steppes. Tin sources are not known from the Caucasus and geologically are not expected to be found there. Thus, what is perhaps even more paradoxical is that by the second half of the second millennium BC, the Caucasus was one of the most prolific metal-producing areas of the Old World and what it was

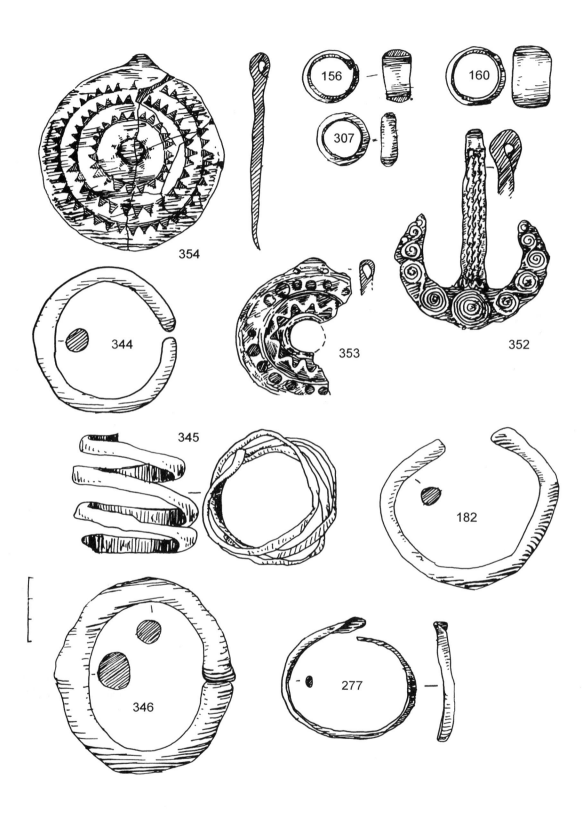

Figure 1.7 Metal ornaments from Velikent.

dominantly producing were tin bronzes, the tin of which had to be imported from sources lying far to the east (see Chernykh 1992: 194) and/or possibly from documented sources in the Taurus mountains farther south (Yener et al. 1989).

Recently, Lloyd Weeks (1999) has reconsidered the West Asian "tin problem" in light of the results of recent lead-isotope analyses of tin bronzes from the site of Tell Abraq in the United Arab Emirates and their comparison with tin bronzes from northwestern Anatolia and the Aegean. More than 500 copper and tin bronze artifacts have been recovered from Tell Abraq, which is located near the Gulf coast on the southeastern Arabian peninsula; tin bronzes actually seem to decrease over time from more than half (53%) of the analyzed metals during the Umm an-Nar occupation at Tell Abraq in the late third millennium BC to the Late Iron Age when slightly less than 40% of the analyzed artifacts were tin bronzes. Exotic luxury items also found at Tell Abraq can be paralleled to materials from Iran, southern Central Asia, and the Indus Valley. The excavator D. Potts believes that such luxury goods accompany and reflect the more basic and extensive organized late third and early second millennium trade in tin/tin bronzes from sources farther east, particularly western Afghanistan; that is, the trade in luxury exotica—interesting and significant in its own right—masks in a sense this more fundamental trade in tin bronzes. We know that farther south near the site of Maysar in Oman there is substantial evidence for the smelting of copper in the late third millennium, and this area often is identified as ancient Magan, which is known to have been one of the main sources of copper for southern Mesopotamia. Tin bronzes are not found at Maysar, suggesting possibly that a maritime trade in tin or tin bronzes from sources farther east reached only the part of the Arabian peninsula bordering the Gulf.

Weeks believes that the source(s) for the copper in the tin bronzes from Abraq was different from the local source(s) utilized for the production of copper artifacts at Tell Abraq, suggesting that at least some of the tin bronzes from Abraq were traded in alloyed form, either as ingots or as finished artifacts. This situation is similar to that for the tin bronzes from Velikent; intriguingly, in both instances the tin bronzes contain concentrations of lead, though it is unclear whether it is the tin or the copper that is contributing the lead. Even more intriguingly, Weeks notes a general "isotopic similarity" between the tin bronzes used

at Kastri, Poliochni, Thermi, Troy, and Tell Abraq and suggests that the bronzes from these sites were obtained from the same sources. To quote him directly:

> This possibility is supported by a number of lines of reasoning. Firstly, geological evidence of the scarcity of tin deposits in Western Asia suggests that a relatively small number of sources could have been supplying the raw material for bronze industries across the region. Secondly, the surviving third and early-second millennium texts from the region indicate that all the major sources of tin used in Western Asia in the Early Bronze Age lay to the east of Mesopotamia. Finally, isotopic and geological evidence has shown that the earliest bronzes in Anatolia, Mesopotamia and the Gulf were obtained through trade, and were produced from metal foreign to any of these regions. Isotopic similarity between bronzes from sites as distant as Tell Abraq and Troy is thus exactly what might be expected in such a situation, reflecting the wide dispersal of a scarce and highly demanded commodity.

Ten metal artifacts from the earlier excavated tomb 1 at Velikent were sent to Lloyd Weeks in Australia and submitted to lead-isotope analysis; five of these were deliberately alloyed tin bronzes. The "linear isotopic array" ($208Pb/206Pb$ relative to $207Pb/206Pb$) of the Velikent tin bronzes essentially matched those of the other analyzed West Asian tin bronzes, though the absolute isotopic ranges varied from site to site, which possibly in the Velikent case may simply be a function of the smaller number of samples (5) tested (Kohl 2003 and Weeks, personal communication). The analyses reveal that the copper, as well as the tin in the Velikent tin bronzes, most likely came from a different source than the copper used in the production of the standard Velikent arsenical bronzes (for a full report of these analyses, see Kohl 2003). These results are more tantalizing than conclusive; many more samples will have to be tested from Velikent and other contemporary West Asian sites before Weeks's hypothesis can be definitively confirmed. Nevertheless, a picture of great interregional complexity, consistent with the early historic record, can be dimly discerned.

CONCLUSION: VINDICATION OF THE THREE AGE SYSTEM?

The actual source(s) of the tin remain elusive, more speculated about than actually known. Crucial aspects of the organization and mechanics of this long-distance trade in tin and tin bronzes will not be understood without precise determination of these sources and the large-scale excavation of Bronze Age sites in their vicinity. It must be admitted that some of this essential work will be very difficult, if not impossible, at least in the short term for the most likely important eastern source is in western Afghanistan. Was the trade somehow balanced between more or less equally powerful and significant trading partners or asymmetrical, and, if the former, how is systemic integration achieved in the absence of dominance or exploitation? It seems to me that an integrated tin bronze "world system" does not necessarily imply dominance by an urban core over an underdeveloped barbarian periphery; if Chernykh is correct, one extremely important center for the production of bronzes during the Late Bronze Age lay far to the east in the nomadic steppe world bordering the southern Urals and in northern Kazakhstan. How was this postulated long-distance exchange in metals directed and coordinated, and what were the changes in its scale from the third through the second millennia BC? When were tin bronzes traded principally as prestige goods and ornaments and when had they become essential necessities that had to be procured through some structured form of organized long-distance exchange? There will not be simple answers to these questions for different areas became structurally integrated into this dimly perceived interconnected Bronze Age world at different times. The Caucasus certainly seems to be a participant by the Late Bronze Age, though it is unclear how best to conceptualize earlier Early and Middle Bronze developments in this area.

For many reasons, the West Asian tin problem is far from being resolved. This tin bronze world system undoubtedly differed in interesting ways from the model Wallerstein postulated for the beginnings of the modern historical era, but it is equally hard to see how the distance-parity model can account for it. It is reasonable to feel a certain satisfaction in the aptness of the well-established Old World archaeological terminology. Christian Thomsen certainly was prescient in organizing his materials into successive Stone, Bronze, and Iron periods. Major transformations in the prehistory of Eurasia were marked by fundamental developments in the production and exchange of materials basic to the reproduction and consolidation of societies stretching from the Eurasian steppes to the ancient Near East and northern Europe. Whatever model one adopts, this certainly was an interconnected world.

CHAPTER 2

Ancient Metallurgy in the Mountain Kingdom:

The Technology and Value of Early Bronze Age Metalwork from Velikent, Dagestan

DAVID L. PETERSON

Copper ore deposits in the Caucasus Mountains appear to have been first exploited by the mid-fourth and perhaps as early as the fifth millennium BC (Chernykh 1992:32-35, 57-67; Kushnareva 1997:196-204). However, it is only with the regularization of metallurgical production in the Early Bronze Age (3500–2500 BC) that we find evidence for the use of metal goods in numerous and varied cultural contexts. During the Early Bronze Age in the early to middle third millennium BC, some 1500 metal objects were assembled in tomb 1 on mound III of the site of Velikent in Dagestan as grave goods that accompanied what was probably a successive series of interments in this collective catacomb tomb (Gadzhiev et al. 1995; 1997; see Kohl, chapter 1). Spectral-chemical analyses of the composition of these objects revealed the presence of tin bronze in approximately 8% of the tested sample (Gadzhiev and Korenevskii 1984). This represents a remarkably early example of the systematic use of tin bronze in Caucasia and much of the Old World in general.[1] If the proportion of objects made of tin

bronze in the sample corresponds to the assemblage as a whole, it may number among the largest known collections of tin bronzes from any Early Bronze Age site.

Technical sophistication in Early Bronze Age metalwork is often judged by the presence or absence of tin bronze within an assemblage. There are good reasons for this, since the production of tin often involved techniques quite different from those that were more widely practiced in copper production (Yener 2000:111–123), while the addition of tin hardens copper and gives it a golden tint (Hamilton 1996:14). However, this position tends to equate cultural value with a somewhat simplistic, unidimensional vision of technical practice, while ignoring that making even the most common metal artifact was a complex and dynamic social enterprise (Yener 2000:9). There is compelling evidence that the Velikent metalwork was manufactured locally, yet the underlying sense in many studies of Early Bronze Age prehistory is that early innovations in metallurgy and other crafts originated in the civilization that was emerging in Mesopotamia during this period, and from there were disseminated to outlying areas including Caucasia (Yener 2000:5–6). That view is challenged here by an approach to the Velikent assemblage from the standpoint of how *value* was assigned to metalwork in local or regional systems of metal production, in which the significance of the Velikent tin bronzes is interpreted in relation to the assemblage as a whole, in an overall assessment of the production of metalwork and a theoretical approach to value. The point is not to reassert an old counter-claim that Caucasia was the true source of metallurgical innovations (Frankfort 1928). Rather, the aim is to reframe the problem to focus less on the origins of raw materials and metallurgical processes and to shift more toward the role of metalwork in social and cultural practices. In doing so, I hope to show that the kind of local perspective on material culture and value offered here has much to contribute to the study of interregional dynamics, an objective of current research on the Early Bronze Age in the Near East and neighboring areas (for example, Kohl, chapter 1; Stein 1998a; 1999b).

This essay begins with a discussion of recent research on the "tin problem" or attempts to identify the provenience of the tin ore that was exploited for the tin and bronze used during the Early Bronze Age in southwest Asia. It then shifts to defining an approach to ancient metalwork as the product of both technical and symbolic systems in which producers and consumers participated in the creation of value. This approach is then applied to an examination of how the different materials in the Velikent assemblage were used, including copper, silver, and alloys of copper with arsenic, tin, and silver. This interpretation addresses the ways in which technical and social practices influenced the formation of the Velikent assemblage locally, rather than situating the materials predominantly in a core-periphery relationship with adjacent regions. While this approach attempts to sidestep problems associated with the current heavy emphasis upon the procurement of raw materials over long distances, I do not mean to downplay the potential significance of imports. Clearly metal resources were moving across the landscape, sometimes in great quantities and over surprisingly long distances. Studies of the provenience of tin and other materials therefore remain essential to understanding the dynamics of long-distance exchange. However, studies of sources and patterns of long-distance flow are no substitute for a well-developed understanding of how imports were used in local material culture systems, which is vital to our knowledge of what was at stake in the local engagement in interregional exchange and its historic effects. In order to develop an adequate account of the relationship between the production and use of metalwork and its broader sociocultural significance, studies of interregional dynamics must be integrated with research on how metals were processed, worked, and used outside the putative centers of power and influence that are most often the focus of syntheses of Early Bronze Age prehistory.

VELIKENT AND THE TIN PROBLEM

The evidence for the production and use of metalwork during the Early Bronze Age at Velikent does not fit a spatial frame that links the appearance of tin bronze in western Asia to an exclusive network of long-distance exchange focused on elite consumption in Mesopotamia. Nor does it fit a theoretical frame of social evolutionism in which the development of bronze technology was a correlate of increasing social complexity in centers of urbanization. Studies of early metallurgy in southwest Asia have often shared an intellectual framework in which the discovery of tin bronze is cited as a pivotal moment in the unilineal evolution of technology and human progress, an understanding embedded in the notion of the "Bronze Age" itself (Yener 2000:4). Following Childe (for example, 1951), archaeologists have often associated the early use of tin bronze with the emergence of a "high technology" that accompanied the appearance of urban civilization during the Early Bronze Age in the Near East. This technology would then have been restricted for a considerable time to networks of production and exchange centered on early cities, which would have been the main beneficiaries of the technical and economic enhancements it conferred. However, in most regions tin bronze seems to have been adopted first for ornamentation—as appears to have been the case in northeastern Caucasia—and it was several centuries before it was exploited for economic and productive advantage (Renfrew 1986:144–145). Childe himself recognized that the widespread utilitarian use of bronze was preceded by the ornamental use of copper, but was mistaken in associating the appearance of bronze with a revolution in the use of metal technology, at least at the onset. The transition from the ornamental use to the "practical" use of copper and bronze would have varied from region to region, and probably involved protracted shifts in production and consumption in which the use of tin bronze in tools and weapons came to rival and sometimes surpass its use in ornaments. In this regard, the role of social values including aesthetic sensibilities in prehistoric economies (for example, Lechtman 1984) has received insufficient attention in Bronze Age archaeology.

The site of Velikent was used intermittently from the Late Chalcolithic to Middle Bronze Age period (ca. 3600–1900 BC) and is located in the Caspian littoral of southern Dagestan (see Kohl, chapter 1: figure 1.1). Spectral-chemical analysis was performed on a sample of 195 metal objects out of a total of approximately 1,500 from mound III, tomb 1 at Velikent, including the full range of tools, weapons, and ornaments in the assemblage (Gadzhiev and Korenevskii 1984; figure 2.1). That study found tin bronze in fifteen items (one dress pin, five rings, and nine bracelets) or 8% of the sample. All are ornaments and all but the pin were most likely intended for wear as bodily adornments. Recalibrated radiocarbon dates from more recently excavated tombs at Velikent have dated their use from 2879–2474 BC at mound V, tomb 1 to 2851–2367 BC at mound III, tomb 11 (2 sigma range; see Kohl, chapter 1). The close similarity of the architecture, collective burial practices, and material offerings of these tombs to mound III, tomb 1 indicates that the latter was probably constructed and used during the Early Bronze Age in the first half of the third millennium BC, and that the metal assemblage dates to this period.

The Velikent site is a combination of a small to moderate size Late Chalcolithic to Middle Bronze Age village with Early to Middle Bronze Age cemeteries on at least two of the five mounds that make up the site, covering a total area of approximately 28 ha (see Kohl, chapter 1). Although archaeologists have traditionally linked the appearance of tin bronze with urbanization, the Velikent tin bronzes still fall within the accepted window for the early adoption of tin bronze and would be a sizable example at that.[2] There are no known sources of tin in the Caucasus Mountains (Selimkhanov 1978; Palmieri et al. 1993). The tin in the Velikent bronzes, like that used in Early Bronze Age urban centers to the south (Stech and Piggott 1986), was probably imported.

The present discussion is less concerned with identifying the physical source of Early Bronze Age tin than with examining why the Early Bronze Age people of Velikent were interested in things from the outside. Ethnographic literature describes how hierarchies of goods are established in their use in broader realms of social experience involving the social organization of space and the control of knowledge. Value is assigned to some things on the basis of the "sheer distance [over

which they are acquired] and the magical or symbolic potency associated with distance or with distant places and polities." Control of the access to the power and esoteric knowledge embodied in those goods is a means of creating political and ideological distance in society (Helms 1988:13, 119). This social distancing often encompasses the special skills and knowledge needed to produce extraordinary goods, that can convey to artisans such as metalsmiths an exceptional status, whether positive or negative. The metalsmith's craft itself may be conceived of as originating from a distant source (Eliade 1978; Helms 1988:12-13). While in some instances the value of tin bronze may have been linked to the source of the tin itself, its real social importance was more likely associated with its role in creating social distance through transfer of a sense of otherness to the owner or wearer. This, coupled with the early dating and number of tin bronzes from Velikent, suggest that they should be not be approached as having been derivative of contemporary developments in the early urban centers of Mesopotamia—where tin bronze was also a novel element of material culture at this time—but as a local phenomenon. The question then becomes, how was tin bronze employed in relation to the Early Bronze Age material culture of the site and region?

First, it is instructive to look closely at recent research on the "tin problem" or attempts that have been made using several lines of evidence (archaeological, geological, and textual) to identify the source(s) of the tin used during the Early Bronze Age in southwest Asia (for a comprehensive summary, see Weeks 1999). Recent research on the tin problem is largely concerned with trying to identify the patterns in which tin circulated in long-distance exchange and their social implications, rather than how tin was used in the localities in which it is found. This distinction is important, since a lack of understanding of the role of tin in local social and cultural practices also limits the possibility of interpreting its significance in local and long-distance interactions.

Archaeologically, the earliest known tin bronzes in Mesopotamia are generally accepted to be a handful of objects from the Y cemetery at Kish dating to the Early Dynastic I period or the early third millennium BC. Tin bronzes were not present in substantial quantities in the region until the Early Dynastic III period (ca. 2600–2400 BC), when a large number were included in the in the royal cemetery at Ur (Moorey 1985; Müller-Karpe 1991). Tin bronze also appears in a cache of small anthropomorphic figurines at Tell Judeidah in northern Syria dated ca. 3000 BC and in a few objects from neighboring sites (Stech and Piggott 1986:52). It also occurs in possibly contemporaneous levels in sites in southeastern and central Anatolia, such as Tarsus and Alaca Hüyük (Yener and Vandiver 1993; Muhly 1993:240-242; see also Yener 2000:28–29). We know now that tin bronze is present in at least 15 objects dating to ca. 2850–2400 BC at Velikent, and probably many more. The alloy is more broadly distributed by the end of the third millennium BC and is present in many sites throughout western Asia during the second millennium BC.

The main textual sources for the early tin trade are cuneiform tablets from Mari in Syria and Kültepe-Kanesh in central Anatolia (Muhly 1973:288–335; Yener 2000:11–12). These date to the Old Assyrian period, ca. 2000–1600 BC (Kuhrt 1995:74–117). The tablets discuss tin traveling by various means to Susa, Mari, Assur, and Assyrian trading colonies including Kanesh, ultimately from some unspecified source somewhere in the East, while tin is also said to have arrived in Mesopotamia together with lapis and jade from Meluhha, presumed to be the Harappan civilization of the Indus Valley. Since there is no evidence for the early exploitation of tin in South Asia, it is unlikely to have been the source. However, Afghanistan (Stech and Piggott 1986:44–45) and the Zeravshan Valley of Uzbekistan and Tajikistan (Boroffka et al. 2000) are possible sources. The reasoning in the archaeological discussions of these texts is that the sources of tin referred to in Old Assyrian text are the same sources that were exploited during the Early Bronze Age. This argument is more convincing if the object is to establish *numerous* possible sources rather than the *sole* source of Early Bronze Age tin, an issue covered more fully below.

From a geological perspective, the crux of the tin problem lies in the small number of verified sources of tin in western Asia. Where they do exist there is little evidence that they were exploited in the Bronze Age (Weeks 1999:50–51). However, metallic ores are widespread in the highland frontiers of the Near East in Anatolia, which some researchers have favored over more distant localities as one source for Early Bronze Age tin. For example, cassiterite has been identified in shafts and galleries that were worked from the Chalcolithic to the Byzantine period in the Kestel mine in the Taurus Mountains of southeastern Turkey and was processed into metallic tin nearby at the Göltepe site (Yener and Vandiver 1993; Yener 2000:71–110). The strength of the evidence for Early Bronze Age tin

production in Anatolia has been questioned on several occasions (Hall and Steadman 1991; Pernicka et al. 1992; Muhly 1993; Weeks 1999:50). Amongst other objections, there has been strong skepticism on the grounds that Early Bronze Age tin mining in Anatolia would have involved dependence on many small sources instead of one large one (Yener 2000:72), the argument being that a system founded on numerous sources would have been too unreliable for the purposes of an elite exchange network centered on Mesopotamia. However, over time a mosaic of nearer and more distant sources would have been much more resistant to unforeseen contingencies in supply than any single source. Tin has been detected geologically in other parts of Anatolia and in other locations on the fringes of the ancient Near Eastern ecumene, altogether representing a multiplicity of potential Early Bronze Age tin sources (de Jesus 1980; Kaptan 1983; Muhly 1993; Rapp et al. 1996; Yener 2000:72).

Recently, attempts have been made to settle the tin problem by linking finished objects to ore sources through lead isotope analysis (Stos-Gale et al. 1984; Stos-Gale 1989; Pernicka et al. 1990; Weeks 1999). Isotopic profiles of sources tend to be distinctive according to the age of the deposit, and are unaltered by the physical and chemical transformations that occur in processing ore into metal. In other words, the isotopic profile of an ore is the same as the metal made from it. Therefore, lead isotope analysis is a potentially powerful method for determining provenience. Because the trace element profiles of ores are often drastically altered in the transformation of ore into metal, lead isotope analysis has become widely favored over trace element analysis in provenience studies. However, trace element analysis is not rendered completely obsolete by the lead isotope method. Lead isotope analysis is more effective in identifying the sources of ore used to produce groups of artifacts and associated metallurgical debris than the source of metal in individual objects, while trace element analysis is still useful for proveniencing the metal in large assemblages of metalwork (Northover 1989). In either case, the larger the sample size, the more accurate the results. Finally, any attempt to determine the provenience of the metal in artifacts is vulnerable to the uncertainties introduced by alloying and recycling, which mixed metals from different sources together. Thus, while isotopic analysis is without question a viable tool for sourcing ancient metal (Tite 1996), care must be taken in its application and archaeologists must exercise their discretion when using its results.

In summary, there is no clear consensus on the source and networks for the distribution of tin in the Early Bronze Age. Although many researchers favor a distant eastern source as suggested by second millennium BC texts from Syria and central Anatolia, there is archaeological and geological evidence that a number of smaller sources were also used during the Early Bronze Age in highland Anatolia and elsewhere at the frontiers of the ancient Near East. While some regard Afghanistan as the likely candidate for this elusive eastern source (Stech and Piggott 1986; Weeks 1999), evidence of early tin mining further north in Central Asia has been discussed in Russian sources since at least 1950 (Litvinskii 1950). Following these leads, a recent expedition found mid- to late second millennium BC Andronovo potsherds in several shafts used in mining cassiterite and stannite in Tajikistan and Uzbekistan (Boroffka et al. 2000), and it is possible that further research will uncover evidence of earlier exploitation. Tin and nephrite from eastern sources is also present in archaeological deposits of the Seimo-Turbino horizon which are spread across the steppes and forest-steppe of Eurasia and date to the first half of the second millennium BC (Chernykh 1992:215–234). This means that eastern tin from Central Asia was also traveling long distances to the northwest at the same time that was reported moving west to the Near East in Old Assyrian texts. Thus, in terms used by Smith and Badalyan elsewhere in this volume (chapter 7), networks for the acquisition of tin were not centered on Mesopotamia like the spokes of a wheel but enveloped most of western Asia in a complex web of trading relationships that extended well beyond the core areas of urbanization.

It is within this analytical context that the Velikent assemblage is currently situated, joining an often contentious debate over the interregional dynamics of the Early Bronze Age metals trade. With the joining of new analytical techniques to theoretical priorities developed out of world-systems theory and colonial studies, the West Asian tin trade has become a hot topic for many American and European archaeologists outside Russia. But the situation is different in the Russian and Soviet tradition of archaeological research within which the Velikent metalwork has been previously studied. Researchers in the Soviet Union conducted more than thirty- five thousand analyses of the composition of copper and bronze artifacts from Eastern Europe, Eurasia, Central Asia, and Caucasia in the collective investigation of historical links between the metallurgical traditions and archaeological cultures in these

areas (Chernykh 1992:16). This work continues on a much smaller scale in the CIS today. Yet despite their differences, there are subtle commonalities between Western research and archaeometallurgy in the former Soviet Union. In the latter, a sharp line has been drawn between *metallurgy* as the production of metal from ore and *metalworking* as the manufacture of metal objects by techniques such as casting, forging, annealing, and drawing, in which metallurgy is viewed as having had greater significance in the history of cultures since it is a necessary precondition of metalworking (Chernykh 1992). Research on the tin problem emphasizes metallurgy in a similar though less obvious way. The study of metal sources is closely connected with metallurgy in that it often presupposes a direct link between objects and ore sources, while less attention is paid to how metals may have circulated for extended periods and in different forms than those in which they have been found. These concerns are more closely tied to metalworking activities that occurred after the initial processing of ore into metal (Northover 1989). Downplaying the importance of metalworking can lead to a false impression that its goals and techniques remained fixed through time and in separate contemporary settings. More important, the privileging of metallurgy over metalworking creates the impression that the value of materials, such as tin and bronze, to the people who used them is rooted simply in the distance that separated consumers from source, or a community's position within the trading network. However, the evidence for how imported metal was worked and used in separate regions may tell a very different story.

METAL TECHNOLOGY AND VALUE

In moving away from a unidimensional "distance= value" model, it is critical that we situate material culture within a local sense of technical and social practice. This involves an understanding of material culture production not simply as manufacturing techniques but, more profoundly, as a process through which meaningful objects are created in productive acts that are at the same time technical and symbolic (Munn 1977, 1986; Lemonnier 1992; Dietler and Herbich 1998). There has been a growing awareness in archaeology of the importance of the concept of value for understanding the role of commodities in ancient economies, but this has generated few explicit discussions of value itself (but see Renfrew 1986; Bailey, ed. 1998; van Wijngaarden 1999). Archaeologists have most often approached value in relation to circulation and consumption (for example, Parker Pearson 1984; Orser 1986; Hodder and Preucel, eds. 1996:106–107; van Wijngaarden 1999), and less frequently by linking changing technologies to historical changes in the cultural value systems that influenced economic activities (Lechtman 1984; Renfrew 1986; Bradley 1988). This tendency to emphasize circulation and consumption mirrors a similar inclination in sociocultural anthropology (for example, Appadurai, ed. 1986; Miller 1995; Douglas and Isherwood 1996), which arose in part as a response to the inflated role that was previously given to production in the social sciences, as in Marxian approaches that viewed the development of human societies as determined by their "productive bases" (Wittfogel 1957; Friedman and Rowlands, ed. 1977). However, rather than arriving at new understandings of production, in some cases there has been a move toward over-determining the role of consumption (Miller 1995).

Artisans create material value by manipulating materials to conform to aesthetic and other social and cultural values in technical practice, value that is affirmed or redefined after production. Given a set of objects for which a coherent social and cultural context can be established—such as the metalwork from mound III, tomb 1 at Velikent, which was assembled through the mortuary practices of people with a shared material culture—value may be interpreted archaeologically from the correspondences between the ways in which objects were made and used, that harken back to the choices and skill with which productive goals were met in technical practice. Objects are also subject to redefinitions in meaning and value in their individual histories, through their role in significant events, changes in ownership, and in crossing social boundaries (Douglas and Isherwood 1996; Kopytoff 1986; Dietler and Herbich 1998). In such cases objects often move from one sociocultural context to another, and thereby enter new fields of associations. In addition, sweeping revaluations of types and classes of things, such as "precious" metals or industrially "useful" materials, may occur through broader shifts in production, circulation, and consumption (Renfrew 1986; Appadurai 1986:34–35). Detailed information on methods of production is often available through analysis of the artifacts themselves, while evidence for the paths that objects took in movements across landscapes and through diverse hands is often less accessible to archaeology. The study of production is therefore as crucial to archaeological research on value as the studies of circulation and consumption that have recently dominated the theoretical horizon of the discipline.

Modern economics generally approaches value in terms of supply and demand, in which value is tabulated as price or a quantity of common currency that is used to commensurate between goods and services. This approach can be traced to historical Western economic theories and definitions of rationality of the eighteenth and nineteenth centuries (Dumont 1977, Young 1978). However, in their ethnographic and textual investigations, anthropologists and historians have encountered widely varying cultural and historical definitions of value. This relativist response to neoclassical universalism has been accompanied by a move toward more "emic" understandings of significance and value. An anthropological definition has emerged in which value is "general and relational rather than particular and substantive"; products and actions embody "a differential proportion of some homogenous potency" that forms a parameter along which their value can be measured (Munn 1986:8–9). Although theories of value differ sharply on particular points, a brief review generally supports the importance of relationality. Aristotle held that the value of things is or should be related to the status of the individuals to which they are due (Polanyi 1971). Smith saw the natural value of products as measurable in relation to the labor expended in production (Smith 1937). Neoclassical economists further developed this theory by arguing that value is determined in the relationship between labor and fixed capital (Young 1978:31) and that rational actors choose between alternatives to maximize preferences and utility (Gudeman 1985:222). While Marx largely maintained the formalism of earlier theories, his discussion of commodity fetishism is a persuasive critique in which he noted that consumers' fascination with commodities is not commensurable in terms of labor or notions of utility attached to use value (Marx 1971). Kopytoff (1986) attributes this fascination to a cultural process of valuation in which the meaning of things is continually redefined in successive episodes of circulation. Material value would therefore be *intersubjective*, arising from the relationship between desiring consumers and objects with their own social lives.[3] For Simmel (1978) value is also intersubjective and arises from the desire for objects and the ways in which they somehow resist those wishing to possess them. The distance between economic objects and those who desire them is overcome reciprocally in exchange, through the sacrifice of some other object that is desired by another (Appadurai 1986:3).

However, skilled labor, technical knowledge, and the physical properties of things all set parameters within which value operates. Marx (1971:48) viewed commodity exchange as the creation of use values for others, suggesting a degree of reflexivity between producers and consumers in definitions of value. Economic anthropologists generally accept that in most societies the relations amongst people are more important than the relations between people and things, an idea first forcefully developed by Mauss, who saw gift giving as a powerful way of building social bonds in which gifts convey something of the giver's self (1990). However, there is a need for greater emphasis on the attachments artisans form with their creations and the ways they may convey the essence of their creators. This dynamic would arguably have been strong in the production of metalwork in Early Bronze Age Caucasia where the spatial and social distance between those who made and used it may have often been quite small (see below).[4] A reexamination of the role of production thus offers the possibility of new insights into the full range of activities through which value is socially constituted in material culture.

Value is, of course, historical. Historical, cultural understandings of the proper ways to utilize materials and techniques in making things, of how a particular kind of object should look, feel, and function, and of what makes some things exceptional in relation to others all influence the social construction of material value. Technical knowledge and practice also structures what is possible to achieve through production. Value and technology are reproduced through interrelated activities of production, circulation, and consumption that are altered through the incorporation of new objects, materials, techniques, and uses of things that are introduced by individuals or groups. Since these are collective activities that are linked to even broader sets of social relations, changes in technology and value have potentially profound social repercussions. The knowledge and practices that structure value judgments can endure for long periods. Alterations in the activities through which value and technology are reproduced can have historically transformative effects with unforeseen consequences.

The physical and chemical nature of metals also introduces theoretical and methodological implications for the study of technology and value. The production of metalwork is a reversible process in which artifacts may be converted into other things through the proper application of heat and force. If someone with metal goods is skilled in metalworking or has access to someone that is, the *convertibility* of metalwork creates a tension between the durability of objects on the one hand and their potential reuse as raw materials on the other. How this tension is resolved is situational and depends not only on knowledge of metalworking but also on how metalwork is valued by those who own it, and how that material value matches the reigning local constellation of social values. In some situations objects are preserved; in others the attraction held by the possibility of creating new material value may result in the recycling of old objects into new. The tension between the durability of metal objects on the one hand and their convertibility on the other matches two ways anthropologists have identified in which people perceive material value: at the level of object in which value is defined by its individual history, and as an attribute of a material or class of objects that is more easily exchanged than things with a singular value (Graeber 1996, 2001). Metalwork partakes of both kinds of value in the sense that a metal object has an individual history as well as a mutability that allows for its transformation into new forms and into new substances, as in the alloying of copper and tin to make bronze.

With the foregoing in mind, it is important that archaeologists approach the value of ancient metalwork as neither a function of any single characteristic, such as the presence or absence of tin, nor the raw distance from consumer to source, but as relational and built up from shifting combinations of meaningful qualities achieved by artisans in technical practice. This vantage point allows for an archaeological investigation of how value was transformed as materials and objects traveled between contexts of production and consumption and across social boundaries, and for an examination of continuity and change in productive techniques in relation to the adoption of new objects, materials, and uses for things. By establishing value conceptually in the relationship between technological and social practices, archaeology may move beyond its traditional exclusive focus on economics to include an account of the symbolic dimensions of value rooted in aesthetics. This is manifest, for example, in the creation of objects of high value through feats of technical virtuosity, in the application of aesthetic sensibilities in technical practice (Gell 1992). As sign vehicles, objects bring up different interpretants—the signs brought to mind—for different subjects, and in their fabrication, objects are instilled with physical characteristics widely evocative of particular qualitative associations. The characteristics so constructed can be said to operate as "qualisigns" (Peirce 1955; Munn 1986:17) that embody multiple, interrelated qualities that are fundamental aspects of a more comprehensive whole, in this case the economic and symbolic aspects of the social practices surrounding the production and use of metalwork. Although there is no strict agreement between subjects on the meaning of things, the social identities of producers and consumers are still coproduced through the value acts performed in the creation of evocative qualities in objects, and in their use in social interactions. However, since the associations evoked by the characteristics of things and related value acts vary from subject to subject, objects are vulnerable to revaluations that can transform structures of value if new associations become incorporated into technical and social practice.

Early Bronze Age metalwork was the product of a complex series of operations that normally included several different activities: the mining of ore, its transformation into metal (by smelting and other processes which varied according to the raw material and metal product), sometimes combining metals to create alloys, and the manufacture of finished objects by metalworking techniques such as casting and forging. Each operation represents an opportunity for the transformation of value (1) through investments of materials, fuel, knowledge, labor, and special tools and installations; (2) in the circulation of raw materials and unfinished products between social units; and (3) in profound redefinitions of the form and significance of metal products in their metamorphosis from raw materials to objects and sometimes from one object, or one material, into another. Metalwork and value are therefore coproduced in a temporally extended and often spatially divided process. The spatiotemporal dynamics of the creation of value through the production and use of metalwork have profound implications for the social identities of the individuals involved, and in their self-other relations within the more comprehensive whole in which value operates (cf. Munn 1986:16–18). Information on the provenience of raw materials gathered through research on the tin problem has been creatively employed in the study of cross-cultural social relations in the Early Bronze Age metals trade. However, understanding the local significance of metals depends as much, or more, upon knowledge of the techniques used to work with *all* the materials present in an assemblage, the goals of technical production, and how metal objects were used, as it does with knowing the source of the metals themselves. After all,

the scarcity of an import may indicate high value in one instance and simply the lack of local interest in another. The correspondences present (or lacking) in different kinds of evidence provide investigators with a potential means of telling the difference between apathy and interest, and for answering a wide range of other equally important questions as well. This approach is applied in the discussion of Early Bronze Age metalwork from Velikent that follows.

THE TECHNOLOGY AND VALUE OF EARLY BRONZE AGE METALWORK FROM VELIKENT

As noted earlier, recalibrated radiocarbon dates from two of the catacomb tombs at Velikent and close similarities in the architecture, burial practices, and material offerings in the dated and undated tombs indicate that they were constructed and most heavily used in the Early Bronze Age, or the early to middle third millennium BC. Twelve catacomb tombs are currently known from three mounds at Velikent (mounds III, IV, and V; see Kohl, chapter 1, figure 1.2). The interiors of the tombs were dug into the natural clay terraces that make up the mounds, and the underground chambers were reached by a *dromos* or vertical shaft connected to a short, slanted entrance tunnel sealed by an upright stone slab suitable for reuse (Gadzhiev et al. 1995:140–141; see Kohl, chapter 1, figure 1.4). The tombs contain a remarkable number of burials and an unusually large concentration of wealth for the Early to Middle Bronze Age in northeastern Caucasia. Mound III, tomb 1 contained some 1,500 metal objects along with the remains of as many as one hundred men and women (Gadzhiev and Korenevskii 1984; Gadzhiev et al. 1995:141).

Previously in the Early Bronze Age, burials throughout Caucasia were usually single or collective inhumations in small pits, within or outside settlements and sometimes under house floors. The dating of the Velikent tombs roughly corresponds to an era when the number of settlements had begun to diminish throughout Caucasia, possibly in association with increased dependence on seminomadic sheep-goat pastoralism (Kohl 1992). There is no strong indication of social stratification among the burials in the tombs; indeed the practice of collective interment suggests strong lines of social solidarity as well as an egalitarian ethos. However, we have no way of knowing what percentage of the deceased from the population at any given time was interred within them. In contrast to tomb 1, tomb 12 on mound III contained the remains of fewer (no more than fifteen) immature individuals that were buried without metal goods but instead with some 340 ceramic vessels, far greater than the 200 pots estimated for metal-rich tomb 1 (Magomedov personal communication 1998). This evidence suggests that metalwork and ceramics were incorporated into Early Bronze Age social practices at Velikent, involving age-graded formulations of equality and hierarchy. Ethnographic research has shown the intimate connection between gender associations and the production of value (Munn 1986:16–18). Representation of gender in burials may have strongly influenced valuations of the metalwork that was placed in the Velikent tombs. Unfortunately, this may never be satisfactorily demonstrated, since these are collective tombs in which objects and skeletal remains have in many cases become hopelessly mixed together.

The vast number of metal objects in the Velikent tombs suggests that there were restrictions in their transfer and circulation among the living, and that they instead became funerary offerings or were a form of personal property that remained with their owners in death. Spheres of exchange (Bohannon 1955) may have been present that would under ordinary circumstances prohibit the direct exchange of metal for other kinds of objects. Metalwork may have moved within a different sphere of exchange than, for instance, some forms of ceramics that, unlike metal, are ubiquitous in living areas at Velikent. Where spheres of exchange are present, social sanctions may bar the use of one potential "currency," such as food, for certain transactions, such as payments of dowry and bridewealth, that may require transfers of less perishable items such as metal. According to Morris (1986) the involvement of metalwork in the "destruction" of wealth in burials is an archaeological register of gift economies, in which the objective is not to gain economic power through the accumulation of wealth but to secure influence through generosity. The acquisition and social use of metalwork probably involved delicate social maneuvering and political savvy, whether for displays of wealth and status, navigation between spheres of exchange, or attaining influence through successful demonstrations of generosity in a gift economy.

All told the Velikent tombs suggest a form of social organization in which lines of solidarity occupied heterarchically privileged positions derived from size and endurance. Some of the tombs were more heavily used than others, and it is plausible that different tombs were used by distinct social groups, possibly corporate groups organized by family or lineage. If so, the greater use of some tombs than others and differences in the quantity and quality of offerings within separate tombs may indicate that some corporate groups were more successful in self-perpetuation, and exercising and maintaining power and influence, than others.

The metal artifacts from mound III, tomb 1 may be broken down into three classes of objects—weapons and tools, ornaments, and bodily adornments—for which specific substances (copper, arsenic bronze, tin bronze, or silver and copper-silver alloys) were selectively used (Gadzhiev and Korenevskii 1984:9; figures 2.1–2.2; table 2.1). Within these three classes, a very limited number of types of objects account for some 1,500 artifacts in the assemblage: (1) tools and weapons are represented by shaft-hole axes, hafted knives, chisels, flat axes, and awls; (2) ornaments include dress pins, anchor-shaped pendants, medallions, tubular beads, spirals, breast cups, and small caps; and (3) bodily adornments are comprised of rings and bracelets (figure 2.1; table 2.1). The marked consistencies in the form and composition of these objects indicates the high level of congruence that existed between the practices of local makers and users of metal goods that would have generated these consistencies.

Spectral-chemical analysis was performed on a sample of over 10% of the assemblage (N=195), encompassing its full range of tools, weapons, ornaments, and adornments (Gadzhiev and Korenevskii 1984:19). Almost the entire sample is represented by three compositional groups: unalloyed copper, arsenic bronze, and tin bronze. The three exceptions are one bracelet containing 90% silver and two others cast in an alloy of 70% copper and 30% silver (Gadzhiev and Korenevskii 1984: table, nos. 29998, 30078, 30079). One-third of the tin bronzes also contain arsenic in levels over 1%, and are perhaps more accurately described as a ternary alloy of copper, tin, and arsenic. However, there is no apparent distinction between the use of tin bronze and this alloy in the assemblage (figure 2.2).

Except for one predominantly silver bracelet, all of the objects are copper-based, and all but the three bracelets containing silver were found to have arsenic in levels from 0.1% to 20%, with the majority in the range of 0.01% to 5% (Gadzhiev and Korenevskii 1984:19, table).[5] Besides the two copper-silver bracelets, the copper-based objects can be said to form two groups: *arsenic bronze*, in which arsenic is present in levels of 1-20%, and *unalloyed copper*, with arsenic content

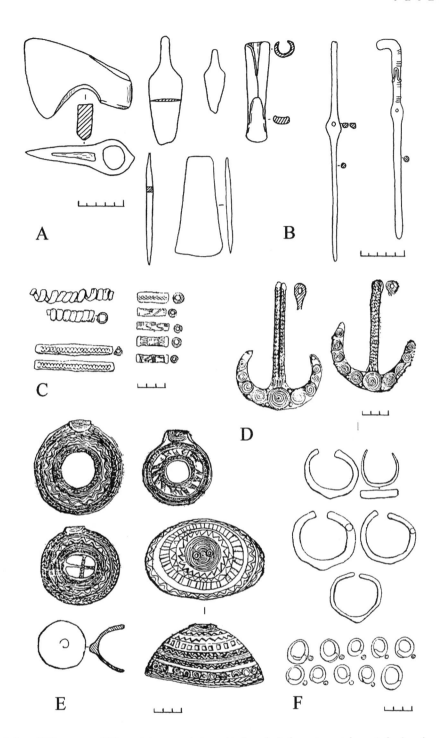

Figure 2.1 Metal finds from Velikent mound III, tomb 1: *a*, axes, knives, chisels, awls; *b*, dress pins; *c*, tubes, spirals; *d*, anchor pendants; *e*, medallions, breast cup, cap; *f*, bracelets, rings. *Figure prepared by D. Peterson after Gadzhiev and Korenevskii 1984:Figs. 2-8.*

below 1% (0.1–0.9%).[6] The concentration of arsenic in the artifacts almost invariably depends on the kind of object that was manufactured. In other words, just provisioning smiths with metal was only one small part of the production of valued goods. Only one of the tools and arms in the sample, a knife, contains arsenic in a level that suggests intentional alloying (2.3%), while a few types of ornaments (spirals, pins, and beads) also tend to be made of unalloyed copper rather than arsenic bronze (Gadzhiev and Korenevskii 1984:19, table, no. 29969; figure 2.2). There was apparently a tendency to reserve arsenic bronze for the other types

Class	Type	Number
Tools and weapons	Shaft hole axe	3
	Knife	6
	Chisel	3
	Adze	4
	Awl	4
Ornaments	Dress pin	46
	Medallion	10
	Breast cup	1
	Cap	1
	Tube	37
	Spiral	7
	Anchor pendant	13
Bodily adornments	Bracelet	30
	Hair ring	30
	Total	195

Table 2.1 Artifacts analyzed by Gadzhiev and Korenevskii (1984) from Velikent mound III, tomb 1, by class, type, and number. *Table prepared by D. Peterson.*

of ornaments as well as bodily adornments (table 2.1; figure 2.2).

The addition of arsenic to copper in arsenic bronze gives copper a silvery tint. Arsenic inhibits the oxidation of copper and also lowers the melting point of copper by several hundred degrees centigrade and reduces the emission of gases as the metal cools, making it superior to unalloyed copper for use in casting (Hamilton 1996:14; Yener 2000). However, the presence of arsenic in levels of 6% or more causes copper to become brittle and unsuitable for tools and weapons, especially those made for use with percussive force, such as axes, adzes, and chisels. The selection of arsenic bronze for ornaments and the tendency to avoid its use in tools and weapons shows that the smiths who made the assemblage knew of the practical dangers of arsenic alloys and consciously manipulated the relationship between form and media. While the arsenic content of ornaments in the sample tends to be much higher than that of tools and weapons, the level of arsenic in ornaments also rarely reaches or exceeds 6%. In combining casting and forging techniques in making ornaments,

the smiths who made the assemblage may have favored the use of arsenic bronze to enhance the castability of copper while avoiding high levels of arsenic because it might be detrimental in forging cast blanks into finished ornaments and adornments. In forging, brittle metal would have required more frequent annealing than a more pliable material. Metallographic research (Scott 1991) is needed to determine the specific metalworking techniques that were applied, and the particular productive goals that were pursued, in working with different metals and alloys in the assemblage.

Similarities in the composition of the items in the sample are strong indications that the metal was produced in the northeastern Caucasus. The objects contain relatively high trace levels of antimony, with the majority falling within 0.15 and 0.3% (Gadzhiev and Korenevskii 1984:19, 23). The addition of antimony to arsenic bronze counteracts brittleness, but the levels of antimony in the objects are well below 1%, suggesting that its presence is probably the result of the geochemistry of the ores that were used. Bismuth also occurs in regular trace levels throughout the sample. It was previously noted that consistently high trace levels of arsenic were detected in objects in which it is only present in levels below 1%, which cannot be characterized as an alloy. The consistent trace levels of arsenic, antimony, and bismuth in the sample, and typological similarities to other Early Bronze Age metalwork assemblages in Dagestan and elsewhere in northeastern Caucasia, further suggest that the Velikent metalwork was made with copper produced within northeastern Caucasia, and that a regional metallurgical tradition—in Chernykh's terms, a "metallurgical focus" (Chernykh 1992)—existed in Dagestan during this period (Gadzhiev and Korenevskii 1984:24–25). Additional source analysis and more systematic investigations of mining and metal production sites are needed to establish the extent to which local ores were smelted for copper during the Bronze Age in the region, and the relationship between ore sources and sites in which copper was worked and used.

Sulphidic ores, which are typically rich in arsenic (Lechtman 1999), are widely available in the Caucasus Mountains (Chernykh 1992:60; Palmieri et al. 1993). However, the Caucasus are a formidable physical barrier in relation to Dagestan. Proceeding almost directly from the Black Sea coast in the west, the Great Caucasus closely approach the Caspian shoreline just south of Velikent at Derbent (see Kohl, chapter 1). At Velikent, a lowland corridor only 20 km in width

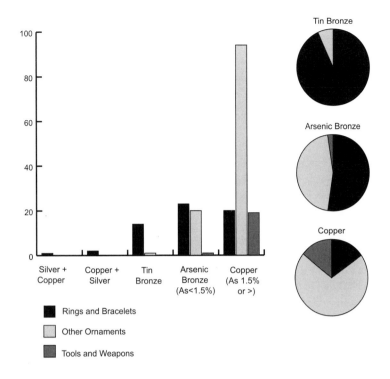

Figure 2.2 Composition of metalwork from Velikent mound III, tomb1. *Figure by D. Peterson based on data from Gadzhiev and Kornevskii (1984).*

separates the Caucasus foothills from the Caspian and was probably even narrower in the Early Bronze Age when Caspian Sea levels were higher (Gadzhiev et al. 1995). While Velikent itself lies in an easily traversed lowland corridor, getting metal or ore to Velikent from even the nearest sources in the northeastern Caucasus would have been a challenging undertaking.

There is evidence that the Velikent assemblage was preceded by a long history of metalsmiths working in the immediate region. An ingot of metal identified as copper was found in an early occupation level in mound 1 (Gadzhiev 1991)[7] and a shaft-hole axe casting mold was found in an early context in a settlement area on mound II (see Kohl, chapter 1). A small sounding excavated at Kabaz Kutan, located only 8 km west of Velikent, yielded a crucible and a casting mold from stratigraphic layers that have been radiocarbon dated to the early third millennium BC, or roughly contemporary to the Velikent assemblage (2 sigma; see Kohl, chapter 1). Prills of copper or bronze have also been found within and near hearths on mound 2 at Velikent. Large numbers of hammerstones occur throughout the settlement areas on mound I and mound II, some of which may have been used to crush ores and fluxes in preparation for smelting or metalworking.

In chapter 1, Kohl discusses new lead isotope analyses that support the conclusion that Velikent smiths used imported tin to make bronze. However, previous spectral-chemical analyses may indicate that imported tin was added to copper made in the northeastern Caucasus to produce metalwork locally (Gadzhiev and Korenevskii 1984). Fifteen of the artifacts from the sample are tin bronzes containing tin in concentrations from about 1% to 10% (Gadzhiev and Korenevskii 1984:24–25, table). The objects are one pin, five rings, and nine bracelets (figure 2.2). Like arsenic, the addition of tin hardens copper and makes it easier cast. The difference is that tin can be added to copper in greater proportions than arsenic (to about 12%) before it causes the alloy to become brittle. Early Bronze Age metalworkers in the region apparently used tin bronze almost exclusively for adornments (rings, bracelets) that were worn directly on the body. The tin bronzes are distinguished from the other objects in the sample by elevated levels of lead and nickel, probably as a result of mixing copper with tin or bronze that was saturated with these elements (Gadzhiev and Korenevskii 1984:24–25). Lead isotope analysis of objects from the sample has indicated that the tin came from the same eastern source as tin in Early Bronze Age metalwork from Oman (see Kohl, chapter 1; Weeks 1999), but more testing is needed to confirm these results. The tin bronzes share the same levels of antimony, bismuth, and arsenic as the rest of the sample, suggesting that they may have been made by mixing imported tin or bronze with copper from northeastern Caucasia (Gadzhiev and Korenevskii 1984:24–25). Copper ores with high nickel content are also thought to have been mined in the Armenian upland by the beginning of the second millennium BC and perhaps as early as the third (A. T. Smith 2001, personal communication), and such ores are also characteristic of Iran and Anatolia, where Kura-Araks-like pottery and other forms of material culture similar to that of Velikent became widespread in the early third millennium BC (Kohl 1992; Kushnareva 1997).

The technical leap embodied in the local adoption of tin bronze at Velikent seems to have been tied to the demand for silver and tin bronze in *status markers*. Status markers tend to be the highest-quality versions of something with no other purpose, such as the well-worn example of a tea service of fine china as it stands in relation to everyday dishes (Douglas and Isherwood 1996:85). There also tends to be an inverse relationship between the rank value and frequency with which an object was used. The lesser value of necessities is belied by their use in frequent, low-esteem events, while luxuries are reserved for highly esteemed, low-frequency events (Douglas and Isherwood 1996:83). The types of objects with the most "versions" at Velikent are bracelets and rings. The rings were made in copper, arsenic bronze, and tin bronze while the bracelets were made in those materials as well as silver and copper-silver alloys (figure 2.2). By analogy this multiplication of versions, and the fact that rings and bracelets had no other apparent use than as bodily adornments, suggest that they served as status markers used in conjunction with funerary events. Moreover, the death of an individual is itself a singular occurrence, and in most cases mortuary ceremonies are known ethnographically to be highly esteemed events (Metcalf and Huntington 1991). The level of mortuary ceremonialism evident in the Velikent tombs supports this analogy.

The "highest quality" versions of these status markers would have been those made with silver and tin. They are the most infrequently occurring materials in the assemblage, and were probably the most difficult to acquire and those likely to have elicited the most interest. However, difficulty of acquisition should not be equated with scarcity in the normal sense. The scarcity of silver and tin at Velikent would have been meaningful only in relation to other positive associations with these materials, and to the positive and negative associations of all of the materials in the assemblage.

I believe that the color of the different materials present in the Velikent assemblage—copper, silver, and alloys of copper with arsenic, tin, and silver—served as qualisigns (Peirce 1955; Munn 1986:17) of the relative value of the objects and materials to the people who made and used them. As qualisigns, the color of metal objects would have evoked a wide range of different but interrelated associations for producers and consumers that were associated with the physical properties of the materials including their relative hardness, brittleness or durability, and the ability to use them to execute productive goals related to collective sensibilities concerning desirable characteristics in metalwork, such as the suitability for use with a specific technique like casting. From an interpretive perspective, there need not be an objective correlation between a particular color and material in each object. For example, the similarity in the color of arsenic bronze to silver, and the selective use of both for ornamentation but not in tools and weapons, suggests that arsenic bronze may have been meant to emulate silver.[8] In some cases the silver color of arsenic bronze may have also been used to dissemble silver as a more valuable material.

Silver was identified in only three objects and is therefore by far the least frequently occurring material and was arguably considered the most valuable metal in the assemblage. Silver is very rare in Early to Middle Bronze Age metalwork from Eurasia and Caucasia (Chernykh 1992:143), and its source is open to question. It is available at various points in the Caucasus Mountains including parts adjacent to lowland Dagestan, but in smaller quantities than copper ores. In this case the difficulty of acquiring silver may be related not to long distance exchange but rather to its limited availability in the physical environment. Knowledge of techniques for winning silver may have also been less widespread than knowledge of copper smelting. The addition of silver, like arsenic and tin, inhibits oxidation and hardens copper (Lechtman 1984), and in the percentages present in the bracelets from Velikent has a much lighter color than copper or bronze. If color served as a qualisign in value judgments, the concentrations of 30% and 90% silver in the bracelets would have been sufficient to distinguish its presence among the other objects in the assemblage.

But if silver was so valuable, why mix it with copper? The metal technology used to make the metalwork from Velikent was largely copper-based, and the silver present may have been derived from copper-silver deposits. In addition, the mixture of copper and silver is desirable in that it forms a harder material than copper and a more ductile metal than silver alone. Although arsenic bronze also has a silvery hue, smiths and experienced consumers would have been able to thwart attempts to dissemble alloys of silver and copper with high arsenic bronze by identifying the greater durability of the former and the brittleness of the latter.

In some ways the metalwork from Velikent is distinct in form from Early Bronze Age metalwork from neighboring regions (Gadzhiev and Korenevskii 1984:11–17). The shaft-hole axes with downward curving blades (figure 2.1) are quite distinct from Kura-Araks shaft-hole axes in southern Transcaucasia. The straight and crosier-shaped dress pins (figure 2.1) are without parallels in Caucasia. Their closest analogies occur in the eastern Mediterranean but in later contexts (ca. 2300–1600 BC).

The metal objects from tomb 1 also share all of the typological parallels that Kohl notes for the metalwork from mound III, tomb 11 in chapter 1. While these objects include forms that are widely distributed throughout Caucasia and southwest Asia in the Early and Middle Bronze Age, our knowledge of the techniques used in making them is much more limited. Formal similarities in the typology of metalwork from different regions may mask differences in productive technologies that may not become apparent until metallographic analysis is performed to identify the metalworking techniques that were used to make these objects (Scott 1991). Since there seems to have been a profound correspondence between technical practice and the meaning and value of metalwork, differences in technology would suggest differences in value. The characteristics that would have made the objects valuable were achieved through technical practice, and it is likely that the techniques, skill, and knowledge of the smiths who made the Velikent metalwork were iconicized (Munn 1986:16–17) as valuable in themselves. The cross-cultural significance of metalsmiths has been well demonstrated by Eliade (1978), but cannot be overemphasized since early metal production in Caucasia is often treated as derivative of technologies that originated in the urban centers of southwest Asia, while the role of local metalworkers is largely ignored.

While all marking of difference should not be read as hierarchy, value conceptually entails a process of hierarchization (Munn 1986:18). This examination of Early Bronze Age metalwork from Velikent suggests that the physical properties of metals, their practical performance both during and after production, and the relative difficulty in acquiring them were involved in the hierarchical ordering of materials and objects. However, the production, use, and value of metalwork underwent profound historical changes in different localities. Dumont's (1980) notion of *situational hierarchy* is a means for conceptually exploring hierarchies of value as structures in process. According to Dumont, idea-values are ranked in such a way that "high" ideas contradict and contain "low" ones, a relationship he refers to as *encompassment* (Dumont 1980:224–225). Another property of the ranking of idea-values is *reversal*. "[H]ierarchy is bidimensional, it bears not only on the entities considered but also of the corresponding situations, and this bidimensionality entails the reversal" (Dumont 1980:224–225). In other words, in certain situations objects of lesser value become more important than those of higher value, a situation that may be accompanied by a reorientation of hierarchical relations. The selection of unalloyed copper for tools and weapons in the Velikent assemblage was related to knowledge of the practical dangers of arsenic bronze, as well as the selection of bronze and silver for use in adornments. Thus the hierarchical priority of those materials was less relevant from the standpoint of the practical use of implements, at least as long as they were reserved for adornment. The bidimensionality of hierarchical values could have been involved not only in temporary reversals as discussed by Dumont but also in broader revaluations of materials and objects, and the principles governing their use.

The hierarchy of value in the Velikent metalwork would have been embodied socially through bodily adornment, a practice closely associated with the social inscription of concepts of personhood, and an important mechanism for naturalizing social categories and behavioral expectations in the formation of social identities among closely interacting members of a group (Dietler and Herbich 1998:242). The bidimensionality of the hierarchy appears to have been manifest in relation to difficulty of acquisition and practical performance. The superior performance of tin bronze over unalloyed copper and arsenic bronze during and after production, and its greater availability in relation to silver, may have opened the way for practical revaluations of the associations evoked by the characteristics of metalwork, and hence the socially prescribed uses of materials.

The distribution of silver and tin was limited and may have been controlled by a privileged few, but the legitimate uses of metals and metalwork were related to practices and associations that may have often been outside the direct control of an elite. Therefore even where an elite instigated contestations of legitimacy, such as the use of tin bronze for its practical advantage in tools and weapons versus a traditional use in adornment, these contests may have led to unforeseen results that would have brought the terms of legitimacy itself into question. For example, the increasing use of tin bronze for tools and weapons over the course of the Bronze Age had its technical and economic advantages, but also promoted the production of greater quantities of the alloy, and thereby lessened its effectiveness in creating or highlighting social distance. The revaluation of the utilitarian uses of bronze in relation to bodily adornment may have also drawn into question the value of other materials reserved for adornment and their legitimizing effect in local social practice.

CONCLUSION

The study of the relationship between the technology and value of Early Bronze Age metalwork from northeastern Caucasia is important for several reasons. Syntheses of the Early Bronze Age in southwest Asia have structured archaeologists' expectations concerning material culture practices in Caucasia during that period. The immense assemblage of metalwork from the tombs at Velikent represents a technological complexity in both metallurgy and metalworking that rivals that of more socially complex Early Bronze Age urban centers to the south. Similarly, the early and systematic use of tin bronze at Velikent indicates that Early Bronze Age societies in northeastern Caucasia had established trade networks necessary to acquire the materials needed to fabricate metalwork on a similar order to contemporary workshops in southwest Asia. Theories of value and ethnographic research on the formation of value indicate that the production and use of objects are joined in the creation of value as a social process, and suggest that even where cross-cultural exchange has a significant role in the acquisition of materials and objects for local production and consumption, their form, meaning, and significance are profoundly transformed in local practice. Developing

an adequate account of the early commoditization of metals and its broader sociocultural significance in western Asia will require further research on how metals were processed, worked, and used outside of urban centers in the south. Doing so will enhance our understanding of the role of metalwork and technology in Early Bronze Age societies, and the nature and historical impact of interregional connections in the material culture practices of distant and diverse social groups.

I have argued that during the Early Bronze Age at Velikent, metalwork was implicated in a social process of hierarchization involving both the production and use of metal objects, in which shifts in production and consumption were linked to changes in joint constructions of value and related technological and social practices. In acquiring tin for bronze, this process would have included interaction with distant polities with potentially transformative effects. However, this influence would have depended on how those interactions were integrated into local practice, so that in many ways this process remained a fundamentally local phenomenon even at the level of cross-cultural interaction.

ACKNOWLEDGMENTS

I wish to express my gratitude to Philip Kohl and to Drs. Magomed G. Gadzhiev, Rabadan M. Magomedov, and other members of the Institute for History, Archaeology, and Ethnology, Dagestan, for introducing me to the Velikent materials and enabling me to participate in the Dagestan American Velikent Expedition in 1997 and 1998. Without them this paper would not have been possible. My thanks also go to David Anthony, Michael Dietler, Philip Kohl, Nicholas Kouchoukos, Jennifer Lundal-Humayun, Kathleen Morrison, Karen S. Rubinson, Adam T. Smith, and K. Aslihan Yener for reading various drafts and generously offering their thoughtful suggestions and comments. Finally, thanks to Michael Stein, Hae-Kyung, and Nicholas Chamandy with the Statistical Consulting Program at the University of Chicago. Their statistical analyses of this material was completed after this article was submitted, but will be included in future publications.

NOTES

1. This paper uses the term "tin bronze," the alloy of copper and tin, rather than the more traditional "bronze" in order to distinguish it from "arsenic bronze," the alloy of copper and arsenic that was widely adopted much earlier in the Old World than tin bronze (in relation to the Caucasus, see Chernykh 1992). It also follows the archaeological convention of identifying an alloy by the presence of a secondary (and sometimes tertiary) elements in levels of 1% or more (for example, Chernykh 1992:145), whether it was achieved through the direct mixture of processed metals or by other means including cosmelting or fluxing (Lechtman 1999; Yener 2000).

2. Care must be taken not to conflate the adoption of the material with its discovery, especially in terms of a unilineal history. For instance, Yener (2000) discusses Chalcolithic copperwork with high tin content (>1%) from Anatolia. As Renfrew (1986) has argued, it is the widespread adoption, and not the discovery, of a technology that is important to the understanding of prehistoric society.

3. Munn (1986) discusses a more specific notion of intersubjectivity in relation to value than the one suggested here.

4. This in no way means that definitions of value derived from the knowledge of producers and consumers were identical nor that they were the same among individuals within those groups. The ramifications of this are dealt with later in this chapter.

5. Their table of data on the composition of all 195 items indicates that although the proportion is unspecified, arsenic *is* present in the objects that contain silver (Gadzhiev and Korenevskii 1984: table. nos. 29998, 30078, 30079).

6. This differs from a bimodal distribution of "low arsenic" at levels of 0.1–1.5% and "high arsenic" in levels of 1.5–5% discussed in the original study (Gadzhiev and Korenevskii 1984). For the sake of simplicity, I have chosen to focus instead on the 1% threshold typically used to distinguish an alloy (see note 2).

7. Whether or not it is an alloy remains to be determined.

8. Thanks to Kathleen Morrison and K. Aslihan Yener for first pointing this out.

CHAPTER 3

On the Origins of the Kura-Araxes Cultural Complex

TAMAZ KIGURADZE
&
ANTONIO SAGONA

Throughout its history Caucasia has stood as a formidable frontier. A complex and often inaccessible landscape, the region is partitioned by the impressive Caucasus mountain range that conspicuously defined the north central boundary of the ancient Near East, separating it from the extensive European steppes to the north. Around 3500 BC, or slightly earlier, one of the most distinctive archaeological complexes of the ancient Near East came into prominence in the lands south of the Caucasus and neighboring regions. Known in archaeological literature as Kura-Araxes, Early Transcaucasian or Karaz, this material culture complex stretched across a remarkably wide area from Transcaucasia (except the westernmost part of Georgia) through northwestern Iran to eastern Anatolia and the Upper Euphrates for more than 1,500 years (Japaridze 1961; Khanzadian 1967; Sardarian 1967; Burney and Lang 1972; Munchaev 1975; Sagona 1984; Kushnareva and Markovin 1994; Kushnareva 1997). A related artifact assemblage occurs in the Levant, where its conspicuous presence comes in a derivative form named after the site of Khirbet Kerak (modern Beth Yerah) in northern Israel (Miroschedji 2000; Philip and Millard 2000). In the Amuq (H–I), Khirbet Kerak ware has been designated Red-Black Burnished ware by Robert Braidwood, a term that has the virtue of emphasizing the distinctive color scheme.

Although regional variants of the Kura-Araxes cultural assemblage have certainly been recognized, unmistakably similar modes of architecture and artifact types are recurrent over an astonishingly wide geographical zone. These traits include rectilinear, subrectangular, and circular houses built of mudbrick or wattle and daub; portable and fixed hearths that are often anthropomorphic or zoomorphic in style; a wide range of hand-built burnished pottery often displaying a contrasting color scheme of black, gray, brown, and red, and sometimes bearing elaborate ornamentation; well-crafted bone implements; standardized horned animal figurines; a simple range of metal objects most of which may be classed as arsenical bronzes; and a standardized stone tool repertoire that is manufactured primarily from obsidian in the eastern areas.

Despite these seemingly crisp brushstrokes, many issues of this cultural complex remain elusive. Perhaps the most intriguing questions concern its origins, which is as problematic today as when B. A. Kuftin coined the term *Kura-Araxes* more than half a century ago (Kuftin 1941). While acknowledging multiple regional adaptations, the homogeneity of the Kura-Araxes complex has led some prehistorians not only to equate the phenomenon with a discrete ethnic group (Burney 1989) but also to the conclusion that the culture was diffused from a single point of origin rapidly throughout the highlands north of the fertile crescent.

So where did this ubiquitous and enduring cultural tradition begin? The purpose of this paper is to examine the archaeological evidence that precedes the earliest manifestations of the Kura-Araxes complex. This is not intended to be a comprehensive survey of the Chalcolithic traditions of the highland area, a subject recently dealt with by Chataigner (1995). Rather it is a discussion of specific sites in Transcaucasia and northeastern Anatolia, broadly datable to the two millennia between about 5000 to 3000 BC, that we believe collectively shed some light on the puzzling issue of Kura-Araxes origins (Kiguradze 2000). In doing so we wish to highlight the little-known data from Transcaucasia and combine them with information that is emerging from Sos Höyük in northeastern Anatolia. The very interesting Late Chalcolithic data from the Upper Euphrates, most especially the recent tantalizing evidence from Arslantepe (Frangipane 2000), will be considered only in the conclusion and insofar as they reflect broad socioeconomic and political developments further east. Instead we shall concentrate on the eastern geographical zone.

The premise of our argument is that a general cultural continuum, albeit a tenuous one given our patchy record, existed from the end of the Transcaucasian Neolithic, represented by the Shulaveri complex, to what may be termed the "Proto-Kura-Araxes" horizon at the end of the Late Chalcolithic period. On present evidence, it appears that during this transitional period a socioeconomic structure was established that was broadly adopted by Kura-Araxes communities of the subsequent third millennium BC.

To clarify the present state of studies on the origin of the Kura-Araxes complex, something will first be said, by way of background, of the nature of the evidence. Then follows a presentation of the information available on the stratigraphy of key sites before, in the final sections, some discussion on the material culture

and the influences, both internal and external, to which the region was subjected.

NATURE OF THE EVIDENCE

Those venturing into the archaeology of Transcaucasia will at once face some daunting though not insurmountable difficulties. The most confounding problem, especially for the prehistoric period, is the lack of a reliable chronology. Compared to some parts of the Near East, such as Palestine or the Turkish Upper Euphrates, where cultural chronologies have been anchored to firm data, the material available for Transcaucasia is pitifully inadequate, resulting in a sequence of human occupation for the prehistoric period that is still largely free-floating. (For detailed discussions on chronological issues see T. B. Kiguradze 1976; Andreeva 1977; Kavtaradze 1981; Sagona 1984; Glumac and Anthony 1992; Marro and Hauptmann 2000). In Transcaucasia, chronology rests mostly on typological rather than stratigraphical evidence and is often characterized by involved and contradictory arguments that seek to distinguish developmental phases with only a handful of trustworthy absolute dates. In dealing with the Chalcolithic period, for instance, we have only a handful radiocarbon dates.[1] Consequently, we are forced to determine the period's absolute lifespan by reference back to the comparatively small number of assessments available for the Neolithic and Early Bronze Age. Many of these dates, in turn, are individual readings that are scattered chronologically and geographically, most with wide standard deviations that offer little statistical reliability. The solution to this problem really depends on a sufficient number of well-stratified and radiocarbon-dated sites in regions that accurately reflect the geographical variations, which are so much part of Transcaucasian cultural mosaic.

For the time being, this situation has been ameliorated somewhat by investigations at Sos Höyük, in northeastern Turkey, which, we must not forget, is geographically closer to Tbilisi and Erevan than it is to Malatya in east central Turkey. We have almost sixty radiocarbon readings from Sos with more than half from secure deposits that yielded Kura-Araxes and related material. Just as the Sos sequence has clarified matters pertaining to the end of the Kura-Araxes complex and its relationship to the period of the *kurgan* (barrow) burials in the Erzurum region (Sagona 2000), it is now beginning to yield evidence on the Late Chalcolithic–Early Bronze Age transition (for the Late

Chalcolithic–Early Bronze Age period at Arslantepe, see Frangipane 2000). Thus we include in this paper some of the data collected in the 1998 and 1999 campaigns, which go some way toward assisting with the interpretations of horizons further east.

Broadly speaking, the Chalcolithic of Transcaucasia, or Eneolithic as it is also referred to, can be divided into three separate zones (Munchaev 1982):

1) East Transcaucasian, including Sioni, Delisi, Berikldeebi, Alikemek Tepesi, Leila Tepe, and Tekhut.

2) West Transcaucasian, represented primarily by the key site of Samele Kldé.

3) North Caucasian, including Ginchi, Galugai 1 and 2, the Nalchik cemetery, and the pre-Martkopian sites such as Meshoko and Skala.

This study will focus on a series of recurring cultural traits and patterns, referred to as "Sionian" (Menadbe et al. 1978) by Georgian archaeologists, after the type site Sioni, that are germane to the matter of Kura-Araxian antecedents. On the basis of data presented here, two broad chronological phases can be discerned at this stage: (1) an Early Chalcolithic phase, stretching from around 4800 to 4000 BC and (2) a Middle/Late Chalcolithic phase covering the fourth millennium around 4000–3200/3100 BC. In northeastern Anatolia, however, preliminary radiocarbon readings are pointing to dates closer to 3000 BC for the end of the Late Chalcolithic. Within this millennium considerable cultural traits and patterns are emerging to warrant the identification of a "Proto-Kura-Araxes" developmental phase around 3600/3500–3200/3100 BC, which, in time, will probably require its separation into a Late Chalcolithic phase proper.

THE SITES

Some fifty sites attributed to the Chalcolithic period have been investigated in Transcaucasia with the vast majority located in Georgia (figure 3.1), a situation that reflects the intensity of archaeological investigations in the central plain more than it does any real concentration of settlements in that region. The most conspicuous features of the Caucasus are geographical division and extreme environmental diversity, a combination that promoted a degree of cultural regionalism in antiquity. To the south of the Greater Caucasus mountain range, for instance, central lowland plains are juxtaposed with a subtropical littoral along the Black Sea coast, steppe lands and highland plateaus.

Geographically, the neighboring highlands of northeastern Anatolia are equally complex with a pronouncedly east-west orientation defined by the Pontic ranges that separate the subtropical Black Sea coastal fringe from the Aras [Araxes]-Kelkit-Çoruh depression, a natural highway that leads to central Anatolia.

A glance at the distribution of Neolithic (Kiguradze 1986: Fig. 1) and Chalcolithic (figure 3.1) sites will reveal immediately a major economic difference. The earliest Neolithic settlers clearly preferred the light-chestnut soils of the Kura depression, presumably because of their proximity to stands of wild cereals. Later Chalcolithic settlements, by contrast, covered a much wider distribution area and more diverse ecological zones. Communities began to spread upland, above the altitude of 400 to 500 m above sea level, and utilize the thin podzolized soils of the foothills and mountains that are most suited to grazing, a practice that continued into the period of the Kura-Araxes complex. From the few available studies, it seems that at most sites domestic animals—sheep, goats, cattle, and even pigs—predominated. That pig bones were recovered at some of these sites certainly argues against a nomadic lifestyle but would not exclude the notion that these communities might have practiced a transhumant subsistence strategy. The view that human groups in this period moved between fundamentally different environmental zones, copying the seasonal movements of the animals on which they rely for food, is supported by emerging evidence on settlement patterns. Moreover, this form of economy appears to have been practiced in the third millennium.[2] Survey work in northeastern Anatolia, for instance, has revealed Kura-Araxes sites in a range of altitudes, suggesting pastoralist farmers and their livestock moved, usually altitudinally, according to changing climate and resource availability.[3] The exception to this pattern is Samele Kldé, where only cattle represented the domesticates in an economy based on the hunting of wild species—goat, bison, red deer, wild boar, brown bear, and wolf (Javakhishvili 1971). Another difference is apparent between Neolithic and Chalcolithic sites, namely the former are generally multilevel mounds with settlements of circular mudbrick houses whereas the later settlements of the Chalcolithic are generally flat with a notable paucity of architectural remains and a preponderance of pits.

Several key Chalcolithic sites are located in the neighborhood of Tbilisi. The most important is Sioni, nestled in the foothills within the village of Sioni located 60 km southwest of Tbilisi (Menabde and

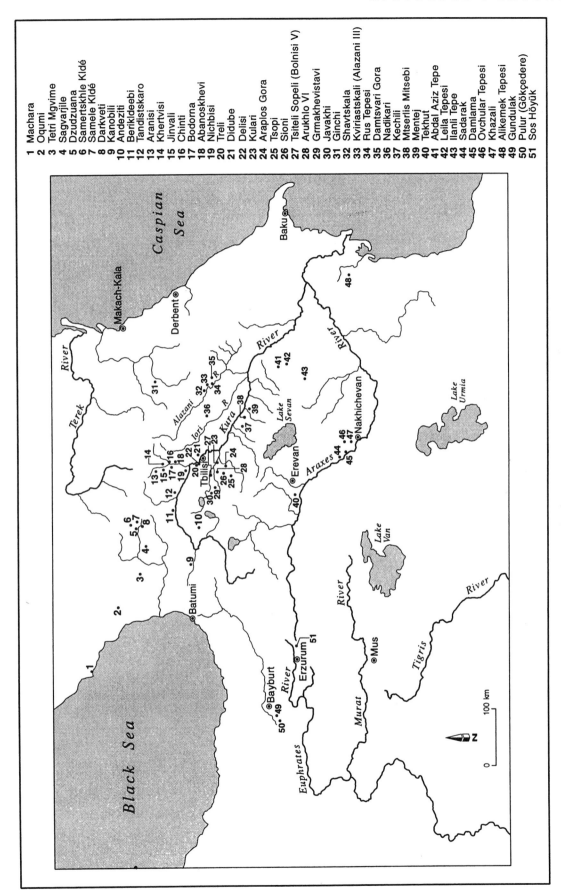

1 Machara
2 Oqumi
3 Tetri Mgvime
4 Sagvarjile
5 Dzudzuana
6 Samertskhle Klde
7 Samele Klde
8 Darkveti
9 Kanobili
10 Andeziti
11 Berikldeebi
12 Tandistskaro
13 Aranisi
14 Khertvisi
15 Jinvali
16 Chinti
17 Bodorna
18 Abanoskhevi
19 Nichbisi
20 Treli
21 Didube
22 Delisi
23 Kulari
24 Araplos Gora
25 Tsopi
26 Sioni
27 Tsiteli Sopeli (Bolnisi V)
28 Arukhlo VI
29 Grmakhevistavi
30 Javakhi
31 Ginchi
32 Shavtskala
33 Kviriastskali (Alazani III)
34 Rus Tepesi
35 Damtsvari Gora
36 Nadikari
37 Kechili
38 Mtserlis Mitsebi
39 Mentej
40 Tekhut
41 Abdal Aziz Tepe
42 Leila Tepesi
43 Ilanli Tepe
44 Sadarak
45 Damlama
46 Ovchular Tepesi
47 Khazali
48 Alikemek Tepesi
49 Gundulak
50 Pulur (Gökçedere)
51 Sos Höyük

Figure 3.1 Chalcolithic sites in Transcaucasus and northeastern Anatolia. *Map by Chandra Jayasuriya.*

Kiguradze 1981). Measuring about 80 x 35 m today, the site has been eroded on the left flank by the Khudis Tskali, a tributary of the Shulaveri River. People settled at Sioni only during the Early and Middle Chalcolithic period and built a large circular structure (10 to 12 m in diameter) with stone foundations (Menabde and Kiguradze 1981: Fig. 1). Although this structure is the largest attributable to the fourth millennium in Transcaucasia, its purpose remains unclear. In later times, especially during the Middle and Late Bronze Age, the function of the site changed to that of a cemetery, which comprised at least sixty graves that were dug into the earlier Chalcolithic deposits.

On the other side of the mountain ridge, some five to six km southeast of Sioni, is the site of Tsopi. A one-period settlement, Tsopi is situated on the left bank of the Banusha stream, near the village of the same name (Grigolia and Tatishvili 1960; Chubinishvili 1971). No architecture was recovered in the course of investigations, though fragments of a wattle-and-daub wall were found in one of the 27 pits that ranged between 0.9 m and 1.8 m in diameter. Nearby is Arukhlo VI, the latest site from a group of six low mounds located at the confluence of the Khrami and Mashavera rivers (Chubinishvili et al. 1979; Gogeliya 1982). Arukhlo VI is Chalcolithic in date and yielded only pits.

Modern building activity within the city of Tbilisi and its neighborhood led to the discovery of three Chalcolithic sites. The earliest of these salvage projects was Didube, a settlement and cemetery site, excavated in 1930–1931 and dated to the late fourth millenium BC (Koridze 1955; see note 1). More recent are the excavations of Treli and Delisi. Treli was investigated as part of the reconstruction of Georgian Military Highway (Abramishvili and Gotsiridze 1978), but, regrettably, most of site was destroyed before it was properly recorded. An early Kura-Araxes settlement was found 3 m below the surface of the ground, which attests to the considerable deposition of silt that has occurred in the Kura valley over the millennia. Moreover, the intensive use of the site as a cemetery during the Late Bronze Age and Iron Age has provided only the sketchiest of pictures of its Late Chalcolithic occupation. Nonetheless, three building levels were defined and contained a considerable amount of wattle-and-daub fragments and post impressions, sections of plaster floor, parts of hearths, six bell-shaped pits each with evidence of burning, and also the corner of a stone-founded structure. The pits reached a maximum depth of 1.1 to 2.0 m, and had a diameter at the top of

0.5 to 0.6 m, whereas their base ranged between 0.8 and 1.0 m. Only two pits, no. 3 and 5, could be attributed with confidence to a stratigraphic level, the third (lowest), but to judge from the homogeneity of pottery all six pits are likely to be contemporary.

Delisi was discovered a little later than Treli, in the winter of 1972, and excavated by R. Abramishvili in 1976, and again a few years later (Abramishvili 1978). Stratigraphically, the cultural deposit was distinguished by an ashy layer again located well below (between 3.5 and 4.6 m) the present ground surface. Although the excavators were not able to discern any coherent architectural plans, more than one hundred postholes and fragments of wattle and daub were suggestive of structures.

One of the latest and most significant Chalcolithic sites is Grmakhevistavi, situated in the village Vardisubani, in the Dmanisi region, 80 km southwest of Tbilisi. It comprises Late Chalcolithic, Late Bronze Age, and Early Iron settlements and cemeteries; Achaemenid graves; and Medieval buildings (Abramishvili et al. 1980). The Late Chalcolithic (Proto-Kura-Araxes) levels were badly damaged by building activities, but floors plastered with clay and fragments of hearths were found. More than one hundred pits, cylindrical and bell-shaped, varying in depth from 0.5 m to 2.5 m, contained much cultural debris that was often sealed by a layer of stones. As we shall see, the excavators grouped the pits into three chronological categories on the basis of pottery. Six pit graves and two stone chambers also belong to this period. One of the latter, measuring 3.0 x 1.8 x 1.0 m (depth), was found intact. It contained five skeletons, four of which were secondary and placed in a corner, and four clay vessels comparable to later Early Bronze Age examples from Samshvilde.

Among the handful of Chalcolithic sites in the Alazani region that demand attention are Alazani I and II, destroyed during farming activity in the mid- to late 1950s, and often attributed mistakenly to the Neolithic (Javakhishvili 1966). Kviriastskali, known in early reports as Alazani III, is the best-preserved settlement in the area (Varazashvili 1992). It is a mound 70 m in diameter at the base, rising at the eastern end to 1 m above the plain, with a further 30 cm of deposit below the valley floor. To judge by the scatter of sherds, obsidian, and groundstone objects, the original settlement may have covered an area 200 x 150 m. The settlement was occupied only during the Chalcolithic and is distinguished by thirteen pits—no traces of architecture

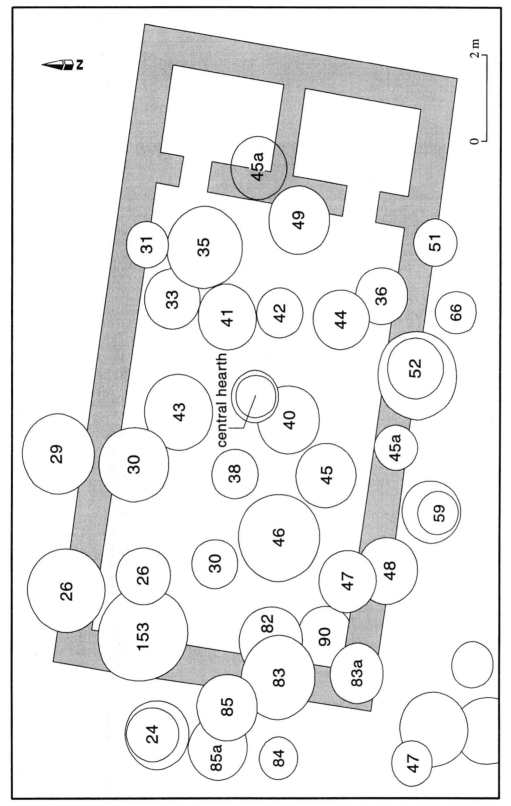

Figure 3.2 Berikldeebi: Plan of rectilinear structure and later pits from Level II. *Illustration by Chandra Jayasuriya after Kipiani 1997.*

were found—cut into a relatively thin (around 30 cm) level of yellow clay level.[4] About 1 km from Kviriastskali is Alazani IV, where pits again feature prominently (Gogeliya and Chelidze 1992: 62-63).

Two kilometers northwest of Kviriastskali is Damtsvari Gora, a small mound, 1 m high and 40 m in diameter (Varazashvili 1992: 32). The excavators distinguished four stratigraphic layers: a yellow clay level, the lowest, followed by the cultural deposit, with a maximum thickness of 30 cm, which was superimposed, in turn, by a layer of weathered soil and burnt red earth respectively. The excavator suspects that the redness was the result of the mound being used as a pyre during the Late Bronze Age. Some 700 square meters of the Chalcolithic settlement were exposed. Twenty-six pits, ranging in diameter from 0.4 to 1.2 m and measuring 0.5 to 0.8 m in depth, were cleared plus three ditches each 1.2 m wide.

Northwest of Tbilisi, in the region of Shida Kartli, are the sites of Nichbisi, Tandistkaro, Berikldeebi, and Khizanaant Gora. Here the key site is Berikldeebi, located on the top of a natural outcrop, not far from Kvatskhelebi, at the junction of the Kura and Phrone rivers.[5] Excavated by A. I. Javakhishvili between 1979 and 1991, the settlement is about 100 m in diameter and rises to about 3 m, though only 2 m of its height were cultural. Javakhishvili exposed most of the site, more than 2000 square m, including a settlement and nearby kurgan, and distinguished five cultural horizons: level I was ascribed to Late Bronze Age deposits; level II comprised Middle Bronze Age graves; level III was attributed the Bedeni period and contained eight building layers; level IV belonged to the Early Kura-Araxes complex; whereas level V, subdivided into two phases (V1, the lowest level, and V2) was dated to the Late Chalcolithic period. A total of 262 pits punctuated the settlements of levels III-V; 33 were dug during period V1, and most of the others were Bedeni (late third millennium) in date.

Level V1 contained a lot of charcoal and ashy debris but, only fleeting remnants of architecture that were distinguished by changes of soil color and a few stone footings, conforming to a circular plan. A rather large pit, measuring 3.25 m in diameter and 50 cm at its deepest point, was curious. At the middle was a roughly circular clay-plastered feature about 1 m in diameter with a hole 25 cm in diameter and 15 cm deep in the center. A few postholes were scattered about in the pit. What purpose this construction served is unclear.

In contrast to the flimsy remains of the earliest settlement, level V2 is represented by a large rectilinear building (figure 3.2), around 14.5 x 7.5 m, designated as the "Temple" by Javakhishvili (1998). The building is orientated east–west and comprises a large open hall and two small rooms at the eastern end. Equally significant is the mudbrick enclosure wall found mostly along the northern edge of the site. The wall is 2 m wide at one point and constructed of seven bricks across, the brick sizes averaging 44 x 20 x 8 cm and 48 x 25 x 8 cm. Although the maximum height preserved is 1 m, Javakhishvili speculated that originally it might have reached up to 4 m in height. Only one entrance that led into the compound was preserved. It was a meter wide and blocked at a later date. A cobble-based ditch 50 cm wide and 1 m deep that may have served as a type of drainage system defined the outside of the wall. Certain sectors of the inner face of the wall had reinforcements that appear to have been built after the wall. Later still, casemate spaces were constructed between the reinforcements. Charcoal collected from pit 172, level V, and analyzed more than a decade later, in 2000, have provided the securest date for the Late Chalcolithic (see note 1). The two-sigma range suggests occupation in the early fourth millennium.

Not far from Berikldeebi is Khizanaant Gora, located in the village of Urbinisi. Within the site's 4 m deposit, the excavator, I. A. Kikvidze, recognized four Kura-Araxes levels designated E–B from bottom to top (Kikvidze 1972). Of these horizons, the lowest two, Khizanaant Gora E and D, are most relevant. No structures were discerned in level E, which yielded only occupation floors, hearths, and pits, like so many Chalcolithic sites. By contrast, in level D, Kikvidze exposed four huts built with posts and daub in-fill, foreshadowing the well-known wattle-and-daub architecture of later periods. Unlike later round-cornered, rectangular huts, the houses of level D conform to a roundish plan redolent of architectural forms, but not construction, of the Neolithic period.

Situated in the Aragvi catchment, Aranisi and Chinti are two of nine Chalcolithic sites excavated as part of the Zjinvali expedition in the 1970s and 1980s (Chikovani 1999). At Aranisi the Late Chalcolithic settlement was cut by later pits, whereas at Chinti, positioned on a slope near the village of the same name on the left bank of the Aragvi River, excavators exposed a ditch without accompanying architecture. Three other sites in the Aragvi catchment within close proximity to each other are grouped together as Abanoskevi

(Chikovani 1999). One was found to have Chalcolithic material in the middle of a 30 to 40 cm organic level. A sterile clay deposit measuring 1.0–1.6 m separated it from the earliest Kura-Araxian material. At Zjinvali, also known as Khertvisi, similar stratigraphic units were identified and assigned to the Early and Middle Chalcolithic (Chikovani 1999).

Samele Kldé in west Georgia does not truly belong to the Sioni complex, but it shares strong affinities with it. The site is a karst cave on the left bank of Gruchula River, a tributary of the Quirila River, which in turn flows into the Rioni (Javakhishvili 1971). Located at an altitude of 630 m above sea level, the mouth of the cave faces east to the river 70 m below. The interior of the cave is dry and well lit, with basic dimensions of 30 m (length), 25 m (width), and 11 m (height). Its cultural sequence is at least 2.5 m in depth, divisible into three horizons based on soil characteristics, in particular distinctive layers of beaten earth. Horizon 1, the uppermost level, was situated between 1.30 m to 2.25 m. It was separated from the second horizon by 7 to 8 cm of beaten earth. Horizon 2 (2.33–3.10 m.) was a very ashy deposit with small inclusions of charcoal. Again a layer of beaten earth, about 10 cm in thickness, lay between this layer and the third, which reached a depth of 3.5 m. The floor level of horizon 3 was not reached owing to rock fall.

One of the northernmost sites of the Sionian cultural complex is Ginchi in Dagestan. Situated in the small gorge of Ginchi in the high plain Gidatli, near the Gideril Or River, the site is located at an altitude of 1600 m above sea level. An extensive area of the settlement measuring 1500 m² was opened and revealed a large wall 2 m wide, 1.15 m high, and 15 m in length, thought by the excavators to serve a defensive purpose. Its foundation date is not clear, though it has been tentatively attributed to the Late Chalcolithic. In these earliest levels there were also a large rectangular structure and circular houses, measuring about 4 m in diameter. The walls of these houses were well built without mortar and were about 1.5 m thick. Simple, open round hearths, 0.6–1.9 m. in diameter, and nine pits also belong to these lowest deposits.

In southern Transcaucasia there are three relevant sites: Alikemek Tepesi and Leila Tepe in Azerbaijan and Tekhut in Armenia. Alikemek Tepesi is located in the Jalilabad district of the Azerbaijan Republic. More precisely, it is situated in the Mugan steppe, near the village of Uchtepe, on the right bank of the Inchechay stream. Excavations began in 1971 and continued for more than ten years (Makhmudov and Narimanov 1972; Narimanov 1987). A modest mound, about one ha in area, Alikemek Tepesi has a 5 m cultural sequence, the lowest of which lay below the valley floor. Six building levels, termed horizons 0–5 from top to bottom, were distinguished on the basis of architecture and ceramics. Houses in all horizons were constructed in mud brick. Horizon 0, disturbed in recent times, yielded a rectilinear house, pits, and very large vessels. Below it, in horizon 1, houses were rectangular in shape, possibly multiroomed, and centered by an open hearth; a curvilinear wall was found attached on both sides to rectilinear structure. Both horizons 2 and 3 had curvilinear and rectangular structures; horizon 3 also had a round subterranean structure. In the lowest two levels, horizons 4 and 5, houses were primarily circular and ovoid, and associated with small, rectangular storage structures. Ten graves were uncovered: one in horizon 0 and nine in horizons 1–3. All skeletons were found in a fetal position, lying on either side and without any specific orientation. All were covered with red ochre. In each case the deceased was laid to rest with a bowl. Little has been published on the settlement of Leila Tepe other than references to rectangular mudbrick houses (Aliev 1991). The Armenian site of Tekhut is a one-period settlement on a small hill, 8 km south of Echmiadzin (Torosian 1976). The cultural deposit, 1.6 m thick, yielded pits and a series of freestanding round structures, used both for habitation and storage. Although the largest circular structure, around 2.6 to 3.0 m in diameter, has been interpreted by some as the remains of a beehive-shaped house, it is often difficult to determine the purpose of these round structures.

Information on the origins of the Kura-Araxes complex is beginning to emerge at Sos Höyük, a multiperiod mound site between Erzurum and Pasinler in northeastern Turkey.[6] Although the area exposed is still relatively small, some 25 m², investigations in 1998 and 1999 on the northern side of the mound, in trenches L17 and M17, have yielded clearly stratified deposits and radiocarbon readings that place Sos firmly within the debate of Kura-Araxes origins (figure 3.3). These Late Chalcolithic deposits belong to what we provisionally term Sos period VA that falls in absolute terms between 3500/3300 and 3000 BC (Sagona 2000).

The most conspicuous architectural feature of this period is a large stone curved wall (figure 3.44) that occupies much of the area in the lower northern operation (Sagona et al. 1997: Plates 11, 12; Sagona et al.

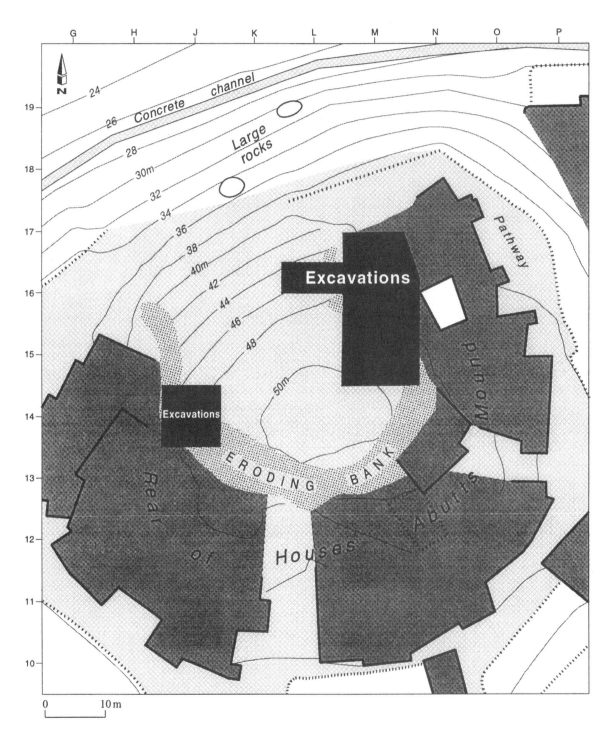

Figure 3.3 Sos Höyük 1999: Plan of central mound showing the areas of excavation. *Plan by Kep Turnour, illustration by Chandra Jayasuriya.*

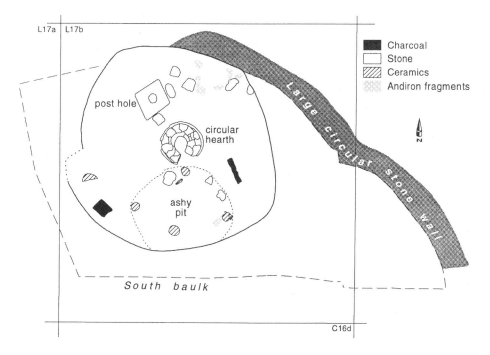

L17a | L17b

post hole

circular
hearth

Large circular stone wall

Charcoal
Stone
Ceramics
Andiron fragments

N

ashy
pit

South baulk

C16d

Figure 3.4 Sos Höyük; Plan of round house (*locus* 4250) from Period VA. *Illustration by Chandra Jayasuriya.*

1998: Plate 5). Only part of the 2.5 m wide wall has been exposed, the remainder disappearing under the northern scarp of the site. The edges of the wall are well defined with large, neatly stacked stones, measuring between 25 to 70 cm in length, whereas its interior packing consists of smaller stones and hard clay. The most recent investigations at Sos Höyük carried out in 2000 have clarified that the massive wall is not part of a large building but rather constitutes a boundary wall of some sort that separated the core of the settlement from the areas outside the wall. In its heyday the structure must have towered above the surrounding plain and had a commanding view in all directions. What this boundary actually represented, whether it defined social, economic, or political zones, is yet to be determined. Whatever purpose the wall served, it must have been important enough to be rebuilt at least twice during the Late Chalcolithic.

After this floruit, the area inside the circular structure was occupied several times, as clearly attested by a series of plaster floors and circular hearths uncovered in the 1999 campaign. The uppermost was a circular freestanding house built of mud bricks laid directly onto the ground (figures 3.4; 3.45–L17b, locus 4250). Within the house a hard-packed surface of clay was superimposed with a layer of burnt debris that contained much carbonized organic matter, including matting. Entering the house on its western side, attention would have been drawn

to the circular hearth built into the center of the floor. To the left of the doorway was the support posthole and portable hearths; across the floor lay a series of ceramic vessels. Later, a pit was dug into the house floor along the southern boundary and filled with pottery and ash. Radiocarbon analysis of charcoal from within the house has given a two-sigma reading of 4440 +/- 50 BP (Beta-135362).

Four more floor levels, each with a circular hearth, were exposed in deposits below the roundhouse. The one immediately below (L17b, locus 4254), a lime plaster surface, belonged to a house that was rectilinear in plan with a stone "bench" built against the east side of the curved wall. Its hearth was set in virtually the same position as that of the roundhouse. The next floor surface (L17b, locus 4270) was distinguished not so much by a clear plan, but as a floor that had been founded on a deposit of pottery sherds that were purposefully crushed on the spot (figures 3.5; 3.46). Sherds surrounded a circular hearth that had been placed against the inner face of the curved wall. Below this level another round hearth was found associated with a hard-packed, burnt-orange floor level (L17b, locus 4279). The lowest deposit reached so far within the area of large curved wall is locus 4299, in trench L17b. This surface did not contain a built-in hearth, but had a fine example of the twin-horned andiron, similar to those illustrated in figure 3.41: 2–3, found among ceramics on a burnt plaster floor. A small deposit of phytolith was collected for radiocarbon analysis, but it did not yield a very helpful date (Beta – 135363: 4290+/- 70 BP) once calibrated. Given the date from the roundhouse, the upper range of this segmented reading should be considered the most accurate.

At the present stage, the earliest material gathered at Sos Höyük comes from outside the large wall where a small exploratory trench was dug in 1998. Excavations in trench M17/L17 revealed a series of burnt layers and some very large stones, superimposing virgin soil, that appear to have been positioned at about the time the large stone wall was established. Radiocarbon readings from the base of the sounding (Beta-120452: 4590 +/- 50 BP) and from a level higher up (Beta-107912: 4390 +/- 70 BP) corroborate the dates inside the curved wall and point to the late fourth millennium BC for the Late Chalcolithic (period VA) occupation at Sos Höyük. More dates are required to expand this series in order to hone this time frame further.

THE FINDS

Pottery has always bulked large in discussions on the cultural developments of Transcaucasian prehistory. In the Chalcolithic, ceramics are characterized by a typological conservatism reflected in the comparatively few vessel forms and a restrained ornamentation. In general, pottery was built by hand, using either coils or slabs of clay. Vessels from Tekhut, Grmakhevistavi, and Treli are reported also to have textile impressions on the interior surface, whereas those from Sioni (figure 3.9:3) and Damtsvari Gora (figure 3.12) have mat-impressed bases. From Didube and Khizanaant Gora (figure 3.25:5), however, we have textile impressions sandwiched between two layers of clay that become evident only when pottery fragments laminate lengthwise. These impressions suggest that certain pieces were either manufactured around a mold covered in cloth or more likely that slabs of clay were laid out on a mat base before being shaped. In the case of the Didube vessels, the survival of the impressions indicates that the slabs of clay were not pressed firmly together during production. This method of manufacture certainly continued into the Kura-Araxes period, as can be clearly seen by impressions in figure 3.47. The fragment from Sos Höyük, like those from Late Chalcolithic Transcaucasia, recall a vessel found at Amiranis Gora, now on display in the Georgian State Museum, which has similar textile impressions between

two laminations of clay. A few vessels from Tsopi are thought to have been wheel-made, but their thick walls and the localization of "striations" (likely to be wipe marks) on the rim argue against wheel manufacture (Kushnareva and Chubinishvili 1970: Plate 9).

One of the most distinguishing traits of Chalcolithic ceramics from Transcaucasia is the micaceous quality of the clay, most noticeable among vessels at the site of Sioni. Although a considerable amount of both silver and gold mica is often present in the fabric and slip, judging by the small particle sizes, it is unlikely that the mica was added as temper, but suggests instead that potters favored mica-rich clay deposits. As yet, the Late Chalcolithic pottery from Sos Höyük VA, on the other hand, has no mica inclusions.

In addition to mica, Late Chalcolithic pottery is often gritty. The inclusions range from sandy mixtures to quartz particles (Berikldeebi, Tekhut, Ginchi, and Sos), or even crushed obsidian (Tsopi and Delisi). Chaff and grog were also used but were not as popular. Chaff-tempered pottery has a wide distribution area, covering western (Samele Kldé), central (Treli and Grmakhevistavi), and southern (Tekhut and Alikemek) Transcaucasia. In contrast, grog appears to be restricted to the environs of Tbilisi, occurring at Delisi, Treli, and Grmakhevistavi. No chronological division on the basis of inclusions is immediately obvious, though chaff temper peters out with the manufacture of Kura-Araxes pottery.

Apart from variations in temper, the fabric of pottery can be divided into four broad groups, still being clearly defined, using the Sos Höyük sequence as a provisional benchmark.

Group A. The first and most common ware in Transcaucasia, sometimes know as "Sioni" ware, is baked quite hard with relatively few voids. It is invariably slipped, and the colors vary widely, though prominence is accorded to pale browns through reds to yellows (10R 4/6 and 2.5YR 4/6, for instance). In cross section, most sherds often display two or three contrasting colors, indicating that vessels were not oxidized fully during firing. At Sos Höyük VA, represented by only a few body fragments of this ware type, sherds display an interior and exterior edge that sandwich a thick pale gray core. Surfaces are usually burnished or smoothed and hardly ever left plain. Certain pieces, in particular from the sites of Khizanaant Gora, Berikldeebi IV, and Ginchi, are highly polished, thin-walled, and well fired. Another treatment of the surface is combing (figures 3.8:2, 4, 7; 3.9:2), a haphazardly executed series of incised lines over the body of

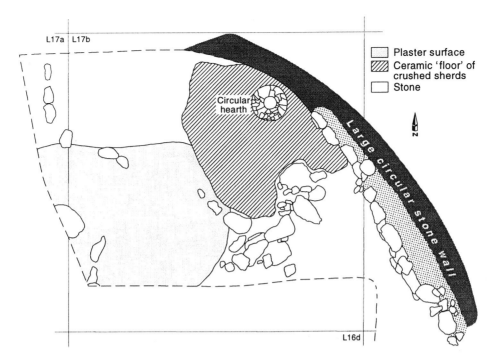

Figure 3.5 Sos Höyük: Plan of period VA floor surface (*locus* 4270) within the large stone wall, showing the extent of the ceramic sherd "pavement." *Illustration by Chandra Jayasuriya.*

the vessel (flint-scraped?) which, at Sioni at least, is mostly restricted to pottery slipped in the paler colors. This type of ornamentation is not found in northeastern Anatolia.

Group B. Found mostly in northeastern Anatolia (at Sos, Gundulak[7] and Pulur [Gökçedere] in the Bayburt plain), group B has a coarse, dark core with a lot of voids and mixed grit inclusions, breaking with sharp angular edges. The exterior surface of these vessels can be a mottled grayish brown (around 10YR 5/4), matte and self-slipped, or rarely, cream-slipped (2.5Y 8/3), or even lightly burnished (figures 3.38:3, 10; 3.39:1, 2, 4; 3.40:1, 4; 3.42:1–11, 13–14; 3.43). In the Sos Höyük reports this group is referred to as "Drab" ware.

Group C. The third group, found in Transcaucasia and eastern Anatolia, has a dark paste, baking orange near the surface, that is generally friable and gritty to touch. Its surface is highly burnished and is slipped in black or dark gray (figures 3.38:1–2, 4, 9; 3.40:5–7); rarely, it has a red-brown burnished exterior (figure 3.39:5). Of the four groups, this would signal to most investigators the antecedents of Kura-Araxes and may well be termed "Proto-Kura-Araxes." It should be stressed, however, that the many stylistic features of this group that link it to the other three argue against any notion of discontinuity.

Group D. Another Late Chalcolithic ware datable to circa 3500/3300–3000 BC has been identified at a few

sites in eastern Anatolia, including Sos Höyük. The quality of manufacture is good with no obvious signs of production. Its fabric is compact and well-levigated with a moderate amount of small, rounded white grit inclusions. The color of the fabric is uniformly dark brownish grey [5YR 4/2]. The slightly friable quality of the paste suggests a low-medium firing. Both surfaces are generally baked black—the exterior is given a good polish whereas the interior is simply smoothed. A range of forms is attested, including tall-necked jars with rounded bodies and small loop handles. Full details of the entire northeastern Anatolian ceramic sequence will appear in A. Sagona and C. Sagona (forthcoming).

Typologically, the four groups share forms. Jars are the most common shape category. Ovoid-bodied jars, with a balanced curvilinear profile, comprising an everted or straight neck attached to a high shoulder were particularly common at Sioni (figures 3.6; 3.7; 3.8:1–4; 3.9:5–6; 3.10). Their bases are narrow and flat, and sometimes bear the impressions of basketry. Hole-mouth jars are also found, especially within groups A and B. Another category of jars, mostly datable to the very end of the Chalcolithic and well represented by group C, is distinguished by a globular body and comparatively tall neck that can be either convex or slightly swollen. These jars are generally fired black-and-red or pale brown. (figures 3.19:3–8; 3.20; 3.23; 3.24:3–9;

3.26; 3.28:1–3; 3.30; 3.32; 3.33; 3.34; 3.36; 3.37:1; 3.38; 3.40:6); many vessels, especially from Transcaucasia, have one or two handles, whereas the one from Nuli is triple-handled (figure 3.37:1). Both the form and color of these jars herald the advent of the earliest Kura-Araxes horizon. A large, well-known jar from Kiketi (figure 3.28:5) displays the same proportions, but its straight neck is that much closer to the Early Bronze Age I horizon. Both the large jar from Didi Akhalisopeli (figure 3.37:2) with its broad base and the tall cylindrical jar from Kiketi (figure 3.28:6) are uncommon shapes. Handles are never attached to the hole-mouthed jars that appear to be more common in northeastern Anatolia than in Transcaucasia (figures 3.8:5-7; 3.39:5; 3.42:1–6; 3.43:3–5). In both regions they are restricted to the Late Chalcolithic period. A similar time range can be attributed to a distinctive beaker with a broad base and convex neck (figures 3.11; 3.14:1–3) that appears to be a purely Transcaucasian product.

Bowls are mostly hemispherical (figures 3.15:1, 3; 3.18:5; 3.25; 3.29: 5–6, 8; 3.35:1–3; 3.39:4; 3.40:7; 3.42:7, 10), or with a short neck that is often everted (figures 3.16; 3.17; 3.29:1–4; 3.31:2–4; 3.35: 4-5). The latter form is more popular in Transcaucasia and generally has a pair of handles.

Conical (figures 3.15:2; 3.16:3; 3.18:1, 4; 3.28:4) and straight-sided (figures 3.24:1–2; 3.31:1) bowls were also produced, but are in the minority. Like the jars, the fabric of bowls varies from coarse drab pieces to those with a crisp and well fired fabric, thin walls and a high burnish. The low tray, sometimes with a pair of horizontal lugs that are occasionally impressed along the edge and attached to the rim (figures 3.13; 3.15: 4, 6–7; 3.21:1–3; 3.40:1–2), is found only in Late Chalcolithic deposits. The zone below the rim may also often perforated with a horizontal row of punctures usually running around the entire circumference of the tray. Lids were made toward the end of the Chalcolithic and are generally flat with a loop handle at the center (figures 3.18:8; 3.39:1–2; 3.40:4). Those from Khizanaant Gora (figure 3.22:1–4) have a central depression and are more akin to the Early Bronze Age type. Finally, attention should be drawn to a number of perforated vessels that are found throughout Transcaucasia and northeastern Anatolia (figures 3.18:3, 6–7; 3.42:8; 3.43:1–2).

Perhaps the most striking feature of Chalcolithic pottery from Transcaucasia, and restricted mostly to group A, is the decorativeness of its rim. The Sioni horizon offers the full range and comprises rims with oblique or transversely parallel incisions that sometimes extend down over the interior and exterior (figures 3.6:7–8; 3.7:4,5,7,8,13; 3.8:1,2–4; 3.9:5); oblique parallel combed impressions (figures 3.6:1; 3.7:1,3); circular impressions on the lip (figures 3.6: 3, 6, 9; 3.7:9); a saw-like lip, or serration; a wavy silhouette when viewed from the top (figures 3.6:5; 3.7:6, 11); a wavy rims when viewed from the side. None of these decorative rims has been found at Sos as yet, indicating that this stylistic trait is either localized to Transcaucasia or that it petered out by the last centuries of the fourth millennium.

Decorative rims aside, Transcaucasian Chalcolithic pottery is rarely and certainly not elaborately ornamented. A few vessels bear single knobs or ledges of varying sizes attached to the rim that may have also functioned as handles (figures 3.15:1,2; 3.16:2–5; 3.23:10,13; 3.25:2; 3.29:1,4; 3.33:1; 3.42:3). Knobbed ornamentation is found at Sos (figure 3.40:5), in the Bayburt plain (figure 3.42:3) and beyond in the Malatya and Elazığ region (Sagona 1994: 7). Variations of this theme are seen in vertical rows of knobs attached to the neck (figure 3.14:4; Miron and Orthmann 1995, Fig. 22), or an all-over ornamentation with small pastilles (figure 3.12). Other relief ornaments come in the form of a horizontal, either plain or with oblique impressions, a zigzag, or a double spiral (figures 3.11; 3.14:1; 3.28:5). Incised patterns are rare and found at Khizanaant Gora (figure 3.23:1–4,8,9) and Samshvilde (figure 3.34:3,7) where rows of zigzags and hatched triangles are pendant from the base of the neck; one of the Samshvilde jars is further decorated with vertical bands along the neck.

At certain sites, especially in the southern regions, the monochrome and variegated pottery is associated with a category of painted ceramics that was clearly foreign to Transcaucasia. The clay of these vessels can be either coarse, chaff-tempered, or a fine paste with no visible inclusions. The designs are usually geometric, especially wavy lines and zigzags, and executed in black or red paint on a pale, polished surface (Munchaev 1982).

Few other Chalcolithic terracotta objects have been recovered. There are no anthropomorphic figurines, but the occasional horned animal figurine does occur and points to the emergence of a standard trait of the Kura-Araxes complex (Sagona 1998). Twin-horned pot stands, too, foreshadow the larger U-shaped portable hearths of later times (figure 3.41:2, 3). Other portable hearths include individual props (figure 3.39:3),

(continued on page 89)

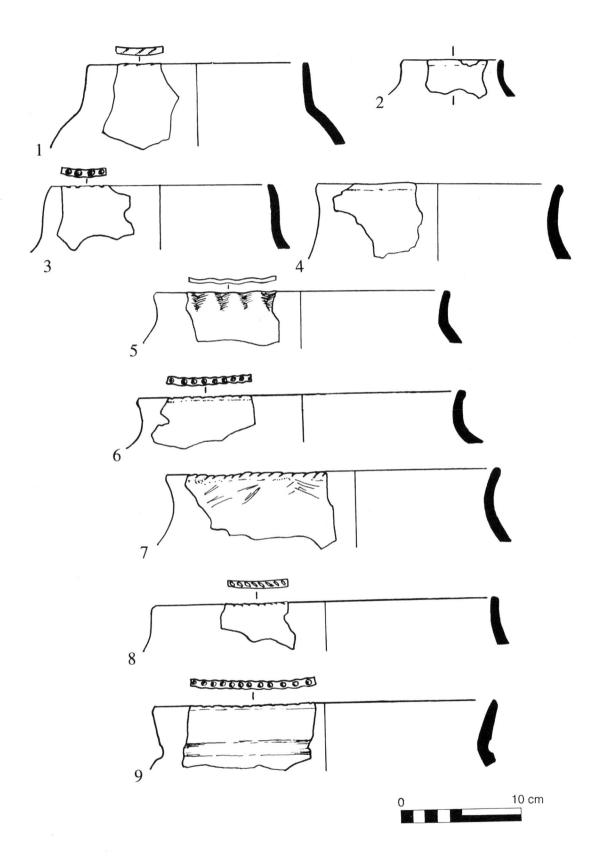

Figure 3.6 Pottery from Sioni. *Courtesy of the Georgian State Museum.*

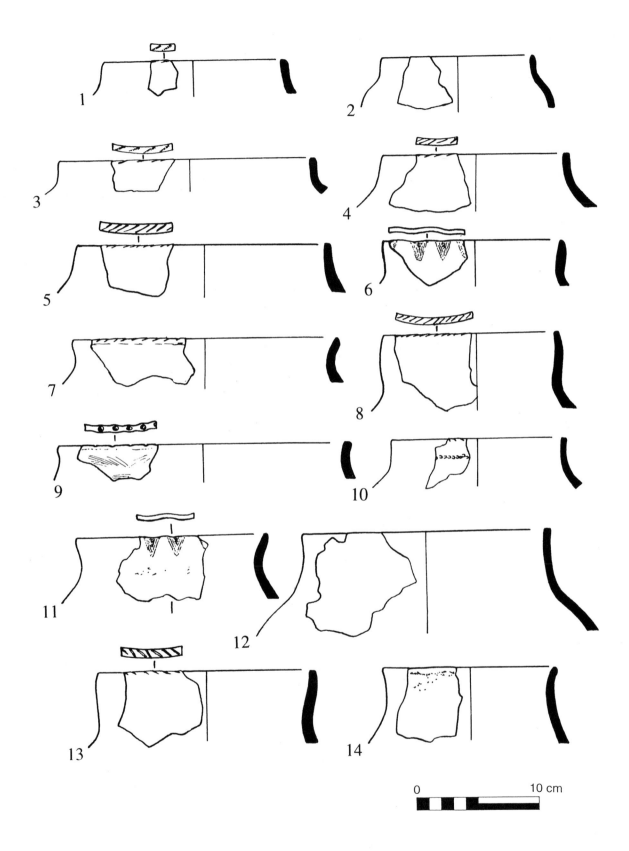

Figure 3.7 Pottery from Sioni. *Courtesy of the Georgian State Museum.*

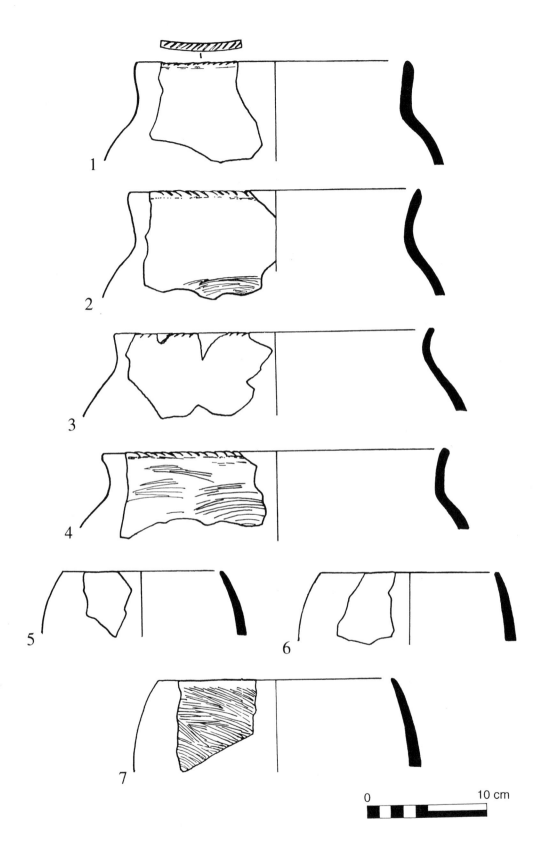

Figure 3.8 Pottery from Sioni. *Courtesy of the Georgian State Museum.*

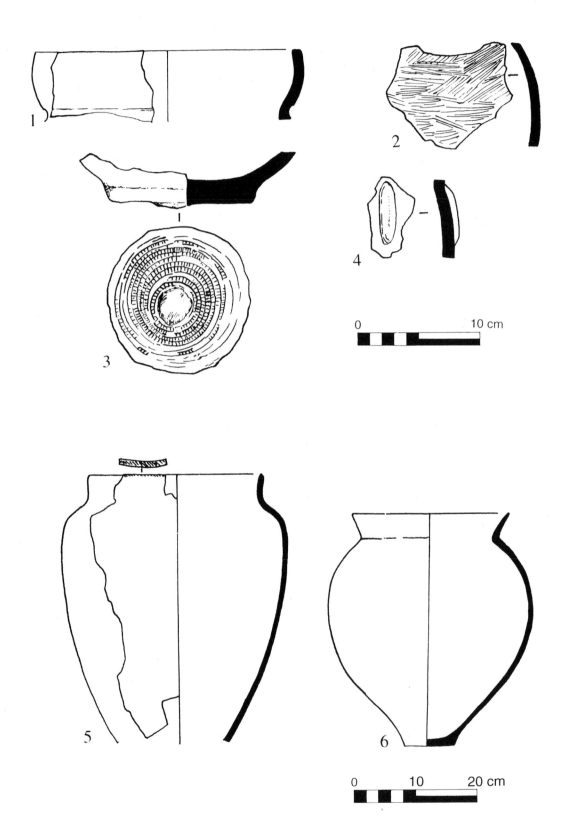

Figure 3.9 Pottery from Sioni. *Courtesy of the Georgian State Museum.*

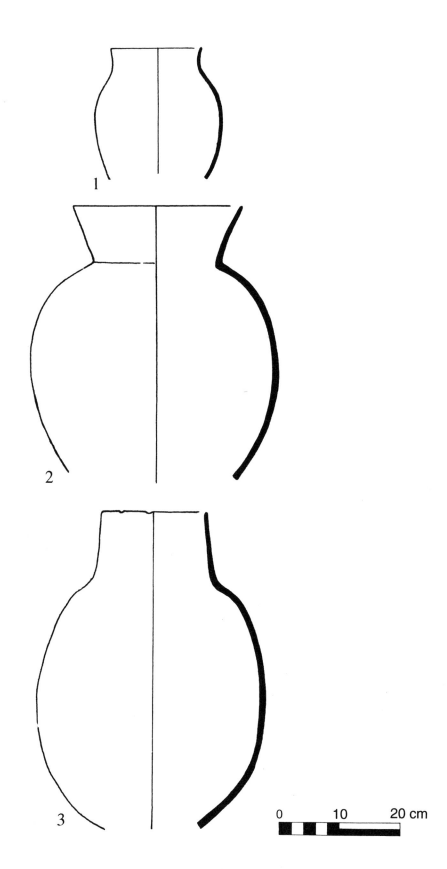

Figure 3.10 *1,3*, pottery from Samele Kldé; *2*, pottery from Samertskhle Kldé. *Courtesy of the Georgian State Museum.*

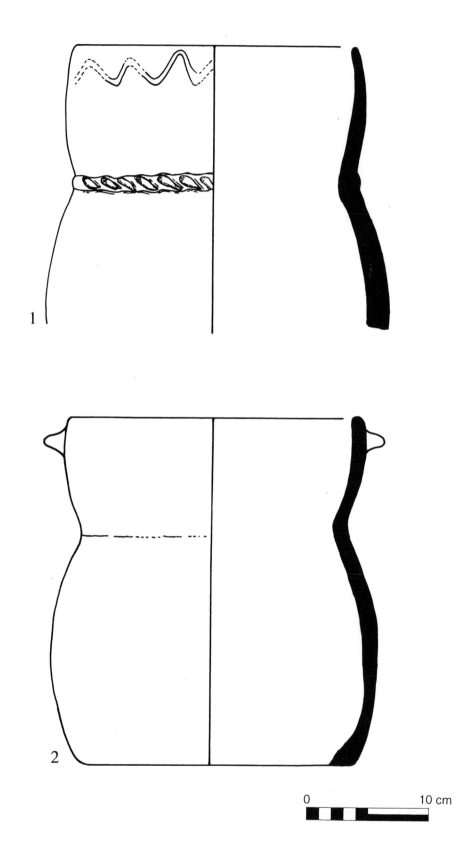

Figure 3.11 Pottery from Damstvari Gora. *Courtesy of the Georgian State Museum.*

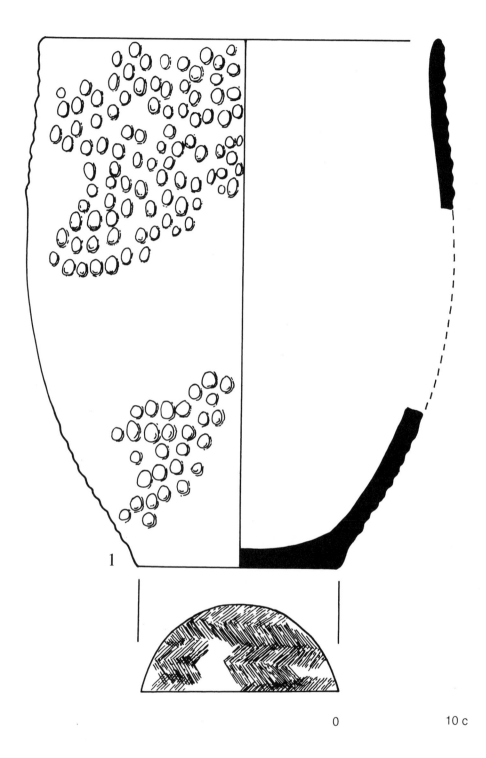

Figure 3.12 Pottery from Damstvari Gora. *Courtesy of the Georgian State Museum.*

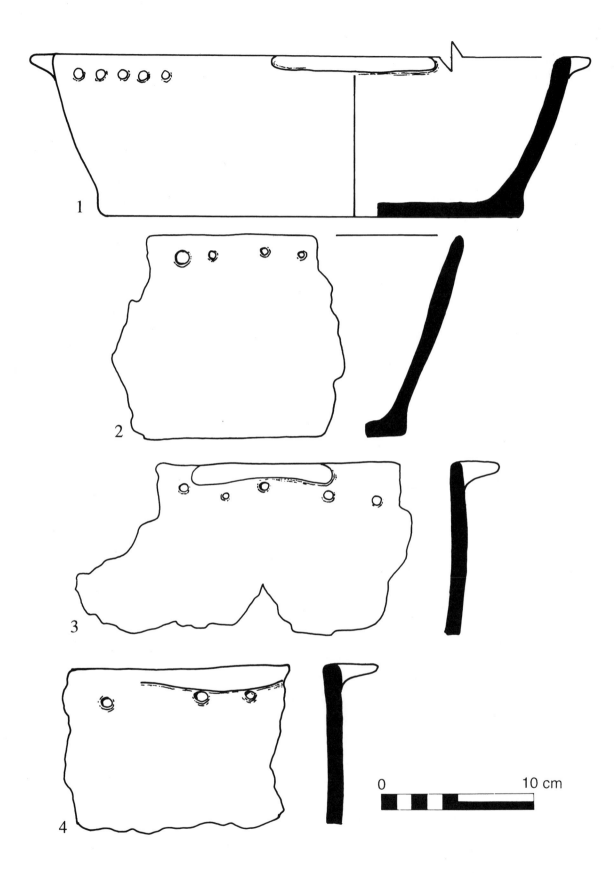

Figure 3.13 *1*, Pottery from Damstvari Gora; *2-4*, pottery from Kviritsvari Gora. *Courtesy of the Georgian State Museum.*

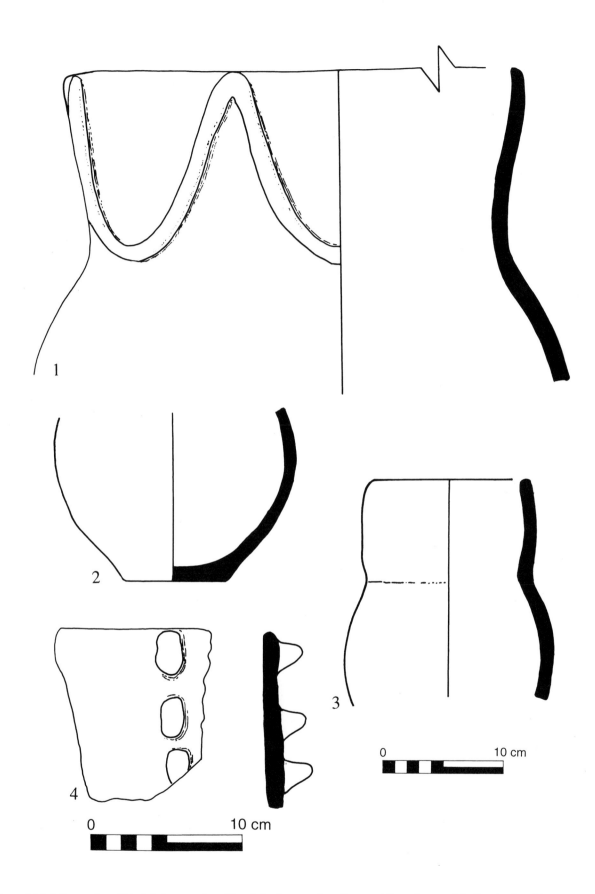

Figure 3.14 *1*, Pottery from Chinti; *2-3*, pottery from Skavtskala; *4*, pottery from Damstvari Gora. *Courtesy of the Georgian State Museum.*

Figure 3.15 Pottery from Didube. *Courtesy of the Georgian State Museum.*

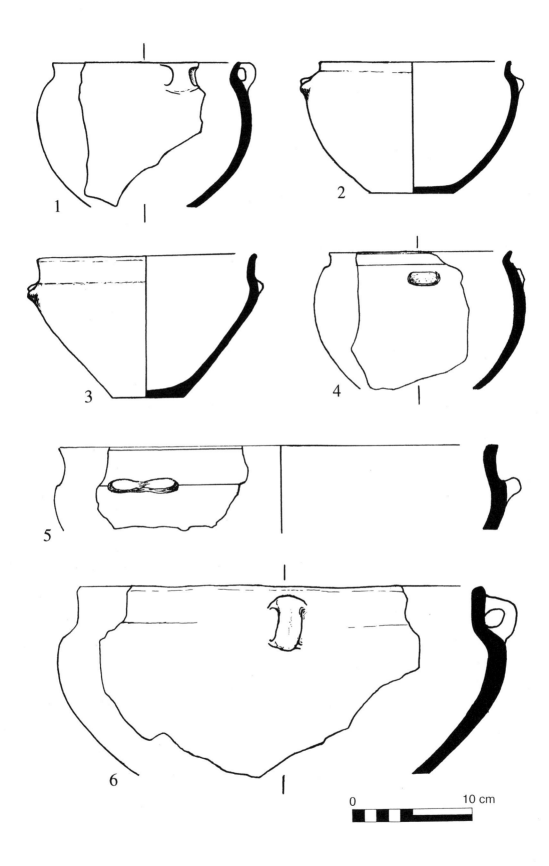

Figure 3.16 Pottery from Didube. *Courtesy of the Georgian State Museum.*

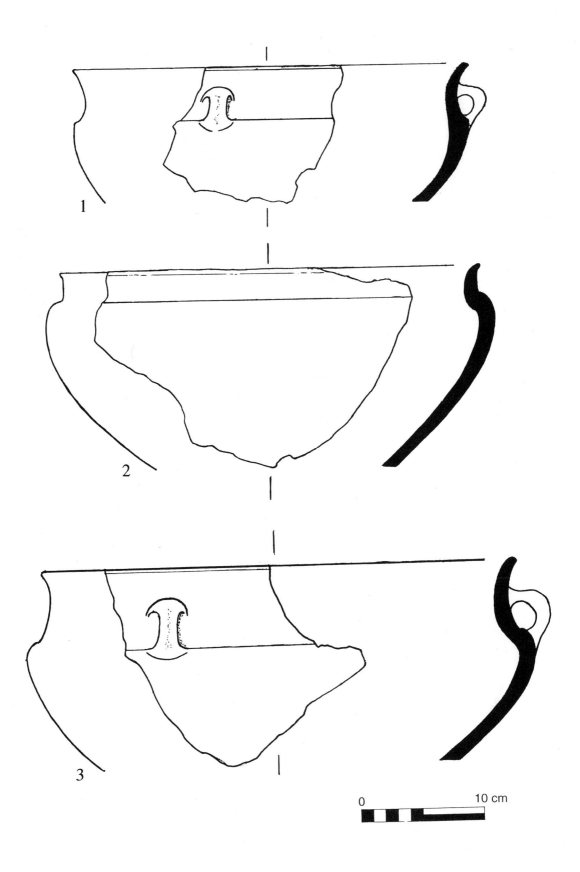

Figure 3.17 Pottery from Didube. *Courtesy of the Georgian State Museum.*

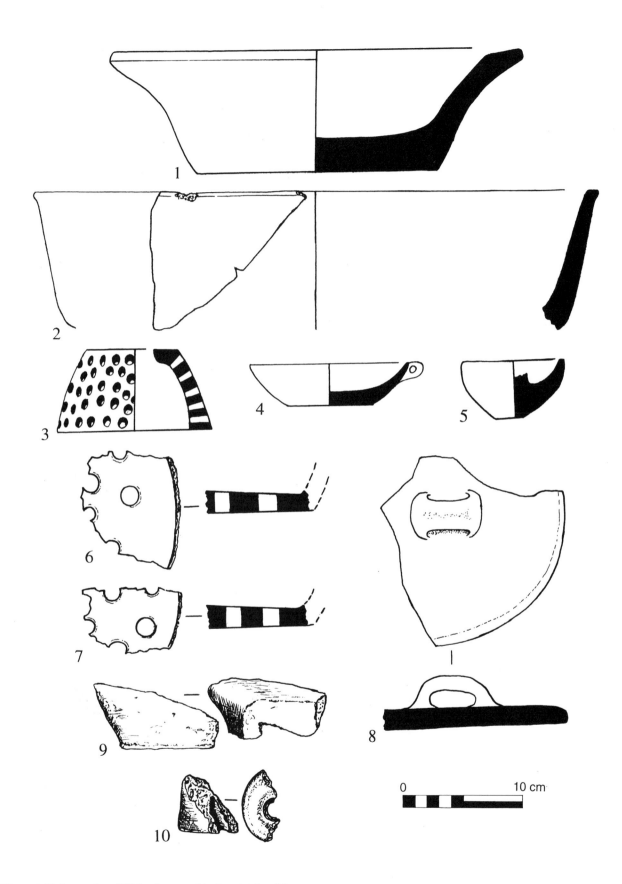

Figure 3.18 Pottery from Didube. *Courtesy of the Georgian State Museum.*

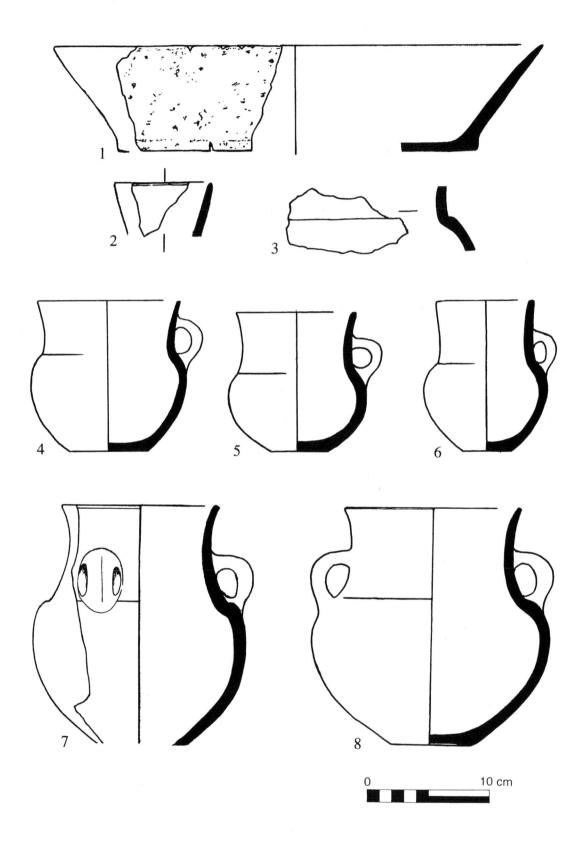

Figure 3.19 *1-3*, Pottery from Samshvilde; *4-8*, pottery from Didube. *Courtesy of the Georgian State Museum.*

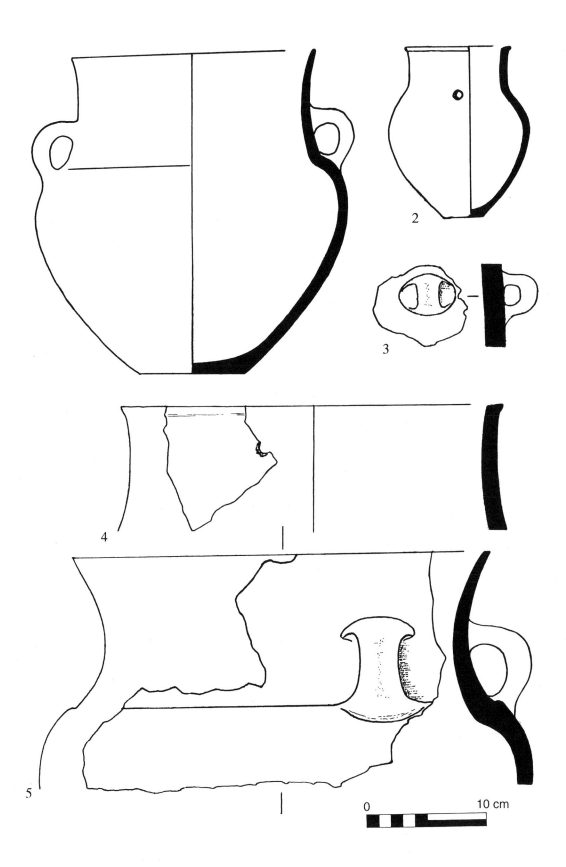

Figure 3.20 Pottery from Didube. *Courtesy of the Georgian State Museum.*

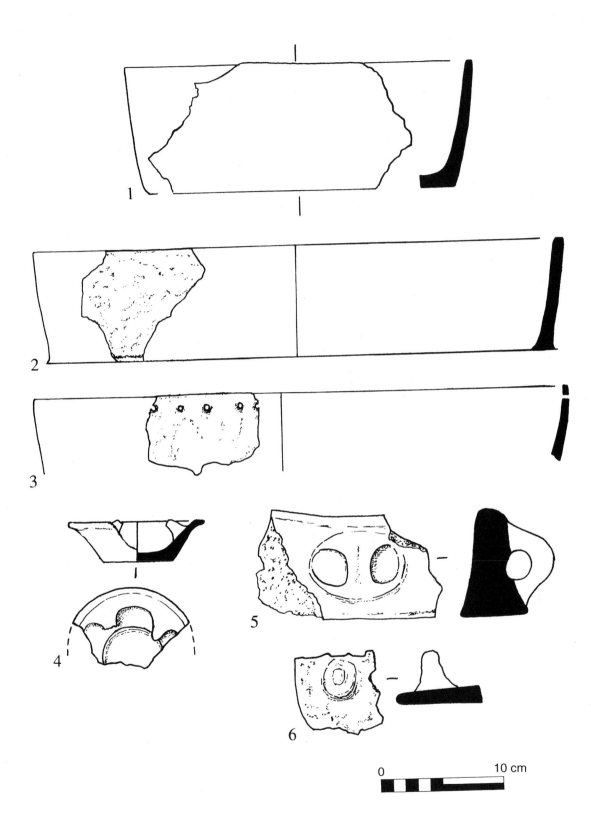

Figure 3.21 Pottery from Khizanaant Gora. *Courtesy of the Georgian State Museum.*

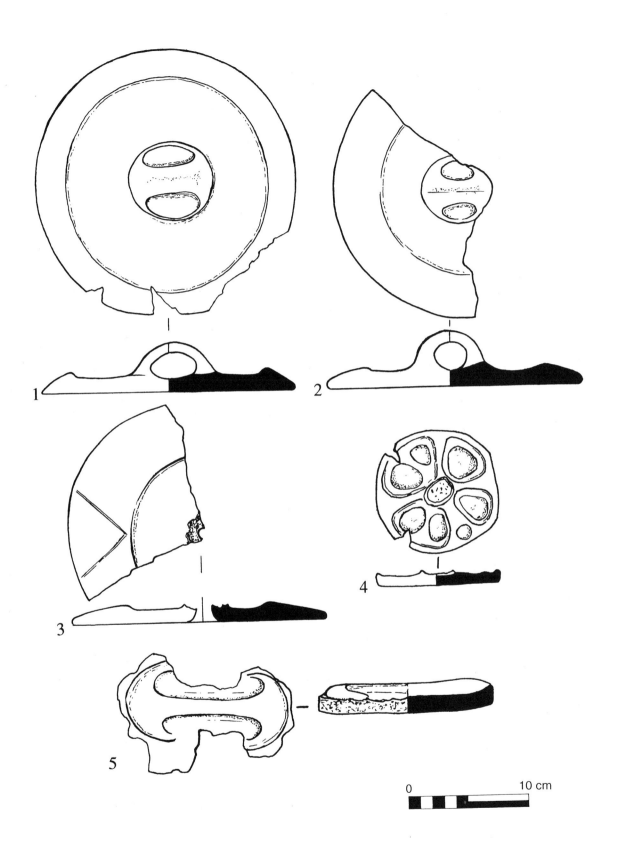

Figure 3.22 Pottery from Khizanaant Gora. *Courtesy of the Georgian State Museum.*

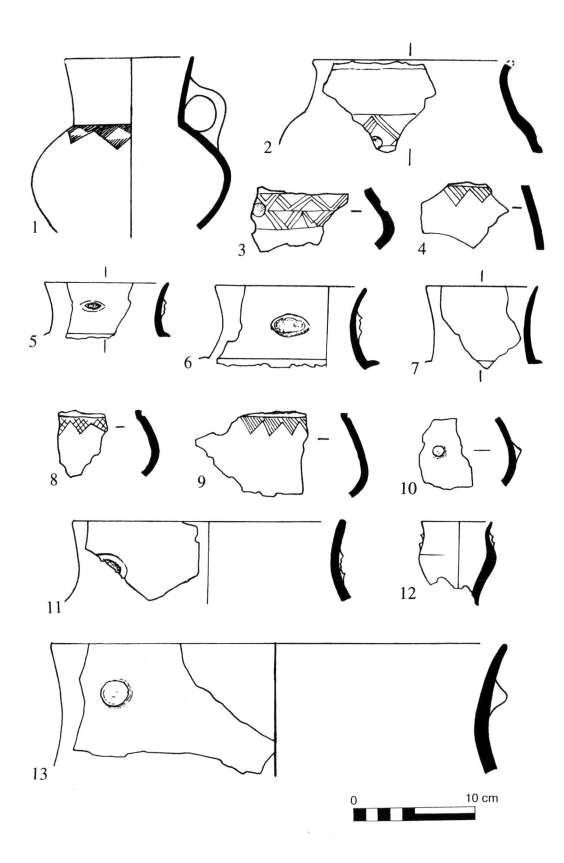

Figure 3.23 Pottery from Khizanaant Gora. *Courtesy of the Georgian State Museum.*

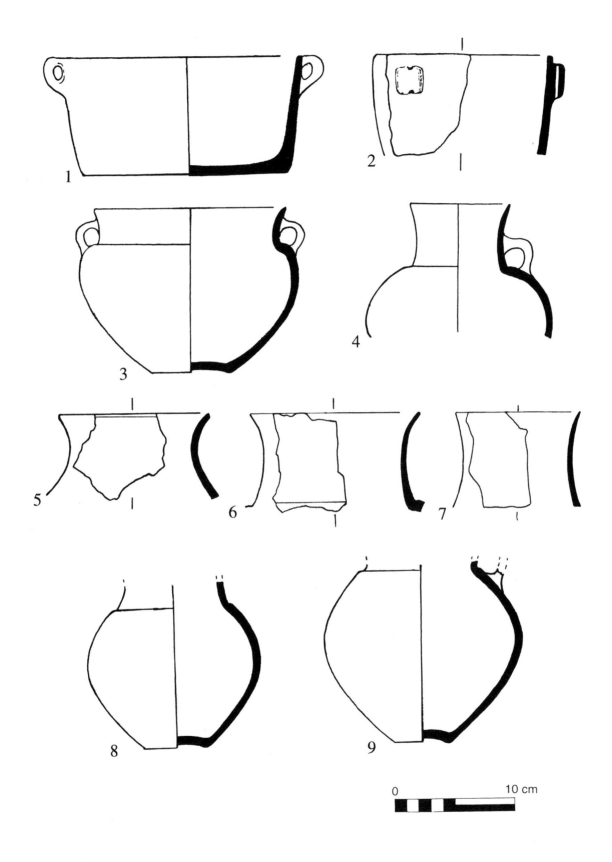

Figure 3.24 *1-2*, Pottery from Kiketi; *3-9*, pottery from Khizanaant Gora. *Courtesy of the Georgian State Museum.*

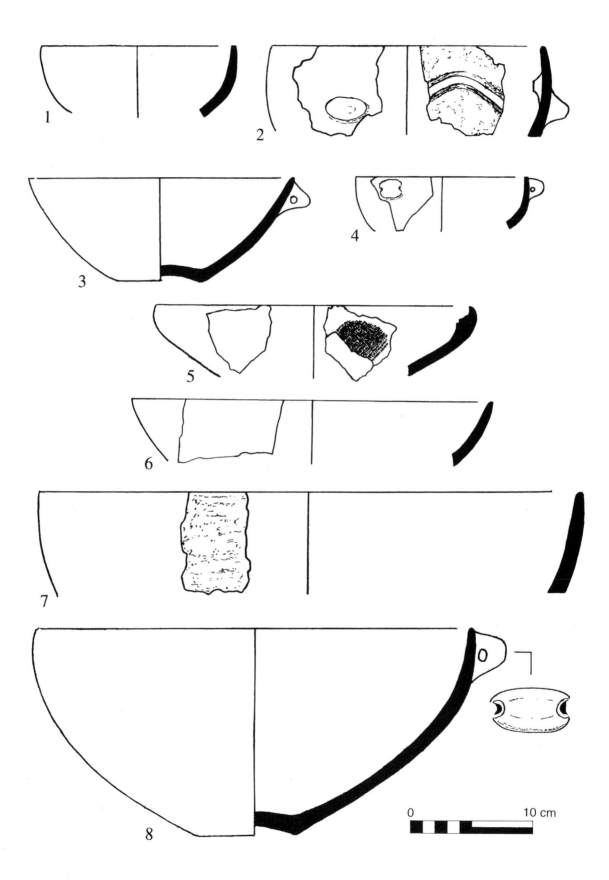

Figure 3.25 Pottery from Khizanaant Gora. *Courtesy of the Georgian State Museum.*

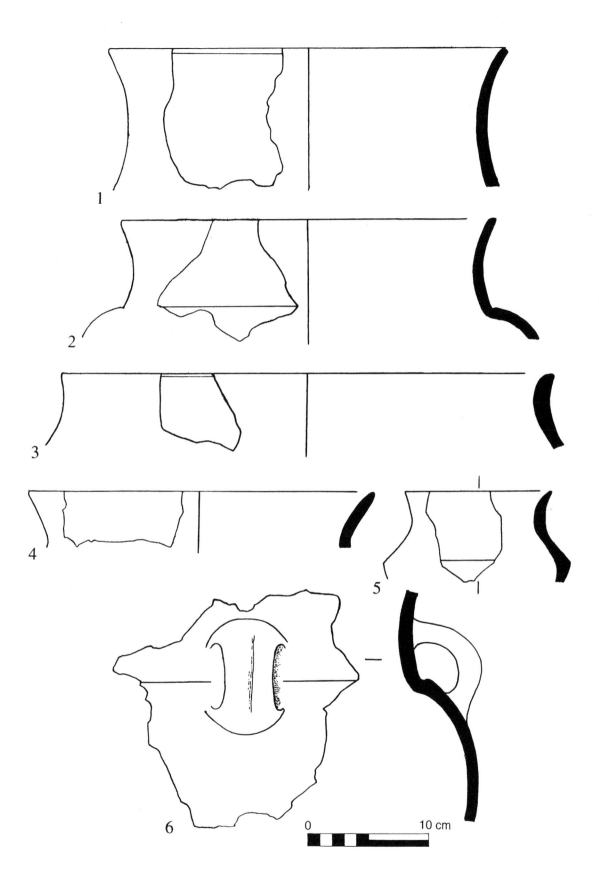

Figure 3.26 Pottery from Khizanaant Gora. *Courtesy of the Georgian State Museum.*

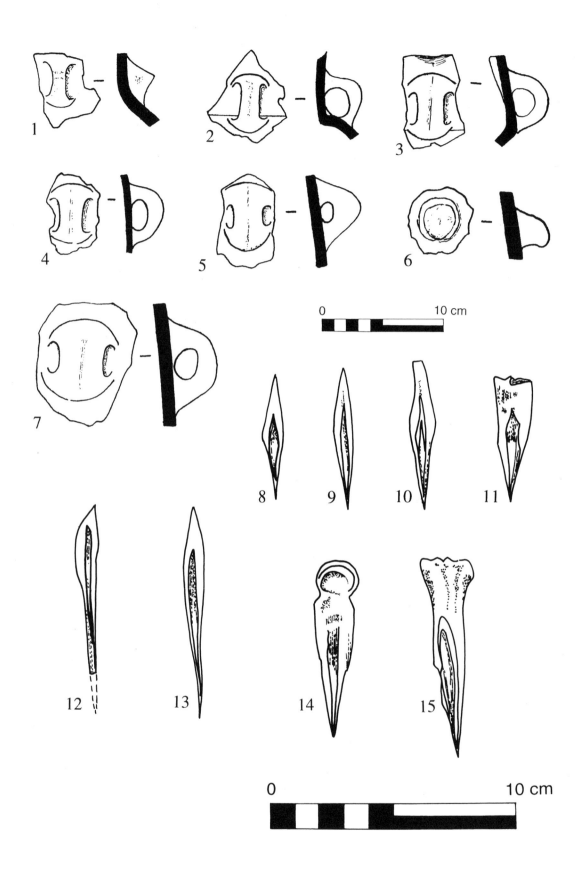

Figure 3.27 Khizanaant Gora: *1-7*, pottery; *8-15*, bone implements. *Courtesy of the Georgian State Museum.*

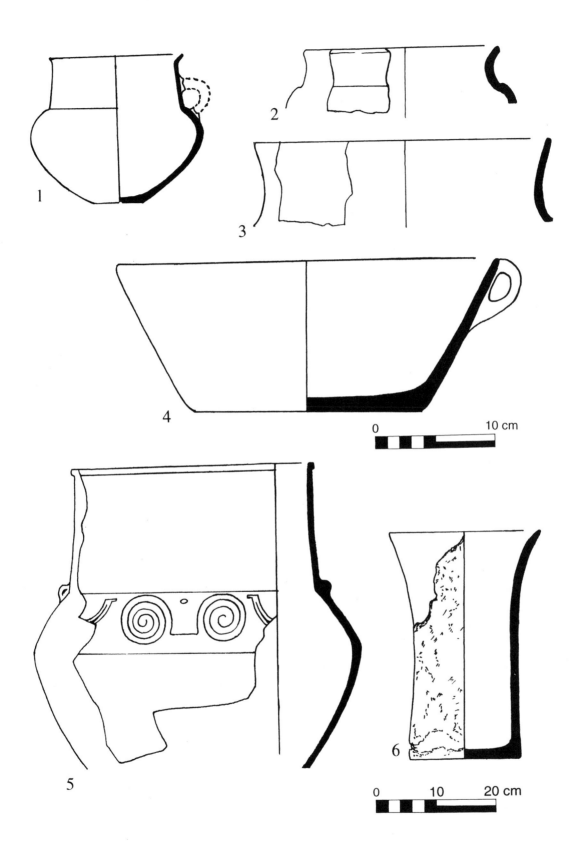

Figure 3.28 Pottery from Kiketi. *Courtesy of the Georgian State Museum.*

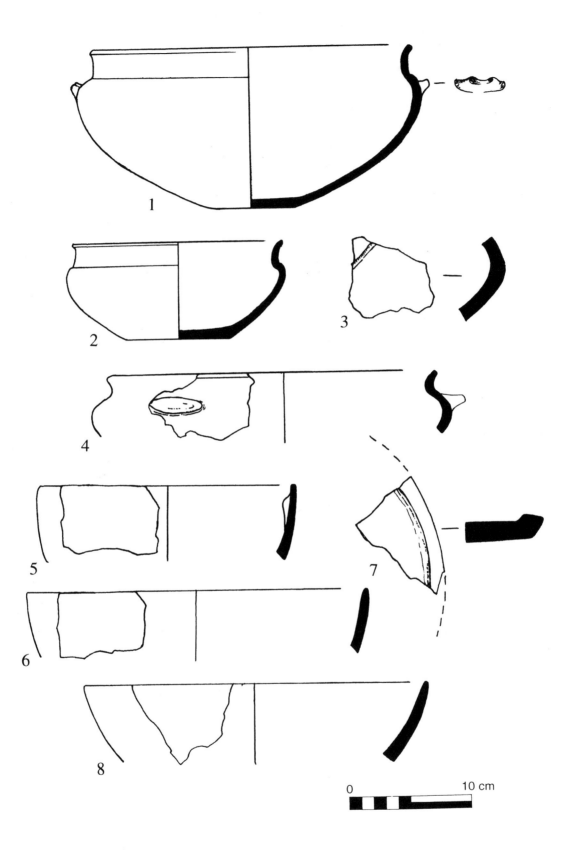

Figure 3.29 Pottery from Kiketi. *Courtesy of the Georgian State Museum.*

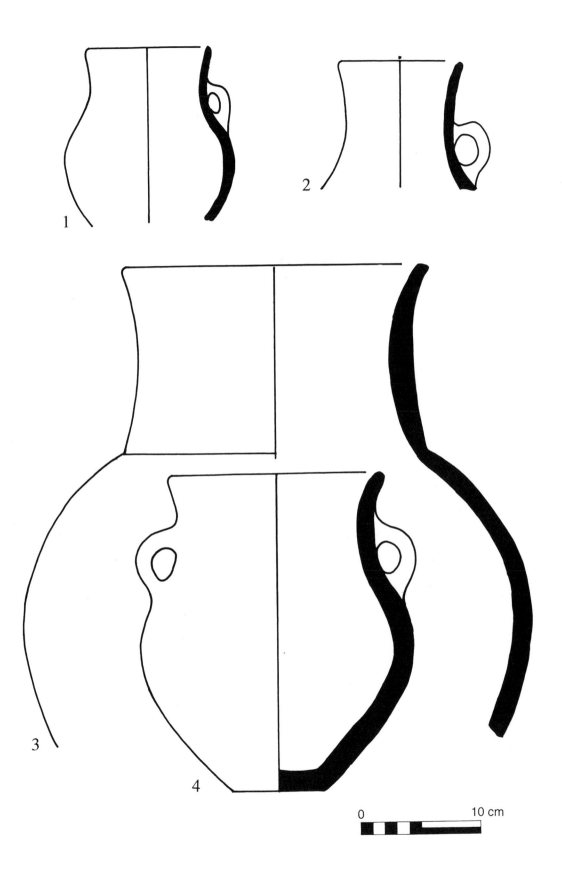

Figure 3.30 Pottery from Treli. *Courtesy of the Georgian State Museum.*

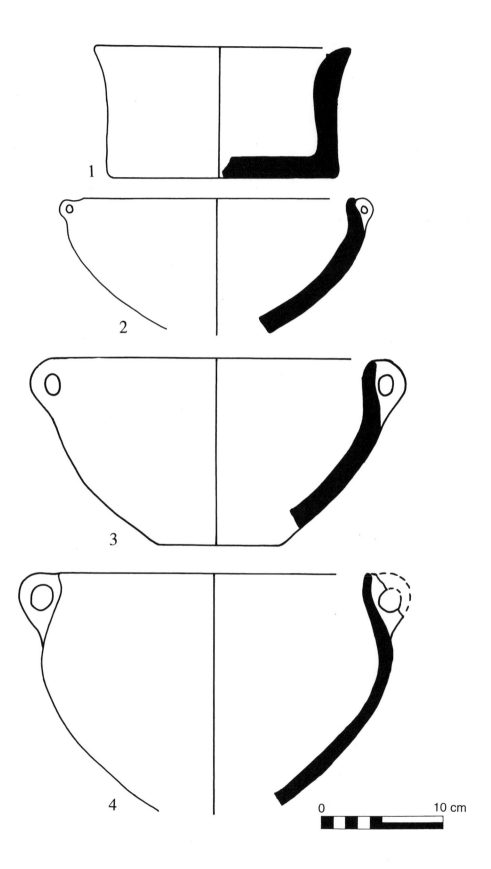

Figure 3.31 Pottery from Treli. *Courtesy of the Georgian State Museum.*

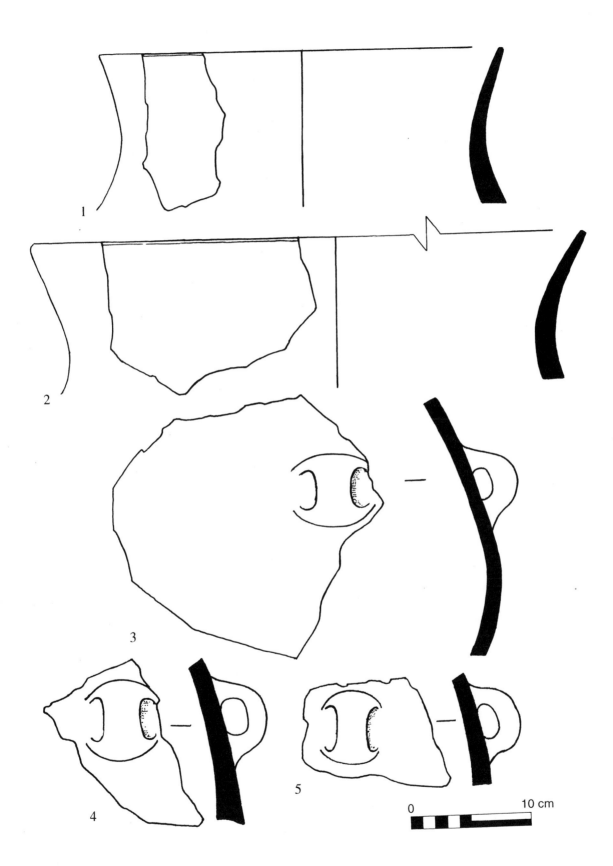

Figure 3.32 Pottery from Samshvilde. *Courtesy of the Georgian State Museum.*

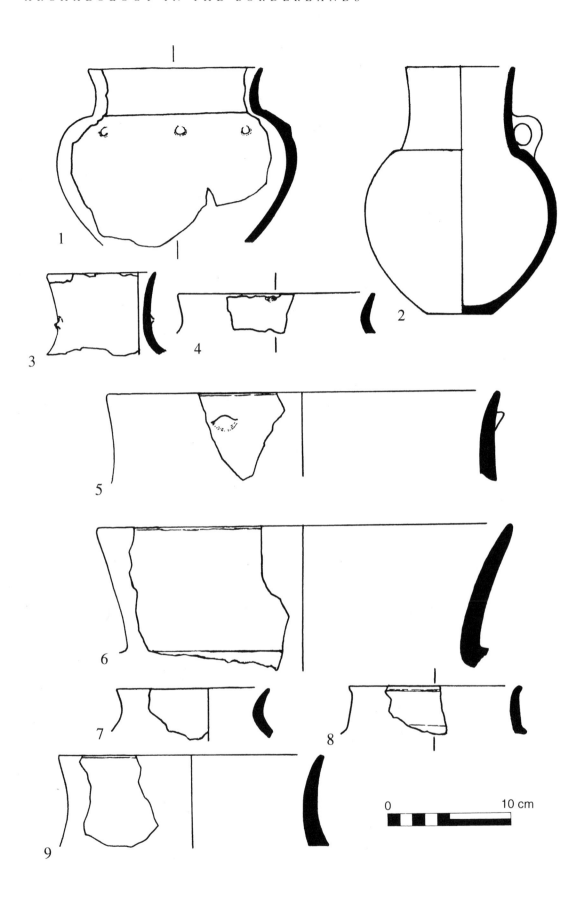

Figure 3.33 Pottery from Samshvilde. *Courtesy of the Georgian State Museum.*

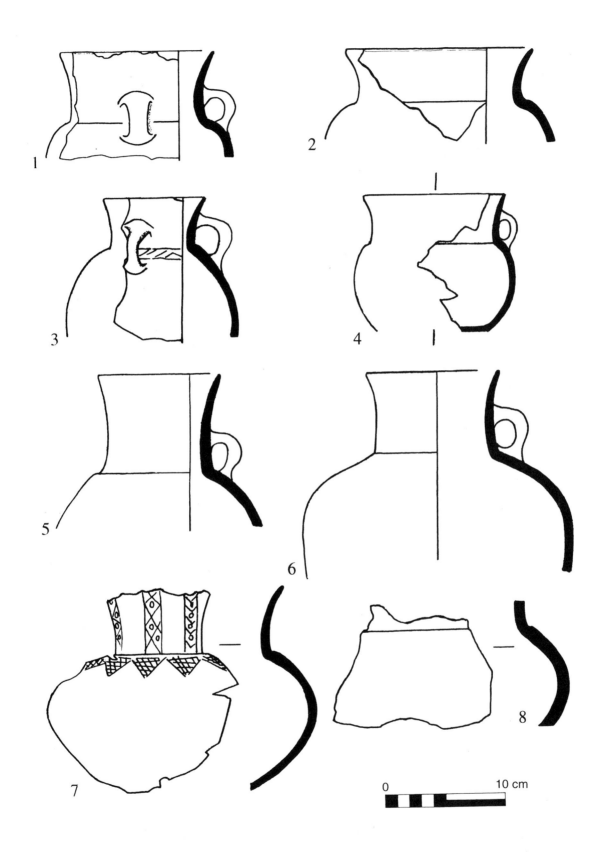

Figure 3.34 Pottery from Samshvilde. *Courtesy of the Georgian State Museum.*

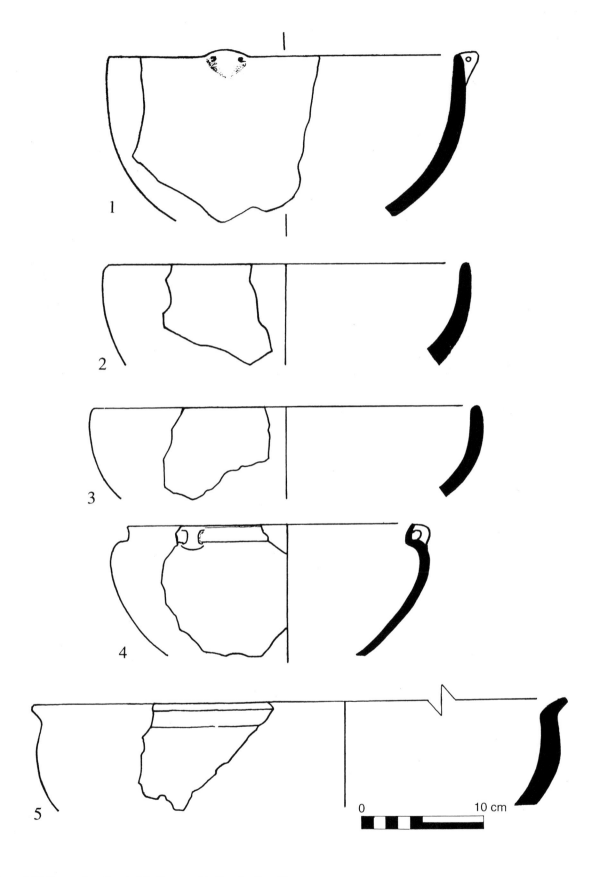

Figure 3.35 Pottery from Samshvilde. *Courtesy of the Georgian State Museum.*

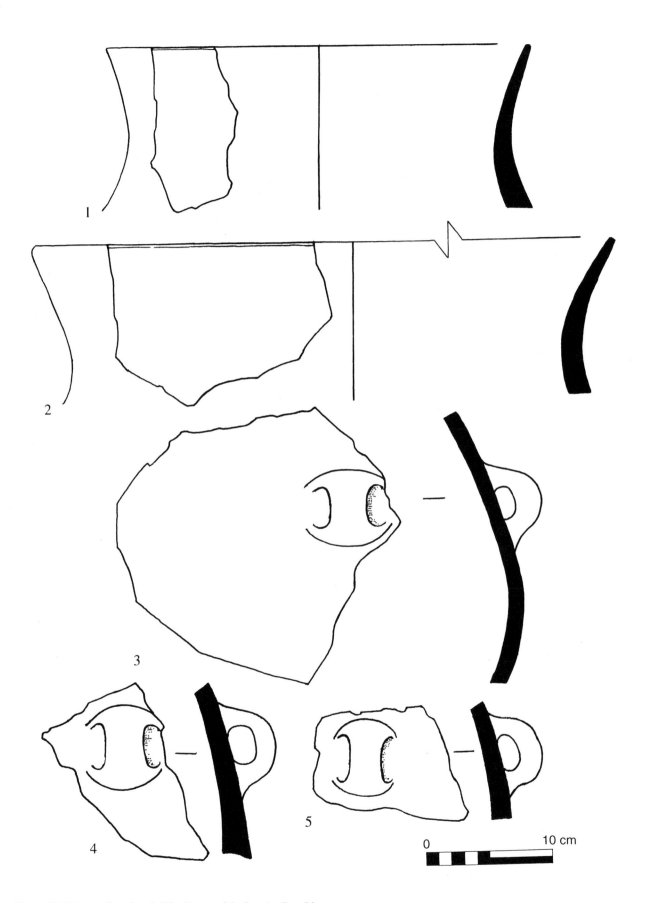

Figure 3.36 Pottery from Samshvilde. *Courtesy of the Georgian State Museum.*

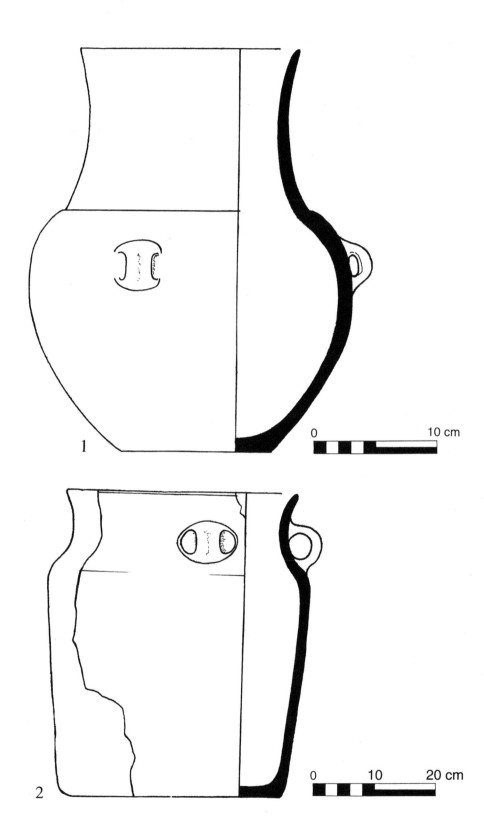

Figure 3.37 *1*, Pottery from Nuli; *2*, pottery from Didi Akhalsopeli. *Courtesy of the Georgian State Museum.*

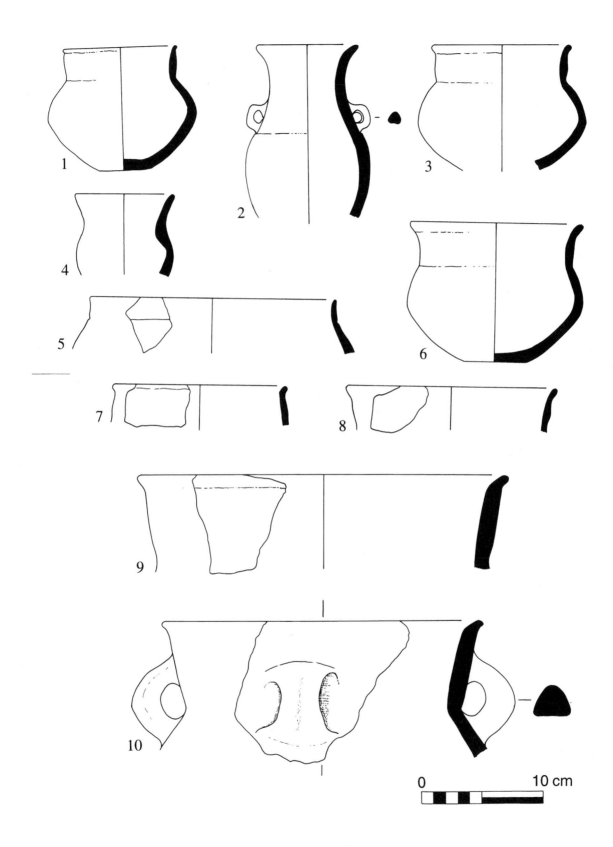

Figure 3.38 Pottery from Sos Höyük, Period VA. *Illustration by A. Sagona, C. Sagona, M. Anastasios-Wilson.*

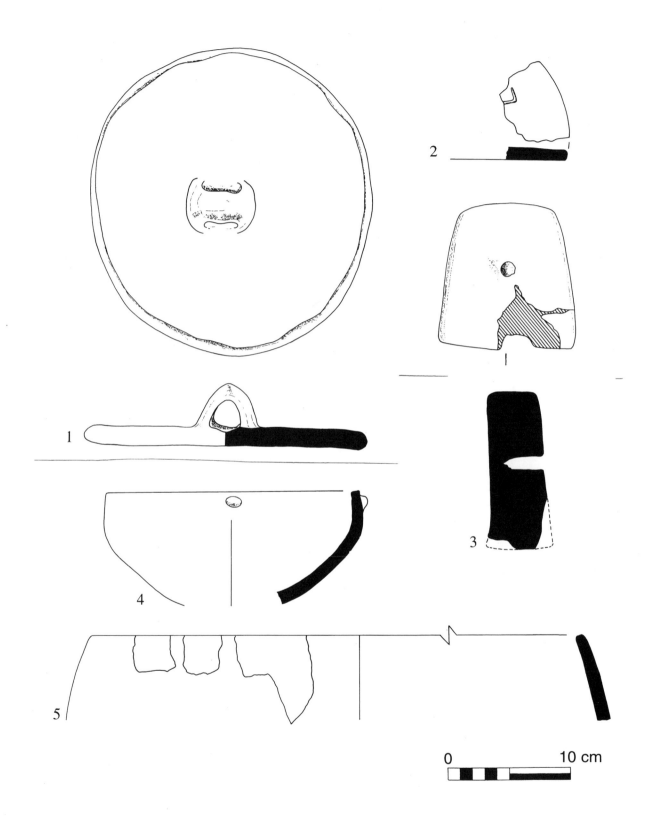

Figure 3.39 Pottery from Sos Höyük, Period VA. *Illustration by A. Sagona, C. Sagona, M. Anastasios-Wilson.*

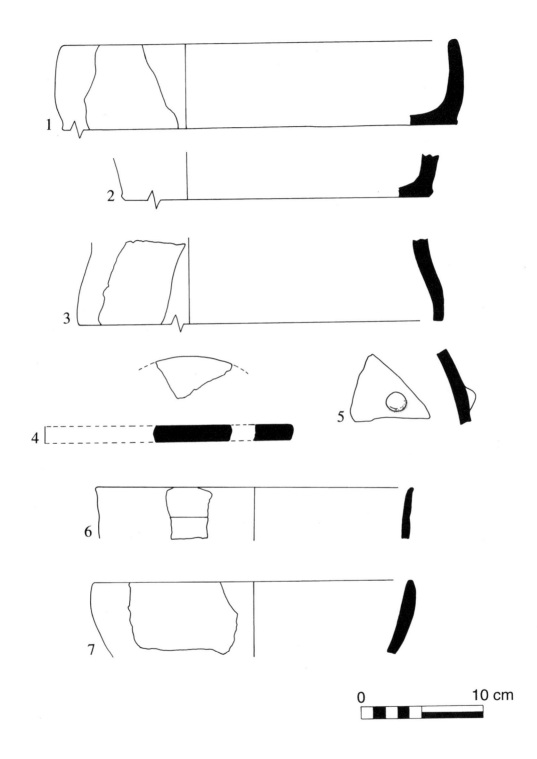

Figure 3.40 Pottery from Sos Höyük, Period VA. *Illustration by A. Sagona, C. Sagona, M. Anastasios-Wilson.*

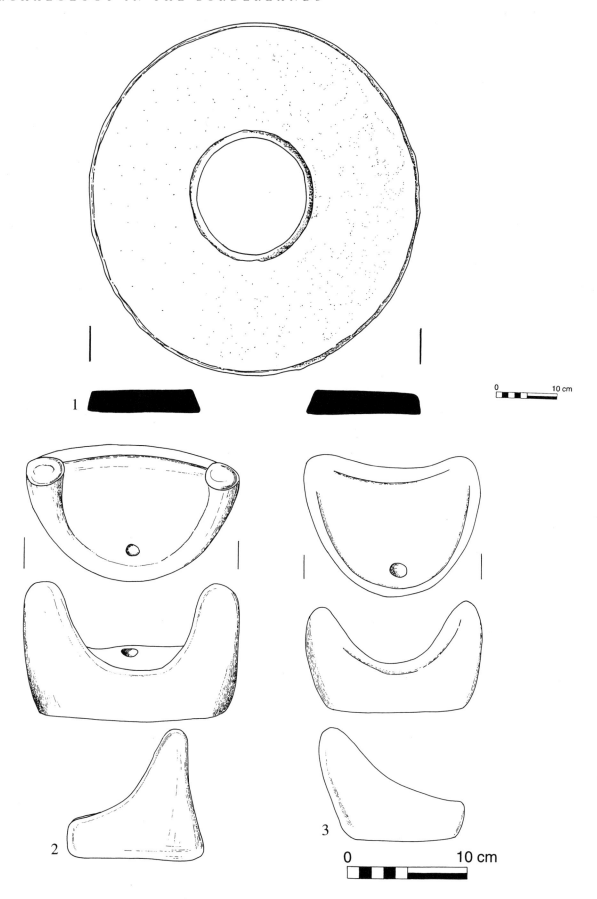

Figure 3.41 *1*, Circular hearth and *2-3*, horned pot stands from Sos Höyük, Period VA. *Illustration by A. Sagona, C. Sagona, M. Anastasios-Wilson.*

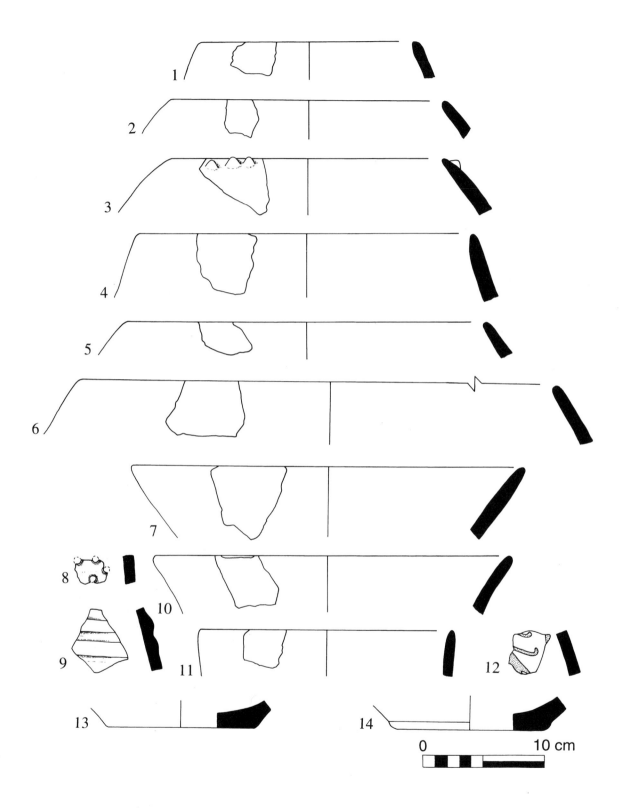

Figure 3.42 Pottery from Gundulak. *Illustration by A. Sagona, C. Sagona, M. Anastasios-Wilson.*

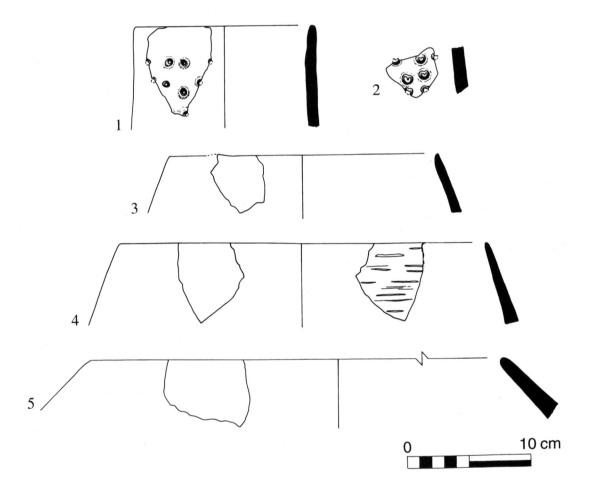

Figure 3.43 Pottery from Pulur (Gökçedere, Bayburt). *Illustration by A. Sagona, C. Sagona, M. Anastasios-Wilson.*

(continued from page 50)

generally found in a group of two or three at Sos, and the clover-leaf-shaped illustrated here by a model from Khizanaant Gora (figure 3.21:4).

The chipped stone industry is overwhelmingly obsidian, except at Samele Kldé where it is entirely flint and chert, and Ginchi and Alikemek Tepesi where obsidian tools are in the minority. Most of the obsidian in Georgia originated at the Chikiani source, except for the region of the Alazani valley where knappers also exploited Armenian sources. Analyses have also shown that the inhabitants of Alikemek Tepesi used Kelbajar obsidian, located some three hundred km away from the site.

Typologically, the tools range from the rich and archaic industry at Sioni, comprising a range of blades, to the comparatively undistinguished amorphous flake tradition at Delisi (Menabde and Kiguradze 1981). Formal types include notched blades from which were manufactured burins, scrapers, and *piece écaille* (flakes with squamous surface). End scrapers are quite common. Only a few blades were backed, mostly for use as sickles. Other rare types include the trapeze-shaped tool with retouched longitudinal edges and a pressure-flaked upper surface and a denticulate blade. Certain tools, knives and scrapers in particular, display fish-scale pressure flaking over most of the surface. Truncated and tanged triangular projectile points are common in western Georgia only, where they characterize the Samele Kldé industry. There are a few bifacial chopping tools, and cores are small and reutilized, or large and conical. Ground stone objects are produced from basalt and include edge-ground axes, saddle querns, and mortars.

The bone industry is characterized by numerous awls (figure 3.27:8–15), spatulae, and some spindle whorls. At Damtsvari Gora a cattle shoulder blade was used to manufacture a hoe. Understandably, antler was also exploited for the manufacture of picks and shaft hole hoes. At Alikemek Tepe a considerable amount of jewelry was found. Numerous circular beads were made from shell (150 from one pit in horizon 1) and pendants from perforated teeth. A few stone beads, including carnelian and turquoise, and a copper bead were also found. Metal objects are few, but significant. An awl with square shaft and knife blade with a high percentage of tin: 3.8 (knife?) and 3.2 (awl?) from Delisi (Miron and Orthmann 1995: S.318). Similar awls were produced at Kviriatskali and Leila-depe, where the analysis of excess metal provided a reading of 2.01% of arsenic and 0. 67% of nickel.

CONCLUSIONS

The data presented above lend themselves to a new developmental sequence for the Transcaucasian Chalcolithic, and, accordingly, point to a number of significant cultural and socioeconomic dialectics that gave rise to the Kura-Araxes culture complex. Two broad chronological horizons can be discerned. The earlier one is best represented by the horizons at Sioni, Kviriatskhali, and Zjinvali and falls between around 4800 to 4000 BC. Occupying regions that were more ecologically diverse and higher in altitude than those settled by their Neolithic predecessors, the Early Chalcolithic communities established a pattern of settlement that was also more dispersed when compared to the aggregated distribution of sixth millennium BC. So meager is our environmental evidence for the Chalcolithic period that we cannot reconstruct its subsistence pattern. But the major shift in settlement patterns and the associated changes in the settlement types to smaller, more temporary villages in the early Chalcolithic period appears to reflect a change in the way communities responded to "risk management." The mosaic of environments in Transcaucasia did offer diversity, to be sure, yet the extremes of temperature and precipitation, especially in adjacent eastern Anatolia, added a degree of unpredictability. To deal with risk in an unpredictable but potentially productive environment, the communities appear to have changed their strategies, traveling to resources that were more dispersed. The flimsy structures of this period and the large number of pits accompanying them are suggestive of such a mobile lifestyle. Transhumance may well have formed a major part of this economic subsistence strategy, but no one is sure of the exact nature of this mobility. Conspicuous in this regard is the large round structure at Sioni that does point to permanency and to a different organization of labor, one that may have been akin to that responsible for the later, large structures of Sos Höyük VA and Berikldeebi V2.

Whatever the changes in socioeconomic strategies, the Early Chalcolithic societies of Transcaucasia occupy a position along a continuum from the Neolithic to the earliest stages of the Kura-Araxes complex. Vestigial influences of the Shulaveri Neolithic are seen at Sioni mostly in cultural features—hole-mouth jars, serrated rims, basket impressed flat bases, and knob decoration. Rims decorated with combed impressions at Tsiteli Sopeli suggest that they, too, belong to this early phase. Complementing these ceramic features is

Figure 3.44 View of Late Chalcolithic (Period VA) stone wall at Sos Höyük, looking east. *Photograph by Bronwyn Douglas.*

Figure 3.45 Sos Höyük: Late Chalcolthic, Period VA, round house (*locus* 4250). *Photograph by Bronwyn Douglas.*

a homogenous bone industry, replete in awls, and an archaic lithic industry largely characterized by burins, scrapers, and squamous retouch. Sickle blades typical of the Shulaveri Neolithic were also found at Sioni. The majority of the features that distinguish this phase such as the distinctive decorative rims from Sioni are localized to Transcaucasia. Zjinvali and Damtsvari Gora, it seems, were established a little later. Although they share many similarities with the earliest Chalcolithic sites, the absence of knob ornaments at Zjinvali together with a lithic industry characterized mostly by flakes, the absence of pottery with wavy rims and punctures, and stone tools with squamous retouch at Damtsvari Gora, point to a later date.

The Middle/Late Chalcolithic phase (around 4000 to 3200/3000 BC) includes the sites of Tsopi, Tekhut, Leila Tepesi, Berikldeebi, Khizanaant Gora E, and Sos Höyük VA. Here one is struck by the presence of the large "public" building at Berikldeebi V2 and the massive boundary wall at Sos Höyük VA. Although only the Sos structure has absolute dates that place it in the late fourth millennium, both are associated with material that is tentatively described in this paper as

"Proto-Kura-Araxes." What is so intriguing about these structures is that they provide a fleeting glimpse of a level of developed sociopolitical organization that disappeared in the subsequent centuries in this region. These two sites show a localized transformation of their respective societies that may have been influenced by new external stimuli. Cross-cultural comparisons are tempting indeed, most especially with the Upper Euphrates valley where the late fourth millennium at Arslantepe (period VIA) saw the emergence of a fully centralized society with strong Syro-Mesopotamian connections (Frangipane 2000). Such comparisons have already been drawn by Javakhishvili (1998), who pointed to architectural and presumed functional similarities between the Berikldeebi building and the "temple" structures in northern Mesopotamia.

It should be pointed out, however, that both the Sos and Berikldeebi horizons lack definitive cultural links with Syro-Mesopotamia. Javakhishvili further attempted to draw Berikldeebi into a southern orbit by suggesting that within its assemblage the thick-walled vessels, tempered with quartz and chaff, and bearing an flared rim attached to an ovoid body, have Amuq F

Figure 3.46 Sos Höyük: Late Chalcolthic, Period VA, ceramic sherd 'pavement' (*locus* 4270). *Photograph by Bronwyn Douglas.*

Figure 3.47 Body sherd from Sos Höyük showing the impressions of a woven mat sandwiched between two slabs of clay. *Photograph by Bronwyn Douglas.*

connections. But without a final publication, it is difficult to judge the tightness of this comparison. Nonetheless Javakhishvili reminded us that although the stratigraphy of Berikldeebi V is divided into two phases, the pottery horizon is basically homogenous, with profiles tending more toward the angular in level V2. Pit 150, located below the structure ascribed as a temple in V2, offers the full range of ceramics. Ovoid-bodied jars with cylindrical necks and a micaceous paste and a combed surface comprise the second type. Most important are a few sherds that belong to tall-necked jars with globular bodies. Their comparatively thin walls, generally well baked to a grayish brown color, prompted the excavator to designate them as Proto-Kura-Araxes.

Although the scale of organizational complexity that developed in northeastern Anatolia and Transcaucasia in no way matched that in the Upper Euphrates valley, both regions followed a similar broad pattern: namely, a rise in sociopolitical organization in the late fourth millennium followed by a "collapse" around 3000 BC

that is represented at both Arslantepe and Sos by the absence of substantial structures, and at Berikldeebi by the abandonment of the site altogether. Given the high level of centralization at Arslantepe in the Late Chalcolithic, the changes accompanying the onset of the Early Bronze Age there, period VIB1, were more dramatic than at Sos Höyük. The large public buildings of Arslantepe VIA gave way to a settlement comprising mostly wattle-and-daub architecture and the diversity of its Late Chalcolithic pottery production narrowed to a repertoire represented by Red-Black Burnished ware only. At Sos, the earliest Kura-Araxes settlements (in period VB) are characterized by a variety of freestanding domestic houses and standardized assemblages that reflect the conservative nature of their makers, who unswervingly preserved the fundamental character of their culture for over a millennium thereafter.

Despite these changes, the new communities of the Early Bronze Age showed cultural continuity with the late fourth millennium BC. This connection is stronger in north-eastern Anatolia and Transcaucasia, regions that were less affected by the social and political flux that embraced their neighbors to the west. The question of continuity is most clearly expressed in pottery manufacture and, in turn, the origin and subsequent dispersal of the distinctive Kura-Araxes pottery, termed Red-Black Burnished pottery at Arslantepe, where excavators have now recorded its presence as early as period VII (Frangipane 2000:443–44). What this signifies in terms of interaction between the Upper Euphrates valley and the lands to the east during the fourth millennium is still rather vague. But the considerable amount of Red-Black Burnished ware in the subsequent period VIA leaves no doubt that by the end of that millennium communities in the Malatya region were in regular communication with the manufacturers of this ware. Then, as we have seen, in period VIB, Red-Black Burnished ware was the only pottery type produced at Arslantepe.

Interestingly, the mode of production whereby a vessel is burnished and then fired to produce a lustrous red and black surface, long held to be the hallmark of the Transcaucasian Kura-Araxes repertoire, may, in fact, have an origin in east-central Anatolia. Following the earlier views of Esin (1979) and Arsebük (1979), Frangipane has suggested that the Red-Black Burnished ware of Arslantepe VIA and related assemblages in the Malatya and Elazığ region may point to a combination of traits from two traditions (Frangipane 2000:447) : (1) a typology of shapes that is largely derived from central Anatolia; (2) a fine red and black fabric (contemporary central Anatolia wares are generally black all over) that points to Transcaucasia. In Transcaucasia, however, vessels with a red and black color scheme appear later, at around the transition between the fourth and third millennia, and then only in very small quantities. Prior to that time, the Sioni complex dominates. On the other hand, at Sos Höyük, positioned between Transcaucasia and the Upper Euphrates valley, the presence of fine red and black burnished vessels is conspicuous in the Late Chalcolithic ceramic assemblage, suggesting that the idea of a red and black color scheme may have been east Anatolian. Yet many of the typological attributes of the earliest Kura-Araxes ceramics such as small handles set at the juncture of the neck and shoulder, or tall, concave or slightly swollen necks are firmly rooted in the Transcaucasian Chalcolithic. What emerged about 3000 BC as early Kura-Araxes pottery was a combination of these two traits.

AUTHOR'S NOTE

This chapter is dedicated to my dear friend Tamaz Kiguradze, who passed away on April 10, 2002, before the publication of this book. Our friendship extended back to the early 1980s when, as a doctoral student bewildered by the complexities of Transcaucasian archaeology, I arrived in Tbilisi. Tamaz immediately took me under his wing and introduced me to the extensive holdings of the Tbilisi State Museum. More recently, we met annually, in eastern Turkey. As a member of the Sos Höyük team, Tamaz was very excited about the Late Chalcolithic material he was finding, especially the light it shed on the elusive origins of the Kura-Araxes complex, a topic that interested us both very deeply. We spent many an hour discussing Transcaucasian prehistory, and I am forever indebted to Tamaz's encyclopedic knowledge and his clear, cautious and well-balanced judgment on material culture. Tamaz relished writing this chapter and saw it as the pilot for a book he was planning to write on the late prehistory of Transcaucasia. Although we will never benefit from that book, Tamaz has left an even more enduring legacy—memories of his friendship and inspiration. He touched the lives of countless individuals, from undergraduate students to senior scholars, and he will be remembered by many with deep affection.

NOTES

1. One reading from Jinvali, 4300±150 BC (TB-326), provides a calibrated range of 5237 to 4637 Cal BC. Two others were analysed recently at the AMS facility at Lucius Heights, Australia. One sample from Berikldeebi V, 5070±40 BP, (OZE595), may be calibrated to a two sigma range of 3955–3778 BC, whereas the other, from Didube (OZF720) has a reading of 3330–3060 BC, within a similar range. The authors would like to thank the Australian Institute of Nuclear Science and Engineering (AINSE) for two AMS grants (00/134P; 01/024) and to Ewan Lawson and Ugo Zoppi, staff at the Australian Nuclear Science and Technology Organization, for their assistance in the analysis. New dates from Late Chalcolithic levels at Aparan III and Aratashen, in Armenia, will be published soon, complementing the late fourth millennium dates already know from Horom.

2. The question of nomadism during the Kura-Araxes cultural complex is discussed by Howells-Meurs (2001), who studied the Early Bronze Age faunal material from Sos Höyük collected during the first years of excavations. The bulk of faunal remains from Early Bronze Age contexts collected in later years and those from the Late Chalcolithic period have yet to be studied.

3. Details of the University of Melbourne survey of the Bayburt region (1988, 1990–1993) will be available soon in a final report. For results of recent survey work in the Erzurum region see Sagona 1999.

4. After the Late Chalcolithic, the site was used as a cemetery. The fourth millennium settlement was superimposed by a kurgan-like mound with a chamber of the Bedeni period positioned within a stone circle originally more than 16 m (plan shows it to be about 13 m) and covered by a mound of earth. Below the chamber were another three graves, but unlike the burial in the chamber they did not contain grave goods. A further two burials, again without grave goods, were located within the circle. Six of the Late Chalcolithic pits were within the kurgan; seven were outside.

5. The final report on Berikledeebi is being prepared for publication. A useful interim report is Javakhishvili 1998 published posthumously. Readers should note, however, that in the illustrations of that report Kura-Araxes material excavated in level IV was incorrectly attributed to the Pre-Kura-Araxes level V. The correct documentation is as follows: figures 3 and 4 belong to level V, whereas figures 5 and 6 should be attributed to level IV.

6. Since its beginning in 1994, the Sos Höyük project has been funded by the Australian Research Council. Radiocarbon dates prefaced by laboratory code OZD were made possible by an Australian Institute of Nuclear Science and Engineering AMS grant (no. 97/189R); those dates prefaced by Beta were funded by the ARC.

7. One fragment (figure 3.42:12) collected at Gundulak, a Late Chalcolithic site, is included here even though it is painted. Whether this sherd belongs to the Neolithic, a period seemingly absent from northeast Anatolia, remains to be seen.

CHAPTER 4

Ripples in the Stream:

Transcaucasia-Anatolian Interaction in the Murat/Euphrates Basin at the Beginning of the Third Millennium BC

MITCHELL S. ROTHMAN

INTRODUCTION

The presence of highly burnished, often incised red-black,[1] black-black, and gray-gray pottery over a wide expanse of eastern and southeastern Turkey and western Iran at the beginning of the Bronze Age has led to a number of theories of what the presence of these cultural artifacts represents. Does this Early Transcaucasian, Karaz, or Kura-Araks ware indicate a massive migration out of the Transcaucasian region where this pottery first appears? Is the pottery carried by traders and reproduced by local Late Chalcolithic populations? Is its presence simply a marker of the spread of new technologies—those include metallurgical techniques and ceramic copies of metal shapes—among Late Chalcolithic and Early Bronze Age populations?

In this chapter I will (1) summarize the current debate on how to understand migration, diffusion, and other forms of interregional contact; (2) briefly describe the current archaeological, chronological,

cultural, economic, and environmental data relevant to the coming of Transcaucasian wares into eastern Turkey; and (3) present a theory to explain this spread and review the relevant survey and artifactual evidence in favor or opposed to it.

I will argue that, in fact, the appearance of Transcaucasian ware in eastern Turkey and, for that matter, in western Iran represents a series of ripples in a stream of movement of pastoral nomads, traders, and small farmers back and forth in this larger region. These small segments of the Transcaucasian population, after wandering into eastern Turkey and western Iran, mixed with pre-Bronze Age populations to create the great variability observed in artifacts of the Early Transcaucasian Culture (hereafter ETC) over this large area. This spread has to do with the particular distribution of natural resources, environmental zones, population, politics, and their adaptations to natural and human environments.

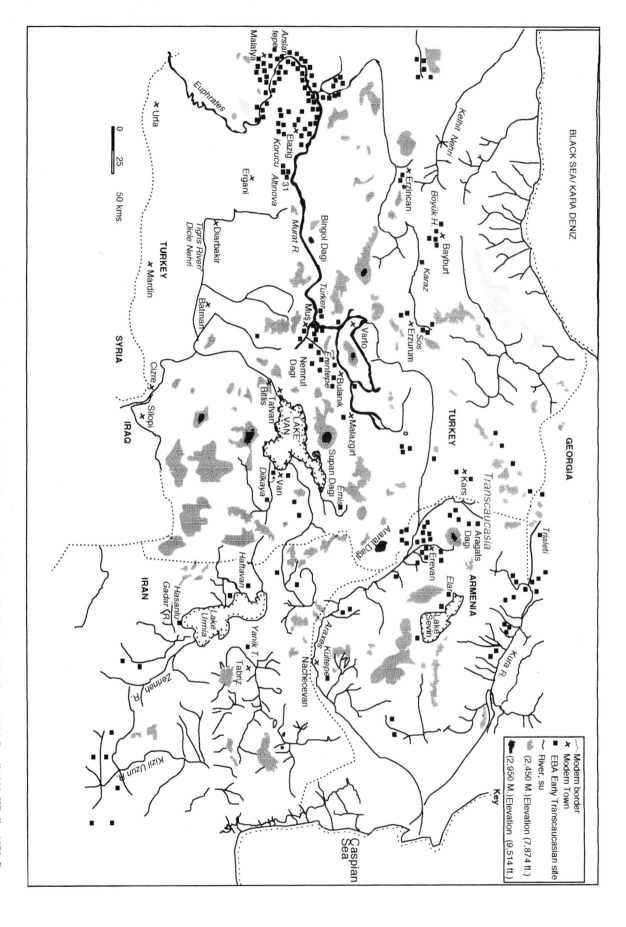

Figure 4.1 Topographic map, Eastern Turkey, Western Iran, Transcaucasus: Early Bronze Age with Early Transcaucasian Culture. *After Rothman 1993, Sagona 1984, Russell 1980, Whallon 1979, Burney and Lang 1971. Map by Mitchell S. Rothman.*

MIGRATION

Theoretical Issues

The issues of migration and diffusion are at the very heart of the discussion of the ETC penetration, diffusion, or influence into the areas to the south, southwest, and southeast of the basins of the Kura and Araxes rivers (see figure 4.1). As an explanatory tool in archaeology and history these elements have had a long and checkered history. As Anthony (1990:896) writes, the idea that the appearance of new types of cultural artifacts in a geographical area must represent "new peoples" was first utilized in the nineteenth century. Kossina and later Childe thought that variability in artifactual remains across Europe could only be explained if archaeological cultures were understood as statistical clusters of similar artifact types. Childe wrote,

> We find certain types of remains—pots, implements, burial rites, house forms—consistently recurring together. Such a complex of regularly associated traits we shall term a 'cultural group' or 'culture.' We assume that such a complex is the material expression of what today would be called a people. [1929:v–vi]

This is the explanatory model that Kramer (1977) describes as pots equal peoples. Biologists used the same trait listing or phenotypic technique to define discrete human races in the nineteenth and early twentieth centuries rather than looking at the deeper or genetic relationships (Gould 1996). Therefore, the appearance of a new corpus of artifact traits and types in an area must represent either the wholesale adoption of items diffused from neighboring groups or the migration of new peoples into the area, carrying the material manifestations of their culture with them.

With the advent of the New Archaeology in the 1970s, this trait-listing, culture historical "explanation" of change was rejected, often out of hand. If the study of archaeology is to be the study of human groups as defined by ethnographers, cultures or "peoples" as sets of traits reflect only a shadow of the actual behavior, ideas, and perspectives of human groups long past. The models thus created paint a false image of the ancient reality. With the real challenges of learning why a particular people change—what Sahlins and Service (1960) call *specific evolution*—the focus was necessarily local. Therefore, "local invention" as opposed to diffusion or migration became the new watchword for explaining change (Chapman and Hamerow 1997:4). Binford, long credited as one of the founders of the New

Archaeology, nonetheless questioned the utility of these alternatives. He wrote (1972:256-258) that by seeing all explanation as fitting into the culture historical processes of diffusion, migration, or local invention, archaeologists were making much the same mistake as Kossina and Childe. They were forced to look at local patterns of artifact type, assume they represented local communities, and therefore decide how much of the variability could be attributed to each of three processes. The important distinctions among technological, functional, and stylistic variability, and also what these factors mean for interpreting the past, became confused. The approach that Binford criticizes is certainly the one Rouse advocates by defining the term *culture* as he does (1986:13, see also Byrne 1978, Kristiansen 1989). At the same time Rouse proposes an adaptation-oriented approach that I discuss below as a useful one (Rouse 1986:12). In all of the traditional approaches to the subject of migration, diffusion, and acculturation, the real fluidity of culture contact, culture change, changing politics, ideology, and adaptations were at best described according to a new set of archaeological categories, but not explained. The very fact that cultures are not closed systems and that the lines differentiating one culture from another are often fuzzy was not taken into account in this analytical orientation. In the end, where the ideas or techniques came from is less important than how they were integrated into the living human groups in any particular area and then modified and adapted to become a "new" cultural system. In other words, a more culturally "genotypic" approach is necessary even to understand migration.

As a starting point, we know from modern and from historically documented cases that migration, diffusion, and independent invention happened in the near and ancient past. For example, no future archaeologist could hope to understand the United States and its role in the world without understanding its migration pattern (immigration). No one could understand the first decade of the twenty-first century AD without understanding the invention of computers, the new organization of labor and time they promote, and their worldwide diffusion. The shelves of research libraries are full of scholarly treatises on modern migration patterns. We also know that although the formula of pots equals peoples is too simplistic, there are elements of style that have meaning symbolic of identity and of cultural perception. In Longacre's (1968) classic study of the distribution of variability in ceramics at the Carter Ranch Pueblo, he used pottery design to monitor postmarital living arrangements. Currently, studies of the "Uruk Expansion" show that style in artifacts does have some cultural meaning, although in the Uruk case that meaning is still much debated (Algaze 1993; Rothman 2001; Stein 1999a). To reiterate, migrations, independent invention, and subsequent diffusion take place in modern times and certainly occurred in the past. Artifact style does have meaning, although not the simplistic meaning formerly assumed.

Our problem of how to analyze ancient societies then remains. How do we determine whether there were migrations of significant size, diffusion, or influence? How do we in the same context explain why such processes are set in motion and how they changed the cultural landscape in the places where they occurred? In other words, we need to see how the needs and opportunities of groups engaged in this process of movement of people, technologies, goods, and ideas were manipulated and adapted to produce the cultures we see later on in time. This is the adaptation approach advocated by Rouse and myself (Rothman 2000).

Methodologies

To begin to understand the role of migration and diffusion as factors in explaining the changes we see in the material record and the cultural reality that lies behind it, we must reject a purely artifactual analysis. That is to say that merely tightening our chronological analysis or a more detailed categorization of artifact types from neighboring geographical areas will not produce a satisfactory method. I could not agree more completely with Anthony when he writes, "How is migration to be identified archaeologically? This is, of course, an important methodological question, but it is not the place to begin" (Anthony 1990:897). As Anthony writes,

> While it is often difficult to identify specific causes of particular migrations, even with the help of documentary data, it is somewhat easier to identify general structural conditions that favor the occurrence of migrations. Moreover, particular structural conditions favor migrations of particular types. [1990:899]

In other words, we need to understand the changing natural, cultural, and sociopolitical environments of the time we are studying. Then, if there were significant movements of human, groups, goods, or information, we can begin to understand how those movements changed the adaptations of all the societies involved (Rouse 1986:12; Rothman 2000). "It is only after the

structure of the migration process is understood that appropriate methods can be identified or developed to detect its archaeological signature" (Anthony 1992:174).

For example, the Seljuk Turks or Oghuz[2] represent a historically attested migration of groups from Central Asia in the first millennium AD. Their homeland was farther east than the ETC, occurring as it did on the borders of Afghanistan east of the Caspian in Transoxiana. These groups eventually migrated into the Kura Araxes basin and eastern Turkey. Modern Turks claim their ancestry from the Seljuks of Rum (Rice 1961). The populace that moved was made up of nomadic pastoralists and small farmers like most believe the ETC populations to have been. Historical records indicate that the initial reason for migration was economic.

> As with most of the great Turkish migrations in history, here too the major impetus seems to have been a lack of land and pasturage. [Kafesoğlu 1988:24]

A number of elements of the natural, cultural, and sociopolitical environments make this a less than perfect model for the ETC migration. However, this case demonstrates how many factors must be taken into account. For one thing, the Seljuks had a travel advantage in having the camel and modern horse available, technological advantages that greatly aided their mobility. Second, the political organization of the Oghuz and their neighbors was much more sophisticated than the ETC group was likely to have been. The Oghuz under Seljuk and his sons were part of a series of competing states with capital cities and sophisticated military organization. In addition to land competition, they were competing with other states, the Khazar state and the Qipchaq confederation. Because of their size and military prowess, they were pulled into Anatolia initially as mercenaries for the Byzantines and early on in their migration made political alliances with Moslems. Kafesoğlu (1988:25) argues that the conversion of Turkic tribes to Islam was really a political move.

The case of the Seljuk Turks, although not a direct model for the ETC, does point to a number of elements of a methodology to study cultures on the move and in contact with other populations. As Anthony points out (1997:22), "Migration is a social strategy, not an automatic response to crowding." Simply to say that the Seljuks lacked enough land in their old homeland and therefore somehow wound up in eastern Turkey is not the full story.

Demographers speak of a "push" and a "pull" in all migrations. There must be some reason to be pushed out of an earlier homeland, but there must also be something that pulls the mobile population in a particular direction. Moch writes of modern migrations,

> I argue that the primary determinants of migration patterns consist of fundamental structural elements of economic life: labor force demands in countryside and city, deployment of capital, population patterns (rates of birth, death, marriage), and landholding regimes. Shifts in those elements underlie changing migration itineraries. [1997:43]

At the same time, Moch admits that configurations of political economy—what anthropologists would call social organization—underlie all the different, possible itineraries. Primogeniture or other customs favoring one family member, one kinship segment, ethnicity, or class over another, for example, may cause the less economically fortunate to migrate. In its extreme form, governmental policies like the expulsion of the Huguenots from France, the Jews from Spain, or the export of African war prisoners and lower class citizens as slaves to America catalyzed mass migrations. Ideology may also factor into the equation. The filling of America's Western frontier was more than population pressure in the east or purely economic opportunity. The philosophies of American individualism and manifest destiny were major pulls for the European population that migrated to the Americas (Billington 1967).

Part of the pull for migrants assumes that they have information about their destination. Rarely does a completely isolated group migrate, except under the greatest duress.

> It is quite clear that the probability that x will migrate to y at time t is partially determined by x's level of knowledge about place y. This, in turn, is largely determined by the prior history of migration between x and y. Earlier migrants return home carrying information about optimal routes and destinations, and as a result these same routes and destinations are targeted by later migrants. [Anthony 1997:23-24]

In the case of the Seljuk Turks, they were familiar with the peoples in the areas to which they eventually migrated. In the seventh and eight centuries AD Arab traders were going "in ever-increasing numbers" into Central Asia (Rice 1961:27). At times this informational pull involves "leapfrogging" (Anthony 1990:902-903). Relatives or others who have migrated may draw migrants over large areas of available territory to a more distant locale. Diffusion of information

along the stream may occur even in areas where the migrants do not settle. The makeup of early migrants may not represent the entire population from which migrants came. For example, Stein (1998) and Badler (1998) propose that male traders may have occupied the fourth millennium BC "colonies" at Hacınebi and Godin Tepe. Lefferts (1977) reports that at the beginning of migrations, especially into frontier zones, the population tends to be mostly male and young. Among the earliest migrants groups, one often emerges as an "apex family" when migration pulls more members of the group into new territory (Anthony 1990:904). These families provide resources for other migrants as they arrive and act as cultural "translators" and liaisons with the native population. If necessary, they serve as organizers of defense and even expansion for their own group. As a result these apex families gain special status among migrant groups.

Because migrants follow established routes to established localities, migration forms more of a stream than a wave. Often because the migrants follow their predecessors, migrations appear to be like links in a chain, each representing a subsequent group migrating along the same stream (Anthony 1997:26). The wave theory of the Neolithic in Europe (Ammerman and Cavalli-Sforza 1973), not accounting for new questions of fact, may be somewhat questionable, because it assumes a gradual and wide band of migration and information flow (diffusion). Alternatively, the migration stream may also consist of a mix of groups all in the same direction and on the same path. This is what in my title I call ripples in the stream, because stones thrown from different directions will set up a confusing pattern of ripples. However these ripples may yet be possible to trace back to their source, the place from which the stone is thrown. Such ripples are most likely the result of a series of homelands, where the social organization consists of identifiable, segmentary units (clans, sodalities, lineages, and other associations). Since internally coherent units that are nonetheless subsets of the larger group break off and move, these segments are more likely to maintain elements of their former group, especially as reflected by cultural identity worked into artifact style.

Last, and certainly not least, the structure of migrations must be understandable in terms of the adaptations of the groups to their natural and human environments. With some rare exceptions like the Tainos of the Caribbean (Rouse 1986:106–155) most migrating groups move into new territories to which they are preadapted. The degree of fit to a particular set of environmental factors can limit or open potential new migration routes. Food production and general subsistence behaviors are naturally the most critical elements of the social strategy of migrations. These are of two types (Cleland 1976). Groups practicing focal subsistence strategies have quite specialized and narrow possibilities. The terrain into which they migrate must offer readily available resources. Alternatively, groups practicing a diffuse subsistence strategy are more readily adaptable to a wider set of resources. The speed of migration often is dependent on whether a focal or diffuse subsistence strategy is practiced. For example, the migration of Bantu groups within the forested zones contiguous with their probable homeland in the Congo proceeded fairly rapidly (Oliver 1970). With fairly advanced agricultural practices and knowledge of iron working and with many rivers as migratory routes, they could and apparently did spread rapidly in the zone where they had the same sort of environment of agriculture as in their homeland. Once at the limit of that ecological zone, their migration into the drier environments—what Africanists call stage III (Hoover 1974:6)—was much slower. Groups already living in the drier zones, although pushed out of some niches, were able to maintain a niche for themselves. The Bushmen and Hottentots are examples of groups that remained after Bantu migration. In the core zone where traditional Bantu agriculture was possible without change, however, the migrating Bantu peoples quickly assimilated local populations.

Indicators of Migration

Above I have argued that to explain changes in antiquity involving migration, it is necessary first to understand the full context, environmental and cultural. I proposed that an orientation that analyzes the movement of human groups as a social strategy and the changes that result over the range of space as a series of adaptations will yield the best explanation.

It is still necessary to establish that migrations did occur. Since migrations are demographic shifts, the first indication of a migration should be population growth in areas to which migrants go. Populations do have a natural growth rate and increase in population does not necessarily mean the introduction of new peoples. The longer the chronological period, the harder it is to assert that increased numbers of sites and occupied hectares represents migration. However, if the numbers of migrants are significant, surveys should show a relatively rapid population growth that cannot

be explained by indigenous population increase. Also, unless somehow the migrants and the native population share an identical adaptation, settlement patterns should vary between groups initially. A migrating group might use ecological niches other than those used by a native group, especially if there is competition between them. Since settlement patterns theoretically represent social and economic patterns that generate them (see Rothman 1987), these too should be distinctive.

In cases where language is recorded, linguistic change can be indicative of a number of elements. The homeland of a particular language can be traced by finding common route words in cognate languages. If linguists map the occurrence of language groups' patterns over space, they should be able to trace the routes or streams of migration. Linguists can also determine the relative dominance of migrants and native speakers by viewing language change as itself an adaptation that mirrors the cultural and political adaptations of human groups. For the ETC, linguistics is of marginal use at best. The two best-known cases, the spread of Indo-Europeans (Renfrew 1987; Anthony 1991, 1997) and of Bantu speakers (Fage 1975; Hoover 1974; Oliver 1970), are not particularly apposite here, so I will not discuss them further.

The remaining indicators have to be artifactual. To the degree that stylistic variation can be attributed to migrating human groups, it must be understood in context. For example, at Hacınebi Tepe in southeastern Turkey, Stein argues that a group of southern Mesopotamians migrated northward into the plains just south of the Taurus foothills as traders (Stein 1999a, 1999b, 2001). These migrant traders moved into an already established community. How, though, do we know that we are not seeing diffused style, or emulation of a known but foreign style? The idea is not merely to note the presence of styles foreign to the Late Chalcolithic, northern Mesopotamian population. The full corpus must be viewed, and the patterns of behavior of the migrants must be contrasted with that of the native population. At Hacınebi the styles of the two populations' pottery are distinct, but so are the ways foods are prepared, the cuts of meat used, and the sources of foods. In addition, the technology of the two groups is different. The older native population used traditional northern Mesopotamian administrative hardware, seals and sealings, while the contemporaneous southern group uses administrative techniques most similar to the cities of the southern alluvium.

Their subsistence practices were largely the same, but the indigenous group used typical chipped stone sickles, whereas the immigrants, despite the easy availability of chipped stone, continued to use baked clay sickles. The clay sickles must have required much more work than the sharper, more durable stone sickles, but the practices of the migrants reflect their homeland. If two groups, a migrant and a native, are hypothesized to live in the same areas, the functional categories of their artifacts need to be carefully monitored. Their inventory of tools and production techniques should be distinctive, as it represents their subsistence practices. If ideological elements are represented in artifact style, they too should be distinct. Diverse groups are unlikely to produce the same exact goods in the same exact way. Their manufacturing waste products should be different. If what the archaeologist observes is a uniform artifactual assemblage, it might be a case of diffusion. That would not be the case with parallel and distinct assemblages. In this effort to determine whether a migration has occurred, artifacts must be viewed not as simple markers of identity but as representatives of contrasting adaptations, economically, culturally, and politically.

With this background in mind, I will examine the ETC of the late fourth and early third millennia BC.

THE CASE OF THE EARLY TRANSCAUCASIANS

Chronology

Chronologically, the Kura-Araks phenomenon is first evident in the fourth millennium BC. The very first signs of the Transcaucasian culture appear outside the Transcaucasus at Arslantepe and at Sos Höyük at this time. The phenomenon has been thought to end no later than about 2000 BC, although Sagona's work at Sos may complicate that end date (Sagona 2000). Considerable confusion in the relative dating of the larger region occurs because of different schemas for assigning Early Bronze dates. Often what is of Early Bronze I date in Georgia, Armenia, and Azerbaijan is still Late Chalcolithic in Mesopotamia and eastern Turkey. This confusion is clear in the dating of Arslantepe VIA to either Late Chalcolithic or to Early Bronze I (see Conti and Persiani 1993, also see Kushnareva 1997:53–54). In the following discussion, I will accept Sagona's division of time into Kura-Araks 1, which is contemporaneous with the end of the Late Chalcolithic or Uruk in Mesopotamia and Turkey (3500–3000 BC), Kura-Araks II (beginning at roughly 3000 BC) for Early Bronze Age I in Mesopotamia and Turkey, and Kura-

Araks III (very roughly 2600–2000 BC) for Early Bronze Age II/III. These three periods are cultural benchmarks from the point of view of this eastern Turkish zone. As Edens (1995:59) points out, in the hilly country from the modern Syrian-Turkish border to the Taurus Gates, the rapidly developing sociopolitical complexity of the Late Chalcolithic/Uruk period is parallel in time to Kura-Araks I (figure 4.1). That period is followed by an apparent decline in societal complexity and return to village life in Kura-Araks II or Mesopotamian Early Bronze Age I (Algaze 1999, but see Rothman in press). After that decline urban society at sites like Tepecik, Titriş, and Norşuntepe emerged in Kura-Araks III (Early Bronze Age III). In the interregnum between the two periods of rapidly increasing sociopolitical development the large-scale influx of Transcaucasian artifacts is thought to occur. The goal of researchers on the ETC is to explain what happened in the Kura-Araks II period particularly.

Geography of the Zone

From the practical perspective of living and moving through eastern Turkey, what was its landscape and geology like? In other words, what was the natural environmental context for the events of the late fourth and third millennia BC? Geologically, the two great east-west upthrust massifs of the eastern Taurus Mountains define eastern Turkey. In the area of Lake Van the lowest altitude is 1300 m (4300 feet) above sea level, the highest about 2950 m (9700 feet). Lake Van provides a center point for the region, in part because in the past the lake covered a much wider area than it does today. For example, before the explosion of the Nemrut Daği volcano a million years ago, the Muş plain was part of the bed of Lake Van (Dewdney 1971). To the east of Elazığ the open plains rest on a large plate of sandstone conglomerate not well suited to drainage and soil accumulation (MTA 1988). The hills north of the plains have a more propitious geology for agricultural production in some places. Large-scale agriculture is not possible in this zone, although small farms are relatively easy to develop. The same can be said for most of the area of small parallel valleys running northeast to southwest, north of the northern Taurus massif. The spring thaw provides farmers with a wealth of runoff streams and rivers, but also extensive swampy areas and frequent flooding. The area of the northern Murat River is agriculturally marginal. Near Karaköse, modern Ağrı, for example, the environment is typified by gravel filled, very poor soils. That area would be largely useless for small farming communities. The Transcaucasian area itself is a very variegated environmentally (Kohl 1992; Burney and Lang 1971) with quite different potentials for food production. However, throughout the region pastureland is and has been abundant. North of the northern massif in the Bingöl Mountain area is one of the largest and finest pasturelands in the whole region (Altınlı 1963:56). No part of eastern Turkey lacks good pastureland. The early history of the Transcaucasian phenomenon highlights the role of pastoralism (Kiguradze and Sagona this volume).

Was the environment like the modern one at the time of Kura-Araks I–III? Based on paleoenvironmental pollen corings (van Zeist and Botema 1982:279–280; Degens and Kurtmann 1978), prior to the fifth millennium BC desert steppe conditions prevailed throughout the region. By the fifth millennium oak-juniper forest—presumably indicating a warmer and wetter climate—blanketed the area, certainly around Lake Van. By the second millennium BC, thick forests typified the region. Rowton (1967) sees the Malatya to Elazığ area as a more likely source of large construction logs discussed in third and second millennium BC Mesopotamian texts. He suggests that the "Cypress Mountain" of Sumerian fables was eastern Turkey, not the Lebanon.

Always necessary to factor into any analysis of contact between Transcaucasia and eastern Turkey is snowfall. In the area of Van, deep snow is typically on the ground for up to seven months a year. For our discussion, the important area of the Altınova and Malatya are at the edge of the maximal snow. That is, in the Van area maximum precipitation is snow in the winter. In the Altınova and westward, the winters are shorter (approximately three months) and almost twice as much of the winter-spring precipitation is rain rather than snow (Whallon 1979:7). There is no reason to believe that seasonal climatic cycles were considerably different in earlier times. In general, extremes of weather are common during any given year, as the region's weather is influenced by the mountain climate of the Taurus and the drier, hotter northern Mesopotamian regime. The area is habitable, but movement during the winter months is difficult either along the edge of the northern massif or along the Murat River, which empties into the Euphrates. In short, for herders and small farmers the intervening zone between the Kura and Araxes basins and the better watered, less climatically severe Altınova and Malatya is a difficult one. It is

habitable, but farmers and cattle grazers would do better to move westward.

Transport in this region is very limited. Within Transcaucasia proper the geology tends to isolate large areas. "The Kura-Araks folk inhabited regions where natural routes of movement are mountain chains running along an east-west axis. The fertile depressions adjacent to these east-west formations with their narrow rocky gorges and torturous courses make these river valleys formidable barriers rather than accessible communications routes" (Sagona 1984: vol. 1:24). Transport from some areas of Transcaucasia may be easier to the southwest into eastern Turkey than east or west within Transcaucasia. Those routes would be along the modern road north of the northern Taurus massif from modern Erzurum through Erzincan and down toward Malatya. A second route, which apparently was not favored at first, was north of Lake Van to the Murat and between the two massifs through modern Muş and Elazığ to Malatya.

Interpreting the ETC

As I argued above, any explanation of the Transcaucasian phenomenon must account for the reasons and means for and scale of such an influx of new artifact styles and possibly of new population. Therefore, in order to understand this phenomenon, or more probably the underlying causes of the phenomenon, it is necessary to take a more global view of the context of pushes and pulls on the populations in the Transcaucasus. Those who study the second half of the fourth and first half of the third millennia BC find ourselves in the midst of a complex and fascinating cultural cauldron. The larger Middle Eastern region, for our purposes, can be divided into four great culture areas: Transcaucasia, Central Anatolia, Mesopotamia, and western Iran. The edges, shape, and size of these culture areas shifted over time, but they appear to have represented some continuing source of cultural and technological traditions. It is from them that armies, migrants, and socioeconomic innovations flow. The question of ETC expansion focuses on the zone where all these somewhat distinct zones intersect. In one sense the hills, mountains, and undulating plains of eastern Turkey are a boundary zone for a succession of cultures in the larger culture areas (Rothman 2003). Whether we are speaking of the Halaf, Early Hittites, Achaemenids, Greeks, Romans, Islam, or the Seljuks, different parts of these borderlands are influenced by or overrun by their neighbors. Of these cultures, the

Urartians, a culture of first millennium BC pastoralists and farmers with commonalities to the ETC (Rothman 2003), is really an indigenously developed culture, although the invasions of the Neo-Assyrians influenced some of Urartu's most easily detected archaeological features (fortresses, armor, writing systems, and sculpture).

To understand the spread of Transcaucasian wares and people, it is necessary to understand the relations of the larger regions, especially Mesopotamia, the foothills of eastern Turkey, and Transcaucasia. Whether or not an economic empire or world system was created in the steppes and foothills of Northern Mesopotamia, including southeastern Turkey during the fourth millennium (Algaze 1993; Rothman 1993; Rothman et al. 1998; Rothman, ed. 2001; Stein 1999a, 1999b), the level of interaction between south and north Mesopotamia increased dramatically from about 3600 to 3000 BC. In part, this contact must involve the exchange of raw materials, products, *and* technology. Metals, especially tool-grade bronze, certainly must have played a role (Kelly-Buccellati 1979, 1990; Burney 1996; Frangipane 1985). Arsenical bronze and copper smelting was well known in the Late Chalcolithic period of the fourth millennium BC (Esin 1982). Copper ores were available at Ergani not far from Malatya and Elazığ. However, some advanced techniques of bronze making seem to have developed early in the Transcaucasian region, and many copper sources are localized in the Black Sea, and Kura and Araxes River areas. Bronze artifacts of Transcaucasian type are found in considerable number in North Syrian sites such as Mozan (Kelly-Buccellati 1990). Possibly, grapes and their wine were involved in exchange as well. A late fourth millennium BC jar from Godin Tepe in western Iran attests the presence of wine at this time (Badler 1995). According to McGovern (1999), Transcaucasia was the homeland of grape-growing and winemaking. Burney (1996:7f.) suggests this and the possibility of textile making with Transcaucasian motifs. The exchange of these goods was certainly a pull factor for groups in the Transcaucasus and also a vehicle through which knowledge of the areas of eastern Turkey and western Iran was carried to the Transcaucasus.

The only theory offered to date for why people would leave the Kura and Araxes basins is the pressure of population because of climate change or overgrazing (Burney 1996; Sagona 1984:138–39). Despite considerable archaeological work in the former Soviet Union (Kohl 1992; Kushnareva 1997), drawing any firm conclusion on this question is not yet possible.

The theory of a single, large-scale migration at the beginning of the Kura Araks II period would imply a gradual movement out of the Transcaucasian homeland, much like the Seljuk migration, in search for new land, but this does not seem to fit the rest of the picture that I will examine below. Kohl (1992:125) does speak of a large-scale decrease in settlement during the second half of the third millennium, but this is already past most of the period we are discussing. Certainly, it does not explain why evidence of ETC presence in places like northwestern Iran and the rich pastureland around Lake Van (Çilingiroğlu 1987; Kozbe 1987, 1990) was not found for the early Kura-Araks II period. A strong push may not be the critical factor initially.

Rather, as I read the archaeological record, the critical factors were at first strong pulls. The strongest pull was economic in terms of new markets for goods. Although the eastern Turkish sites remained small and scattered, the Khabur sites of Tell Brak and Hamoukar were major urban enclaves in the fourth millennium BC New excavations at Brak indicate that it was very probably over 45 ha in size at 3500 BC (calibrated), and perhaps as large as 100 ha (Oates and Oates 1997). Hamoukar was probably similar in size. Frangipane (1997a) proposes that the size of these sites resulted from the greater agricultural potential of the lower Khabur. Certainly, that size would rival any contemporaneous Mesopotamian city. Both were clearly urban centers with large markets for trade. Southern migrants at sites like Habuba Kabira—migrants and not primarily traders in my opinion—also served as part of a conduit for goods to and from southern Mesopotamia. Within the highland zone, sites like Arslantepe were nodes for production and exchange, although relatively small and controlling a very small territory (Frangipane 1997a). Burney (1993) aptly calls Arslantepe a gateway to the highlands.

There were few barriers to movement across this large area of open land from the Transcaucasus over the northern massif of the Taurus Mountains to the Euphrates at Arslantepe. Aside from the Khabur triangle, the area where Transcaucasian pottery appears was fairly lightly populated. No major centers with sufficient power to control larger areas existed. The opposition of organized polities was not a concern for migrants. The probable domestication of the horse and donkey by this time makes such long distance movements with cargo practicable (Bokonyi 1987). Nomadic pastoral groups have historically ranged far afield and have often played the role of traders,

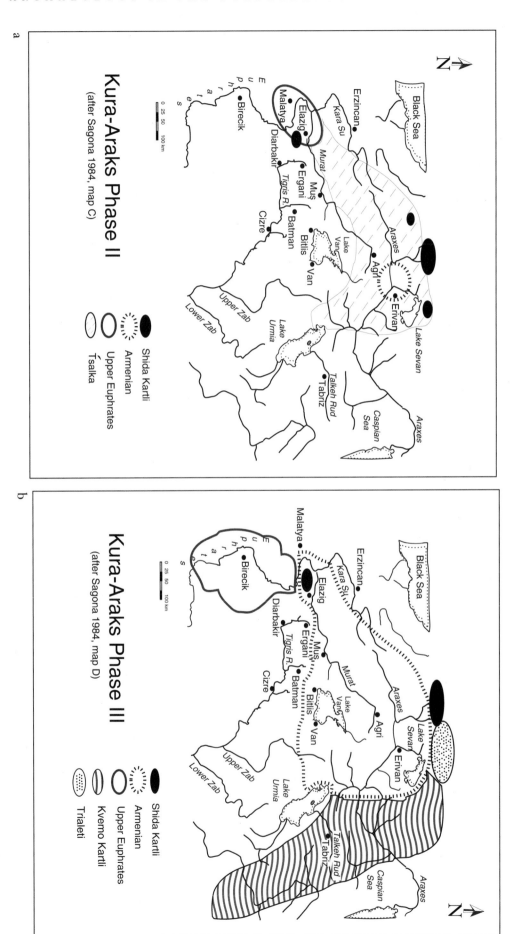

Figure 4.2 Distribution of Kura-Araxes Culture in the third millennium BC. *Map by Mitchell S. Rothman.*

whether the products they transported were uniquely from their homeland or picked up along the way (Ferdinand 1962).

Movement out of Transcaucasia into Anatolia and perhaps into Mesopotamia may well have begun earlier than formerly thought. Findings from Sos Höyük (Sagona 2000) indicate that the beginnings of contact and perhaps small-scale back-and-forth migration began already in the Kura-Araks I or Late Chalcolithic period at Sos. A few pots of a clearly ETC type were present at Sos in period Va. Sos is already fairly deep into eastern Turkish territory (see figure 4.1).

In a real sense, however, Malatya is key to understanding the opening of the first stream of traders or ETC migrants. As a gateway, it was serving as a center of communication and cultural influence from two directions. The very first influx of what would be the Transcaucasians is seen in Arslantepe VIA near the end of the fourth millennium. Figure 4.2a illustrates two key patterns for what must have been the first significant contact between the Euphrates Basin and the basins of the Kura and Araxes Rivers. Artifacts with Transcausian elements represent the first pattern. There are two distinct sources for these elements: the one Sagona (1984) identifies as coming from the Shida Kartli ETC grouping and the other from the Tsalka ETC variant. From figure 4.2a it appears that Transcaucasians from the Shida Kartli area leapfrogged into the Euphrates Basin, a pattern more likely to involve trade or back and forth movement, not long term migration. This second Tsalka variant dominates the intervening area between the Transcaucasus and Euphrates Basin. Already near the beginning of significant contact there are ripples from different areas. The second important aspect of this early contact is its characteristic stream, not wave, pattern. Contact with the western and also the southeastern areas was directed along a route north of the more northerly Taurus massif or down the Araxes River valleys toward Lake Urmia in modern Iran.

The area of Arslantepe in modern Malatya therefore seems the destination for this earlier contact. Evidence of this movement in the form of ETC pottery and metal technology is apparent in Arslantepe VIA (Frangipane and Palmieri 1983). The subsequent Arslantepe VIB1 finds at Arslantepe tell a story of increasing movement into a cultural vacuum (Palmieri 1985). The very end of the Uruk period saw increasing migration from the southern alluvium all along the Euphrates Basin. Although determinedly local in culture, the influence of Mesopotamian administrative techniques and cultural

markers of status is very evident (Frangipane 1997a; Frangipane and Palmieri 1983). The fourth millennium BC ends with the final monumental architecture of the Uruk Age at Arslantepe VIA, whose pottery was typified by Early Reserved slip wares and a few red-black sherds. This very long period of growth and elaboration of north–south Mesopotamian interaction changes after VIA. I view it less as a collapse than as a re-orientation.[3] Over top of the massive palace of VIA, the third millennium BC began with a series of wattle and daub houses, that is, with a squatter village of earliest VIB. This house type is typically ETC and the pottery associated with them was almost exclusively ETC red-black ware.

It is into the terracing fill over VIA at the very beginning of the VIB1 period that the recently excavated chiefly tomb was excavated (Frangipane 1997b). This tomb of clearly Kura Araks II date shows cultural links to Transcaucasia and to Arslantepe's Mesopotamian-influenced period VIA (figure 4.3). A stone slab sealed the tomb. Four bodies in unnatural positions—that is, they were probably sacrificed—were found on the top

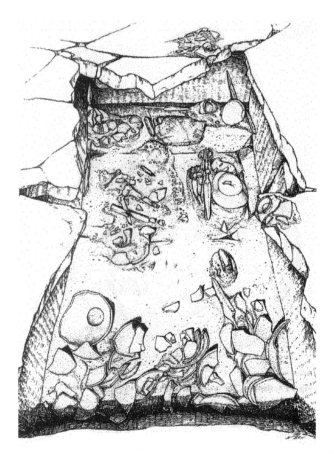

Figure 4.3 Arslantepe Early Bronze 1 tomb. *After Frangipane 1997b, fig. 4.*

of the tomb. At what would be the foot of the tomb were two individuals buried with no artifacts. On top of the slab were two individuals, facing each other, with diadems and spiral hair ring pins made of an unusual silver copper alloy. Copper pins were found at their shoulders. In the tomb one individual was buried in a flexed position on its side with a large number of objects. The pottery was of two varieties. Vessels buried near the head were the Transcaucasian red-black hand-made vessels. Those near the feet were Arslantepe VIA, north Mesopotamian reserve slip jars. At the individual's back were a large number of metal objects, mostly swords, spears, and daggers. He/she wore a diadem similar to the skeletons on the slab, only larger and more elaborately decorated, and spiral pins. Two unusual copper vessels were also found, made of arsenical copper (9% arsenic plus iron and antimony). Stylistically, most of the metal artifacts have are technologically similar to VIA material. Frangipane notes,

> the presence of northeastern Anatolian-type [ETC] ware together with Mesopotamian-type pottery, and the typological and technical similarities between the metallurgy found in the tomb and period VIA metallurgy may be evidence of close interaction by the end of the fourth millennium between people living in the Euphrates Valley and groups from the regions south of the Caucasus. [1997b:297]

The presence in a tomb of an individual clearly mixing symbols of Transcaucasian and Arslantepe's Mesopotamian cultural connection represents a new cultural form. Frangipane assumes that the individual is a Transcaucasian. With the nearby wattle and daub houses, that is a tempting conclusion. However, it may not indicate foreign persons as much as it represents a new format for leadership on the part of the residents recombining new cultural elements and new ways of showing status and authority.

After this period of wattle-and-daub houses and the tomb, a small, well-laid out village of Arslantepe VIB2 date, parallel to early Ninevite V in the Jazira steppes and the beginning of the Early Dynastic period in the southern alluvium, was established. Late Reserved Slip ware and some red-black pottery typify this occupation. Interestingly, the Late Reserved Slip ware period was concentrated north of Ninevite V sites and south of the southern Taurus massif with its large concentrations of ETC ware. According to Palmieri, Late Reserved Slip period sites tend to cluster around copper mining source area (Palmieri 1985:209).

So, we have Transcaucasian pottery originating in the basins of the Kura and Araxes Rivers during Kura-Araks I, parallel in time to the Late Chalcolithic/Uruk period. It appears very early at Arslantepe, but as far as I can determine it was only infrequently found at that early date in the intervening areas between Erzurum and Malatya, and certainly not in the Lake Van area or far into western Iran. What follows in the later Kura Araxes II and III periods is a new pattern.

As figure 4.2b shows, the pattern of distribution of Transcaucasian wares changed dramatically in the Kura Araks III period. Obviously, the area covered by ETC wares was much greater. Also, the source of the styles in the newly included ETC range differed. The Armenian types, which were limited to the Armenian Plateau in Kura-Araks early period II (IIA) are now found over a very wide area. Sagona categorizes western Iranian ETC types in the Kura-Araks III period as Kvemo Kartli.

My own survey in the Muş Province may explain some of the processes involved (Rothman 1992, 1994a). In this area between the two Taurus massifs along the Murat River, which flows into the Euphrates, the earliest discovered occupation is of sixth millennium BC Halaf date (see figure 4.4). In the Late Chalcolithic period the center of the plain was sparsely occupied. The sites with Transcaucasian pottery, all of Kura-Araxes II date, represent new patterns of occupation and land use. For the first time, sites along the higher hills, adjacent to the Murat's natural road up toward northeastern Turkey and the Transcaucasus were occupied. Erentepe/Liz in Bulanık is one such site. That the position of Erentepe is on the modern route to the great pasturelands near Lake Van hardly seems coincidental. The Transcaucasian pottery from Liz is among the earliest in date from Muş. It falls into what Summers (1982) classifies as Kura-Araks IIA with typical rail rims, incised designs and grit tempering. During the long third millennium BC occupation at Erentepe, typical Transcaucasian types continue to evolve. In short what the settlement pattern of Muş indicates is that there was an influx of population in the Early Bronze Age and that it seems to be coming from the direction of the northeast, and occupying the hills, not yet the plain.

Pottery from the plain is best dated to Kura Araks IIB and III, based on the "groove and circular groove" and "groove and dimple" incised designs (Summers 1982:116). As study of this material by Kozbe (Rothman and Kozbe 1997) indicates, however, it is technologically different from other Transcaucasian pottery in eastern Turkey and is similar to the pastes

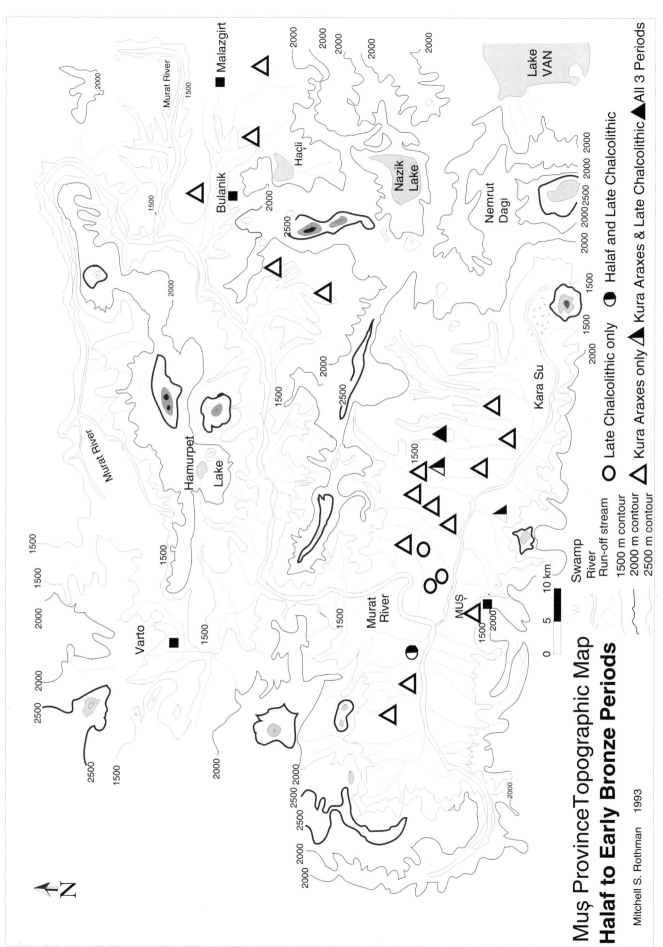

Figure 4.4 Muş Province topographic map, Halaf to Early Bronze periods. *Map by Mitchell S. Rothman.*

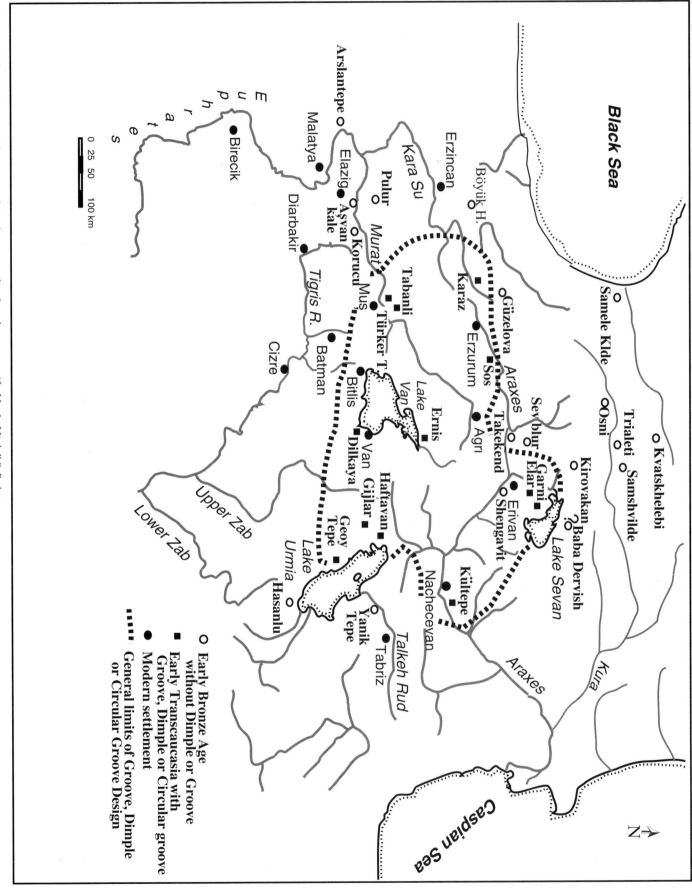

Figure 4.5 Kura-Araks sites with groove and circular groove, dimple and groove motifs. *Map by Mitchell S. Rothman.*

of earlier and later Muş ceramics (Rothman 1994a). Muş is certainly an example of the admixture of earlier local traditions and Transcaucasian forms and techniques, as Sagona notes,

> it has become increasingly apparent that cultural developments in the Chalcolithic and Early Bronze Age owe much to both local and foreign influences. [1994:15]

Its pottery is certainly different from, for example, Bayburt material found on Sagona's survey and excavation (Sagona 1992; Sagona et al. 1992). In the Altınova and Malatya, local pottery styles exist alongside ETC wares in the village period of Kura Araks II and III. What is perhaps most interesting about the pottery from the Muş plain is that its closest connections are to the area from Ernis, north of Lake Van, east to Haftavan Tepe, on the western side of Lake Urmia. This is not the great agricultural zone, but a heartland of pastures.

Although the stream of migrants continued along the route from the Transcaucasus toward Malatya, what was new in the Kura-Araks IIB and III periods was the opening of new streams into some of the best pastureland relatively close by the Transcaucasus. There were more ripples in new streams.

Was It a Migration?
One of the first indicators I proposed above for migrations of significant size was an unexpectedly dramatic demographic shift. Conti and Persiani (1993:408) suggest that the population of the Malatya area was only about 20,000 people in the Early Bronze Age. The distribution map of Transcaucasian sites (figure 4.1) seems to support the contention of a concentration of new population in the Keban and Malatya. Whallon (1979) demonstrates a marked increase in the number of sites in Early Bronze Altınova Plain. Visible settlement is less well evidenced to the east, although much of the area north of the northern Taurus massif has not been surveyed (but see Özfirat).

In Muş as well, the number of sites jumped dramatically in the Kura-Araks IIB and III periods (figure 4.4). In terms of artifactual remains, not only were new styles introduced into the area but they existed next to older, native styles. House forms and tool kits that fit the pastoral and small farming patterns in the Transcaucasus appeared as well. New technologies in metallurgy were introduced from the Transcaucasus; probably raw materials from that region were brought

with traders and migrants in increasing numbers. It is possible, though not yet verifiable, that the intrusion of ETC materials, technologies and peoples affected the re-orientation of the post-Uruk economic and political systems in the foothills of southeastern Turkey.

Given the weight of the evidence, a series of migrations is the most likely interpretation. Each period's migrations were probably of a different scale and resulted from a different set of pushes and pulls. The Kura-Araks III migrations seems most likely a search for new lands for pasture, perhaps because of climate change, perhaps because of new adaptations favoring a different mix of food resources. Bahşaliyev (1997:99) suggests that the residents of the Nakhichevan area in Transcaucasia changed from animal resources reliant on cattle in the Kura-Araks I and IIA periods to sheep and goat in Kura-Araks IIB and III. The Kura-Araks period I and IIA migrations seem to be of a smaller scale and appear to have been impelled more by economic opportunity than from the pressure of population on resources.

What Was the Long-Term Effect?
The migrations of Transcaucasians over a number of centuries certainly affected the societies and cultures of what Kelly-Buccellati (1979) calls the Outer Fertile Crescent. How pervasive was their influence over the longer term? In the later Early Bronze Age, when urbanization and a new economic and political order is evident at sites like Korucutepe, Titriş, and Norşuntepe, did these Transcausian groups continue to move in and out of the region and leave a long-term mark? The answer may best be seen in the area of probably the largest population movement, the area around Lake Van to the western edge of Lake Urmia and then to Lake Sevan (figure 4.5). Whereas outside of this area, marked by the so-called groove and circular groove and dimple and groove design (Rothman 2003; Rothman and Kozbe 1997), saw a rapid period of change and development, this area remained pretty much as it was. While orange wares appeared south of Lake Urmia, and the painted wares of Malatya and Elazığ appeared in more urban societies, this core area of the Kura-Araks IIB and III migration and admixture remained largely unchanged well into the second millennium. It is interesting to note that the heartland of the first millennium BC Urartian heartland was almost identical to the extent of the groove and circular groove and dimple and groove design (see Rothman 2003a).

CONCLUSION

Using a method that looks first at the context for migration, both in the natural and human realms, I believe I have been able to show that it is possible to get beyond the pots equals people approach of an earlier time. By looking first at the structural reasons for migrations and by taking an adaptation-oriented approach, I think archaeologists have begun to make some sense of what is a wonderfully complex past. Until we have much more publication of excavated sites, more excavations of sites with Transcaucasian artifactual remains, new research on ancient climates and ancient subsistence, we still are very far from a verifiable answer. That explanation will require finer chronological analysis and a global analytical point of view, which takes in all of the adjacent ancient culture areas. We have come to the bridge of explanation. We are not quite ready to cross it all the way.

NOTES

1. This pottery is red on the interior and black on the exterior.
2. Seljuk was the name of the leader of a number of sections of the tribal group known as the Oghuz. Rice (1961:26) sees Seljuk as part of the Kabak tribe of the princely house of Afrasiab.
3. The only abandonment in northern Mesopotamia was in the Middle Euphrates—these are the migrant sites of Habuba Kabira and Jebel Aruda and just over the Turkish border with Syria. Samsat, Tell-al Hawa, Brak, Nineveh, and other sites continue to grow into the Early Bronze 1. Even Arslantepe, after a very short period of decline in VIB1, is reestablished in VIB2. Frangipane reports that a large EB1 wall has begun to emerge at Arslantepe surrounding the VIB2 town (personal communication).

CHAPTER 5

Social and Economic Shifts in the South Caucasian Middle Bronze Age

MARINA PUTURIDZE

The Caucasian corridor, a cultural crossroad since ancient times, has played an important historical role as a bridge joining the Russian steppe and the Near East. It is therefore unsurprising that in the later eras of the region's prehistory, this small land mass hosted several distinct cultural zones (figure 5.1). From the beginning of the second millennium BC to the high Middle Bronze Age (an era roughly contemporary with the Old Assyrians, Mycenaeans, Old Hittites, and Hurrians in the Near East and Aegean), the South Caucasus was populated by the bearers of several distinct archaeological cultures (figures 5.4–5.5), including the Sevan-Uzerlik, Karmir-Berd (formerly called Tazakend), and Kizil-Vank cultures (Japaridze 1994: 75-92; Kushnareva 1985; Kushnareva 1993:106–132; Kushnareva 1994a, b, c). Yet the most famous and elaborate among the Middle Bronze Age archaeological cultures of southern Caucasia is the so-called "Trialeti Culture of the brilliant kurgans" (Japaridze 1969:99), which played a perceptible role in the ancient history of the Caucasus and Asia Minor. As a result, the essential cultural and socioeconomic shifts of the Middle Bronze Age are most evident in its archaeological remains.

The fluorescence of the Trialeti culture marks not only the second (II), developed, stage of the South Caucasian Middle Bronze Age but also of major changes in the societies of that region. An intensification of social stratification is quite evident in the more than three hundred burial sites of the Trialeti Culture, as indicated most significantly by the dimensions of the giant kurgans. These burial tumuli can be as large as 5 m in height and in one (Trialeti kurgan 36) covers a colossal "sepulchral hall" 175 m² in area. Under these giant kurgans, some sepulchral chambers were sunk to a depth of 8 m below the surface of the soil, with a diameter as large as 5 m (for example, Trialeti kurgan 10). Other burial chambers (such as Trialeti kurgan 17) reached up to 14 m in length, 8.5 m in width, and 6 m in depth (Kuftin 1941: 79, Fig. 5.8). These immense mortuary structures provide evidence for an unprecedented concentration of power and wealth in the hands of a new ruling elite and signal important

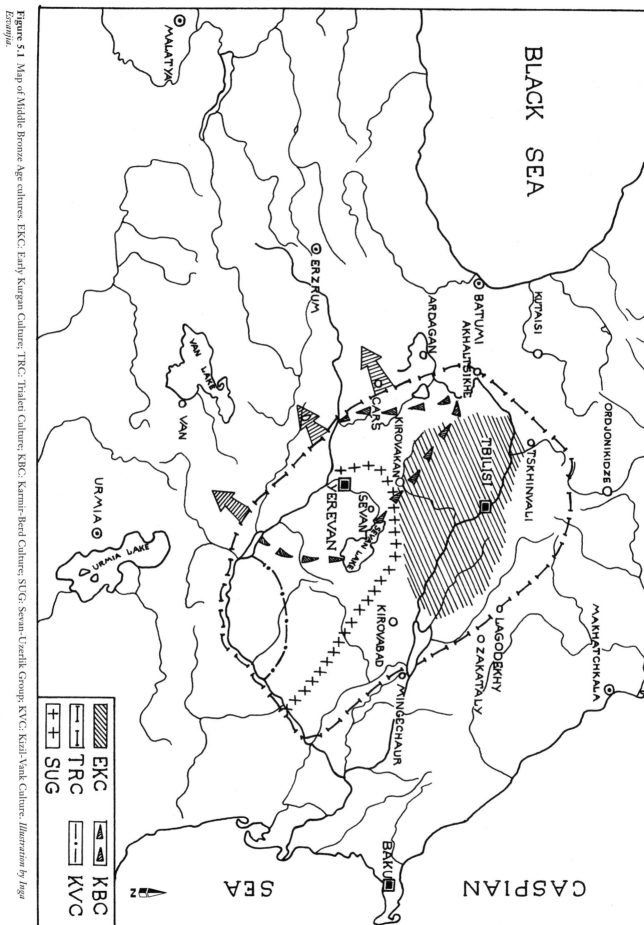

Figure 5.1 Map of Middle Bronze Age cultures. EKC: Early Kurgan Culture; TRC: Trialeti Culture; KBC: Karmir-Berd Culture; SUG: Sevan-Uzerlik Group; KVC: Kizil-Vank Culture. *Illustration by Inga Evanjia.*

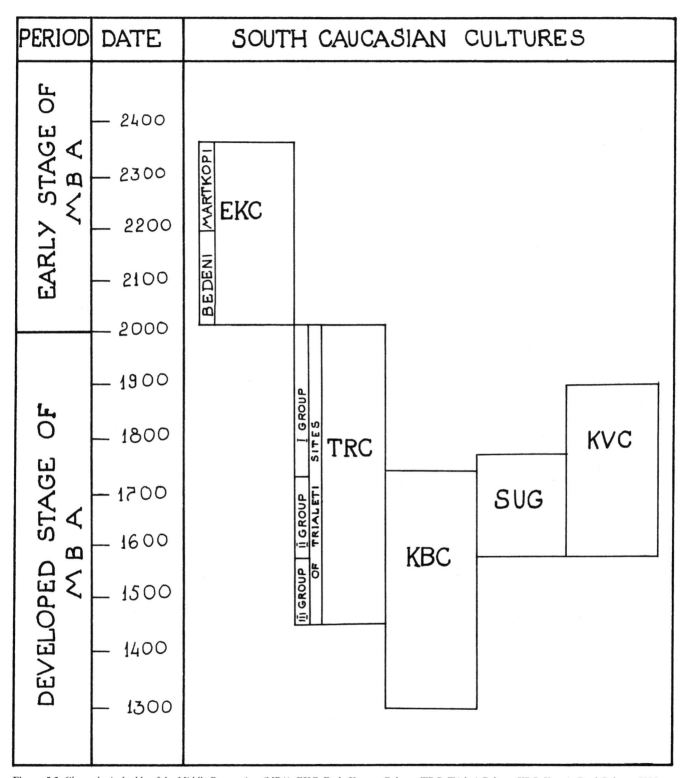

Figure 5.2 Chronological table of the Middle Bronze Age (MBA). EKC: Early Kurgan Culture; TRC: Trialeti Culture; KBC: Karmir-Berd Culture; SUG: Sevan-Uzerlik Group; KVC: Kizil-Vank Culture. *Illustration by Inga Esvanjia.*

ideological and social changes in Middle Bronze Age societies. Unfortunately, changes in the political structure in the South Caucasian region cannot be determined with the same degree of certainty that is possible for neighboring polities in the Near East, where texts provide more detailed information about rulers and administration. However, we should not exclude the possibility that the visible changes that take place under the auspices of the Trialeti archaeological culture indicate the start of a regional process of early state formation.

Questions concerning the genesis of the Trialeti culture and its links to both its contemporary neighbors and historical predecessors have provided critical foci of archaeological research since the discovery of the earliest sites. As a result, diverse and often controversial opinions have accumulated in the literature. Investigations of the connections between the Kura-Araxes and Trialeti cultures have a long history, but nevertheless remain a topic of considerable debate. Kuftin (1941), Piotrovskii (1949: 46), and several other scholars (see Japaridze 1969:270) have argued in favor of formal genetic ties between these two cultures, suggesting that Trialeti must be understood as an indigenous phenomenon that grew primarily out of local roots. At the time when this point of view predominated, only a very small number of Early Kurgans Culture complexes from the earliest stage of the Middle Bronze Age were known. Following the discovery of a large number of Early Kurgans Culture sites (and the clear definition of related material culture repertoires), it became quite evident that the Early Kurgans Culture arose after the collapse of the Kura-Araxes Culture and before the rise of the Trialeti Culture (figure 5.2). Thus, the Kura-Araxes and Trialeti cultural horizons are both chronologically and culturally distanced from one another. According to Melikishvili (1965b: 95), materials from the "brilliant kurgans of Trialeti" bear obvious traces of the strong influence and possibly the expansion of Hurrian tribes. Melikishvili (1999) had long argued that Kura-Araxes and Trialeti cultures were not genetically related. Instead, the formation of the latter, he argued, was in large measure determined by the invasion of a new ethnic group from the Near East at the very beginning of the second millennium BC.

Materials from the Trialeti region provide a great deal of information about the innovations and changes in social life during the Middle Bronze Age (figures. 5.6, 5.7, 5.10). Specific features include the appearance of precious gold and silver vessels and other examples of high artistic craft (indices of unexpectedly advanced goldsmithing), new forms of metallurgical products, new forms of burial construction, four-wheeled wagons, a shift in the economy toward stock breeding, the occupation of foothills and mountainous parts of the landscape and the comparative depopulation of the lowland areas of South and Central Caucasus, and an intensification of social stratification. Unfortunately, settlements dating to this period have not been excavated. This bias in the archaeological record thus precludes us from developing a more exhaustive inventory of the characteristics and innovations of the Trialeti Culture. With this caveat, the following discussion will examine the most essential changes that took place during the Middle Bronze Age and provide interpretations of their causes.

ON THE TRANSITION FROM THE EARLY TO MIDDLE BRONZE AGE

A detailed analysis of the available archaeological data indicates that the changes described above initially appeared during the early period of the Middle Bronze Age rather than during the time of the Trialeti Culture. Features characteristic of both the Early Kurgans Culture and the Trialeti Culture include closely analogous burial rites centered on kurgan burials, shared metallurgical techniques (from both stylistic and metallographic points of view), a similar paucity of settlement sites (as compared with their Kura-Araxes predecessors), economic foundations rooted in stock breeding, and close cultural and economic relations with the Near East. This Near Eastern influence can be seen most notably in the metallurgy, goldsmithery, and elements of burial rites of southern Caucasia.

The chronology of the Early Kurgans Culture (figure 5.2) is most clearly defined based on stratified layers of the final phase of Kura-Araxes Culture at Berikldeebi, Tsikhiagora (Makharadze 1994:44-66), and two related unpublished sites, where investigations have documented the coexistence of Kuro-Araxes and Bedeni wares (see Kushnareva 1997: 90-92 for further discussion). Thus, the available archaeological data suggest that during a very short period the Kura-Araxes and Early Kurgans cultures coexisted. Afterward, the latter, which inaugurates the Middle Bronze Age, continued to develop independently (Martkopi and Bedeni phases) until the appearance of the Trialeti Culture around 2000 BC. The group of Bedeni kurgans

(continued on page 120)

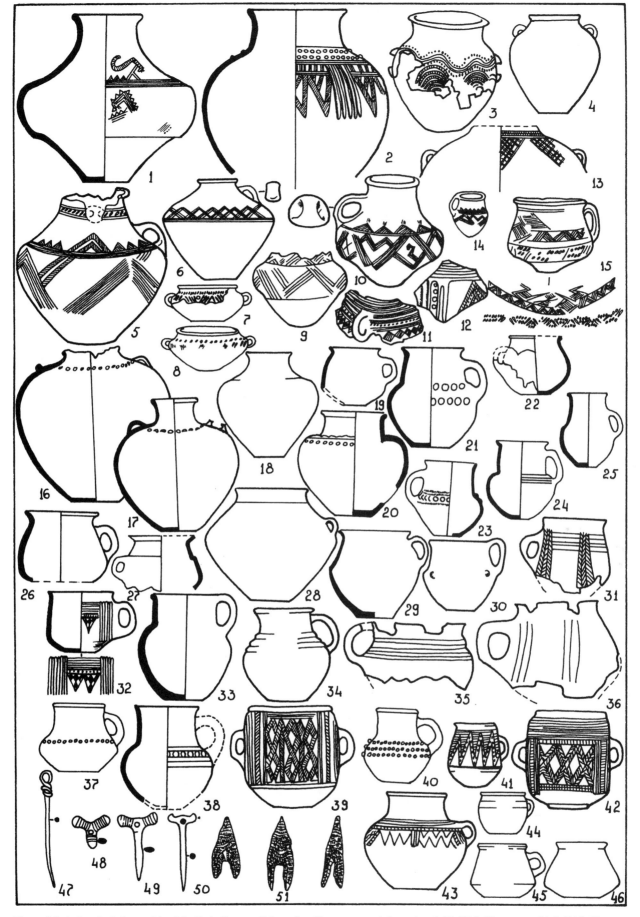

Figure 5.3 Archaeological materials of the Early Kurgans Culture. Specific provenance information: 1, 15, Trialeti barrow no. 24; 2, Trialeti barrow no. 46; 3, 5, 14, Trialeti barrow no. 19; 4, 7–8, Trialeti barrow no. 25; 6, Trialeti barrow no. 12; 9, Trialeti barrow no. 4; 10, Trialeti barrow no. 13; 11–12, Trialeti barrow no. 11; 13, Trialeti barrow no. 27; 20, 23–24, 32, 38, the great barrow no. 5 of Bedeni; 16–17, 19, 21, 26, black-burnished pottery from Alazani barrows; 18, 28, barrows from Kheltubani; 22, 27, 31, 35–36, barrow no. 2 from Zilicha (lower burial); 25, 29–30, 33, 47–50, barrows from Korinto; 34, 37, 40, 43–46, barrow from Bakurtsiche; 39, 41–42, Martkopi barrow no. 5; 51, barrow from Tsnori. *Illustration by Inga Esvanjia.*

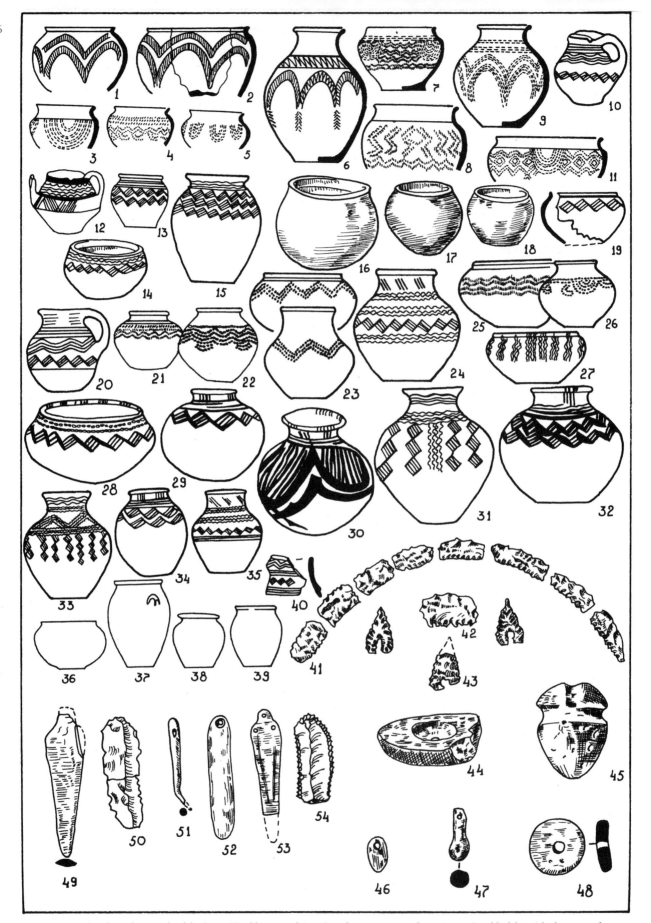

Figure 5.4 Archaeological materials of the Sevan-Uzerlik group of sites. Specific provenance information: 1–2, 6, black burnished pottery of stratum I of Uzerlik-Tepe; 3–5, 7–8, 11, black burnished pottery of stratums II-III of Uzerlik-Tepe; 10, 12–18, Lchashen barrow no. 6; 19, Sjuni-Berd; 20, Karchakhpjur; 21–22, 25–26, Sevan-GES; 23, Nor-Beyazit; 24, 35, Kamo; 27, Achlatyan; 28–30, 32, Garni; 31, 33, burials from Zolakar; 34, Astapat; 36–39, pottery of stratums II-III of Uzerlik-Tepe settlement; 40, painted pottery of stratum III of Uzerlik-Tepe; 41–48, 50, 52, 54, characteristic stone artifacts from Uzerlik-Tepe settlement; 49, 51, 53, characteristic bronze artifacts from Uzerlik-Tepe settlement. *Illustration by Inga Esvanjia.*

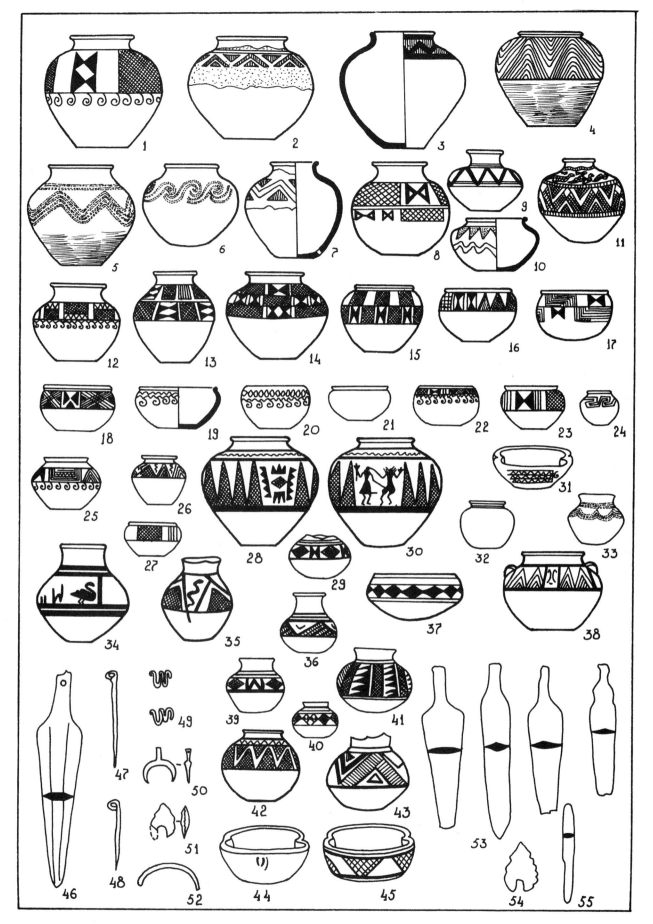

Figure 5.5 Archaeological materials of the Kamir-Berd and Kizil-Vank Cultures: 1–27, 31–33, 46–52, Karmir-Berd Culture; 28–30, 34–45, 53–55, Kizil-Vank Culture. Specific provenance information: 1, Karmir-Berd cemetery, barrow no. 2; 2, 6–8, 17, 50–52, Verin-Naver cemetery, barrow no. 12; 3, Keti cemetery, burial no. 18; 4–5, 14, 23, Karmir-Berd cemetery (collection of P. Charkovsky, 1896 excavations); 9, 25–26, Karmir-Berd cemetery (excavations of M. Zacharyants); 10, Arich cemetery, burial no. 9; 11, Elar cemetery, burial no. 32; 12, Arich cemetery, burial no. 14; 15, Elar; 16, Karmir-Berd cemetery, barrow no. 13 (excavations of P. Charkovsky); 18, Arich cemetery, burial no. 31; 19, Arich cemetery, burial no. 12; 20, Karmir-Berd cemetery, barrow no. 2; 21, 27, 32–33, 46–49, Verin-Naver cemetery, barrow no. 9; 22, Karmir-Berd cemetery, barrow no. 1; 24, Arich cemetery, burial no. 85; 31, Nor-Bayazet (Kamo); 28–30, 34, 45, 53–55, artifacts characteristic of the Kizil-Vank culture. *Illustration by Inga Esvanjia.*

118

Figure 5.6 Trialeti Culture ceramics from barrows at Trialeti. Specific provenance information: 1, barrow no. 1; 2, 8, 15, barrow no. 15; 3, 6–7, 9, 12, 14, barrow no. 17; 4, barrow no. 6; 5, 24, barrow no. 7; 10, barrow no. 5; 11, barrow no. 8; 13, barrow no. 28; 16, 20–21, barrow no. 45; 17, 22–23, barrow no. 36; 18, barrow no. 23; 19, barrow no. 34. *Illustration by Inga Esvanjia.*

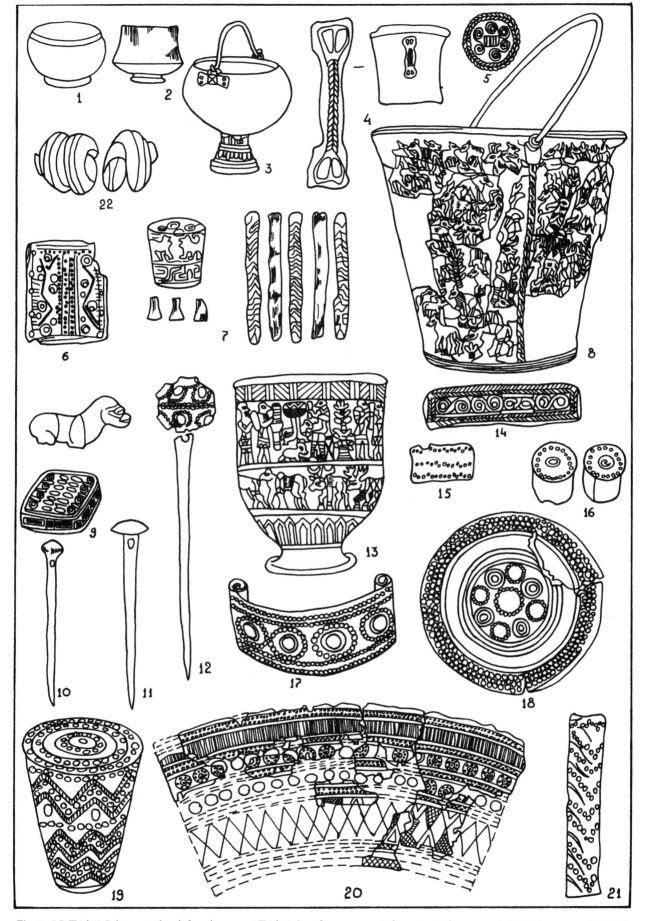

Figure 5.7 Trialeti Culture metalwork from barrows at Trialeti. Specific provenance information: 1, barrow no. 7; 2–3, 7, barrow no. 15; 4, 20, barrow no. 16; 5, 16, barrow no. 45; 6, 15, 22, barrow no. 8; 8, 10, 12, 18, barrow no. 17; 9, 11, 13, 17, barrow no. 5; 14, barrow no. 9; 19, 21, barrow no. 6. *Illustration by Inga Esvanjia.*

(continued from page 114)

(figure 5.8a) is considered by most scholars to be the developed, later, phase of the Early Kurgans Culture rather than a distinct culture in itself. The first appearance of Bedeni materials in Kura-Araxes sites marks the advent of radical changes in the life of South Caucasian populations, after which the Kura-Araxes Culture declined and disappeared. During the Bedeni phase, the Early Kurgans Culture reached the zenith of its development and was ultimately succeeded by the "Trialeti Culture of the brilliant kurgans."

The fluorescence of the Trialeti Culture was predetermined by several factors, among which we must include increasingly brisk contacts with the Near East (Puturidze 1991:216–217; Rubinson, chapter 6). In our judgment, the extant data indicate the following observations on the relationship between the Early Kurgans and Trialeti cultures. First, the Trialeti Culture does not, in essence, differ from the culture of early Middle Bronze Age (Early Kurgans Culture). By adopting the innovations listed above, the Trialeti Culture faithfully imitated the model of Early Kurgans society (Puturidze 1991: 208–220). As social systems, Martkopi-Bedeni (Early Kurgans Culture) and the Trialeti Culture are of the same essential orientation. While the latter represents a more developed cultural model, it is very similar to the culture of the early Middle Bronze Age in its content.

At the same time, the manifest differences between the ceramic assemblages of the Early Kurgans Culture and the Trialeti Culture (including the appearance of painted pottery in the latter) as well as differing elements in both jewelry and some new types of metal weapons and vessels do not permit us to assume complete uniformity between them. Nevertheless, we assume that the Trialeti stage of the Middle Bronze Age, in every one of the above-mentioned characteristics, offers a continuous stage in Middle Bronze Age development rather than a fundamental alteration of the inherited cultural model. For example, there are no essential changes in socioeconomic system; social stratification was only intensified and the economic orientation toward cattle breeding continued. Continuity is also observable in some aspects of the material culture assemblages of the two cultural eras; the main types of bronze and stone weapons and some categories of jewelry are identical. We conclude then that these historical processes, underway during the Early Kurgans and Trialeti periods of the Middle Bronze Age, represent a complete replacement of the Early Bronze Age (Kura-Araxes) cultural model, a so-called

"cultural changeover" (Puturidze 1991:217), marked by radical shifts in the socioeconomic systems of the southern Caucasus.

At the same time, we cannot fail to give some consideration to the fact that investigators have long been well aware of the Trialeti developments and the differences between the Kura-Araxes and its Middle Bronze successors. Much more complex is the relationship between the Early Kurgans and Trialeti cultures. Despite the numerous similarities, an essential visual distinction between the ceramics of the two is readily apparent. These differences, without a doubt, provide a good argument not only for distinctions between ceramic types in themselves but also for the absence of genetic interrelation between Early Kurgans and Trialeti peoples, despite the cogent similarities in their economic bases, cultural orientation, and historical line of development. It should be emphasized that the growing influence of the ancient Near East and the high level of development in all spheres of the Trialeti Culture in large measure determined the magnitude of the divergence from the earlier Martkopi-Bedeni culture. Aside from the ceramic evidence, important differences can also be observed in goldsmithing and bronze metallurgy. Early Kurgans Culture assemblages include neither the precious metal vessels, jewelry (Kuftin 1941: Plates XCI, XCIII, XCVII, CI, CII), nor the bronze artifacts (cauldron, rapier) characteristic of the developed (II) period of the Middle Bronze Age—the Trialeti Culture. Yet, in our view, these stylistic differences in pottery and other elements of the Middle Bronze assemblages cannot outweigh the essential sociocultural similarity that indicates the integration of the two cultures within a single socioeconomic model.

Explanation of the differences and traditional features of the Early Kurgans and the Trialeti Cultures is a complex archaeological problem. An account of their relationship cannot be based solely on typological and comparative analyses of examples of material production. Differences between objects of the same type of each individual culture can be assayed, yet the nature and causes of their divergence remain unclear. A useful point of departure for an evaluation of archaeological cultures is a comparative account of their economic foundations since it is this sociological element that strongly determines the historical direction of any given course of cultural development. When a definite stage of cultural development is characterized by an imbalance of traditions and innovations (such as that presented by the end of the Early Bronze Age and the

a

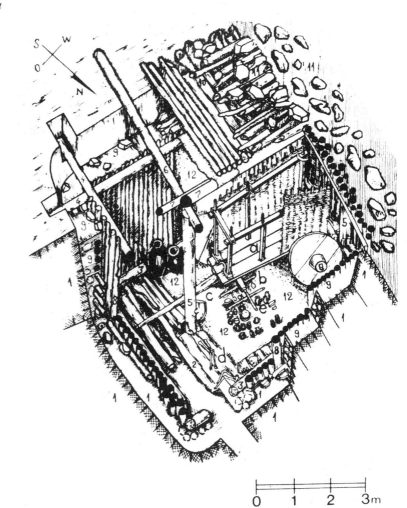

Figure 5.8 *a*, Burial no. 5 at Bedeni, reconstruction drawing of the burial chamber. *After O. Lordkipanidze (1989:110, Fig. 50); b*, Stone walls of barrow no. 3 at Zurtaketi. *After O. Japaridze (1969:29, Plate IXa).*

b

beginning of the Middle Bronze Age) and innovations outweigh traditional elements, pressures toward cultural transformation logically arise. Therefore, in our opinion, the pivotal cultural transformations of the Middle Bronze Age occurred not at the start of the Trialeti Culture but earlier, at the beginning of the Early Kurgans Culture. It was in the collapse of the Kura-Araxes Culture that critical elements of this new archaeological complex first appeared, including a new burial type (the kurgan) and new mode of transportation (the wagon), which radically altered settlement patterns (the occupation of the foothills and mountains instead of the lowland areas).

Unfortunately, the socioeconomic side of the Trialeti Culture has not been studied in great detail. For this reason, we cannot yet provide answers to all of the questions being posed. Typically, such an analysis would include a comparison of different but contemporary settlements, as well as their cemeteries within a circumscribed region. In our case, all discussion and analysis of the Middle Bronze Age Trialeti society can be based only on mortuary sites. Study of the socioeconomic aspects of the Trialeti Culture is considerably hindered by the lack of excavated settlements. Most concretely, the lack of available archaeological materials related to production and economic relations precludes a discussion of economy from any perspective except that of consumption as viewed from cemetery contexts.

The limitations of the extant data result in serious interpretive problems. Despite the sixty years of investigation that have passed since the discovery of the Trialeti Culture (Kuftin, 1941: 78–105), we remain uncertain about the Middle Bronze Age economy beyond the domain of mortuary consumption. Until stratified settlements are excavated, broader visions of the Trialeti economy will and indeed should be debated. In this spirit, even though many critical aspects at present remain unclear, we must try to reconstruct the economy beyond the confines of the grave site. In spite of the careful surveys carried out in Tsalka-Trialeti region, where rich burial mounds are located, contemporary settlements have not been found. Only in the most eastern zone of this culture have several thin, unsubstantial Middle Bronze Age layers been revealed by a series of sondages excavated at a handful of archaeological sites. Surviving painted pottery fragments from these Middle Bronze Age layers belong to the Trialeti tradition (Mansfeld 1996: 365–380, Plates 25, 26). Although it seems safe at the moment to assume that multilayer tell sites were largely deserted during

the Trialeti era (Kikvidze 1976; Japaridze 1969: 10–11), we should keep in mind the existence of these thin Middle Bronze Age strata known exclusively from eastern Georgia. This absence of more robust forms of settlement suggests quite strongly that from the abandonment of (most) Early Bronze Age settlements in lowland areas (Japaridze 1969) until the start of the Late Bronze Age, populations made significant movements toward high mountain zones. The appearance of a great number of animal bones in burial contexts and the nearly total absence of tools from Trialeti contexts can serve as an indication of an attendant change in the region's economy toward stock breeding centered in highland pastures.

VARIABILITY IN TRIALETI ECONOMIES

Trialeti populations most typically have been described as practicing animal husbandry without an associated domain of agricultural production. The primary data indicating an intensification of the role of cattle breeding in the Middle Bronze Age southern Caucasus comes from burial sites, where significant numbers of animal bones are regularly unearthed as elements of grave assemblages. However, given recent advances in our understanding of the character of stock breeding, it seems more plausible that the Trialetians managed a variable economy, where the leading role of cattle breeding was combined and coordinated with agricultural activities (Kikvidze 1976). The above-mentioned layers of settlement in eastern Georgia provide some evidence for the continuity of life in some lowland areas where fertile soil certainly opens the potential for a complementary agricultural economy. We suggest that the depopulation of the lowland areas was only in specific areas and did not cover the entire ecological zone. For example, the Ararat valley, the most eastern part of Georgia, and a very small part of inner Kartli continued to be inhabited as evidenced by the distribution of kurgans as well as the Trialeti levels recorded in eastern Georgia (Pitskhelauri 1984:8–20).

There is some reason to believe that the essential transformation of the economic sphere in Middle Bronze Age South Caucasus began in ecological niches situated in foothill and highland areas. These areas, critical for cattle breeding, come to be occupied from the beginning of the Middle Bronze Age, more intensively by the Trialeti Culture period. Occupation of these areas by Trialeti tribes is confirmed by the existence of cemeteries or individual kurgans in these areas.

From these locations, Trialeti groups moved into a wide array of ecological zones. If we were to outline the distribution of Trialeti materials on a geomorphological map of the Caucasus, we could see quite readily that these populations occupied various and diverse ecological zones: lowlands, foothills, mountains, and even desert areas (Udabno) in the eastern part of Georgia (Lisitsina and Prishepenko 1977).

The character of a manufacturing economy depends in large measure upon regional geomorphology and other prevailing conditions shaping available resources. This is especially the case at early stages of human community. It is only natural that the course of economic development could not be the same in regions that differed greatly from each other geomorphologically. Thus it is important to note that important zones of Trialeti occupation—such as the Tsalka-Trialeti plateaus, the eastern Georgian valley, the Ararat valley and foothills, the northwest Armenian highland—boast highly contrasting geomorphological characteristics. If we add to this source of diversity in Trialetian forms of manufacturing, both some agricultural production and the dominant tradition of stock breeding, we must admit a significant degree of regional variability within Middle Bronze Age economies. On the basis of ecological and palaeozoological analyses, we can describe a number of economic types within the Trialeti Culture:

- Type one is characterized by the dominant role of cattle breeding in the economy, with agriculture relegated to an insignificant auxiliary role.
- Type two is characterized by an equal proportion of cattle breeding and agricultural production. Typically, communities of this type occupied lowland areas.
- Type three is characterized by an economy in which agricultural production plays a highly significant role, though perhaps remains slightly subordinate to stock breeding in the life of the community.

The proposed typology represents the first attempt to describe axes of variability within the Trialeti economy. Looking toward the future, it is hoped that when Trialeti settlements and tool complexes are located, the study of tool function will clarify and extend the economic types described above. Such investigations will undoubtedly also expose other sources of economic variability.

It is our hypothesis that diversity within local economies is one of the causes of variation within Middle Bronze Age archaeological assemblages. At present, we can only provide an outline of the major regional variants within the Trialeti economy. Apparently, the major Trialeti cattle-breeding regions were the Tsalka-Trialeti region and the Kvemo-Kartli Plain (the most southern part of Georgia). The economies of these regions most likely belong to type one, with a heavy emphasis on cattle breeding. In contrast, the lowland regions of Shida Kartli, the Iori-Alazani basin, and the Ararat valley were, in our view, occupied by tribes whose economic base more closely corresponded to type two, with a more equal reliance on cattle breeding and agriculture. Last, type three was likely most characteristic of the economy of the tribes that inhabited the Bedeni area, northwestern Armenia, and Meskheti (Puturidze 1983a). It is important to restate that agricultural traditions of the previous period were not absolutely lost, an observation based on the occurrence of burials within the fertile lowland zones that had been used for agricultural production in the Early Bronze Age. Another supporting line of evidence is now emerging from the palynological and climatological data collected from the Ararat valley and Kakheti in eastern Georgia (Lisitsina and Prishepenko 1977).

Despite the variability underlying Middle Bronze Age economies, it remains clear that a profound shift in settlement did occur at the end of the Early Bronze Age that led to an intensified occupation of highland areas relative to lowland zones. Furthermore, the highlands must certainly be understood as the vital center of Middle Bronze Age life since the richest burial sites were discovered mainly in these areas. A number of explanations have been forwarded to account for this movement from lowland to highland and the concentration of the Trialeti kurgans in the latter. Some scholars have linked the shift to climatic changes at the end of the Early Bronze Age (Kushnareva 1999: 18). Other scholars have suggested that the shift in habitation areas was provoked by dramatic events, such as large-scale invasions of new populations. At present, there is little archaeological evidence to support such a scenario. We think it more likely that the development of a cattle-breeding economy in itself forced the Middle Bronze Age populations to leave the well-inhabited places and move toward the highlands. Admittedly this explanation does beg the question of what forces drove populations across the southern Caucasus to move toward cattle breeding. One possible explanation is that the highland zones were attractive to Middle Bronze Age communities because of their rich ore sources and the possibilities these resources offered for metallurgical production. The kind of

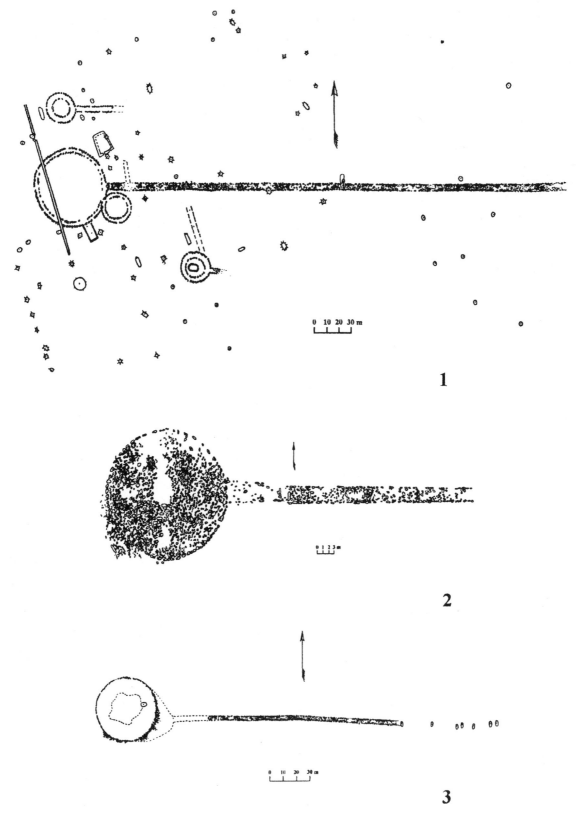

Figure 5.9 Barrows with processional ways from Tsalka. *After Narimanishvili 2000: 51, plate 1.*

a

b

Figure 5.10 *a*, necklace from Trialeti barrow no. 8, 20th–19th centuries BC; *b*, gold bowl with incrustation from Trialeti barrow no. 17, 18th–17th centuries BC.

nomadic pastoralism practiced by the Trialeti tribes was constrained by the geography of the Caucasus and the nature of their herds. Unlike the open steppe areas to the north, the pastures of the southern Caucasus are quite limited, thus confining the movement of herds to a limited territory. Until more evidence of settlement occupation is excavated, the precise nature of the presumably seasonal movements cannot be mapped.

Of special importance are the questions of whether rich burial groups had their equivalents in settlements and how individual settlements and cemeteries were organized. Like other problems associated with the Trialeti Culture, these questions require further study. The absence of Middle Bronze layers in stratified settlements is only an indirect indication of the shifts in settlement pattern. It is possible that the Trialetian populations had quite different types of habitations, at least in the highland areas. Regional surveys to look for settlements in those areas must be continued.

TRIALETI SOCIAL ORGANIZATION

In contrast with the uncertain perspective that the Trialeti burials provide on the Middle Bronze economy, the mortuary sites provide an excellent view on Trialeti social hierarchy and structure. At present, burial sites can be divided into at least four categories. First are the richest kurgans, which are also the most impressive in size. For example, kurgan 3 at Zurtaketi (figure 5.8b) is 100 m in diameter with a 40 m long dromos; the stone "sepulchral hall" is 150 m² in area (Japaridze 1969: 24–25, Plates VII, VIII, IX). Another example of this category is kurgan 36 at Tsalka, which includes a "sepulchral hall" of 175 m² (Kuftin 1941:79, Plate LX). Usually, these extremely large kurgans contain a greater variety of precious burial goods than other groups, represented primarily by gold work and richly ornamented ceramic assemblages. One of the key distinguishing indicators for this type of kurgan is the presence of a ritual route for funeral processions. These processional routes, such as the one recorded at Tsalka (Narimanishvili 2000:47–51), lead directly to the barrow and can be as long as 356 m and as wide as 6 m (figure 5.9). These routes evidently characterize only a handful of kurgans and provide an indication of the privileged status of the interred.

Members of a second social group were also buried in large kurgans accompanied by luxury goods (for example, kurgans 6, 7, and 15 at Tsalka). However, these burials reveal less honor in ritual ceremony and a re-

duced number of precious items (Gogadze 1972a: Plates 18, 19, 22). A third level in the Trialeti social hierarchy seems to have been occupied by specialized craftsmen, such as goldsmiths and pottery masters. Burials of these individuals can be identified with some certainty. For example, recent excavations in the Dmanisi region by Kakhiani (unpublished materials) have revealed burial pits that include partially finished gold products of goldsmithery.

A fourth group of burials was occupied by the least privileged level of Trialeti society. These burials are most notable for their small size and undistinguished assemblages of grave goods. Such burials have been excavated in Shida Kartli (for example, Nuli, Kvasatali; Kuftin 1948) and eastern Georgia (for example, Gumbati [Puturidze 1983b] and Shiraki [B. Maisuradze, personal communication]). In general, these graves contain only ceramics (usually without rich ornamentation) and a few bronze items. The suggested lines of division are general and preliminary and require further refinement through additional archaeological work.

While the processes of social stratification within Middle Bronze Age society were perhaps most conspicuous during the Trialeti stage, evidence for emerging social hierarchy appears in the archaeological record of the southern Caucasus during the preceding era of the Early Kurgans Culture. At the time of the Early Kurgans Culture, the preeminent social group does not appear to have been strongly differentiated from others in the general population (Japaridze 1998). But while intense concentrations of wealth in the hands of a limited elite appear only in the developed stage of the Middle Bronze Age, we suggest that an elite was already emerging, creating the conditions for privilege, during the Early Kurgans stage. The expansion of wealth during the Trialeti era was a result of a formalization of the ruling group and full hierarchical differentiation from other social groups. It seems to us that the Middle Bronze Age ruling elite of the southern Caucasus tried to adopt the style of life of ancient Near Eastern rulers, imitating them in many respects. Thus the explosion of wealth was highly determined by contacts with the world beyond the South Caucasus. Clues to these contacts can be found in the luxury goods recovered in the burials of the highest strata of Trialeti society (figures 5.7, 5.10). The highly artistic and well-crafted materials clearly show that local goldsmiths were familiar with the achievements and traditions of old Near Eastern, especially Anatolian, civilizations (see Rubinson, chapter 6).

CONCLUDING REMARKS

In this discussion, we have argued for an understanding of the nature and sources of cultural and economic diversity within South Caucasian Middle Bronze Age societies. Special attention has been paid to the historical significance of pivotal changes and innovations seen in the archaeological record of the Trialeti Culture. However, we have suggested that the roots of Trialeti social life lie in the extensive transformations in the latter part of the third millennium BC (indicated by the huge barrows at Tsalka, the Bedeni plateau, and Tsnori) that marked the end of the Kura-Araxes Culture and beginning of the Early Kurgans Culture (Kuftin 1941: 101–105; Dedabrishvili 1977; Gobedzhishvili 1980). These transformations we suggested may indicate the inauguration of a process of state formation in the region. New discoveries in the Tsalka region and northern Armenia we suspect will, in the future, allow us to confirm or reject this hypothesis.

With the rise of the Trialeti Culture we find, for the first time in the South Caucasus, large amounts of precious materials (figures 5.7, 5.10) that reflect a close interaction with the Near Eastern world. We have argued here that these interactions had a profound influence not just on material production but also on the course of Trialeti social formation and development. It is clear that the people of the Trialeti Culture were familiar with the achievements of Anatolian, Sumerian, Aegean, and more distant civilizations and their traditions. Yet the nature of these ties remains unclear. Presumably such connections can occur in a variety of ways: indirectly through regular cultural influence or more directly through exchanges of "diplomatic gifts" or occasional traveling merchants (it is unlikely that the wide variety of "alien" trade goods known from Trialeti contexts would have resulted from highly regularized trade since we find artifacts of different styles and origins in numbers that rarely exceed one to three items).

The dynamic of cultural changes of remote prehistory usually cannot be recaptured as unambiguous social processes. As a result, we must proceed cautiously when describing an era of such momentous transformations as the South Caucasian Middle Bronze Age. The extant archaeological record does not suggest that these transformations were the result of a migration of alien tribes, since there appears to be continuity in regional cultural development. A complete account of the origins of the famous Trialeti Culture and the main factors that deflected the local Transcaucasian tribes from their traditional Early Bronze way of life remains to be written. While we see no evidence of a wave of ethnic migration into the South Caucasus at the beginning of the Middle Bronze Age, we do think it is critical to emphasize the significant importance of developing ties to the Near Eastern world in the formation of the Middle Bronze Age Trialeti Culture.

CHAPTER 6

Silver Vessels
and Cylinder Sealings:

Precious Reflections of Economic Exchange in the
Early Second Millennium BC

KAREN S. RUBINSON

Until relatively recently, the southern Caucasus has for the most part existed on the periphery of the consciousness of Near Eastern archaeologists, except for the many beautiful objects of gold and silver excavated there.[1] And when precious objects with pictorial images have been excavated in Caucasia, it is to the Near East that their excavators have often looked for understanding and interpretation of those images (Kuftin 1941:88–91, 163–165; Oganesian 1992a:86–90). Scholars not only have looked at formal similarities but also have relied on the visual connections to explain many possible ancient realities, primarily economic interaction (Kushnareva 1997:92–93, 213–214; Boehmer and Kossack 2000:15–16) and ethnic relationships (Oganesian 1992a:97–100). In this chapter, after looking once again at three silver vessels with decoration in relief from the Trialeti Culture (Rubinson 1976, 1977, 1999, 2001), I too will compare them to Near Eastern objects of artistic production. Because of a cluster of distinctive iconographic and stylistic parallels, together with other archaeological materials, I will

suggest that the images decorating the vessels are markers of interaction of the peoples of the southern Caucasus and Anatolia in the Middle Bronze Age.

Looking at objects of artistic production to reveal historical/cultural/economic information is a frequent exercise among ancient art historians, since, as Wolff has said, "Art is a social product," "the complex product of economic, social and ideological factors, mediated through the formal structures of the text (literary or other), and owing its existence to the particular practice of the located individual" (Wolff 1984:1,139). Marcus clearly laid out the issues in her study of the Hasanlu seals and sealings, when she posited:

> …that there is a functional relationship between art and culture. Art objects are viewed…as integrated cultural manifestations, reflecting and reinforcing the basic values of the culture in which they function….Art *styles* are related to social conditions and can therefore serve as media of information exchange… By style is meant "the formal similarities among artifacts that can

Figure 6.1 Karashamb goblet, detail.
Courtesy of the State History Museum of Armenia.

be related to factors other than raw material availability or mechanical efficiency" [Davis 1983:55]; and that it is considered to be peculiar to time and place. In addition, as is commonly assumed in art history and archaeology, the similarities between works of art from historically related contexts are seen as being directly related to the degree of social interaction among individuals or groups [Marcus 1996:2].

An approach to defining the special importance of iconography in cultural settings such as Middle Bronze Age Caucasia is presented in Rubinson (in press).

The Middle Bronze Age in the southern Caucasus is customarily dated from the end of the third millennium or beginning of the second through the first half of the second millennium BC.[2] Because the data from Georgia and Armenia discussed here come from tombs, and we generally lack accompanying settlements, the dating is not precise. There are some carbon dates from earlier and later settlements in Transcaucasia and a relevant sequence of dates from Sos Höyük in Turkey (Sagona 2000:339); they suggest more or less the same time range. We are still left with external parallels for the grave goods to refine the chronology of the Trialeti Culture, a process that has been undertaken since Kuftin's first excavations, but that will not explicitly concern us here (Kuftin 1941:81–100, 162, 164–165; Rubinson 1976:134–142; Kohl 1992:127–128; Oganesian 1992a:100, note 1; Kushnareva and Rysin 2001). These external parallels may tell us something about the cultural/economic interaction as well, as will be discussed below.

Figure 6.2 Karashamb goblet, detail.
Courtesy of the State History Museum of Armenia.

TRIALETI CULTURE SILVER VESSELS

The Trialeti Culture is named for the type site in southern Georgia, but burials assigned to the culture occur over a broad area of southern Georgia and parts of Armenia, Azerbaijan, and eastern Anatolia as well (Kushnareva 1997:85, map 1, 89–108; Özfırat 2001:120; Sagona 2000:337–338; and Puturidze, chapter 5). The material culture from the tombs is rich and varied, including distinctive ceramic types and many kinds of luxury goods (Kuftin 1941; O. Japaridze 1969; Martirosian 1964:64–70, Plates 1, 2; Oganesian 1992b). Here I will examine in detail three embossed silver objects found in Trialeti Culture burials: a small bucket from kurgan 17 and a goblet from kurgan 5 excavated in the late 1930s from Trialeti itself and a goblet excavated in 1987 from the site of Karashamb in Armenia (figures 6.1–6.12) (Kuftin 1941:87–90, Plates 88–92; Miron and Orthmann 1995:238, Figures 10, 68; Soltes 1999:61, 66–67, 146; Oganesian 1988, 1992a; Santrot 1996:65–66, Plates 6-7; Kévorkian 1996:27,228; Boehmer and Kossack 2000).

The three silver objects are distinctive in Middle Bronze Caucasia for many reasons. The two goblets both display human figures, which are not characteristically represented in the preceding period in Caucasia nor widespread during the Trialeti Culture (figures 6.1–6.8). Both goblets are divided into registers and the figures on the vessels are shown standing on ground lines (figures 6.1–6.9), a new feature in Caucasian art (N.O. Japaridze 1988:15). The hunting scenes on the Karashamb goblet and Trialeti bucket are also new to Caucasia in this period (figures 6.5, 6.11, 6.12).

There is no question that these objects, found in elite burials, bore meanings within the culture where they were found (Hays 1993:82–83; Smith 2001) and that they were items of prestige and value (Helms 1993:149). It also seems that the origin of some images that appear on these objects lay in Anatolia, as will be detailed below. What specifically inspired the individuals who crafted these objects and what local dynamics specifically existed that caused the exotic images to be received and reproduced are unknowable, but many of the borrowed images were characteristic of central Anatolia, and it is this relationship that will be explored here.[3]

The Karashamb goblet is related in iconography, shape, and technique of manufacture to the one from Trialeti. Both goblets are made of thin silver plate, with hollow foot and flat bottom, and are decorated by bands of ornament separated by narrow plain bands. The lower parts of both goblet bowls bear similar rosette ornaments (figure 6.1, figure 6.9). The Karashamb goblet is 13.2 cm high, 10.5 cm in diameter, and weighs 215 grams (Santrot 1996:65), slightly larger and heavier than the Trialeti example, which stands 11.3 cm high and 9.8 cm in diameter and weighs 163.39 g (Miron and Orthmann 1995:238). The human figures on both share large eyes, prominent noses, and receding chins, as well as footgear with turned-up toes. However, the humans on the Trialeti goblet have hair and beards indicated, unlike those from Karashamb, and the puffy style of the Karashamb figures contrasts with the more angular Trialeti style (figure 6.5, 6.8). Nevertheless, the strong similarities point to more or less contemporary manufacture. Whether the goblets were buried near their time of manufacture is certainly unknown. However, the pottery from the Karashamb kurgan also appears to be approximately the same period as other Trialeti Culture burials such as that from Zurtaketi kurgans 3 and 4 (compare, for example Oganesian 1992b: Plate 25, 4 to O. Japaridze 1969: Plate XV, upper right and Oganesian 1992b: Plate 25, 3 to O. Japardize 1969: Plate XX, two examples lower left, and Fig. 36), so the goblets can be said to have been more or less both contemporaneously made and more or less contemporaneously buried.[4]

From its first publication, the Trialeti goblet has been compared to imagery from Anatolia, particularly rock reliefs (Kuftin 1941:89–90). Many years ago, I pointed to similarities between the decoration on the goblet (and bucket) and Anatolian-style seals of the Assyrian Trading Colony period (Rubinson 1976:194–

196). The more elaborate program of ornamentation on the Karashamb goblet provides an opportunity to reexamine the stylistic and iconographic parallels with Anatolia and consider the implications, beyond chronology, of the apparent similarities.

GOBLET FROM KARASHAMB

Because the Karashamb goblet has had less exposure in Western literature than the material from the Trialeti type site, I describe it here in some detail (and see Oganesian 1988; Oganesian 1992a; Boehmer and Kossack 2000). On the goblet, three registers are primarily animals, although the top register does contain one human figure hunting (figure 6.5); the lower register of the goblet body is an animal procession and the foot has a series of heraldic animals and one lion *en face*. The two wider registers show a presentation/ritual/banquet scene and various apparently military encounters, along with other elements. The edge of the foot is decorated by a herringbone pattern (figures 6.4, 6.6).

When looked at from the point where the figure seated before the offering table is centered (one of the two largest humans, and the figure toward which the human figures converge from both directions), the frontal figure of the lion-bird[5] is centered as well, suggesting that this is the principal focus of the imagery and thus the center of the goblet (figure 6.1). This assumption leaves the boar hunt in the uppermost register in a subsidiary position embedded in what is otherwise a file of animals, like the fourth register. The foot has four pairs of heraldic animals with their heads turned back and a single lion in profile with an *en face* head, the single animal almost directly below the archer at the top.

The hunt scene of the top register is seen as the first in a narrative sequence by the excavator (Oganesian 1992a:96–97) and by Santrot (1996:66), generally involving a leader or hero whose exploits are shown in the first three registers, beginning with a symbolic/sacred hunt. While this is certainly a possibility, the formal organization just noted suggests that there may be other ways to read the information on the goblet. Rather than attempt that here, however, I will instead explore the formal, stylistic, and iconographic elements.

The one human figure in the top register is a kneeling archer, with his near leg back and the foot at right angles to the ground line, with the upturned toe of the shoe parallel to the ground. He is holding a bow with his far arm and pulling an arrow back with the near one. Kneeling, the figure fills the register and the bow

Figure 6.3 Karashamb goblet, detail. *Courtesy of the State History Museum of Armenia.*

is almost as tall. Before the human figure is a lion bit-ing the ear of a boar, whose shoulder is marked by an arrow head. The lion's mane is indicated by a pointed ruff. Biting the rear of the boar is a spotted feline ani-mal, which has engraved triangles at the neck similar to the lion at the boar's front. Like the boar's body, the body of this following feline is marked by overall punched dots, which also fill the body surfaces of five of the other animals in this top register (figure 6.5). Beyond the active combat of this group of three ani-mals are another ten, nine of them facing toward the archer and the tenth, next to the human figure, facing in the opposite direction, toward the man's back (fig-ures 6.1–6.6). The animal facing the back of the archer is identified as a dog by Oganesian (1992a:86), Santrot (1996:65), and Boehmer (Boehmer and Kossack 2000:17), which is certainly plausible in the context, de-spite feet and tail like the feline animals in this register.[6] Of the ten animals, all have turned-up tails but one, whose long tail hangs down (figure 6.2). This same animal has feet that appear to be more hooflike, simi-lar to the boar's, unlike the large feline-like clawed feet of the others. The nine animals facing the archer are alternating lions and spotted felines, with two excep-tions: the third and fourth in the file, the third being a spotted animal with a fully expressed mane and the

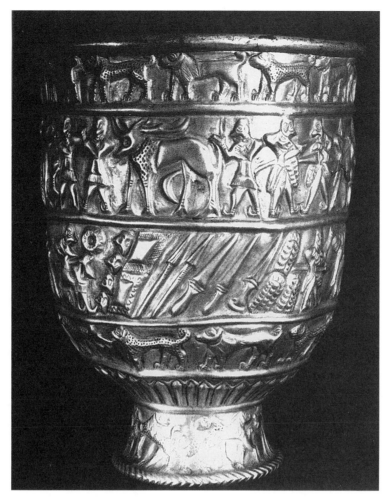

Figure 6.4 Karashamb goblet, view. *Courtesy of the State History Museum of Armenia.*

fourth the spotted animal with long tail and more hooflike feet just mentioned (figures 6.1, 6.2). The remaining lions, together with the spotted feline with mane, have manes filled with parallel incised lines filling the area of the neck and front chest, and at the end of the mane, on the trunk, a band of attached angles pointing toward the back. The felines in the fourth register are rendered in the same fashion, and the lion in register 3 is treated similarly except for the pose (figures 6.1–6.6). Details of the felines on the foot are not clear from the photographs I have seen, but the *en face* lion lacks the pointed element at the body/mane join. (Santrot 1996:67).[7]

The second register contains, as the focal point, a large figure in a fringed robe seated on a stool with crossed struts, his feet on a plinth decorated with crosshatching, holding a vessel by its long narrow base. The flaring upper part of the vessel is near the lower part of the figure's face; the mouths of the human figures on the goblet are not generally shown (figure 6.1). Before him

stands a table with hoofed feet, and lying on it a fish or fish-shaped object, a beaker, and an object made up of two or three interlocking triangles. An animal described as a dog (Oganesian 1992a:89; Boehmer 2000:19) stands behind the table. Approaching the seated figure is a man dressed in a short-skirted fringed garment with a central panel of hatching (presumed to be a tunic), carrying a goblet in his raised arms (figure 6.1). Behind him is another table with two hoofed legs separated by a hatched band from table top to ground, the legs each descending vertically from the table top, in contrast to the first table. Both legs have lines down their centers; on one, those divided areas are filled with V-shaped hatching. This second table has three vessels on top: a jar marked with an X and an open bowl in front of a second jar (figures 6.2, 6.3). Nearby is a bowl in a stand, the bowl having a somewhat pointed bottom, echoing the V-shape of the top of the stand (figure 6.3). Approaching the seated figure are three more men with uplifted hands, two preceding a stag and one following

Figure 6.5 Karshamb goblet, detail.
Courtesy of the State History Museum of Armenia.

(figures 6.3, 6.4). All the standing figures in tunics, in-cluding these, are shown with the shoulders and garment frontally and the legs (or at least the feet) and the heads in profile. They all share with the animals joints marked with (usually) three parallel lines (figures 6.1–6.6).

The head of the stag is marked off from the body, char-acteristic of all of the animals on the vessel. The shoulder of the animal is filled by punched dots and the leg joints indicated by groups of parallel lines. A crescent is placed vertically between the legs of the stag (figures 6.3, 6.4).

On the other side, behind the principal figure, are two apparently kneeling figures, the lower edges of their garments marked by zigzag lines. They are placed one above the other. (figures 6.1, 6.6) Since in the same reg-ister an animal is shown behind the table (figure 6.1)

and in the register below the lion is shown in front of the horned animal it is fighting (figure 6.5), it is worth noting this visual choice. The kneeling figures are hold-ing stemmed objects with rounded ends that might be fans, spouted vessels, or musical instruments (Boehmer and Kossack 2000:20). Behind them is a seated stringed instrument player. He sits on an X-shaped stool, wears a long fringed garment, and fills the register, seated, in the same manner as the drinking figure (figures 6.5, 6.6). Although it is possible that the size of the musi-cian, like the figure seated before the table, indicates that he is more important than the other figures, it seems more likely, based on the overall composition, that the practice of the maker of the goblet was to fill the entire register with each human figure, regardless

Figure 6.6 Karashamb goblet, view. *Courtesy of the State History Museum of Armenia.*

of pose. The kneeling pair holding fans (?) are the only exceptions to this practice. Even the headless figures in register three fill the entire register (figures 6.5, 6.6).

Approaching the central scene are three armed figures, with another male figure, unarmed, in front, being encouraged forward by a spear point in his back. The armed figures carry spears, hold ovoid shields, and wear scabbards at their waists; they are shown in garments without skirts, thus perhaps trousers (?).[8] The unarmed figure wears a tunic (figures 6.5, 6.6). Formally, this group of walking figures balances the deer and walking figures approaching the central scene from the other direction.

The remaining part of this register is filled with two pairs of battling figures, dressed similarly, apparently in trousers and with ornamented scabbards behind them, but using different weapons: the figures to the viewer's left of each pair use spears, held at a rising angle, and the figures to the right, swords or daggers held horizontally. The left-hand pair have ovoid shields divided in half by a line and filled with lines of hatch marks (like the shields of the three figures holding spears with the prisoner [?]) and the right pair hold rectangular shields with an extended corner toward the body at the top, the three sides toward the body edges with hatched bands (figures 6.4, 6.5 and see Santrot 1996:67; Boehmer and Kossack 2000: Fig. 4). This conflict could be read as preceding the procession of victors and vanquished just adjacent. However, the parsing of these scenes remains ambiguous, in my view. For example, the "victors" carry spears, like the left-hand figures of the two fighting pairs, yet they also carry ovoid shields, like both figures fighting each other in the right-hand pair. None of the four fighting figures wear the tunic of the figure being prodded by a spear in the back, so the precise reading of the story remains elusive. All one can say with certainty is that about half of this register shows scenes of fighting and prisoner-presentation.

The register below seems to have several discrete elements clearly tied together by their violence; however, the order and specific relationship of each element is not clear, at least to me. From the lion-bird, which I assume to mark the center because of its position below the focal individual in register two, the images may be read as follows. Two figures are fighting at the right, with the warrior carrying a spear and rectangular shield and wearing a scabbard, getting the best of a possibly helmeted figure who has fallen to his knees and is dropping his rectangular shield (figure 6.1).[9] The kneeling figure is shown filling the entire register, effectively much larger than the figure who attacks him. His head is shown thrown back, his nose in the air. The top of the head is pointed and striated; it is possible this represents headgear of some type. His arms are shown extended on the frontal torso; the legs and head are in profile. He wears crossed straps on his chest, which extend from a band of vertical lines at the "waist" and a hatched band from his belt, which has been interpreted as a tail, analogous with the Trialeti goblet (figures 6.1, 6.2, 6.8).[10] Next is a figure seated on a stool with crossed struts and hatched top and bottom. The figure wears a long garment fringed at the bottom and with a band of cross-hatching from hem to shoulder. He holds a large axe, above which is a wide disk decorated with a plain center surrounded by a hatched circle and an outer circle filled with a zigzag line. In front of the seated figure are four heads, shown stacked one above the other (figure 6.3). Behind the heads is a group of armaments: two rectangular shields (one with cross-hatched border, as occurs elsewhere on the goblet, and one with a zigzag filled border), two spears, three daggers or swords, and three ovoid shields (figures 6.3, 6.4). Another pair of fighters follows the armaments. This battling pair again has a spear wielder (with an ovoid shield) in the winning position over an unarmed man with crossed straps on his chest and a hatched band (tail [?]) extending from his waist along his back to the ground. The attacker extends one arm to touch the forward-bent head of the attacked, whose own arms are outstretched (figures 6.4, 6.5 and Santrot 1996:67).

The next pair of figures is also fighting, but these figures are a lion and what seems to be a goat. The two animals extend in opposite directions, the lion in front

of the horned animal. The neck and belly of the horned animal are marked with parallel hatching, as is the lion's mane (figure 6.5). Between this battling group and the lion-bird are three headless figures with crossed straps on their chests and hatched bands (tails[?]) dependent from their waists. Their torsos are frontal, with outstretched arms, and their trousered (?) legs are shown in profile (figures 6.5, 6.6).

The animal file of the next register has nine walking animals, alternately lions, with plain bodies and striated manes, or spotted animals (figures 6.1–6.6). Where two spotted animals follow each other, they are separated by a rectangular shield with hatched border (figure 6.3). The register at the bottom of the goblet bowl is a rosette with pointed ends (figures 6.1–6.6). The foot has four pairs of felines with forelegs off the ground. The lions to the right have their forefeet on the shoulders of the spotted animals without manes (one "lion" is also spotted). Their heads are turned back. Between two of the addorsed groups is a lion en face, like the one in the third register but with all feet on the ground (figures 6.4, 6.6 and Santrot 1996:66–67; Oganesian 1992a:92; Boehmer and Kossack 2000:Fig. 4).

Santrot suggests that the goblet images are a hero/priest/divine person first hunting in preparation for battle, then in a ceremonial setting where victory in battle is assured by ritual playacting, and then holding the axe of victory in front of the spoils of war (1996:65–66). Oganesian suggests that the second register is a victory banquet after the battle shown on the third register which was started by someone hunting a boar in defiance of its sacred role (1992a:97). Both follow Areshian, who suggests that all figures with wolf tails are dead, a suggestion made in the course of his analysis of the Trialeti goblet, which he suggested was an afterlife scene (Oganesian 1992a:95 and fn. 42; Areshian 1988). Until we more fully understand the cultural contexts in which these vessels were made, it remains difficult to know their full meaning.

INTERNAL ARTISTIC RELATIONSHIPS

In contrast to the complex scene on the Karashamb goblet, the Trialeti goblet is very simple. The upper register contains a row of twenty-two males wearing short tunics with long striated tail-like elements suspended from the lower part of the garments behind their back legs. They are approaching a deity or elite person who sits on a stool, holding a goblet. Before him

Figure 6.7 Trialeti goblet, detail, top register. *Rubinson photo, with gracious permission from the State Historical Museum, Tbilisi.*

Figure 6.8 Trialeti goblet, detail, top register. *Rubinson photo, with gracious permission from the State Historical Museum, Tbilisi.*

Figure 6.9 Trialeti goblet, detail, second register. *Rubinson photo, with gracious permission from the State Historical Museum, Tbilisi.*

Figure 6.10 Trialeti bucket, detail, lower section. *Rubinson photo, with gracious permission of the State Historical Museum, Tbilisi.*

Figure 6.11 Trialeti bucket, detail, fragment.
Rubinson photo, with gracious permission of the State Historical Museum, Tbilisi.

Figure 6.12 Trialeti bucket, detail. *Rubinson photo, with gracious permission of the State Historical Museum, Tbilisi.*

Figure 6.13 Seal from Kültepe karum Kanesh. *After Özgüç 1965: pl. XVII, 50.*

is a hoofed table and a stand holding a bowl. Two animals, perhaps felines, flank the table. Behind the seated figure is a plant or tree (figures 6.7, 6.8). The lower register displays a procession of five female deer and four bucks. At the base of the goblet body is a rosette pattern with pointed ends (figure 6.9). The foot is undecorated.

The two goblets share many iconographic details. The two authority figures and accompanying paraphernalia are quite similar. If we look at the seated principal figures on both goblets, we note the crossed struts of the stool, the footrest, the hoofed table, the animals beside the table, the drum-shaped stand topped by a bowl (figures 6.1–6.3, 6.7, 6.8).

In contrast to the goblets, with human representations as well as animals in registers, the silver bucket from Trialeti kurgan 17 has an all-over pattern of animals and plants (figures 6.10–6.12). According to the excavator Kuftin's analysis, it is a hunt scene, based on the fact that two animals stuck with arrows are preserved, although the figure of a hunter does not remain (figures 6.11, 6.12). Since the bucket is preserved in very fragmentary condition, Kuftin's suggestion is certainly possible.[11] In fact, the arrowheads near the animals on the Trialeti bucket are similar in form to that which hit the boar on the Karashamb goblet, although the relationship between the animals and the arrowheads is different, with the Trialeti animals shown with arrows against the background and only beginning to hit the animals, in contrast to the Karashamb goblet,where the arrow is outlined against the body of the boar (figures 6.5, 6.11, 6.12). The side seam of the bucket is closed by an applied guilloche of gold (figure 6.12) and has a basket handle (Kuftin 1941:p. 88) and a metallic ring at the base (figure 6.10).

There are interesting questions for further study about the interrelationship of the three silver pieces. Kuftin pointed out that the Trialeti goblet shows a pair of walking animals which is very close in pose and body markings to a pair of animals at the base of the bucket (figures 6.9, 6.10). He suggested that the animals on the goblet were copied from those on the bucket, since the figures on the bucket were more lively and less static than those on the goblet (1941:88, Fig. 93). When looking at the two goblets, the similarities in iconography are striking (such as the elements of the footed table and stand, human figure in fringed robe seated on a stool with crossed struts, walking figures in short fringed tunics and footgear with turned-up toes shown with faces and legs in profile and torsos frontal, the human heads

with large noses and pointed-oval eyes and no visible mouth), form of object, and organization of decoration (in registers separated by plain bands with rosettes at the bottom of the cups' bodies). The differences between the goblets are also noteworthy: hair and beards on the Trialeti human figures and not on the Karashamb ones, the more elaborate program of the Karashamb goblet, the presence of what may be tails seemingly attached to the garments of all of the Trialeti walking figures, and what are possibly tails attached to the waist of only headless or defeated figures on the Karashamb goblet. Whatever the sources of the imagery on these objects, it is as clear as it can be from only three examples that the manufacture of silver objects for elite persons or purposes in the Trialeti Culture shared a common set of images and perhaps ideas (see Helms 1993:4–5, 14–15).

EXTERNAL VISUAL COMPARISONS

Elements of the imagery on both the goblets and the bucket share many details with Ancient Near Eastern imagery, as already noted by many, beginning with the excavators. Most recently, Boehmer has collected extensive visual parallels primarily from Mesopotamia and Iran (Boehmer and Kossack 2000). Although many of these parallels are interesting and provocative, in most cases they are not internally consistent chronologically nor are they within a coherent cultural/historical framework. In my opinion, the closest detailed parallels are with seals from the Anatolian group of the Assyrian trading colony period, in the first few centuries of the second millennium BC (N. Özgüç 1965). For example, ritual tables with hooved feet and stools with crossed struts on which major figures sit are common in Kültepe karum Kanesh seals of the Anatolian group (see, for example, N. Özgüç 1965: Plate 4:11a; Plate 5:15a,b). Both seals also show a standing figure with upraised hands held at an angle, as on the Karashamb goblet, approaching the seated figure, and there is a dagger in the field against a plain ground on the latter seal and a ritual fixture on the former seal consisting of a conical base topped with a bowl-shape (in this case with flames arising from it). Animals on the seals of the Anatolian group have vividly decorated surfaces, with the parts of the body striated in varied directions (for example, N. Özgüç 1965: Plate 12:34 [this seal also has a human head in the field]), also seen on the bucket (figures 6.10–6.12) and echoed in the animals on the Trialeti goblet (figure 6.9). In some combat scenes on the seals, the lion is shown en face, though the rest of the animals are shown in profile (N. Özgüç 1965: Plate 17:50) (figure 6.13), like two of the lions on the Karashamb goblet. Further, the overall character of the bucket's surface, covered with many figures in different orientations, is quite similar to the organization found on the Anatolian group seals from Karum Kanesh (for example, figure 6.13).[12] The guilloche pattern along the side of the bucket is found on Karum II seals (N. Özgüç 1965: Plate 31:97) and becomes a distinctive feature of Karum 1b and Hittite period seals (Rubinson 1977:243).

One could note that many of the elements described above occur on seals of other styles from Kültepe, which is indeed the case (as well, of course on Mesopotamian seals as Boehmer suggests [Boehmer and Kossack 2000: passim]). However, the largest cluster of parallels is with the Anatolian group. In fact, the single seal impression illustrated here (figure 6.13) has many details which recall elements on the Karashamb goblet; they are complex enough to be a strong indication of some type of connection. The depiction of the headless bodies is quite similar, with stalk necks, arms and legs akimbo (figures 6.6, 6.13). The figure with the spear killing a person in the lower left of the seal recalls in pose and organization the fellow having his head taken off on the Karashamb goblet. Although the figure being speared is more vertical on the goblet than the seal, the kneeling pose, the outstretched arms, the torso shown frontally, and the legs and head in profile reflect each other (figures 6.1, 6.2, 6.13). The individual doing the spearing holds a detached human head in his hand. As noted above, this seal also contains a lion with an *en face* head attacking a horned animal, although the composition is quite different from that on the goblet (figures 6.5, 6.13).

That this imagery was native to the creators of the Anatolian style seals at Kanesh and borrowed into the Southern Caucasus cannot be proven. However, much of the other iconography certainly is, such as the specific detailed elements of the banquet/ritual scenes, as well as many details of style. Further, nowhere in the early imagery of the Northern and Southern Caucasus do we have a tradition of human representation in this kind of narrative setting. So I am inclined to see the source of the imagery as Anatolia, transformed within the Southern Caucasus to locally contextual meanings.

There are other objects excavated in Kültepe karum Kanesh that reflect Trialeti Culture finds. One connection between Trialeti and Anatolia was pointed out some years ago by Collon: the type of handle on the silver bucket—a basket handle attached via a "split-pin" to a separate piece of metal attached to the body of the vessel (Collon 1982a). With more publication of the Kültepe material, it appears that this kind of vessel occurs relatively frequently at the site (T. Özgüç 1986:73; Akyurt 1998:Fig. 103, j,k,l,m). Other finds from Kültepe, which may bear on the question of the source of the images on the goblet, include a rhyton in the shape of a fish (T. Özgüç 1986:67 and Plate 117, 1), axes and axe molds with triangular blades and ribbed haft which recall the axe on the Karashamb goblet (T. Özgüç 1986:44–45, Plates 87:11,3, 88:7,8, 134:2) (figure 6.3), and even perhaps a pendant mould found in a workshop of Karum level 2, which is shaped like a disk with a central impressed area surrounded by a disk decorated with a zigzag line, echoing the pattern on the disk above the man with the axe on the Karashamb goblet (T. Özgüç 1986:42-44, pl 87,4).[13]

CULTURAL INTERCONNECTIONS

What might these visual connections be a marker of? We know that active long distance trade is the reason for the existence of the karums at Kanesh and other sites, which represent the Assyrian-Anatolian ties so clearly outlined in the texts. Is it possible that there was an active, important trade in the early second millennium between the Anatolian trading centers and the Southern Caucasus, of which these metal objects are a reflection? I think that is likely.[14] We have insufficient evidence to fully understand the nature of the elite society and the appeal of these once-foreign images, so must leave a detailed exploration of that question aside here (but see Smith 2001 and Puturidze, chapter 5).

Despite suggestions that objects in the Trialeti kurgan burials reflect Mesopotamian influence or contact (N. O. Japaridze 1988:56–59; Boehmer and Kossack 2000:26), it appears from the evidence above that in the early second millennium, South Caucasian–Anatolian interaction was paramount. Painted pottery from Trialeti in this period is ornamented with spirals like those on Anatolian seals, which may be further evidence for contemporaneity and contact (Kuftin 1941: Plate 78, top).

What kinds of goods might have been sought in the southern Caucasus to bring the area into active participation in some part of this early second millennium trading network (see Peterson, chapter 2, for a discussion of multifocal trading networks)? It might have been minerals of some sort—perhaps even tin. There have been reports of exhausted tin mines at Borzhomi Gorge, along the Kura River, although this is controversial (Kohl 1995:1056). Tin is also reported from various Central Asian areas, which could have passed through the Caucasus on the way into the Near East (See Peterson, chapter 2). Chernyk suggest that Transcaucasia was an important source of arsenical bronze and antimony in the Middle Bronze Age (1992:113, 157, 159–62).

Might obsidian have played a role? Almost one-third of the obsidian tested to date from the Kafteri period deposits at Tal-i Malyan in the Fars province of Iran comes from Caucasia (Blackman et al. 1998:222). This is not to say that Caucasian obsidian was sent to Anatolia, where many obsidian sources exist. But it is an indicator that Transcaucasia was connected into the long-distance trading system. At this stage it is not possible to solve the problem of the material reasons for the contact, but it does appear, based on visual evidence, that the trading network, of which the Assyrian colonies were a significant if not seminal part, included some kind of exchange between Anatolia and the southern Caucasus, reflected in these silver objects.

NOTES

1. The material excavated at Trialeti was published almost immediately after the appearance of Kuftin's report (1941) by Schaeffer, first in a series of articles and then in his exhaustive survey of Near Eastern archaeology (1943, 1944a, 1944b, 1948). The Trialeti silver goblet was used as comparanda by Porada when she first published the Hasanlu Gold "Bowl" (1959). In the classic survey of ancient Near Eastern art by Frankfort, he includes from the northern Caucasus figural metalwork from Bronze Age excavations at Maikop (1963[1954]:115–116, Plate 124).

2. A summary of the chronological discussion is found in Kushnareva, who includes carbon dates from sites before and after the Trialeti culture and points to the role of external parallels for the general dating of the Trialeti culture (1997:82–83,114). Recent archaeological work in eastern Turkey has yielded additional dates based on carbon dating of sites including Trialeti culture ceramics (Sagona 2000:339). And see Badalyan et al., chapter 7, this volume.

3. For an exemplary study of a corpus of archaeological material and the cultural/historical understandings which can be gleaned from study of a local style in relation to external artistic sources, see Marcus 1996. For a monograph on a single excavated (uninscribed but decorated) object from which much was learned through an art historical investigation, see Winter 1980. In discussing the Hasanlu breastplate, Winter says it "is a unique object in its own right and is also part of a particular archaeological context; through it we are provided with a tantalizing glimpse of a cultural and historical moment. The plaque is a work of consummate skill, in which several traditions have been united into a dynamic whole....It stands further as a microcosm of the influences absorbed by the region at that time. If one understands influence to be not merely an overlay upon a passive culture but rather a reflection on some level of active acceptance—embrace, even—of desirable qualities, the breastplate then reflects clear cultural attitudes of northwest Iran in the early first millennium BC in relation to the large and powerful states of Assyria to the west and Elam to the south. By extension, the breastplate then provides material witness to the fact that ideas and information must have been fundamental, although non-material, agents in and results of the process" (1980:31). Much more is known about the historical context of the Hasanlu material than of Caucasia in the Middle Bronze Age, but Winter's perspective is a useful framework for the Caucasian objects as well.

   Another excavated decorated object that has inspired much chronological and cultural scholarship, with many differing conclusions as to both date and cultural (as opposed to archaeological) context, is the Hasanlu Gold "Bowl" (Barrelet 1984 and Winter 1989), a situation similar to that of these Middle Bronze silver pieces.

   That Near Eastern objects found their way into the Caucasus is known. Two imported objects, a cylinder seal and a weight, were excavated at Metsamor in Armenia (Khanzandian and Piotrovskii 1992; Khanzandian et al 1992). An old Babylonian seal comes from Nakhichevan (Khazandian and Piotrovskii 1992:73–74). At least one Mitannian cylinder seal was found in the Northern Caucasus (Uvarova 1900: Plate 127, no. 47) and three seals of "Mitannian style" were excavated in the southern Caucasus (Avetistyan et al. 2000:24; Badalyan et al., chapter 7, this volume).

4. Oganesian suggests different ceramic affinities, to the earliest phase of the Middle Bronze Trialeti burials, such as Trialeti kurgans 8, 9, and 18 (1992b:32). For the purposes of this discussion, the problem of a refined chronology has been put aside to ask a different question. However, the few ceramics from the Karashamb kurgan need to be compared in detail to the rest of the corpus.

5. The lion-bird consists of a lion's head and legs, together with a bird's body and wings. This combination of features is characteristic of the figure of the lion-headed eagle Anzu, known from Mesopotamian monuments such as the bitumen relief from Girsu (Amiet 1980:447 and Figure 327). Oganesian notes this iconographic relationship (1992a:91). One should not assume, however, that the image as used in the southern Caucasus shares anything with the figure known from Mesopotamian myth except the combination of formal elements. Boehmer's suggestion that the figure marks a mythical realm on the Karashamb goblet is certainly possible (Boehmer and Kossack 2000:24), but it is premature to assume the context and/or the precise Mesopotamian meaning of the image was carried into Caucasia together with the image itself.

6. It is important to keep in mind that the context here is not the Ancient Near East, from which much of the imagery on the goblets is borrowed. Habitual, specific details of Near Eastern iconography, such as "feline feet," may not signify the same concept on the goblet. For another example, Boehmer, in looking at the next register, defines the principal figure as a prince since he has no "divine attributes" (Boehmer and Kossack 2000:18), thus defining the imagery in the context of the Ancient Near East. This approach removes the focus from the local context (and see Smith 2001). I have made an effort here to use context-neutral terms of description.

7. I have not had an opportunity to study the Karashamb goblet first hand, so all observations are from photographs. I am grateful to Ruben Badalyan, Stephan Kroll, Adam T. Smith, and Laura Tedesco for help in obtaining some of the photographs I have used in this research.

8. Oganesian (1992a:91) designates the garments as shirt and trousers. Boehmer says the clothing cannot be trousers, based on Near Eastern parallels and the occurrence there only in Achaemenid times (Boehmer and Kossack 2000:22). I find that argument unsatisfactory, underscoring the importance of examining the vessel in terms of both the borrowed iconography and the local context.

9. For a very detailed discussion of whether this is a helmeted figure, see Boehmer and Kossack (2000:22).

10. Boehmer suggests that the "tails" are in fact extra hanging parts of tunics known in imagery from Anatolia (Boehmer and Kossack 2000:35, Figs. 53, 54). Although the comparisons are apt, I believe that the images on the Karashamb and Trialeti goblets may have been inspired by such representations of Anatolian garments but represent something different on the goblets.

11. The bucket is quite fragmentary, with only areas near the top and bottom and parts of the body along the side seam preserved. This can be seen in a photograph taken prior to restoration (Japaridze 1988: Plate XVIII). The watercolor in Kuftin's publication gives a sense of how the bucket must have appeared when intact (1941: Plate 88). It has seldom been published since except in illustrations based on the Kuftin watercolor (see for example Collon 1982:Fig. 2, b; Japaridze 1988: Plate XVII). I am grateful to the American Philosophical Society for a grant which permitted close study of this object, the Trialeti goblet, and other Trialeti-culture material. I wish here to mention how supportive and helpful Tamaz Kiguradze was, not only during the time I was making this study but through the years of my work in Georgia. His untimely death was a great loss to the scholarly world, and also a personal loss for me and others with whom he worked and with whom he shared his passion for archaeological study.

12. In fact, the surface organization of the images on the bucket, together with the surface treatment of the animals, raise the issue of whether this object, unlike the goblets, was made outside the Trialeti culture, perhaps within the sphere of the Anatolian trading colonies and brought into the southern Caucasus from outside.

13. There are other areas for future investigation, such as a study of the rock crystal beads from the Karashamb tomb. Rock crystal was used for decorative ornaments in the trading colonies, and rock crystal workshops have been found at Kanesh and Acemhöyük (T. Özgüç 1986:50–51).

14. The various ways to think about such interconnections and transformations are cogently laid out by Helms (1993).

CHAPTER 7

The Emergence of Sociopolitical Complexity in Southern Caucasia:

An Interim Report on the Research of Project ArAGATS

RUBEN S. BADALYAN, ADAM T. SMITH,
&
PAVEL S. AVETISYAN

In the fifth century AD, the Armenian historian Moses Khorenats'i offered an historical account of the emergence of complex societies in the Armenian Highlands (southern Caucasia and eastern Anatolia; figure 7.1). The template for such political formations, he posited, was imported to the region when Queen Semiramis of Assyria conquered the plain of Van, erecting a stone-walled fortress to rule the land, a great canal to irrigate it, and inscribed stone markers to delineate its boundaries.

Passing through many places, [Semiramis] arrived from the east at the edge of the salt lake [Lake Van].... [She] ordered forty-two thousand workers from Assyria and other lands of the empire...to be brought without delay to the desired spot.... First she ordered the aqueduct for the river to be built in hard and massive stone, cemented with mortar and sand, of infinite length and height;...within a few years she completed the marvelous [city] with strong walls and bronze gates.... And not only this, but also in many places in the land of Armenia she set up stelae and ordered memorials to herself to be written on them.... And in many places she fixed the boundaries [of the kingdom] with the same writing. [Khorenats'i 1978: I.16]

Although epigraphic research in the late nineteenth century demonstrated that Van (and numerous other fortresses strewn across the region) were built by the kings of Biainili (a polity known to the Assyrians as Urartu) not by Semiramis, Khorenats'i's suggestion that the critical stimuli to social complexity in the Armenian Highlands lay somewhere beyond its peaks and valleys has proven remarkably enduring.

Even as cultural diffusionist approaches to emergent complex societies fell into disfavor under neo-evolutionist and Marxist critiques during the mid-twentieth century, the Highlands continue to be thought of as a region most profoundly shaped by those who lived around it—Assyrians, Mittanians, Hittites, Mannaeans, Cimmerians, Scythians—rather than those within it. As a result, explanations of social complexity have often

Southern Caucasia and Its Surroundings

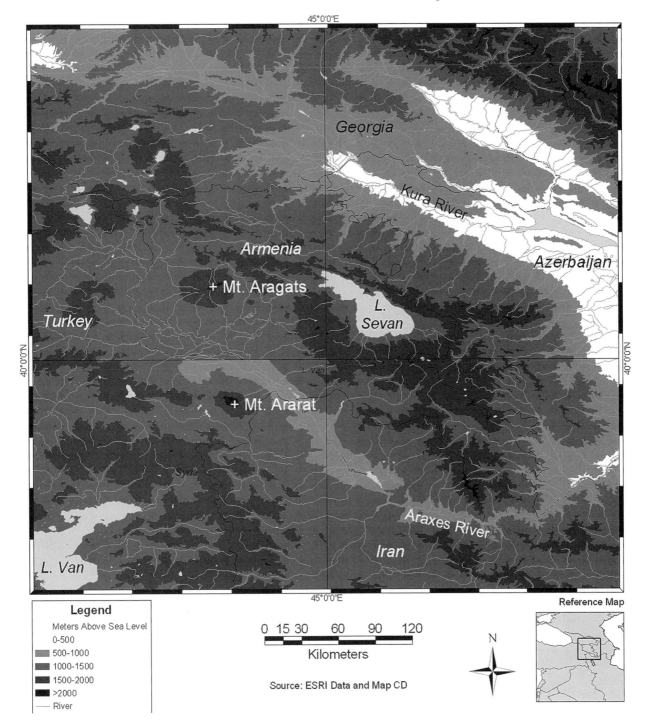

Figure 7.1 Elevation Map of Southern Caucasia and Surroundings.

been transposed into accounts of the political and cultural expansion of neighboring polities into the Highlands or the migration of ethnic or linguistic groups through the region. The tendency to view social complexity as an import to southern Caucasia has shaped archaeological investigations in the region to both good and ill effect. The regular ebb and flow of peoples across the Caucasian isthmus necessitates an appreciation of the cosmopolitanism of the region, forged in dynamic links to surrounding areas that profoundly influenced technological, social, political, and cultural transformations throughout the *ecumene*.

Unfortunately, this cosmopolitan point of view often boils down to an overweening "typologism," a preoccupation with artifactual morphology to the exclusion of an account of the anthropological and historical significance of formal and stylistic parallels. Thus the reigning preoccupation with the determining role of external stimuli in the formation of complex societies has come at the expense of more regional and local accounts of political and social transformation. The observation of morphological parallels between Caucasian materials and artifacts from various regions of western Asia or eastern Europe cannot suffice as a framework for thinking about the rise of complexity for (at least) three reasons. First, description of stylistic and formal similarities tends to obscure underlying differences in systems of production and exchange. That is, there are numerous ways to produce similar implements. What is critical for archaeological understanding is less simple similarities in form or design than shared or dissimilar approaches to the social organization of manufacture, trade, and consumption. Second, accounts of morphological parallels often mistake emulation or adoption of material culture characteristics as an embrace of original uses and meanings, unwisely assuming stability in the cultural significance of artifacts (Kramer 1977; Stein 1998). Last, as a result of the reigning typological cosmopolitanism, the primary theoretical stakes in the investigation of complexity in the region are, within the current dominant intellectual constellation, exceedingly low, limited to amplifying the local reverberations of traditional centers of cultural development in southwest Asia and on the Eurasian steppe.

Since the collapse of the Soviet Union, vast sociopolitical changes have transformed the parameters of archaeological field research in southern Caucasia, offering a new opportunity to raise the stakes in the study of early complex societies throughout the Highlands.

On a practical level this ongoing transformation has resulted in the expansion of the range of methodological procedures employed in field research and promoted the articulation of material culture sequences that transcend traditional geographic boundaries. However, what has yet to emerge from this collaborative enterprise is a new understanding of the impetus to investigation, of the intellectual agenda orienting investigations of complex societies in southern Caucasia, in particular, and the Highlands as a whole. In the absence of such an orienting framework, approaches to complex societies in the region remain hamstrung by the enduring theoretical priorities of a now bygone era—an era where southern Caucasia and eastern Anatolia were severed from each other by a well-patrolled boundary created by geopolitical rivalries that fragmented inquiry into the region's prehistory and early history. In such a climate, it is no wonder that archaeologists largely trained in the academies of rival "great powers," each with such profound strategic interests in the region, came to follow Khorenats'i, reconstructing political complexity as an import, a gift of imperialism (or at least adventurism) rather than a homegrown phenomenon.

Although we must be careful not to allow the pendulum to swing too far in the other direction and encourage isolationist or nativist revisions of ancient sociopolitical history (see Kohl and Tsetskhladze 1995), the advent of newly independent states in the Caucasus provides us with the opportunity to achieve a more evenhanded account of sociopolitical development in the region. Such balance requires that we reframe the problem of complexity in southern Caucasia as one that arises at the intersection of local communities and the wider ecumene.

FRAMING COMPLEXITY

Due to the political fragmentation of the Highlands during most of the twentieth century, the investigation of pre-Urartian episodes of political coalescence has a very different research history in eastern Anatolia than in southern Caucasia. Exploration of the rise of complex polities in eastern Anatolia has been limited by a dearth of archaeological investigations in the region focused specifically on the Late Bronze and Early Iron Ages that might flesh out the thin references to political coalescence contained in Assyrian written sources. As a result, archaeological models of early complex societies in the region focus primarily upon the formation and expansion of Urartu with little reference to its predecessors (*pace* Burney and Lang 1972).

In contrast, the study of pre-Urartian societies has a long and rich history in southern Caucasia, beginning with the architectural surveys of T. Toramanyan (1942), A. Kalantar (1925), and N. Marr (Khachatryan 1974) in the late nineteenth and early twentieth centuries and continuing through contemporary surveys and excavations by Biscione (chapter 8), Kafadarian (1996), Khanzadian (1995), and Petrosyan (1989) to name only a few. Yet despite this research history, as in eastern Anatolia it is the arrival of Urartian armies in the Ararat plain that marks the founding moment of the state in southern Caucasia in both the scholarly and popular imaginations. The centrality of Urartu in the popular imagination of modern Armenia is most visibly expressed in the numerous monuments that employ Urartian artifacts and imagery to commemorate contemporary events. The ceremony held in 1968 to commemorate the 2750th anniversary of the founding of the Urartian fortress of Erebuni as the origin of modern Yerevan clearly marked Urartu as the progenitor of the modern state in southern Caucasia. In the scholarly imagination, one need only note the restricted scope of the 1985 summary volume in the Arkheologiya SSSR series *Drevneishie Gosudarstva Kavkaza i Srednei Azii* (Ancient States of the Caucasus and Central Asia; Koshelenko 1985), which begins its survey with Urartu in order to understand the marginal significance traditionally accorded pre-Urartian complex societies.

Before proceeding further, it is important that we clearly define what is meant by the term *complex*. The term is most often used to refer to a general set of sociocultural features such as inequality in access to resources, variability in social roles, differentiation of decision-making bodies, permanence of institutions, and the distribution and flow of symbols, meanings, and practices (Hannerz 1992; McGuire 1983; Tainter 1988:23-31). In contrast to the categorical descriptor "state," a noun with pretensions to describe a structurally real social form, complex is an adjective describing the *relative* extent, heterogeneity, and differentiation of sociocultural formations. Since the revival of evolutionary theory in the 1950s, archaeological examinations of archaic states have been primarily concerned to define trajectories of social formations to render translucent the general conditions under which polities coalesce, transform, and collapse (for example, Adams 1966; Childe 1950; Harris 1979; Service 1975).

This approach has served relatively well in constructing operational typologies of political forms (Fried 1967;

Johnson and Earle 1987; Service 1962; Southall 1965), outlining structural axes along which change occurs (Claessen 1984; Flannery 1972; Haas 1982; Wright 1977), and articulating a handful of variables (economic, demographic, ecological, and sociological) that may affect directions of long-term political change (Carneiro 1970; Renfrew 1975; Wittfogel 1957; Wright 1978). However, as a number of writers have observed (Marcus and Feinman 1998; Shennan 1993; Southall 1991), this agenda has left us with a surprisingly underdeveloped sense of what early complex societies actually did—how regimes formed, organized institutions, and established sovereignty—and the relationships they established. Southern Caucasia, on which the marks of sociopolitical relationships are deeply etched, provides an ideal setting for an archaeological examination of these relationships.

Because current models of emergent sociopolitical complexity in southern Caucasia hinge upon the origins of the Urartian Kingdom and its defeat of local "tribes" north of the Araxes River, it is important that we briefly reflect upon the extant accounts of Urartian origins in order to open both historical and theoretical space for a discussion of complexity in the Late Bronze and Early Iron Ages.[1] The formation of Urartu has been described as primarily a side effect of Assyrian imperial expansion, either by invoking displaced trade routes (Barnett 1956), struggles for control over resources (Levine 1976:178; Saggs 1962:114), or pressures to political aggregation resulting from a sustained, if circumscribed, military threat (Zimansky 1985:3).[2] It is difficult to underestimate the prominence accorded to Assyria in Urartian political formation. Art historical studies have taken the lead in locating the source of Urartu, as a unified political aesthetic, in Mesopotamia:

> ...at least the art of Urartu, like the art of the Neo-Assyrian Empire, arose on the foundations of a common Near Eastern culture, the intellectual contents of which originated from southern Mesopotamia, but the material acquisition of which had its roots often in Syria and Phoenicia. [van Loon 1975b:454]

> ....Urartian was at its beginnings a provincial but successful variation (=German *Abart*) of the classical Assyrian style. [Akurgal 1968:63]

The effort to envelope Urartian art within a broader category of either Assyrian or southwest Asian traditions represents a particular approach to the aesthetic that tends to focus on tracking formal and stylistic resonances rather than modeling the practical reasons for emulation or the transformation in cultural meanings of a given style that accompany transplantation from one locale to another. A recent study of its political aesthetics by Smith (2000) suggests that while Urartu may indeed have borrowed representational techniques from traditions to the south, as van Loon and Akurgal rightly point out, they were deployed within very different, and perhaps internally inconsistent, political strategies.

Beyond the purely artistic, both Zimansky and Dinçol have forwarded more embracing accounts of the role of Assyria in Urartian political formation. In one of the first anthropologically oriented studies of Urartian political organization, Zimansky argues that:

> Urartu's political and economic institutions may be better understood as an adaptation to an environment that was shaped by…the might and proximity of the Assyrian army, and the potential for defense offered by east Anatolian climate and topography. [Zimansky 1985:3]

In a similar, though more historicist, spirit, Dinçol has suggested that Assyrian pressure might not have been sufficient to stimulate the "tribes" of eastern Anatolia to state formation:

> We have already mentioned that the constant Assyrian threat to the ore deposits may have been a reason for the foundation of the Urartian state….However, this

does not explain why the center of the new state was removed to the east of Lake Van. Was the constant Assyrian pressure from the south the only reason, or was there an immigration of southern tribes with experience in the organization of the state? [1994:17]

There are two difficulties with the essentially diffusionist account of Urartian political formation in general, and with Dinçol's rendering in particular, that we wish to point out.

The first is the description of Assyrian pressure upon Highland polities and resources as "constant". The earliest references to Assyrian military adventurism in the Highlands date to the reign of Shalmaneser I (1273–1244 BC),[3] who referred to campaigns in the lands of "Uruatri" (table 7.1; Salvini 1967). Shalmaneser's successor, Tukulti-Ninurta I (1243–1207 BC) also campaigned in the mountains to the north against the "forty kings of Nairi" (Barnett 1982:329), a geographic referent that was later incorporated into the Urartian royal titulary. In some inscriptions (Grayson 1987:A.0.77.1), Nairi and Ur(u)atri appear to be general geographical designations while in others (Grayson 1987:A.0.87.1), they appear to denote polities, or confederacies of polities united in their resistance to Assyrian hegemony.

References to both Nairi and Ur(u)atri are rather infrequent in Assyrian royal inscriptions until the mid-ninth century BC.[4] In the earliest known reference

Assyrian King	Date B.C.	Campaign Against	References
Shalmaneser III 858-824 B.C.	858, 856, 844 858	Aramu the Urartian Kakia king of Nairi	Luckenbill 1989: 232 Luckenbill 1989: 200-210
Ashurnasirpal II 883-859 B.C.	Early 9th century	Nairi Urartu	Grayson 1987: A.0.101.1,17,30
Adad-nirari II 911-891 B.C.	Late 10th century	Uratri Nairi	Grayson 1987: A.0.99.2
Ashur-bel-kala 1073-1056 B.C.	c.1070	Uruatri	Grayson 1987: A.0.89.2
Tiglath-pileser I 1114-1076 B.C.	c.1114	23 kings of Nairi 60 kings of Nairi	Grayson 1987: A.0.87.1,3,4,15, 16
Tukulti-ninurta I 1243-1207 B.C.	late 13th cent.	40 kings of Nairi lands	Grayson 1987: A.0.78.5
Shalmaneser I 1273-1244 B.C.	c. 1273	8 lands of Uruatri	Grayson 1987: A.0.77.1

Table 7.1 Assyrian Campaigns in the Armenian Highlands, 1300–844 BC according to Assyrian Sources (from Barnett 1982; Salvini 1995)

Years B.C.	Periodization		Horizon Style	Key Sites
500	Middle Iron Age	Achaemenid	Achaemenid	Erebuni, Armavir
600		Urartu	Urartu	Erebuni, Karmir-Blur, Oshakan, Aramus, Argishtihinili
700				
800	Early Iron Age	Early Iron II	Lchashen-Metsamor Horizon	Horom, Elar, Keti, Metsamor
900				
1000				
1100				
1200	Late Bronze Age	Early Iron I/ Late Bronze III		Metsamor Artik (group 3) Dvin (burnt level)
1300		Late Bronze II		Lchashen Artik (groups 1-2) Karashamb, Lori-Berd
1400				
1500		Late Bronze I/ Middle Bronze IV		Shamiram (burials) Karashamb, Horom, Talin
1600	Middle Bronze Age	Middle Bronze III	Sevan, Karmirberd, and Karmirvank Horizons	Karmir-Berd, Lchashen, Horom, Uzerlik 2-3
1700				
1800		Middle Bronze II	Trialeti-Vanadzor Horizon	Karashamb (kurgan) Vanadzor (Kirovakan) Trialeti (groups 1-3) Lchashen (120-123) Lori-Berd Uzerlik 1
1900				
2000				
2100		Middle Bronze I/ Early Bronze IV	"Kurgan" Horizon	Trialeti (group 1) Berkaber (burials 1-2) Stepanakert
2200				
2300	Early Bronze Age			
2400		Early Bronze III	Kura-Araxes Horizon	Shengavit (3-4) Garni, Dvin, Karnut, Harich
2500				
2600		Early Bronze II		Mokhrablur Shresh-blur
2700				
2800				
2900		Early Bronze I		Djervesh (Kurgan 1) Harich (early phase) Keti (burials 1-6) Horom (tomb C1)
3000				
3100				
3200				

Table 7.2 Chronology and Periodization of Southern Caucasia, 3300–500 BC.

to an individual ruler of a coherent and unified Urartian polity, Shalmaneser III claims to have attacked and destroyed the royal fortress of "Aramu the Urartian," a much-touted victory recorded on the Black Obelisk (Luckenbill 1989:202) and Kurba'il Statue (Wilson 1962) from Nimrud and depicted on the bronze gates from Balawat (King 1915). However, by this time, Urartu seems to have already emerged as a polity of considerable regional power. Assyria's sporadic expeditions to the highlands are thus of questionable import to the political development of the region. Indeed, rather than Urartu coalescing in response to Assyrian incursions, it seems quite possible that Assyrian campaigning in the highlands quickened during the ninth century BC as a belated response to the full fluorescence of a threatening new rival on its northern flank.

The second difficulty with the diffusionist reading of Urartian origins lies in the assumption that complex polities did not already exist in the Highlands—that "expertise" in state building would have to come from the south or that episodes of complexity in western Asia must directly articulate with a singular tradition rooted in Mesopotamia. In part this interpretive impulse to link all histories to Mesopotamia arises from a failure to adequately theorize the problems associated with cultural exchange and transmission. However, the tendency to seek explanatory determinacy for Highland social formations in the "grand tradition" also arises from a lack of familiarity with the south Caucasian archaeological record. The great weight of archaeological evidence from southern Caucasia strongly indicates that the emergence of sociopolitical complexity has roots that run as deep as the Middle Bronze Age of the early second millennium BC within a related, yet distinct, sociopolitical tradition (table 7.2).

Under the auspices of the Kura-Araxes material culture horizon, southern Caucasia became closely tied into an Early Bronze Age regional ecumene which extended from the Caucasus to the Taurus mountains. The communities of this ecumene not only shared similar material culture complexes and landscapes but also were closely conjoined in the tempo and rhythms of sociocultural transformations. The end of the Early and beginning of the Middle Bronze Age within southern Caucasia was marked by the disappearance of the Kura-Araxes horizon and the large-scale abandonment of settled village communities. This transformation in settlement patterns is perhaps the most conspicuous feature of the Middle Bronze Age transition. Except for the late third millennium BC layers from the Bedeni

sites, there is little evidence for continuity in Early and Middle Bronze Age occupations and, indeed, very few Middle Bronze Age settlements have been documented in southern Caucasia. As a result, the vast majority of the archaeological record for the Middle Bronze Age comes from mortuary sites. The tombs and kurgans of Shengavit, Trialeti (old group), Martkopi, Shulaveri, Berkaber, Maisian, and Bedeni trumpet profound social, cultural, and political transformations underway during the third quarter of the third millennium BC. With the collapse of the Kura-Araxes horizon in southern Caucasia, the close interregional ties that had drawn the area together also fray and break as several discrete material culture horizons divide the highland ecumene following the staggered close of the Early Bronze Age. The monumental architectural complex at Norşuntepe indicates a still flourishing Kura-Araxes horizon in the southwestern part of the ecumene even as Middle Bronze Age burials had already made their appearance in southern Caucasia.[5]

The shift in settlement patterns in southern Caucasia during the Early to Middle Bronze transition is traditionally interpreted as evidence of the advent of increasingly nomadic social groups predicated upon pastoral subsistence production. The appearance of ox and horse sacrifices in numerous Middle Bronze I and II burials further attests to the increased prominence of pastoral production and equestrian mobility within these communities. The shifting subsistence economy was also accompanied by fundamental transformations in the social milieu, changes that center on emerging radical inequality between a martial elite and the remainder of the social body. The rich inventory of the enormous kurgans of the Middle Bronze Age signify a profound departure in social relations indicated by the collective burials of the Kura-Araxes phase (such as those documented at Velikent, see Kohl, chapter 1). Even more dramatic expressions of this inequality are visible in the Middle Bronze II period when a great part of highland Caucasia was enveloped in the so called Trialeti-Vanadzor (Kirovakan) horizon, which, despite local territorial and chronologically distinct groupings, still presents burial complexes of unprecedented wealth (differences along the eastern border of this horizon do not change the whole picture). The monumental construction and rich mortuary goods of tombs from Vanadzor, Karashamb, and Lori Berd, as well as the iconography of elite privilege portrayed on the metal vessels from Karashamb and Korukh Tash, testify to profound changes in the social orders of southern

Caucasia and provide the initial indications of emergent sociopolitical complexity in the region. In addition, it is during this period that cuneiform texts from Kültepe and Mari refer to small kingdoms in the western districts of the Armenian Highlands.

During the Middle Bronze III period the fragmentation of the Highlands into distinct material culture horizons produced new divisions within southern Caucasia itself. If the Trialeti-Vanadzor sites present us with a relatively homogeneous horizon style for the Middle Bronze II phase, transformations in burial construction and the forms and styles of painted and black ornamented pottery during the succeeding period indicate the differentiation of the region into at least three contemporary, yet geographically distinct, archaeological horizons: Karmir-Berd, Sevan-Uzerlik, and Karmir-Vank. Karmir-Berd materials largely prevail in the Ararat and Shirak plains and on the slopes of Mt. Aragats; the Sevan-Uzerlik horizon tends to predominate in the Sevan, Artsakh, and Syunik regions up to the margins of the Karabakh highlands and the Mughan Steppe; and the Karmir-Vank horizon is best known from Nakhichevan and the painted pottery of Haftavan Tepe. These general regional divisions cannot be taken as rigid geographic mosaics. Sevan basin sites have also yielded evidence of Karmir-Vank and Karmir-Berd painted pottery; Ararat plain sites have included both Karmir-Berd and Sevan-Uzerlik materials and Sevan sites contain both Karmir-Berd and Sevan-Uzerlik ceramics. In Georgia, the Trialeti-Vanadzor horizon persists at sites such as Treli, Tsavgli, Natakhtari, and Pevrebi, but it is also possible to detect Sevan-Uzerlik complexes as well, represented by the typical black pottery with dotted lines. In contrast to these mixed assemblages, several Middle Bronze III settlements do present occupation layers boasting ceramics only of specific horizons, such as Mukhanat Tapa, Aygevan, Jrahovit, Metsamor, Lori Berd, and Shirakavan.

During the Middle Bronze III phase, the wealth of the burial inventories seen in the preceding phase begins to diminish such that in the complexes represented by Karmir-Berd or Karmir-Berd/Sevan Uzerlik pottery one can discern only limited bronze artifacts. Furthermore, in the complexes that signify the end of Middle Bronze Age, the distinctive painted vessels become increasingly rare, yielding to the incised gray and black ware ceramics that came to predominate under the Lchashen-Metsamor horizon of the Late Bronze Age.

There remains considerable disagreement over the causes and extent of the Middle Bronze Age social transformations. A great deal of debate in the 1960s and 1970s centered on the sources of the Middle Bronze archaeological horizons and the extent of the break with Early Bronze Age traditions. A number of scholars, particularly G. A. Melikishvili (1965a:22), argued that there was no continuity between the two periods and that the advent of the Middle Bronze Age should be traced to the incursion into southern Caucasia of ethnic communities from southwest Asia. In particular, Melikishvili implicates an expansion of Hurrian groups in the founding of the Trialeti horizon. C. A. Burney (1958) earlier argued a similar position, suggesting that the Kura-Araxes collapse might be attributable to the advance of an Indo-European population from the Eurasian steppe.

Counterposed to these theories of ethnic replacement are a number of studies that downplay the extent of early second millennium material culture change in order to document the local roots of the Middle Bronze Age. Gogadze (1970, 1972a), Kuftin (1940), Piotrovskii (1949: 46), Japaridze (1969:270), and Martirosian (1964:48), among others, have argued that the Middle Bronze Age horizons, and Trialeti in particular, rested firmly on a local cultural tradition. While various groups did move into and through the Caucasus, such migrations did not, these researchers argue, fundamentally transform the trajectory of local historical development.

More recent investigations have sought to interpret the Early to Middle Bronze Age transition less in terms of an historical genesis and more in light of sociocultural processes. The prominence of equestrian artifacts in the archaeological record of the Middle Bronze Age led I. M. Diakonoff (1984:16) to explain the radical change in settlement patterns in reference to the advent of horse domestication, suggesting that a new variant of nomadism built around equestrian skills led to the exploitation of mountain pastures remote from settlements and the dissolution of the social structures of the village (see Puturidze this volume). The accumulation of wealth represented in the Middle Bronze Age kurgans, Diakonoff argues, indicates an emergent stratified class order dominated by an elite closely identified with the activities of battle and long-distance trade. The fluidity of movement encouraged by this new way of life would have severely tested any established claims to territory established in the more sedentary Kura-Araxes period, a challenge Diakonoff suggests led in turn to an increasing concern with metalwork and weaponry.

Kushnareva (1997:207–208) forwards a synthetic position, where a transition to pastoralism centered in mountain zones rather than on the highland margins exploited in the Early Bronze Age, perhaps driven by a newly arid climate, was exacerbated by new waves of migration. These migrants left their mark in the archaeological record in the form of numerous burnt levels at settlements such as Uzerlik Tepe and Ilto. The invocation of a relatively poorly assayed climatic change as a driving force in such dramatic social change is not particularly satisfying in accounting for the particular direction of sociopolitical transformation taken by communities at the end of the Early Bronze Age (nor is the assumption that ethnic conflict invariably follows ethnic contact). However, Kushnareva does effectively integrate a sense of the global forces at work on a microscale.

The chronology and periodization of sites and material culture horizons remains a lingering problem in the interpretation of post-Kura-Araxes social transformations. Sites signifying the end of Middle Bronze Age have been ascribed to the beginning of this period and vice versa, distorting the panorama of economic and cultural developments of the region. While we find the move to more processual accounts of the Early to Middle Bronze Age transition heartening and ultimately more convincing than earlier historicist interpretations, a full discussion of late third and early second millennia BC social transformations must await a different forum. What is most critical for this discussion of the emergence of sociopolitical complexity in southern Caucasia is the observation that Middle Bronze Age horizons indicate an increasing degree of social inequality, predicated upon an elite culture of martial heroics. Yet there are few indications at present that this social stratification was formalized into an institutional matrix. For this we must turn to the succeeding Late Bronze Age.

It is during the Late Bronze Age that we see the first clear evidence for sociopolitical complexity in southern Caucasia—what Kohl (1993:128) has referred to as "a Late Bronze/Early Iron state formation" and Piotrovskii (quoted in Khachatryan 1975:127) described as "a period of cultural blossoming and independent development." The Late Bronze Age is marked most conspicuously by the reappearance of numerous permanent settlements in the form of variably sized stone-masonry fortresses built atop hills and outcrops. The transition between the Middle and Late Bronze Age is also marked by the gradual

introduction of new ceramic forms and decorative styles—most notably the disappearance of painted pottery and punctate designs in favor of suites of black, gray, and buff wares with incised decorations—as well as new approaches to metallurgical production. With the opening of the Late Bronze Age, the social inequalities visible in the kurgans of the early second millennium appear to have been formalized into a tightly integrated sociopolitical apparatus where critical controls over resources—economic, social, sacred—were concentrated within the cyclopean stone masonry walls of powerful new centers. What is most notable about the era is the unprecedented transformation of the built and unbuilt environment, a process likely focused in fortified political centers but projected well into the hinterlands through large-scale irrigation works, deforestation (promoted by increasing energy needs of metal producers), and new mortuary rituals and burial architecture. It is the florescence of sociopolitical complexity four centuries prior to Assyrian incursions into eastern Anatolia and seven hundred years before Urartian forces crossed the Araxes that is the central concern of the remainder of this chapter. Before proceeding with a discussion of the character of sociopolitical complexity in the region, it is important that we establish the chronological parameters of the era and its archaeological signatures.

ADVANCES IN CHRONOLOGY AND PERIODIZATION OF THE LATE BRONZE AND EARLY IRON AGES

Examinations of Late Bronze and Early Iron Age fortresses in southern Caucasia began in the late nineteenth and early twentieth centuries when archaeologists and architectural historians embarked on a series of nonsystematic surveys to document the settlement history of the region (Adzhan et al. 1932; Kalantar 1994; Piotrovskii and Gyuzal'yan 1933; Toramanyan 1942). Subsequent explorations have greatly expanded our understanding of fortification architecture under the Lchashen-Metsamor horizon (Esaian 1976; Kafadarian 1996; Mikayelyan 1968; Pitskhelauri 1979). Unfortunately, only a handful of Late Bronze or Early Iron Age fortresses, most notably Elar (Khanzadian 1979), Horom South (Badaljan et al. 1992, 1993, 1994), Keti (Petrosyan 1989), and Metsamor (Khanzadian et al. 1973), have hosted intensive research to date and evidence of unfortified settlements remains scarce. Archaeological investigations have focused more resolutely on late second/early first millennia BC cemeteries. Large mortuary complexes at Lchashen (Mnatsakanyan, 1960, 1961,1965), Artik (Khachatryan 1963, 1975, 1979), Horom (Avetisyan and Badalyan 1996), Keti (Petrosyan 1989), Lori-Berd (Devedzhyan 1981, 1986), to name a few, have provided our most extensive orientation to the

material culture of the era as well as providing the primary basis for archaeological chronology.

A number of archaeological chronologies have been proposed over the last half-century for both the era of the Late Bronze and Early Iron Age as a whole and for specific sites and material categories.[6] However, these efforts have consistently stumbled on three significant constraints in the available data: the lack of stratified

Provenance	Lab Code and Number	C14 age (BP)	Calibrated Age B.C. 1 Sigma	2 Sigma
Tsakahovit, West Terrace 1	AA 31034	3015 ± 45	1380-1130	1400-1120
Tsakahovit, West Terrace 1	AA 31035	3040 ± 45	1390-1210	1410-1120
Tsakahovit, West Terrace 1	AA 31036	2975 ± 50	1300-1110	1380-1020
Horom, South M-7	AA-12859	3145 ± 55	1450-1310	1530-1260
Horom, South M-7	AA-12858	3045 ± 75	1410-1130	1450-1040
Horom, North C-3a	AA-10193	2975 ± 55	1310-1090	1380-1010
Horom, North,B-2,4	AA-12860	2850 ± 55	1130-920	1220-830
Horom, North,B-2	AA-11129	2770 ± 55	980-830	1050-800
Horom, E-3	AA-21287	3240 ± 50	1600-1430	1680-1400
Horom, tomb 53	LE-3596	3480 ± 70	1890-1690	1980-1610
Horom, tomb 111	LE-3597	3090 ± 40	1420-1260	1440-1210
Horom, tomb 116	LE-3598	2890 ± 70	1210-940	1310-890
Horom, tomb 151	LE-3928	2825 ± 432	1600-400	2200BC-AD100
Horom, tomb 124	LE-3930	2641 ± 266	1150-400	1500-100
Artik, tomb 223	LE-818	2850 ± 50	1120-920	1220-840
Dvin	LE ?	2670 ± 70	900-790	1010-590
Metsamor, burnt level	IGN-9340	2750 ± 40	920-830	1000-820
Metsamor, burnt level	IGN-9341	2750 ± 110	1040-800	1300-550
Metsamor, burnt level	IGN-9342	3300 ± 360	2150-1100	2700-700
Lchashen, unknown	MGU-29	3500 ± 100	1950-1680	2150-1500
Lchashen, unknown	MGU-30	3630 ± 100	2140-1820	2300-1650
Dates calibrated using atmospheric data from Stuiver et al (1998) with OxCal v. 3.5 (Ramsey 2000) AA – University of Arizona AMS Facility; IGN - Institute of Geological Sciences; Moscow; LE - Leningrad Institute of Archaeology; MGU - Moscow State University.				

Table 7.3 Radiocarbon Dates from Southern Caucasia for the Late Bronze and Early Iron Ages.

Late Bronze/Early Iron Age occupation layers, an underdeveloped understanding of variation in ceramic form and decoration from the Late Bronze Age through the locally made wares of the Urartian era, and a lack of absolute dates to anchor periodization (table 7.3).

Recent investigations in the region have dramatically broadened the extant archaeological sources for the Late Bronze and Early Iron Ages and provided new ground for chronological refinement. Increasingly systematic applications of radiocarbon dating and calibration allow us to propose a revised periodization and chronology for the Late Bronze and Early Iron Ages of southern Caucasia. The Late Bronze Age in the region differs from the preceding Middle Bronze Age in numerous respects, but is most prominently marked archaeologically by the appearance of "cyclopean" fortified settlements, an explosion in the number and extent of cemeteries, shifts in technologies of metallurgical production, and broad alterations in the volume, morphology, and decorative aesthetics of a broad range of artifacts.

The data currently available allow us to divide the Late Bronze Age into three sequential phases, each of which is characterized by distinctive features. The first phase of the Late Bronze Age is characterized by a combination of decorative and formal elements from the Middle Bronze Age with new elements that emerge in succeeding phases as characteristic of the Late Bronze Age (hence its notation as the Middle Bronze IV/Late Bronze I transitional phase). One can trace these combinations of features in the material remains from several cemeteries and multi-component settlements (for example, Lchashen, Lori Berd, Shirakavan, Aparan 2). The stratigraphic positioning of these transitional complexes allows us to establish the Late Bronze I as a discrete phase within the relative chronology of the region. Calibrated radiocarbon dates from the Middle Bronze Age layer on the north hill at Horom and the early Late Bronze level on that site's southern hill indicate that the beginning of the first phase of the Late Bronze Age should be assigned to the middle of the sixteenth century BC.

The Late Bronze II phase is characterized by classic examples of Late Bronze industry, such as battle axes of the "Transcaucasian type," daggers with cylindrical handles, flanged hilt daggers, wheel-shaped bits, and metal statuettes of the Lchashen type. A set of exotic finds, most notably, Mitannian "common style" cylinder seals from the Lchashen (no. 97), Artik (nos. 53, 422), and Shamiram (no. 5) cemeteries suggest parallels with finds from Nuzi and the Levant.[7] Radiocarbon dates from levels at Horom South that bear analogous Late Bronze II materials have led Avetisyan et al. (1996) to suggest an approximate date for the Late Bronze II from the fifteenth to the early thirteenth century BC.

The Late Bronze III phase is distinguished by a repertoire of metal forms unknown in Late Bronze II contexts, including swords with a blunt head, bronze daggers of the Sevan type, hooked arrowheads of the Transcaucasian type, ornamented and plain belts, and bronze knives with curved tips. Radiocarbon dates from an Early Iron I burial (no. 223) at Artik provides a terminus for the Late Bronze III in the late twelfth century BC. Therefore we can posit a relatively short Late Bronze III period extending from the mid-thirteenth to mid-twelfth centuries BC. New radiocarbon dates from Tsakahovit fortress from levels replete with Late Bronze II and III ceramics confirm that these phases should be established between the fifteenth and twelfth centuries BC (Avetisyan et al. 2000).

The florescence of the Early Iron Age, an era marked technologically by an expansion of the repertoire of iron implements, was brought to an end in the region by Urartian imperial expansion in the early eighth century BC, providing a rather emphatic terminus for the period visible in the destruction levels at Metsamor (Khanzadian et al. 1973) and Dvin (Kushnareva 1977). Pottery from Early Iron Age levels is substantially different from both LB III and Urartian wares. Examinations of materials recovered from mortuary contexts suggest that the Early Iron Age can be divided into two distinct phases: a transitional Early Iron I, dated conventionally to the late twelfth and eleventh centuries BC, and an Early Iron II phase during the tenth and ninth centuries BC. At present, we lack absolute dates for marking this transition more accurately and well-stratified contexts for thoroughly describing the formal dimensions of material change.

In now moving to the extant archaeological data bearing upon the emergence of complex societies in the Tsakahovit plain of western Armenia, it is important to keep in mind the remaining chronological limitations in our understanding of the second and early first millennia BC as these restrictions profoundly shape the temporal resolution of potential models for sociohistorical transformations.

Project ArAGATS

**Late Bronze and Early Iron Age Fortresses
of the Mt. Aragats Region, Armenia**

Source: Landsat 7 ETM

Figure 7.2 Late Bronze and Early Iron Age Fortresses of the Mt. Aragats Region (An Annotated Landsat 7 Earth Thematic Mapper Image).

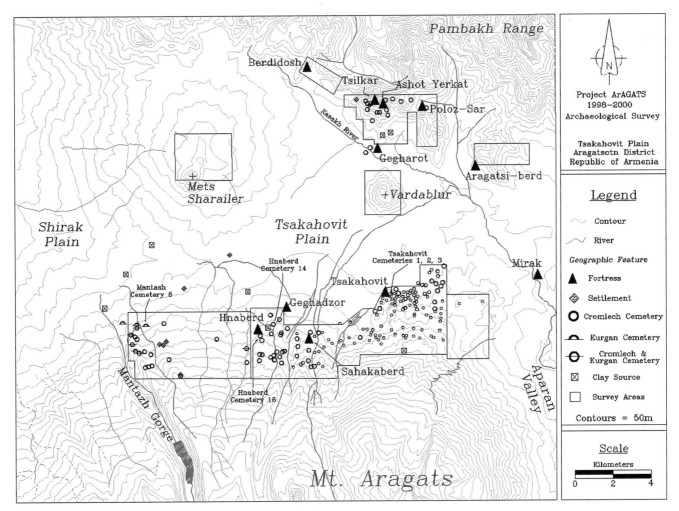

Figure 7.3 Late Bronze Age Sites of the Tsakahovit Plain, Armenia.

THE TSAKAHOVIT PLAIN AS A CASE STUDY

The Tsakahovit plain is set between the northern slope of Mt. Aragats (4090 m), the southern slopes of the Pambak range, and Mt. Kolgat in central western Armenia (figures 7.2 and 7.3). The Tsakahovit plain (2000 m above sea level), 10–12 km across at its maximum extent, was filled in by Middle Quaternary lava flows and Middle Pleistocene and Holocene riverine and glacial deposits (Zograbyan 1979). The regional landscape is classified as mountain-steppe yielding to alpine conditions near the summit of Mt. Aragats. The plain is used today for irrigation-based cultivation while the surrounding mountain slopes offer pasture for livestock. The Tsakahovit basin was selected as the focus of our investigations into the roots of complex societies in southern Caucasia for three reasons: 1) some research had been done in the region previously, lending a foundation for continued work and alerting us to the pronounced and well-preserved remains attributable to the early phases of complex sociopolitical formation in the Late Bronze Age, 2) the region offers a relatively self-contained locale bounded on all sides by mountains but articulated with surrounding regions through well-worn trade routes, and 3) the research area was outside of the areas of direct Urartian occupation, a significant concern given the Urartian tendency to tear down the fortresses of their predecessors.

Archaeological research in the Tsakahovit plain began with a brief visit to the region by Nikolai Marr in 1893 who recorded several large fortresses, including Hnaberd and Tsakahovit, as well as numerous cemetery complexes (Khachatryan 1974). Marr's passage through the region provided a template that was repeated by Toramanyan (1942), Adzhan et al. (1932), and Kafadaryan (1996), who rerecorded the "cyclopean" fortresses in the region in increasing detail. The only excavations conducted in the Tsakahovit plain prior to the commencement of our investigations in 1998 were those of Martirosian (1964:89–93), who opened five Late Bronze Age graves in the modern village of Gegharot in 1956, and Esaian, who examined three additional graves from the same complex in 1960.

During the summers of 1998 and 2000, a joint Armenian-American team led by the authors conducted regional archaeological investigations in the Tsakahovit Plain, the initial phase of a planned multiyear program focused on the roots of sociopolitical complexity in southern Caucasia (Avetisyan et al. 2000; Smith et al. 1999). This initial phase of the research program was centered on a systematic archaeological survey of 85.36 km² of the highlands surrounding the plain (to our knowledge the first intensive walking survey conducted in the Caucasus). Test excavations at five fortresses—Hnaberd (figure 7.4), Tsakahovit (figure 7.5), Gegharot (figure 7.6), Tsilkar (figure 7.7c), and Poloz-Sar (figure 7.7b)—and four cemeteries—Tsakahovit 1, Hnaberd 14 and 18, Mantash 8 (figure 7.3)—complemented the results of the survey, providing depth to the sequences detected on the surface. These investigations were further augmented by targeted examinations of the plain proper, utilizing satellite imagery (Corona, SPOT, Landsat) and two series of aerial photographs (1948 and 1989) complemented by field inspections and subsurface probes (test pits and augur probes). Taken together, this research program has provided the most detailed description to date of the communities forged by early complex societies in the Late Bronze Age and their position within a wider ecumene.

THE TSAKAHOVIT PLAIN IN THE WIDER ECUMENE

Discussions of the ties between local second millennium communities and the wider world have traditionally focused on spectacular finds of exotic artifacts in Caucasian contexts, such as the Kassite weight (Khanzadian et al. 1992) or the New Kingdom Egyptian cylinder seal (Khanzadian and Piotrovskii 1992) found at Metsamor. While such finds are important reminders of the larger world within which southern Caucasian communities were situated, they tell us very little about what kind of part the region played in this global order or about the formal ties that bound the players together. In order to investigate these questions, we must examine more regularized networks of trade and exchange.

Field investigations in the Tsakahovit plain have been amplified by a series of ongoing compositional analyses of obsidian and ceramics/clays from Late Bronze Age contexts. These studies are focused on elaborating the movement of the former into the plain and the latter around the plain. While the Neutron Activation Analyses of the ceramics and clay sources remain at present incomplete, early results of the obsidian source analyses provide intriguing clues as to the links between the Tsakahovit Plain and the wider world.

Seven obsidian samples from Tsakahovit fortress and three from Gegharot fortress were analyzed using X-ray fluorescence techniques.[8] All of the Gegharot obsidians were surface finds while four of the Tsakahovit samples were from the surface and three from the Late Bronze Age occupation level excavated on the citadel. The results of analyses on the Tsakahovit materials indicate that four of the seven samples (three surface and one in situ) originated in the deposits of the Damlik volcano in the Tsakhunyats range, 15 km to the east. Two samples (the last surface find and one from in situ) came from the Arteni volcano on the southwest periphery of the Aragats massif. The remaining sample (from the citadel trench) was traced to the Ttvakar volcano, also part of the Tsakhunyats range, 20 km east of Tsakahovit. All three samples from Gegharot were from the Damlik source.

The connections between the Tsakahovit plain and the Tsakunyats sources were spatially rather immediate but would have nevertheless required exchange relationships with either neighbors to the northeast in the Lori-Pambakh region or to the southeast with polities in the Kasakh river valley. Indeed the Tsakahovit plain was a likely transshipment point for Tsakunyats obsidians known from pre-Urartian contexts in the Shirak plain to the west (Horom and Harich). The Arteni source is comparatively distant and materials would most likely have been brought to the Tsakahovit plain via the Shirak plain. Arteni obsidians are well attested in Shirak plain sites. These very preliminary results suggest that we may begin to position the Tsakahovit region polities during the Late Bronze Age as mediators within exchange networks that looked both east, across the Pambakh range, and west beyond the Shirak plain, for sources and provided distribution ties west to sites in the Shirak plain that also boast Tsakhunyats obsidians. It is important to note that the Tsakhunyats and Pambakh ranges also host considerable copper ore deposits and evidence of mining during the third millennium BC

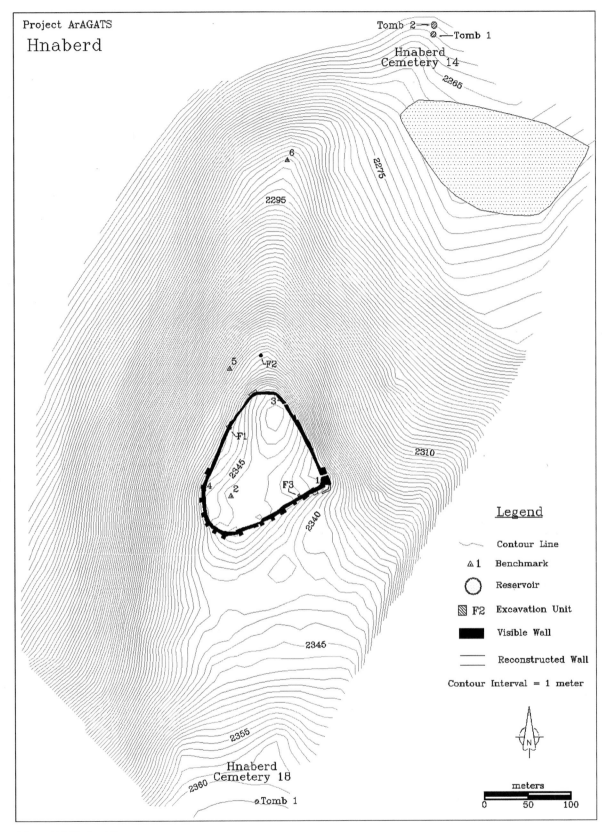

Figure 7.4 Hnaberd Fortress.

(at Fioletovo). In addition, a recent geological survey in the Pambakh hills, in the vicinity of Gegharot, has indicated the existence of copper sources which may have been utilized during the Bronze Age. We suggest that further studies of the metals and ore sources of the region may indicate that Late Bronze Age metallurgical and obsidian trade routes were closely mapped upon each other.

SOVEREIGNTY AND REGIONAL ORGANIZATION

Analysis of patterns of exchange between the Tsakahovit plain and the wider ecumene raises the problem of defining the local scale of sociopolitical integration in the region. That is, at what spatial level was sovereignty, and hence the authority to open and close access to resources both internal and external, organized? Was each fortress effectively an independent polity, sustained by the agricultural and pastoral resources of its hinterland. Or were political communities organized amongst several interlinked fortresses that together ruled larger regions?

Both survey and excavations indicate that the Tsakahovit plain was intensively and extensively occupied during the Late Bronze Age. Surface ceramics and the morphology of fortification architecture suggest that fortresses at Berdidosh, Tsilkar, Ashot-Yerkat (figure 7.7a), Poloz-Sar, and Mirak were all built and occupied during the Late Bronze Age. Excavations at Gegharot,

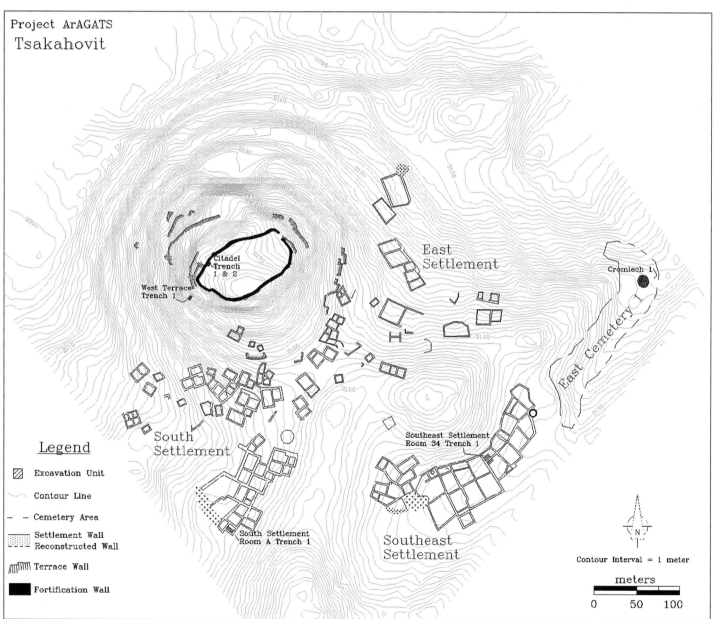

Figure 7.5 Tsakahovit Fortress.

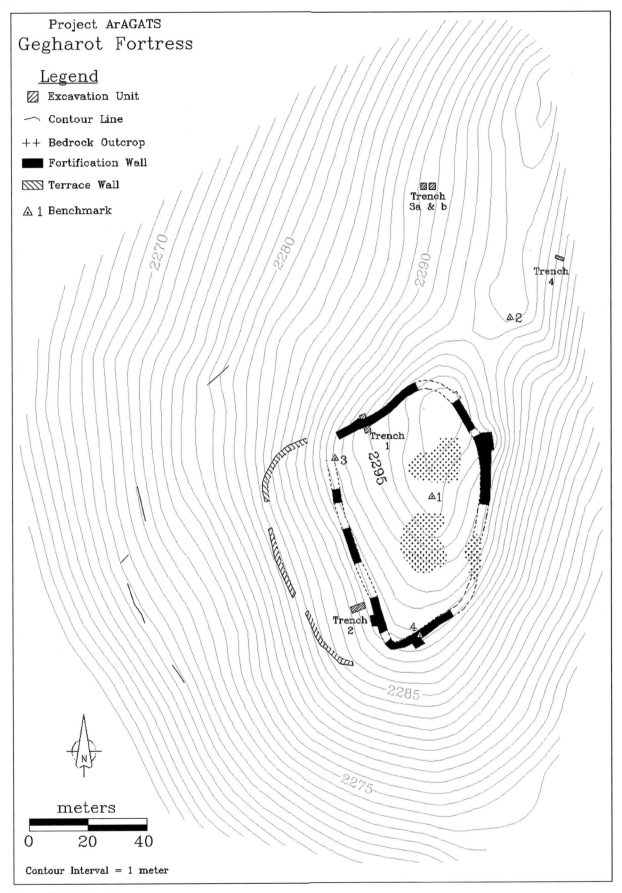

Figure 7.6 Gegharot Fortress.

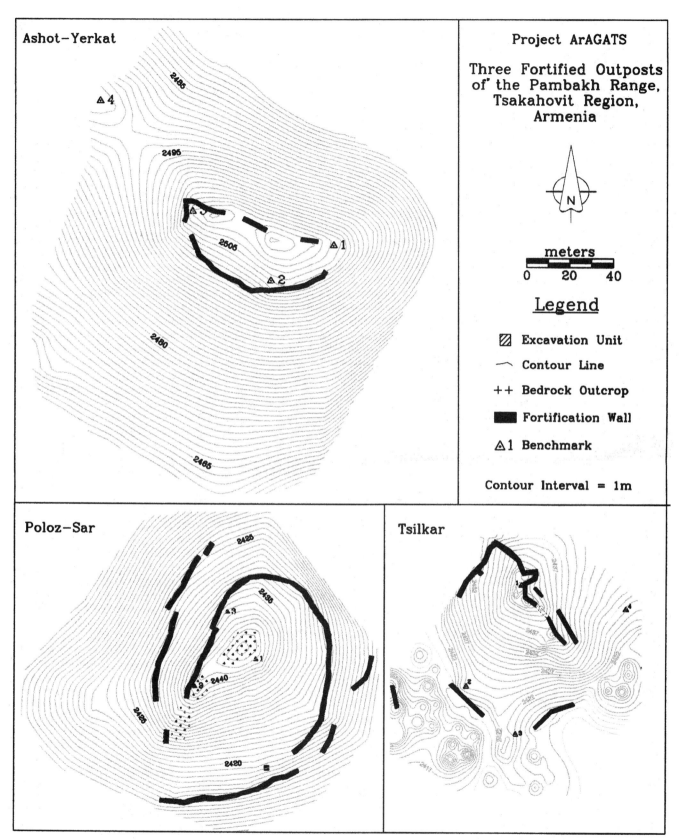

Figure 7.7 Outpost fortresses of the Tsakhaovit Plain: a) Ashot-Yerkat, b) Poloz-Sar, c) Tsilkar.

Tsakahovit, and Hnaberd confirm this assignment of the earliest period of fortress-centered sociopolitical communities to the Late Bronze Age. Radiocarbon dates from a burn layer at Tsakahovit date the destruction of at least a portion of that site to between the early fourteenth and late twelfth centuries BC. Indeed the burn layer at Tsakahovit seems to mark a more dramatic terminus for complex societies in the plain as a whole since none of the fortresses boasted clear evidence for similarly significant Early Iron Age occupations. Indeed, following the Late Bronze Age fluorescence, the next period of major settlement in the region is in the late Urartian/ Achaemenid period of the seventh to fifth centuries BC.

Although our excavations are not particularly extensive at present, investigation of four tombs in the cromlech cemeteries of the central north Aragats slope—Tsakahovit 1, Hnaberd 14 and 18—all uncovered interments dating to the Late Bronze Age. The earliest of these tombs, tomb 2 of Hnaberd 14, included pottery diagnostic of the initial phase of the Late Bronze Age while artifactual complexes from tomb 1 of Hnaberd 14, tomb 1 of Hnaberd 18, and tomb 1 of Tsakahovit 1 embrace the diapason from the Late Bronze I up to the transitional Late Bronze III/Early Iron I phase currently associated with the burned level at Tsakahovit fortress. Indeed, we have found no indisputable indications of an occupation of the region during the early first millennium BC until the reemergence of large settlement and fortress complexes at Hnaberd and Tsakahovit during the late Urartian or Achaemenid era.

The apparent temporal synchronization of settlement across the plain during the mid-second millennium BC provides one indication that the Tsakahovit plain might have been more broadly integrated as a coherent sociopolitical community than we had originally thought (Smith 1996:147). If the plain was fragmented amongst various communities, it would be unusual, though by no means unprecedented, for the rhythms of settlement to so neatly coincide. Conversely, if several fortresses were integrated as part of a larger sociopolitical community then we would expect their occupational sequences to more closely coincide.

More tangible indices of the scale of sociopolitical integration during the Late Bronze Age emerged from the results of the archaeological survey. On the slope of Mt. Aragats, we recorded 162 discrete cemeteries composed of cromlechs (earthen or stone-lined tombs surrounded by stone circles) typical of mortuary architecture under the Lchashen-Metsamor horizon, an overall density of 2.64 cemeteries per km². Although

a true census of the cemeteries is not feasible due to site formation processes, a conservative estimate of 30 cromlechs per cemetery yields a total of 4860 burials within the survey area. Despite the impressive size of the region's Late Bronze Age mortuary population, the most compelling feature of the cromlech cemeteries is their spatial distribution. While the cemeteries are tightly packed within the central 30 km² of the north Aragats slope, extending in an east-west line from 0.5 km west of Hnaberd fortress to 3 km east of Tsakahovit fortress, they virtually disappear beyond these limits. West of Hnaberd fortress, this hiatus in Lchashen-Metsamor horizon mortuary architecture persists up to the eastern bank of Mantash gorge; east of Tsakahovit fortress, the hiatus extends southwest into the Kasakh river valley.

The unexpectedly crisp boundaries of cromlech cemetery construction combined with the current evidence for a chronologically compact explosion of occupation in the region during the Late Bronze Age hint at a broader scale of sociopolitical integration than previously suspected. We suggest that the extent of the mortuary landscape on the north Aragats slope reflects social boundaries established during the Late Bronze Age that index the spatial extent of sovereignty in the region (compare discussions of social boundaries in Stark 1998). That is, the entire north slope of Mt. Aragats was part of a single political formation differentiated from both a southwestern Shirak plain formation (denoted by the mortuary landscape that extends between Mantash gorge, Harich, Artik, and Horom) and a Kasakh river valley formation (incorporating Mirak in the north and likely centered on the large fortress at Aparan).

While the eastern and western thresholds of this formation emerge from the distribution of cemeteries, the extent to which it extended across the plain is less clear at present. The distribution of Late Bronze Age remains in the other sectors of the Tsakahovit plain is highly variable. The flanks of Mt. Kolgat (Mt. Sharai Ler), although strategically located at the intersection of the Tsakahovit and Shirak plains, proved to host extremely low densities of archaeological materials; systematic survey documented only two isolated cromlechs diagnostic of Lchashen-Metsamor horizon mortuary architecture. Mt. Vardablur, which rises out of the eastern center of the Tsakahovit plain, offers a similarly strategic vantage point on its surroundings. Yet it too was found to be largely devoid of archaeological materials. In contrast, our investigations on the slopes of the Pambakh range, on the northeastern edge of the plain, encountered a number of sites with Late Bronze Age occupations. The fortress of Gegharot (Avetisyan et al. 2000) is the largest in this sector of the plain, with stone masonry fortification walls encompassing 0.36 ha. Test excavations at the site uncovered foundational Late Bronze Age levels on both the citadel and western terrace contemporary with, if not slightly earlier than, the occupations at Tsakahovit fortress.

Looming above Gegharot, perched atop several high peaks of the Pambakh range, our survey recorded three previously undocumented fortresses. These three sites—Tsilkar, Ashot Yerkat, and Poloz-Sar—along with the fortress of Berdidosh to the west and Aragatsi-Berd to the southeast, are encircled by stone masonry fortifications typical of Lchashen-Metsamor horizon architecture. Although none of the five sites boast a well-preserved occupation level—a consequence of erosion and deflation—the few materials recovered from the surface and in our soundings supports the assignment of the sites to the Late Bronze Age. These sites are significant as they indicate a somewhat different form of fortified site than that known from the margins of the plain. These sites, situated along the primary routes into the Tsakahovit plain from the north, are substantially smaller than their neighbors on the plain and highly inaccessible. These formal differences suggest that they served not as sociopolitical centers hosting a diverse array of activities but rather as frontier posts, dedicated to defense and protection of circulation routes.

The unique nature of the Pambakh group of fortified outposts suggests two possible models of sovereignty for the Tsakahovit plain region during the Late Bronze Age (figure 7.8). The first describes Berdidosh, Tsilkar, Ashot-Yerkat, and Poloz-Sar as part of a northeast Tsakahovit polity, centered at Gegharot and autonomous from, perhaps in conflict with, the southern Tsakahovit polity on the slope of Mt. Aragats. In support of this reconstruction we can note that the cromlech cemeteries on the Pambakh slopes are tightly clustered around Gegharot and do not extend southwest toward Tsakahovit. This interpretation would require that we describe the Late Bronze Age fortress at Aragatsi-berd as a border post between rival Tsakahovit plain polities (an interpretation supported by the lack of cemetery sites around Aragatsi-berd that might indicate a more enduring commitment to the site than simple geopolitical necessity).

A second model of Late Bronze Age sovereignty takes the entire Tsakahovit plain as a single sociopolitical community with interlinked centers at Hnaberd, Tsakahovit, and Gegharot. This model can muster support from the preliminary results of the materials analyses. Gegharot and Tsakahovit appear to have been tied into the same obsidian trade network and a large portion of the ceramics from Tsakahovit contain silicate inclusions that mark them as produced from Pambakh clay sources. It also seems somewhat more plausible that the numerous outpost fortresses in the Pambakh hills were not simply defending the single center at Gegharot but rather oversaw threats to the plain as a whole coming from the north. This model would interpret Aragatsi-berd as the southeastern anchor of this chain of frontier posts that extends to Berdidosh—a highly plausible suggestion given that it commands views both south into the Kasakh valley and northeast.

At present we do not have sufficient evidence to adjudicate between these rival models (or integrate them into a historical account of sociopolitical development). However, these reconstructions do suggest that as early as the Late Bronze Age, multi-centered polities able to rule large territories and patrol political frontiers had already arisen in southern Caucasia.

ELITES AND INSTITUTIONS

The progress made in modeling the extent of sovereignty during the Late Bronze Age forces us to consider the much more difficult problem of the constitution of the political regimes on the Tsakahovit plain. If the signal transformation from the Middle to Late Bronze Age sociopolitical communities lies in the increasing formalization of social inequalities that emerged upon the collapse of the Kura-Araxes horizon, then what were the sources of elite power and the structure of governmental institutions? What could have made such regularization legitimate? During the Late Bronze Age, the ostentatious displays of social inequality known from the grand kurgans, such as those at Lchashen, moderate considerably. This is not to suggest that social inequality ameliorated. Quite the contrary, the demands placed by rulers quartered in fortified settlements likely intensified the social distance between elites and subjects. However, the expression of this distance in mortuary contexts took on less outwardly demonstrative forms, suggesting that the legitimacy of rule no longer rested as heavily in conspicuous displays of wealth but rather had been regularized into an enduring institutional order.

While the institutional order of Late Bronze Age regimes on the Tsakahovit plain is, as yet, not well assayed and detailed analysis must await more exten-

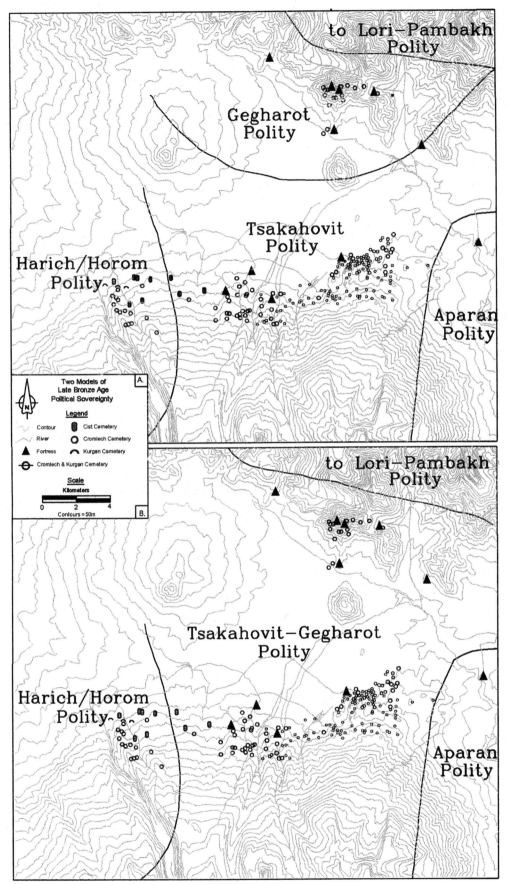

Figure 7.8 Two Models of Political Sovereignty for the Late Bronze Age Polities of the Tsakahovit Plain.

sive excavations, exploratory soundings at Tsakahovit fortress have provided hints regarding the overall outlines of Lchashen-Metsamor horizon polities. While excavations at the site have thus far been limited in their extent, they do provide a basis for opening a discussion of Late Bronze Age institutional orders.

Excavations at Tsakahovit fortress have thus far been limited to three operations—two atop the citadel and one on the upper terrace of the west slope. The terrace excavation encountered a thick burned level (complete with the outlines of burned beams) capping a well-preserved occupation level. In this occupation level we uncovered two large storage jars (*pithoi*) and a butter-making vessel. Indeed, the range of wares recovered within and below the burnt level was tightly restricted to large jars and pithoi. The butter-making vessel was set into a ring of stones embedded in the floor suggesting that it was a rather permanent "appliance."

The citadel operations also uncovered substantial evidence of a burnt layer capping the Late Bronze Age occupation, although the destruction level was not as thick or consistent as on the terrace. In contrast to the terrace operation, the Late Bronze Age levels on the citadel produced no large storage jars, only an array of fine wares and bowls. The division of a set of storage vessels on the terrace and more delicate wares on the citadel suggests a basic segregation of functional areas at the site. This apparent spatial differentiation of functions at Tsakahovit is echoed by investigations at other Late Bronze Age sites (for example, Horom South, Metsamor).

The suggestion that Late Bronze Age societies were ordered by tightly integrated religious, political, and economic institutions located in fortified political centers holds historical significance in addition to anthropological utility. In a recent study of the built environment of Urartian political centers on the Ararat plain, Smith (1999) argues that Urartian political organization was predicated upon tightly knit religious, political, and economic institutions that served as a thoroughly integrated apparatus of governance. While such a model greatly differs from the looser ties between temple, palace, and market that typify ancient Mesopotamian societies, they bear a very close resemblance to the preliminary model forwarded here for sociopolitical communities in the Tsakahovit plain during the Late Bronze Age. While much work remains to be done in order to test and further flesh out the very bare bones of the model offered here, the extant data is certainly enough to support a reframing of the problem of sociopolitical complexity in southern

Caucasia from a question of locating the external stimuli to complexity to one of assessing the processes of social differentiation and institutional formation of which the kingdom of Urartu was an integral part, rather than a radical divergence.

CONCLUSION: FRAMING COMPLEXITY IN SOUTHERN CAUCASIA

The problem of emergent sociopolitical complexity in the Highlands is exceedingly important to the general study of western Asian cultural and political history for at least three reasons. First, Caucasia and the highlands provide not just a road between the Near East and the Eurasian steppe but also a point of cultural articulation that provides a critical archaeological setting for examining the constitution of sociopolitical boundaries and the endurance of long-distance economic ties. Second, early complex societies in Caucasia bear very little resemblance to those of either southern or northern Mesopotamia, suggesting that the region could provide the outlines of a complementary, yet unique, tradition of sociopolitical formation that would enrich our understanding of cultural transformations in western Asia. Third, the unique nature of the enduring economic contacts between highland polities and their neighbors—extensive and intensive exchange without direct political rule—offers an opportunity to examine sets of social relationships within ecumenes bound together less by rigid orders of dominance and exploitation than by shifting patterns of authority and reciprocity. By examining early complex societies in southern Caucasia in their own right, rather than as pale reflections of neighboring ways of life, we not only attain a less reductive understanding of sociocultural dynamics within the "borderlands" but also open new possibilities for defining transformations in adjacent areas that arise from the dynamic interdigitation of differing approaches to social life.

NOTES

1. Diakonoff (1984:44) has cogently argued that Hittite, Assyrian, and Urartian sources rarely mention "tribes" in the highlands—a term that has been read, inadvisably, as equivalent with the neo-evolutionary social type describing geographically dispersed groups united by kin and ethnicity. Diakonoff suggests instead that these sources describe the region as organized into "countries" each with at least one major town.

2. While Assyria is generally the prime mover implicated in Urartian political formation, a number of other polities along the margins of the Highlands have also been cited as possible "inspirations" to imperial coalescence, including Mitanni and Mannaea (Burney and Lang 1972:126).

3. Accession dates for Assyrian kings before 1132 BC are those suggested by Harper et al. (1995). Dates for kings following 1132 BC, beginning with Ashur-resh-ishi I, have been taken from Curtis and Reade (1995). Spellings of Assyrian names have also been taken from these sources.

4. For complete accounts of references to Uruatri and Nairi in Assyrian inscriptions see Melikishvili (1954), Salvini (1967), and Wartke (1993).

5. We understand the monumental constructions to be fixed in levels VIII-VI with three construction stages (EB III B-C). According to Hauptmann, in the EB IIB level of Norşuntepe the "Karaz-Kirbet Kerak" pottery (Schwarzpolierte Keramik) comprises 50% of the total material. In the EB IIIA, the painted ceramic (Bemalte Keramik, Gruppe D) with its decorations and forms repeats the ceramic of the late (Karnut-Shengavit) stage of Armenian Kura-Araxes. In the EB IIIB-C stage the Schwarzpolierte Keramik comprises 90% of the material, testifying to the continuance of Kuro-Araxes culture in Norşuntepe in the time of VIII-VI levels (Hauptmann 1969, 2000).

6. In addition to the general chronologies outlined by, among others, Areshian (1974), Martirosian (1964), and Pogrebova (1977), several works have addressed the material chronologies of more restricted areas such as the Shirak plain (Khachatryan 1975) and northeast Armenia (Esaian 1976). A number of analyses have focused on temporal change in a single material type (such as Esaian [1966] on weapons and Piggott [1968] on wheeled vehicles) or in a single site inventory (such as Kuftin [1941, 1946] on the Trialeti material and Esaian and Oganesian [1969] on the materials from the Dilijan collections).

7. The seal from tomb 422 at Artik repeats elements of the so-called "Mitannian style" of seals. The positioning of the central figure of the seal, a winged goddess with the tree of life, recalls seal number 619 of the Marcopoli collection (Teissier 1984: 293). The other flanking figures in the Artik seal—figures with bird heads and the bisecting body line—and the astral images evoke similar parallels with numbers 608, 611–617 of the Marcopoli group. The author considers these seals as falling within the parameters of the Mitannian type. The Artik seal also has parallels to the Alalakh seals with bird headed human figures (Collon 1982b: 110 [# 97]; compare Louvre examples in Contenau [1922: pl. 36: 238, 265, 272] and a similar seal from Enkomi in Collon [1987: 74]).

8. X-ray fluorescence analyses were performed by J. Keller (Institute of Mineralogy, Petrology and Chemistry, University of Albert-Ludwig, Freiburg, Germany).

CHAPTER 8

Pre-Urartian and Urartian Settlement Patterns in the Caucasus, Two Case Studies:

The Urmia Plain, Iran, and the Sevan Basin, Armenia

RAFFAELE BISCIONE

The Institute for Mycenaean, Aegean, and Anatolian Studies led a systematic survey in the Urmia (then Rezaiyeh) plain, Iran, in the years 1976–1978 (Pecorella and Salvini 1984) and has been conducting another in the Sevan Lake basin, Armenia, since 1994 (Biscione et al. 2002) (figure 8.1). Both surveys were aimed at the archaeological-philological study of the Urartian expansion in those regions and at the study of the settlement organization, both in the Urartian and pre-Urartian periods.

The two areas are fruitful to compare since they are reasonably different from the ecological point of view, rather different from the cultural one, entered the Urartian empire at different times, and had different functions within the empire. The Sevan basin was a fortified frontier of the Urartian empire, while Urmia plain was not on the border. Furthermore, the pre-Urartian settlement patterns were different in the two areas. Therefore a comparison of the data from the two surveys, done according to the same procedure, will enable us to determine the degree of disruption caused by the Urartian conquest in each area and the effect of the insertion of the local polities into a large, supraregional state.

THE URMIA PLAIN

The size, the abundance of surface water, and the relatively high amount of rainfall, 370 mm/year (Ganji 1968:249), make the Urmia plain (figure 8.2) one of the major agricultural areas of the region (Zimansky 1985:21) and one of the key areas in the long-term population shifts within northwestern Iran.

There are no precise data on the Urartian conquest of the Urmia plain (Salvini 1984a). The data—from the stele of Karagündüz (Salvini 1984b:57-62), Kelishin (Benedict 1961; Salvini 1984b:63-64), and Qalatgah (van Loon 1975a), dating back to the joint suzerainty of Ishpuini and Minua circa 820–810/805 BC, and by the later inscriptions of Minua at Tashtepe (Salvini 1984b:65-69) and Ain-e Rum (Salvini 1984b:71-76)—suggest that it was already part of the Urartian empire

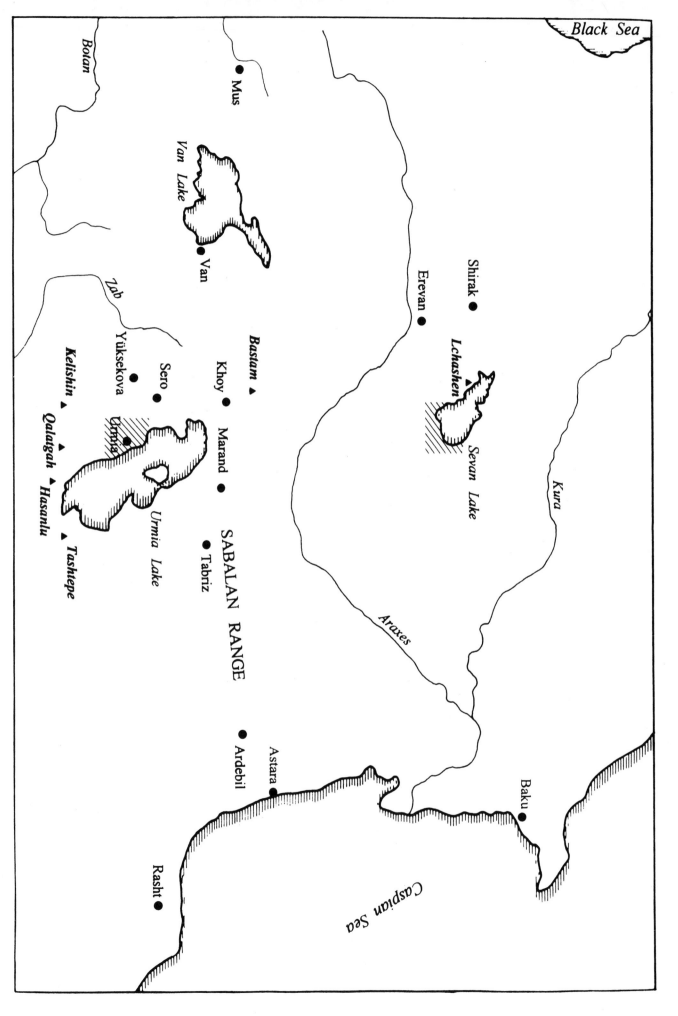

168

Figure 8.1 Eastern Anatolia, Transcaucasia and North-western Iran. Dots mark the modern cities and triangles indicate archaeological sites; hatched areas are the survey areas. Areas surveyed by the Institute for Mycenaean, Aegean and Anatolian studies are hatched. *Drawing by A. Mancini.*

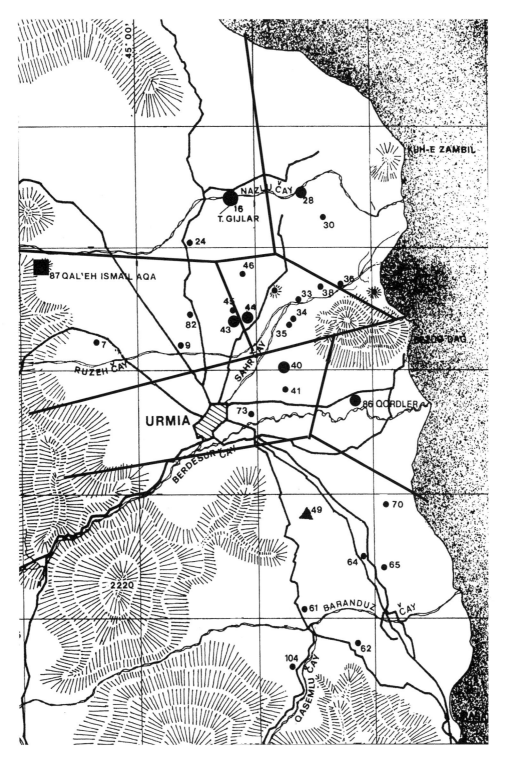

Figure 8.2 The settlement pattern of the Urmia Plain in Iron Age I-II. The triangle indicates Geoy tepe (rank 1) and the size of the dots is proportional to the rank of the other settlements. The square indicates Qal`eh Ismail Aqa. *Illustration by A. Mancini.*

in the end of the ninth century BC. This is corroborated by the destruction of Hasanlu IVB, dated 810–805 BC on purely archaeological grounds (Dyson and Muscarella 1989:22) and the dating by Kroll (Kleiss and Kroll 1977:108) of the first Urartian settlement at Qal'eh Ismail Aqa to the age of Ishpuini and Minua.

The data about the sites have been taken from the published sources (Kleiss 1971, 1972, 1973, 1974, 1975a, 1975b, 1976; Kleiss and Kroll 1977; 1979; Belgiorno et al. 1984a, 1984b; Belgiorno and Pecorella 1984). Archaeological evidence for the Iron Age of the Urmia plain, which follows the sequence and the dating of Hasanlu (Dyson and Muscarella 1989; Dittman 1990), has been divided into Iron Age I (Hasanlu V, circa 1500/1400–1250 BC), Iron II (Hasanlu IVC-B, circa 1250–800 BC) and Iron III or Urartian (Hasanlu III A-B, circa 800–600 BC). The main problem with the sequence lies in the well-known fact that is very difficult to distinguish between Iron I and II survey materials, except for a few diagnostic shapes, because of the strong cultural continuity from Hasanlu V to

Hasanlu IV (Dyson and Muscarella 1989:1). Therefore in the present study Iron I and II have been treated together under the caption Iron I-II (that is, pre-Urartian). Furthermore, in the absence of very specific, very diagnostic sherds, it is almost impossible to determine small chronological variations within Iron Age I-II and III. As a result all the sites of a given period have been treated as contemporary and existing for the whole time span of the period.

Attribution to the pre-Urartian or to the Urartian period has been based on the number of diagnostic sherds. Sites that had a relevant amount of pottery of the two periods have been attributed to both and sites that yielded only a small number of nondiagnostic Iron Age sherds have not been taken into consideration.

Settlement pattern has been determined only on the basis of the extent of surface deposits at a site,[1] of information from excavations, and/or on the perimeter of the fortresses' walls calculated from the published maps, depending on the archaeological evidence at hand. In the Urartian period, red-polished ware

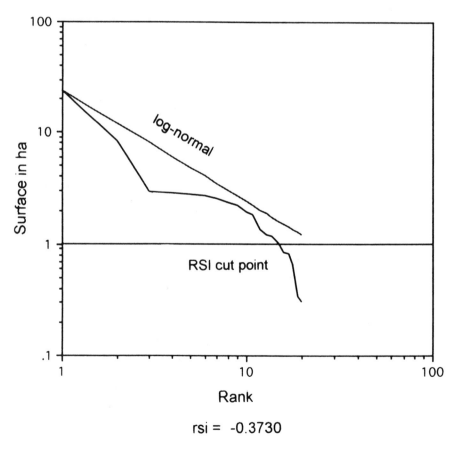

Figure 8.3 Rank-size graph of the Iron Age I-II settlements in the Urmia plain. *Illustration by A. Mancini.*

(Toprakkale ware) can be an important source of evidence in some areas, as it is a component of the elite complex we identify with Urartian material culture. Unfortunately, in the Urmia plain, Toprakkale ware was found mainly in the Urartian fortresses and its distribution in the settlements was so sporadic and erratic that it does not give any evidence besides chronology. All the settlements are located in the plain, between 1280 and 1400 m above sea level, mainly in the fans of the small rivers flowing into the Lake Urmia.

PRE-URARTIAN PERIOD IN THE URMIA PLAIN (IRON AGE I-II, CIRCA 1500/1400–800 BC)

Hasanlu gives full evidence for the existence in pre-Urartian times of a state, at least in period Hasanlu IV. Excavations in the Urmia plain itself did not reveal another site comparable to Hasanlu IV. Among the several possible explanations are either the fact that the Urmia plain was part of the Hasanlu regional state (although the settlement pattern seems to contradict this explanation) or the need for further research.

In the pre-Urartian period nineteen sites are known in the Urmia plain, distributed in four hierarchical levels (figure 8.2). The uppermost is formed by one site only, Geoy Tepe (n. 49), with a surface of 24 ha,[2] that lies in the southern part of the plain, approximately 12.5 km from the southern hills. Gijlar (n. 16), with a surface of 8.29 ha, constitutes the second level and lies in the northern part of the plain, about 25 km (more or less a day's walk) as the crow flies from Geoy and 10 km from the northern hills. Most probably Geoy Tepe was the main center of the whole Urmia plain and controlled directly the southern part, while Gijlar was the secondary center and controlled the northern part. Approximately midway between Geoy and Gijlar flows the Ruzeh Çay that, if its course did not shift much in the last three thousand years, could have marked the dividing line between the two areas of control. Both Geoy and Gijlar are located approximately in the centers of their areas of control.

The third hierarchical level is formed by five sites ranging from 2.927 ha (Shurkand, n. 43) to 2.188 ha (Jarchalu, n. 40), with an average of 2.6 ha. These sites, predictably, are mostly located in the central part of the plain, not far from the border between Geoy's and Gijlar's areas of control. Only Sharbat (n. 28) is located far to the north of this median line. The fourth and lowest hierarchical level is formed by eleven sites, ranging from 1.894 ha (Qishla`shuq, n. 82) to 0.294 ha (Sayedlu, n. 46).

Geoy controls eight sites located in the southern part of the plain, ranging from 2.77 ha (Kordler, n. 86) to 1.03 ha (Turkman, n. 65). Gijlar controls twelve sites, ranging from 2.92 ha (Shurkand, n.43) to 0.29 ha (Saiedlu, n. 46). The larger surface of the sites of the southern part of the plain shows that the total population in the part of the plain directly controlled by Geoy was larger.

The rank-size curve of the sites (figure 8.3) is remarkably concave (primate), with a rank/size index (rsi) of -0.3730. In fact the second-rank site (Gijlar) is well inside the line of the log-normal distribution, as is the third-rank site of Shurkand and all the others. The cluster of 5 third-level sites (ranging from rank 3 to rank 8) gives the impression of a curve more convex than reality. In fact the average size of 2.6 ha for the average rank of this hierarchical level lies well inside the expected line of normal distribution.

This concave distribution is evidence of a strong administrative control of Geoy over the smaller sites and over the activities taking place in the Urmia plain. Therefore the settlement pattern, both with the four hierarchical levels and with the primate distribution, supports the hypothesis of the existence of a local (proto)state.

Military sites do not seem to play a relevant role in Iron Age I-II. Geoy and Gijlar do not show any trace of fortifications or citadels, and Iron I-II sherds have been found only in two fortified sites, namely Qal`eh Ismail Aqa, n. 87 (Belgiorno and Pecorella 1984:323-25) in the northern part of the plain and Qal`eh Pir Chopan, n. 119 (Kleiss and Kroll 1978:46, Fig. 22; 66) in the southernmost part.

URARTIAN PERIOD IN THE URMIA PLAIN (IRON AGE III, CIRCA 800-550 BC)

The open settlements
The Urartian period registered the greatest number of settlements in the Urmia plain, twenty-seven sites (figure 8.4). They range from Geoy Tepe, again with a surface of 24 ha (Iron III pottery comes from all the excavations), to Danqeralu (n. 26), 0.16 ha. Eight sites out of nineteen survived into Iron III, including Geoy Tepe and Gijlar. Material culture shows a remarkable cultural continuity with Iron I-II.

The uppermost level of the settlement hierarchy is occupied by Geoy Tepe, again the largest site. The second level, nonexistent in Iron I-II, is filled by Dizajtakye (n. 51), 11.51 ha; Gijlar (n.16), again with

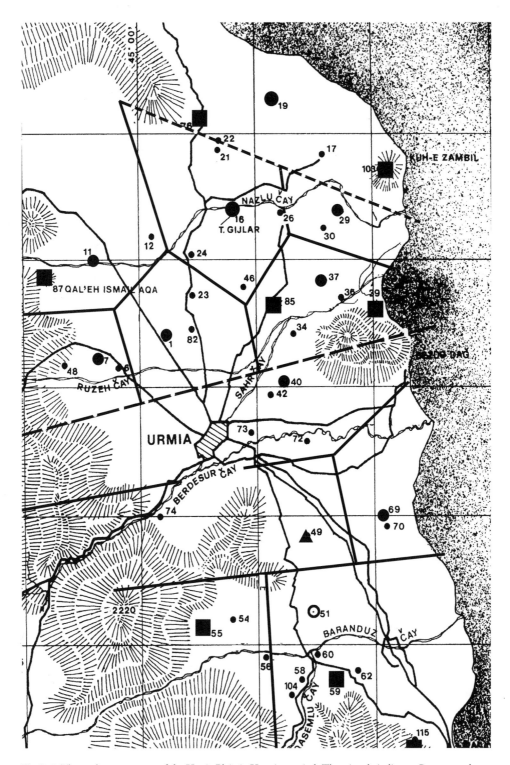

Fig.8. 4 The settlement pattern of the Urmia Plain in Urartian period. The triangle indicates Geoy tepe, the circle Dizajtakye (rank 2) and the size of the dots is proportional to the rank of the other settlements. The squares indicate fortifications. *Illustration by A. Mancini.*

a surface of 8.29 ha, is in the third level. The fourth level is represented by Anganeh (n. 19), 4.65 ha; the fifth level has eight sites, ranging from 3.40 ha (Qara Tepe, n.69) to 2.04 ha (Balajuk, n.7). The lowest level, the sixth, has fifteen sites ranging from 1.29 ha (Ashkerabad, n. 23) to 0.16 ha (Danqeralu, n. 26).

The picture we have here is quite different from that of the pre-Urartian period. In the Urartian period, the sites which occupy the second and fourth levels did not exist previously and, if settlement hierarchy is connected with territorial control, subdivide the areas of control of the first and third levels in what looks like an unsuitable fashion. In fact Dizajtakye, the second-rank site, is not the secondary center, capital of the northern part of the plain, but seems to control the southern part of the area of Geoy Tepe. Anganeh controls the northern part of the area of Gijlar, but with a very small number of sites. Furthermore the areas are now much smaller, as Dizajtakye is about 6 km from Geoy (slightly more than a one-hour walk) and Anganeh is 9 km (slightly less than a two-hour walk) from Gijlar.

As in the pre-Urartian period, the northern part of the plain has a larger number of sites: fifteen settlements lie close to Gijlar and two close to Anganeh, for a total of nineteen sites. In the southern part of the plain, seven settlements are within Geoy's theoretical sphere and six within that of Dizajtakye, for a total of fifteen sites. The sites of the southern part of the plain have a larger surface and therefore a larger population than those of the north, like in the pre-Urartian period.

The rank-size curve for Urartian period (figure 8.5) shows a remarkable change (rank/size index =-0.1862). The second rank site, Dizajtakye, lies on the line of log-normal distribution; the third rank site, Gijlar, is slightly beyond it. The sites of the fourth to ninth ranks are very close to the log-normal line and the tenth rank lies again on it. Thus the distribution of the smallest sites again follows a primate distribution.

The breakdown of the Early Iron Age settlement system indicates that, when the Urmia plain ceased being an independent political-economic entity and was incorporated into the Urartian kingdom, a

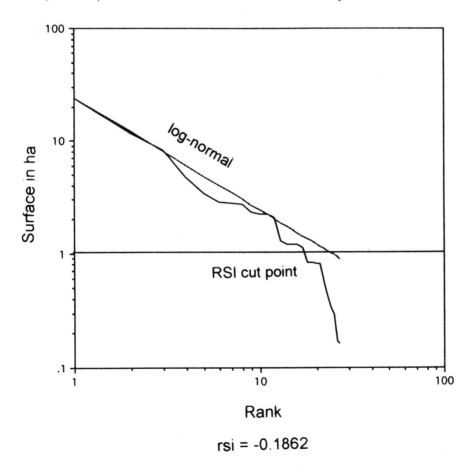

Figure 8.5 Rank-size graph of the Urartian period settlements in the Urmia plain.
Illustration by A. Mancini.

super-regional state and a large political-economic structure, the degree of local control of the large sites was lower than in the previous period. The evidence suggests that at least some of the administrative functions were transferred either to supralocal sites of a higher hierarchical level or to other types of settlements. In fact it is known that in the Urartian kingdom the administrative functions were concentrated in the *É.GAL* (in Urartu, this word means a fortress with palace and administrative center, in contrast to Mesopotamia, where the same word means palace. The literal translation is "big house."), which also had military functions. Evidently the degree of interest and intervention of the Urartian king (and on his behalf by the governor situated in the local *É.GAL*) in the daily life and economy of the Urmia plain was different from, if not less intense than, the presumably direct intervention of the local ruler of early Iron Age. In the settlement pattern of the Urartian period "...more than one hierarchy was at work, and... a complex interaction of several components determined the character of each site" (Zimansky 1985:35). The analysis of the settlement pattern of Iron Age III in the Urmia plan must therefore take into account also the fortresses.

Fortifications

The Urartian system of fortification of the Urmia plain has been reconstructed with a reasonable degree of certitude, mainly thanks to Kleiss and Kroll's surveys (Kleiss 1971, 1972, 1973, 1974, 1975a, 1975b, 1976; Kleiss and Kroll 1977; 1979). In this study, only the fortresses directly overlooking the plain or very close to it will be included, since it is this group that could have been administrative centers and could have militarily controlled the plain. Therefore all the minor fortifications in the mountains, guarding the main roads, have not been taken into account here (figure 8.6).

The main problem facing us is the fact that little work has been done on fortresses. There is no satisfactory ranking system, because surface area, used for ranking settlements, does not have a very relevant meaning in fortifications,[3] which undergo significant strategic, tactical, and locational constraints. Here we propose to take into account the perimeter of all fortification works. This is a reasonable index of the amount of labor invested in the fortress and therefore of the importance of the fortress itself. Therefore in this attempt the perimeter of the existing walls (not including hypothetical or reconstructed ones) was measured on the most detailed published maps. Also other

labor-intensive characteristics can help to assess the importance of a given military site. In our case only the fortress of Qal`eh Ismail Aqa shows one of these characteristics, namely chamber graves carved into the rock.

The fortresses are divided into two groups. The northern one consists of five sites, the largest being Qal`eh Ismail Aqa (n. 87), formed by a lower and an upper castle, with fortification walls connecting the two. The total perimeter of the defensive walls is 1700 m. This fortress controlled the road to Sero, Movana,[4] and finally to Yüksekova.

Qiz Qal`eh (n. 76), perimeter 510 m, controlled the road toward the north to the plain of Salmas (Shahpur); Kuh-e Zanbil, n. 103 (Kleiss 1983:285), perimeter 757 m, and Aqil Tepe (n. 39), perimeter 580 m, are located in the northern part of the plain, close to the lake shore; Qal`eh Sarandil - Bashqal`eh (n. 85) lies on an isolated hill in the plain and is much destroyed, but it is clear that it is a small fort.

In the southern part there are three sites. The largest is Lumbad, n. 115, whose concentric walls have a perimeter of 1300 m. Tepe Baranduz, n. 55, a fortified settlement[5] here grouped with the military emplacement, perimeter not determinable, controls the valley of the Baranduz Çay and the road to Movana and Ushnuviyeh. Zendan-e Safavi - Qal`eh Zendan, n. 59, perimeter 563 m, blocks the valley of the Kazemlu Çay and the direct road to Ushnuviyeh.

Further south, outside the Urmia plain proper, there are the small fort of Kamana, n. 120 (Kleiss 1983:286, Fig. 1), and the fortress of Qalat, n. 121 (Kleiss 1983:289, Fig. 4), approximately the same size of Lumbad.

We can easily see that the most important fortress is Qal`eh Ismail Aqa with a perimeter of 1700 m, followed by Lumbad with 1300 m, both of them "medium size" according to Kleiss's classification (Kleiss 1983:285, 286, Figs. 1, 2, 4). The other forts, ranging from 757 m (Kuh-e Zanbil) to 510 m (Qiz Qal`eh) cannot easily be divided into hierarchical levels.

Judging from the extant data, Qal`eh Ismail Aqa was probably the provincial capital and controlled the northern group, while Lumbad was the secondary administrative center controlling the southern part of the plain and southern group of sites. The smaller forts had presumably only military purposes and closely controlled the subjected territory and natural roads.

The two main fortresses are located about 21 km as the crow flies from one another, and the median line between them lies not far from the Berdesur Çay. It is

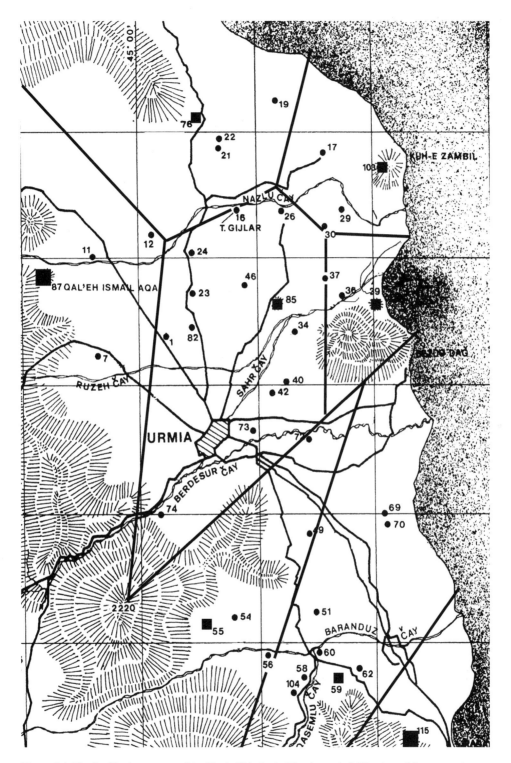

Figure 8.6 The fortification pattern of the Urmia Plain in the Urartian period. The sizes of the squares that indicate the fortifications are proportional to their respective rank. Dots indicate settlements. *Illustration by A. Mancini.*

possible that the river marked the demarcation line between the areas of control of the two fortresses, if the ancient course was not far from the present one.

The demarcation line between Bashqal`eh (n. 85) and Qiz Qal`eh (n. 76) also lies very close to the Nazlu Çay and therefore it is possible that this river also marked the boundary between two zones.

An examination of the distribution map and the calculation of the average distance between the fortifications (about 4.5 km) show that the distribution of the forts in the northern group is unbalanced. Probably a fort is missing, which possibly could have been located south-southwest of Qal`eh Ismail Aqa, between the Ruzeh and the Berdesur Çay. Such a fort would also reduce the area of control of Bashqal`eh, that is very large for such a small site.

As already noted, fortifications, unlike settlements, have not been studied connecting their hierarchy to specific types of human societal organization, like chiefdoms or states. There is no need to determine the existence of the Urartian state on the basis of the settlement/fortification hierarchy because philological and other archaeological data provide all the needed evidence. On the contrary, the information from the Urmia plain can give a first rough correlation between type of social organization and fortification hierarchy.

The three ranks of the Urartian fortified sites in the Urmia plain fall in the "medium" and "small" fortresses of Kleiss (see above). Evidently the "large" fortresses should constitute at least another hierarchical level. A first cursory calculation of the perimeter of Bastam, the largest Urartian fortress in Iran and one of the largest of the kingdom (from Kleiss 1988:35, Fig. 26), gives the result of at least 3000 m. It is evident, therefore, that the Urartian state had at least four hierarchical levels of fortifications, a number coinciding with the four levels of the settlements indicative of the presence of a state. This is not casual because, as already mentioned, administrative and decisional functions of the Urartian state took place not in cities and villages but in fortresses and forts. Therefore the four decision-making levels of a state are reflected not in the Urartian settlements but in fortifications.

The correlation fortification-settlement should logically be true also for the other areas of Transcaucasia and eastern Anatolia where administration was located

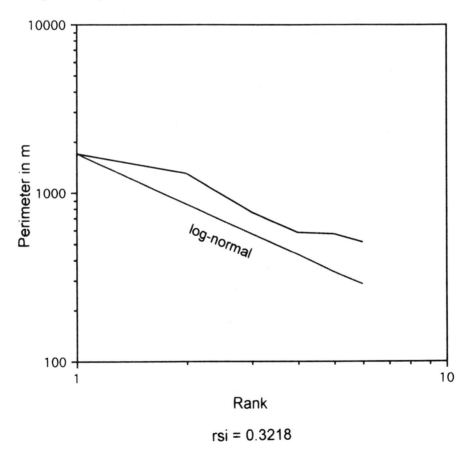

Figure 8.7 Rank-size graph of the Urartian fortifications in the Urmia plain. *Illustration by A. Mancini.*

in fortifications and not in settlements. Of course further study of other polities is required in order to draw a definite conclusion. Furthermore the large extension of the Urartian state could require a fortification hierarchy larger than that of a subregional state.

The distribution curve of the fortification is convex (figure 8.7), with a rsi of 0.3218. This is to be expected, because any fortification work larger than a watchtower implies a substantial perimeter and because it is to be expected that in case of war such an emplacement can be cut off from its customary administrative sites and be forced to a degree of administrative and tactical autonomy. Therefore it seems logical that the differences in size between the various ranks of fortifications should be generally smaller than that between civil settlements, and that a convex curve in this case should not imply the organizational patterns singled out for nonmilitary sites.

URMIA PLAIN—SUMMARY

Summing up the evidence so far gathered it is possible to reconstruct the existence in Iron Age I-II of a settlement pattern with a four-tiered hierarchy and a concave curve of distribution, evidence of a centralized structure probably connected with regional or subregional (proto) state system.

This system crumbles in the Urartian period, when we face a six-tiered settlement hierarchy, with a slightly convex curve, or in any case close to the log-normal distribution. It is evident that there is a lesser degree of centralization and a lesser degree of local control by the large settlements. This reflects the end of the independent local polities after the insertion in the Urartian empire, and the fact that administrative functions are located in the fortresses and not in the cities anymore. The larger settlements like Geoy Tepe and Dizajtakye probably survived into the Urartian period, but with reduced administrative functions or no administrative responsibilities at all.

The fortresses, in their turn, show a three-tiered hierarchy, the first two in the class of medium-size Urartian fortresses and the other classified as small.

THE SEVAN BASIN

Today, Lake Sevan lies at about 1900 m above sea level; in the past, variations of sea level were dramatic. For example, in quaternary times the lake dried up almost totally; in 1932 it was possible to reach the Tsovinar inscription, now about 17 m above the lake level, only by

boat; in the early Bronze Age and then again in the late Bronze and Iron Ages and Urartian period, the lake was very close to the present level.

The basin of Lake Sevan, as pointed out by Zimansky (1985:24), is the rainiest part of the Urartian kingdom, with about 500 mm/year, and the area is extraordinarily rich in archaeological remains.

The first historical information goes back to around 782 BC with the first Urartian expedition by Argishti I. The conquest was completed by Argishti's son Sarduri II, who toward the end of his reign (Salvini 1995:77) finally subjected the southern shores. The northeast coast apparently was never conquered by Urartians. Sarduri's son, Rusa I, fought again in the southern Sevan basin, evidence that with the death of Sarduri II Urartian control came to an end. These facts are testified by the inscriptions of Argishti I at Lchashen, Sarduri II at Atamkhan Adiyaman[6] and at Tsovak, Rusa I at Nor Bayazet/Kamo/Gavar and Tsovinar/Kelagran.

The survey began in the southeastern corner of Sevan Lake and to date the whole of the southern shore has been explored. About seventy sites, ranging from the Early Bronze Age to the medieval period, have been examined and documented.

The data about the sites have been taken from the survey archives (Biscione et al. 2002). In the Sevan region there is a very strong cultural continuity in the time span between Late Bronze Age and Early Iron Age (circa 1500–750 BC). There are only a small number of diagnostic types which allow archaeologists to discriminate between the two periods; in the majority of the cases the diagnostic sherds here indicate a prevalence of Early Iron Age occupation. It is in the Early Iron Age when the protohistoric settlement and fortification systems reached their peak: only few sites with Urartian pottery were new foundations.

All known pre-Urartian sites are forts or fortresses, with the exception of the fortified village of Sot`k` 2. In this case also the settlement pattern has been determined on the basis of the perimeter of the fortification walls.

THE EARLY IRON AGE IN THE SEVAN BASIN (CIRCA 1200–750 BC)

Early Iron Age sites are located both close to the perilacustrine plain and in the high valleys. Those on the lake shore, under the 2000 m line, were transformed into Urartian fortifications. Therefore we cannot rely on them to gather information other than their existence, since the Urartian construction obscures information about the size of the Early Iron Age fortifications. The majority of the Early Iron Age fortresses, however, are concentrated around the Martuni plain and in the upper reaches of the Argichi river, between 2100 and 2400 m, without traces of Urartian presence.[7]

Pottery scatters outside the Early Iron Age fortresses are minimal, about one sherd on 10–12 m², while the concentration inside is much higher. Dwellings were evidently located inside the fortresses and nothing or very little was outside. It is obviously possible that open, scattered settlements also existed, but none have been found to date. The chances of spotting them on eroded mountain tops or in heavily alluviated plains are minimal. A sample of the various erosion terraces has already been explored without results while looking for sites; therefore we have to rely on fortifications as the basic surviving units of the settlement pattern.

The Early Iron Age forts and fortresses are ranked in hierarchical levels and distributed in groups, each formed by one large fortress and two or more smaller forts. The best defined ones are located around the Martuni plain. From west to east they are (figure 8.8):

1) Yeranos group, with the fortress of Sangar, perimeter 875 m, and the forts of Negh Boghaz, 534 m, and Berdi Dosh, 275 m. In the plain the indeterminable site of Kra was settled in Early Iron Age, but the later Urartian fortress destroyed any trace of the perimeter walls.

2) Nagarakhan group, located about 15 km south-southwest of the first group, in the upper valley of the river Argichi. It is composed of the fortress of Nagarakhan, 1303 m, and the forts of Kʿare Dzi, 183 m; Belyy Klyuch, 175 m; and Tatev, 130 m.

3) Martuni group, about 19 km southeast of the Yeranos group and 16 km northeast of the Nagarakhan group, with the fortress of Mtʿnadzor, 899 m, and the forts of Joj Kogh, 640 m; Aloyi Kogh, 323 m; Kyurdi Kogh, 270 m; Heri Berd, 132 m; and Al Berd. The last site was restructured, possibly rebuilt, in Urartian times and therefore it is not possible to determine the dimensions.

Further east, a group of Early Iron Age sites, located at lower altitudes and very close to the plain, were destroyed and rebuilt in the Urartian period; therefore it is not possible to draw definite conclusions about their scale in the Early Iron Age. At Tsovak, about 32 km east, an Urartian fortress overlies an Iron Age site and only the ruins of the outer, Urartian walls are preserved. It is situated on a promontory with steep slopes on three sides, a type of location typical of large pre-Urartian fortresses.

Therefore it is possible that another group of Early Iron Age forts was centered on Tsovak and to it may belong the forts of Bruti Berd, with a perimeter of 247 m, and Tsovinar, overbuilt in Urartian times. The keep of the Urartian fortress at Tsovinar is probably nothing other than the original Early Iron Age fort (Sanamyan 2002:323), which had a perimeter of 355 m. As the existence of this group is not certain, it was not included in the reconstruction of the settlement pattern (figure 8.8).

In the mountainous lands east of Tsovak, near the Masrik plain, is located the well-preserved group of Norabak, without traces of Urartian presence. It is formed by the fortress of Norabak 1, with a perimeter of 955 m, by the fort of Norabak 2, 337 m, and by the fortified settlement of Sotʿkʿ 2, perimeter not determinable and the only Early Iron Age fortified settlement identified up to now.

The examination of the perimeter lengths reveals the existence of various hierarchical levels:

1) The first level is occupied by the fortress of Nagarakhan, with a perimeter of about 1300 m. It was probably the capital of its own group and of the whole southern Sevan basin.

2) Three smaller fortresses, Norabak 1, 955 m, Mtʿnadzor, 899 m, and Sangar, 875 m, constitute the second level. They are the secondary capitals of each group.

3) Joj Kogh, 640 m, and Negh Boghaz, 534 m, possibly constitute a lower, very ill-defined, level. These forts, with the same peculiar shape and location, almost without pottery, occur only in the Martuni and Yeranos groups. Following Kleiss's suggestion (1983:284, 287) they could be *Fluchtburgen* (that is, refuges) used to shelter the population in difficult times. If so their relevance in a study of the settlement pattern is very limited. It was thought advisable not to consider them as a separate level and therefore in the study they were grouped with the following one.

4) Eight smaller forts range from 323 to 130 m.

To these should be added one fortified settlement and at least other five sites overbuilt in later periods and therefore impossible to rank. The location of these overbuilt sites, however, lack the topographical characteristics generally associated with large fortresses, with the possible exception of Tsovak.

Therefore in the southern Sevan basin there are four groups of fortifications, or perhaps five, with a convex distribution, rsi = 0.3429 (figure 8.9) (for convex distribution in fortifications see above); and three

179

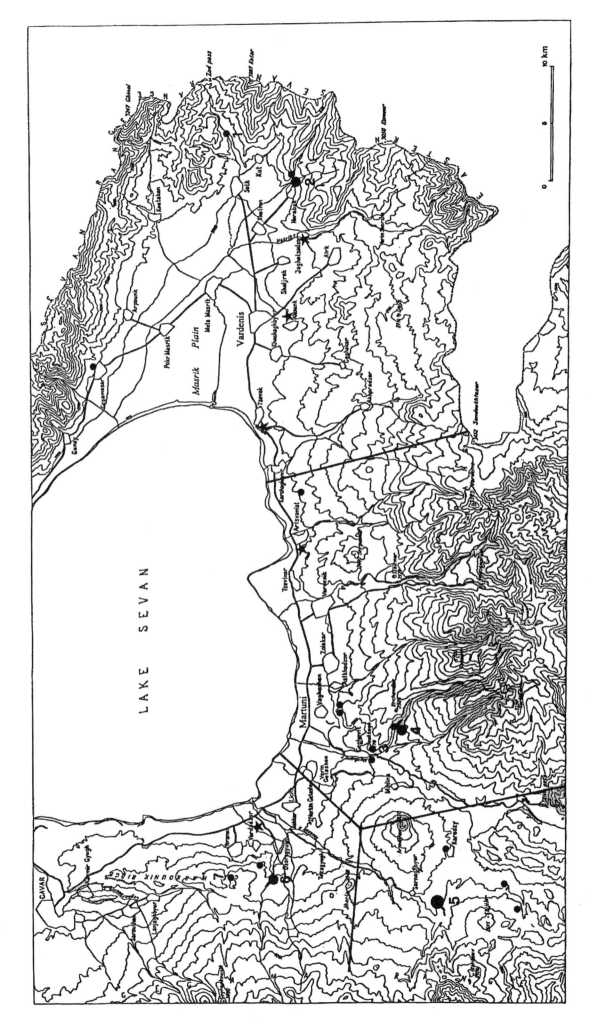

Figure 8.8 The Southern Sevan basin in the Early Iron Age. The stars indicate Early Iron Age fortifications destroyed and/or restructured in later periods and the size of the dots is proportional to the rank of the sites. 1: Sotʻkʻ 2; 2: Norabak 1; 3: Joji Kogh 2; 4: Mtʻnadzor; 5: Nagarakhan; 6: Sangar. *Illustration by A. Mancini.*

clearly distinguishable hierarchical levels plus another possible one for which the evidence is rather hazy and confused. A three-level hierarchy is thought to signify a chiefdom when settlements are considered; up to now there are no studies on fortification works. The archaeological border between complex chiefdom and protostate is notoriously difficult to draw, but summing up evidence from graveyards (very high levels of craftsmanship, chariots with spoked wheels at Lchashen, a high level of metallurgy, and very unequal distribution of wealth), data from locational analysis and other hints like the finding of a jewelry mould in the second-level fortress of Mt`nadzor, we can safely assume the presence in the Sevan basin of societies with a high degree of complexity in pre-Urartian times.[8] These are very good examples of the Caucasian type of social development, a non-urban way, described by Masson (1997), with their rich burials, large sites (fortresses in Transcaucasia), where also artisanal activity went on, and military-aristocratic rule. However, even if concentration and organization of a large amount of labor was present, in a degree not smaller than that of Mesopotamia at the beginning of urbanization, and even if the larger Caucasian sites could have generated protourban organizations (Masson 1997:128, 132), these societies did not develop into a state.

The locational evidence gathered in the southern Sevan basin suggests that in the Early Iron Age the area was under the suzerainty of Nagarakhan and formed one polity, subdivided into four (five?) "provinces." Urartian inscriptions, however, make no reference to a single political structure and list three to four "lands" in this area. This discrepancy between the written and survey evidence can be explained in various ways. It is possible, for instance, that the fusion of various polities into one was a late response to the menacing Urartian presence in the Araxes valley at least sixty or seventy years before the Urartian conquest of the southern Sevan shore and that the Urartian kings in their inscriptions preferred to refer to the period before the conquest. An alternative possibility is that an original large polity was destabilized and fragmented by the Urartians before the conquest and the "lands" mentioned in the inscriptions are its independent remains.

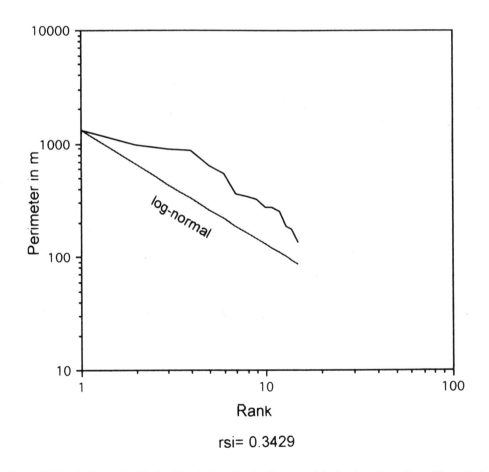

Figure 8.9 Rank-size graph of the Pre-Urartian Iron Age fortifications of the Southern Sevan Basin. *Illustration by A. Mancini.*

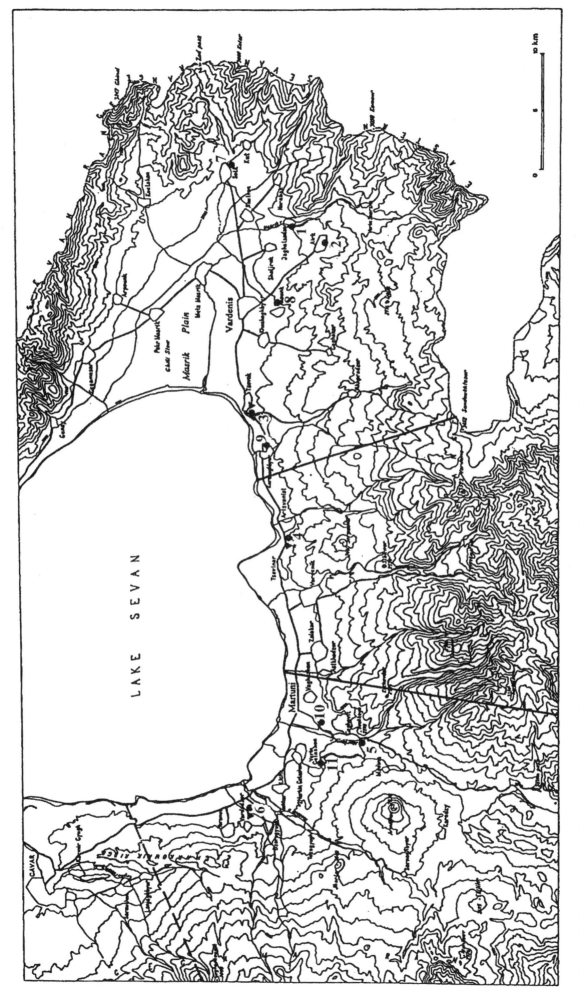

Figure 8.10 The Urartian sites of the Southern Sevan basin. Triangles indicate inscriptions. 1: Jaghats'adzor; 2: Ayrk'; 3: Tsovak; 4: Tsovinar; 5: Al Berd; 6: Kra; 7: Sor'k'; 8: Kol Pal; 9: K'ari Dur; Martuni; 11: Ishkhan Nahatak. Stippled line indicates the border between the territory controlled by Kra and that controlled by the fortress with inscription of Nor Bayazet/Gavar/Kamo. *Illustration by A. Mancini.*

URARTIAN PERIOD IN THE SEVAN BASIN

In the Urartian period, as in the Early Iron Age, the most significant elements of the settlement pattern are fortresses and forts (figure 8.10). Fortified settlements are present, but they are only four sites out of twelve. One of them, Kol Pal, lies on a flat spur overlooking the plain, the others on gentle slopes with one side protected by a canyon.

Urartian sites are concentrated around the Masrik plain and on the road between this and the Martuni plain. The Masrik plain is the larger of the two, in the vicinity of which is the rich gold mine of Sot`k` and possibly these are the reasons for the conspicuous Urartian presence. Urartian sites are generally under the 2000 m line, on the first spurs of the hills, immediately overlooking the plain. Two fortified settlements (Ayrk`, Jaghats`adzor) are above this line, but they are "psychologically" on the plain, because they are on very gentle slopes, at the edge of the plain itself and not in the hilly area. The only Urartian post not immediately overlooking the coastline or the plain is the fort of Al Berd, about 5 km uphill, that closed the road to the Selim pass and to the Araxes valley.

A dimensional examination of the Urartian sites is unfortunately impossible. In fact one of the fortresses, Tsovak, was almost totally destroyed and therefore any reconstruction of the perimeter of the walls would be purely theoretical, and all the minor forts and fortified settlements were overbuilt and/or destroyed in later times, with the exception of K`ari Dur and Martuni. However, the presence of the royal inscriptions associated with Tsovak, Tsovinar and Kra (see note 6) marks them as the most important fortresses. The examination of the remains supports this assumption, because they are clearly the largest Urartian sites in the southern Sevan basin. The easternmost of them is Tsovak, and the line of demarcation with Tsovinar (about 12 km to the west) was probably close to the river Karchaghbyur, almost midway between them; Kra lies about 24 km west-northwest of Tsovinar and the border possibly lay close to the river Astghadzor.

Tsovak lies close to the lake, closes the westernmost end of the Masrik plain and controlled it. From Tsovak depended the fort of Sot`k` 1, that guarded the road to the gold mine and to a mountain pass; the fortified settlements of Jaghats`adzor, Ayrk` and Kol Pal; and the fort of K`ari Dur. This is the only site of this group that could be measured.

It is probable that Tsovinar was the most important of the three fortresses and the administrative center of the southern Sevan basin, because a large amount of labor was invested in the extensive terracing and substructures for walls on the northeastern side of the hill on which it was built. These labor-intensive structures are absent at Kra and Tsovak, but the impossibility of getting numerical data unfortunately does not allow drawing precise conclusions. Oddly enough, in the supposed radius of control of Tsovinar, the survey did not find other Urartian sites.

Kra lies on a low hillock on the plain and its location is not as strong as that of the other fortresses, but the extensive walls and the inscription show clearly that it was not a fortified settlement but a fortress. From it depended the forts of Martuni and Al Berd, plus the fortified settlement of Ishkhan Nahatak.

From the incomplete data at our disposal emerges the presence of a two-tiered system of fortifications that, as stated, were located in the immediate vicinity of the lake shore and of the plain, the main objects of control. The corollary is that Urartians were not interested in the close control of the mountainous areas beyond the plain.

This is reflected by the evidences we gathered in the highland Early Iron Age sites. The eight forts and fortresses that continue their existence (seven of them in the western part of the area we surveyed) have Early Iron and Achaemenid-Hellenistic pottery. It is not reasonable to think that the sites were abandoned in Urartian period and resettled at its end, and this opinion is supported by three or four Toprakkale ware sherds, among the hundreds Early Iron Age and Hellenistic, found at Nagarakhan and Sangar (both of them large fortresses). It is probable, therefore, that local culture continued undisturbed under the Urartian rule, the only appreciable effect being some luxury ware added to the table sets of the local chiefs. Urartians, like almost all conquerors in mountain lands, left the highland people alone, looking only to control the main roads, the richest areas, and the most important natural resources.

SEVAN BASIN—SUMMARY

Summing up the evidence gathered up to now, in the Early Iron Age we witness the existence of a settlement pattern based on forts and fortresses, distributed at least in three hierarchical levels, concentrated around the Martuni plain and in the upper reaches of the Argichi river. In Urartian times the settlement pattern, always based on military installations, seems to show two hierarchical levels of fortifications, concentrated under the 2000 m line, along the coast of the lake and around the Masrik plain. The amount of disruption brought by the Urartians was high in the lowland areas, where they overbuilt all the previous sites, possibly razing most of them, but there was not a change of model. Open settlements did not exist in any of the periods, fortified settlements were only slightly more common in the Urartian period than earlier, and the lower city around Tsovinar is later than the Urartian period (Biscione et al. 2002:128). The highland sites were left undisturbed and the Early Iron Age settlement pattern there continued also in Urartian and later times.

CONCLUSIONS

Comparing the results from the two case studies we can find analogies and dissimilarities. Both in the Urmia plain and in the Sevan lake basin Urartian fortifications are located at low altitudes and not in the hilly areas (in fact no Urartian site was found in the high Movana-Zeyveh valley near Urmia, even if it is well-suited for stock raising and mountain agriculture). This is analogous to what was found in the Mus̡ plain in Turkey (Rothman 1994a: Fig. 14) and in the Ararat-Shirak plain in Armenia (Smith 1999:53, 56). It is therefore evident that Urartians were interested in controlling primarily major roads and plains and other areas favorable for agriculture. This can be considered a typical characteristic of the Urartian settlement pattern. Pre-Urartian sites, instead, climb to higher altitudes both in the Mus̡ area and in the Sevan basin.

As we saw, the impact of the Urartian conquest was not very heavy in the area of the Sevan lake, where the pre-Urartian settlement pattern and social structure somehow survived. In contrast, it was quite strong in the Urmia plain, where the Early Iron Age settlement pattern changed remarkably with the collapse of the administrative functions of large towns and with the introduction of the fortresses as administrative centers. The system brought in by this substitution was totally alien to local tradition.

In fact, on the basis of the evidence we have, it is possible to consider the Urartian system the continuation of a nonurban Caucasian settlement pattern, exemplified in the Sevan Basin. The exact definition of this peculiar system and the determination of its geographical extension is a task for the future. Suffice to say that at present it can be identified in Transcaucasia and in Iran north of the approximate line Astara -

Ardebil - southern slope of the Sabalan Range - Marand - Khoy.[9] In this part of Iran, in fact, tepes are present in scanty number, while fortifications and necropolises constitute the greater amount of pre-Urartian and Urartian remains. Data about easternmost Anatolia and the core area of Urartu are lacking, but this phenomenon could be present there, too.

The structure of the Urartian state has characteristics typical of the nonurban, Caucasian system (military-aristocratic leadership, mighty fortifications) and of the urban systems of the Near East (emphasis on the exploitation of agricultural resources, hydraulic works, administration, writing). The main fortresses also combine characteristics of both systems, with monumental architecture and administrative and religious functions, plus an emphasis on the military aspect. This combination, reflecting the peculiar structure of the Urartian state, is in short a military emplacement with all the functions of a city but without its population.[10]

In the Urartian empire, therefore, coexist two types of settlement patterns: the local variation of the usual, urban Near Eastern settlement pattern, clearly identified only in the southeastern areas of the empire, and the Caucasian one, on which in the case of the Urartian *É.GAL*s (administrative fortresses) were grafted Near Eastern characteristics and techniques needed for the survival of the state. The originality and the importance of Urartu lies in this combination of different systems, which made possible the emergence of a state and civilization in the highlands south of the Caucasus that was the basis for the later developments.

NOTES

1. The surfaces were calculated by Studio Azimut for Mr. A. Zucconi's diploma dissertation (Zucconi 1993:31, 60), using the ARC/INFO program for the automatic generation of Thiessen's polygons related to some Urartian fortresses overlooking the Urmia plain, namely Bashqal`eh, Kuh-e Zanbil, Qal`eh Ismail Aqa, Qiz Qal`eh, Zendan-e Safavi (Zucconi 1993:62–66). It was preferred to use the present surface of the sites, because a geometrical reconstruction of the original surface is not so different as to cause major changes in ranking, calculations, and so on.

2. The surface of Geoy Tepe was calculated on the map, which is not very clear, and other data by Burton Brown (1951:11, 15, Fig. 2), on the sketch and information given by Kleiss (Kleiss and Kroll 1977:78-79, Fig. 31) and on data of the

Pecorella-Salvini survey. On the basis of this evidence, an approximate surface of about 24 ha has been reconstructed (calculation by A. Mancini).

3. For example in the Sevan basin the largest Early Iron Age fortresses (Norabak 1, Mt`nadzor, Nagarakhan, Sangar) cover a surface as great or even greater than the surface of the large Urartian fortresses with royal inscriptions, like Tsovak, Kamo and Tsovinar.

4. Recently an Urartian inscription by Rusa I (about 730–714) was found there (Bashash Khanzaq 1996). This is the third inscription by this king found in the area, the other two were found at Mahmudabad, not in situ but clearly not far from the original location (Salvini 1977; Salvini 1984b:77-78), and at Mergeh Karvan (Salvini 1984b:80-95; Khatib-Shahidi 1998).

5. In this work "fortified settlement" has been defined as a site whose main purpose is intuitively not military, built in a location not particularly strong (for example, in the bottom of the valley, on a gentle slope), and lacking the intensive fortification walls of a fort or of a fortress.

6. The inscription was found near the village of Atamkhan on a cliff overlooking a small valley, toward the lake. At the end of the nineteenth century it was cut away and moved to the Tbilisi Museum; no record was kept of the original location. The Urartian fortress of Kra, 2 km east (toward the lake) from Vardadzor, has a small valley on its northern side, and there are cliffs on the other side of the valley. It is therefore a likely location for the Atamkhan inscription, as already suggested by Piotrovskii and Gyuzal`yan (1933:51–55).

7. In the Middle Ages and later on, villages up to 2500 m were inhabited permanently, until the twentieth century. They were abandoned only in late 1940s–1950s because by law the population of villages at such high altitudes had to move down to lower elevations. Therefore ancient high settlements were probably permanent and not seasonal during the whole sequence.

8. It is significant that the perimeter of Nagarakhan (1300 m) is identical with that of the Urartian fortress of Lumbad in the Urmia plain (Biscione 2003), defined medium-size by Kleiss.

9. The data for Eastern Azerbaijan are gathered systematically in Kroll (1984). There is no general work for Western Azerbaijan, data can be found in various articles by Kleiss (1970:107–120; 1971:51–72, Fig. 1; 1972:135–178, Fig. 1; 1973:9–41, Fig. 1; 1978) and in Kleiss and Kroll (1978:34–41, 52-59, 63-65, 70–71). The data from Western Azerbaijan were only cursorily examined, so a future in-depth examination could change the line west of Marand.

10. The lower cities sometimes found around the large Urartian fortresses are often a scatter of potsherds, evidence of a dispersed population living in insubstantial structures.

CHAPTER 9

The Early Iron Age in the Van Region

VELİ SEVİN

The basin of Lake Van in eastern Anatolia is of particular importance in the first half of the first millennium BC as the birthplace of the Urartian kingdom. At the same time there is little information about the situation of the region in the period leading up to the Early Iron Age. While there is mention in the Assyrian royal annals from the thirteenth century BC onward of the existence in this region of tribes such as Nairi and Uruatru, little material remains of them today. This leaves us somewhat ignorant of the forces that were effective in the founding of the Urartian kingdom. In this chapter we will try to give a general evaluation based on the findings of both recent and old Turkish excavations in the Lake Van region.

In this study we will not be making use of the Iron Age chronology established by R. H. Dyson (1965) in the 1960s and accepted for many years. The reason is that there is still virtually no evidence for what Dyson called the Iron I period in the Lake Van basin, and its existence in western Iran is also open to question (Pigott 1977:211 ff.; 1980:417 ff.; Kroll 1984; Lippert

1979:134 ff.). In the cemeteries of Karagündüz and Ernis, which are situated on the eastern and northern shores of Lake Van respectively, the sudden appearance of iron objects in vast quantities suggests the existence of an earlier period when the first steps in the development of iron technology should have occurred. Yet excavations and finds in the Van region so far have not provided us with any proof that the use of this metal can be dated back toward the mid-second millennium BC.

It is clear that there are four easily distinguishable separate periods within the Iron Age of the Lake Van region. These are the Early Iron/pre-Urartian kingdom (1200? –850 BC), Middle Iron/Urartian (850–650/600 BC), Post-Urartian, and finally Late Iron (400 BC) periods. The excavations at Karagündüz, Van Castle Mound, Dilkaya, and recently Hakkari have provided us with solid evidence for this conclusion. In this work we will be looking at just the first of these three periods.[1]

The earliest information on the Early Iron Age in the Lake Van basin resulted from the excavation in the 1960s of the cemetery at Ernis (Ünseli) on the north

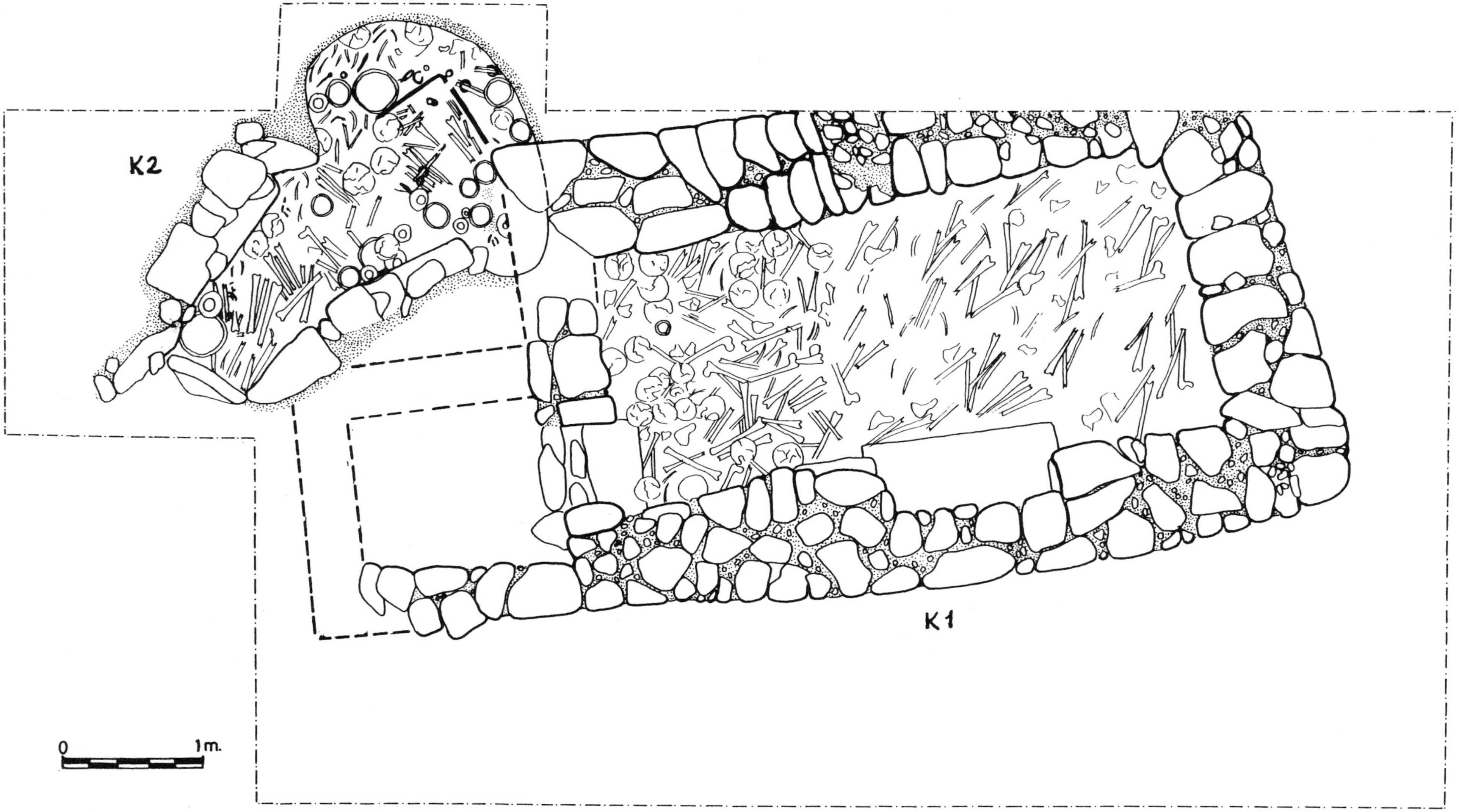

Figure 9.1 Karagündüz cemetery, tombs K 1-K 2. *Courtesy of Karagündüz project.*

shore of the lake (Sevin 1987). Our knowledge of the Early Iron Age increased in the 1980s with the work on the cemetery of Dilkaya on the southeastern shore of the lake (Çilingiroğlu 1991), and again in the 1990s with work on Karagündüz on the shore of Lake Erçek (Sevin and Kavaklı 1996a, 1996b; Sevin and Özfırat 2000) and finally Yonca Tepe near Van (Belli and Konyar 2000). Furthermore, it would appear from the number of similar small finds being bought by the museum of Van (the result of unmitigated plundering) that there are a great many more such cemeteries in the area. It is apparent that all materials come from graveyards and not from settlements. Stratigraphy is lacking, therefore, and only the evidence from tombs can provide material for study. But at the least a detailed analysis of the evidence from the graveyards is necessary to identify a material development in the culture of the Early Iron Age.

The cemeteries identified in the Lake Van basin do not usually appear to be attached to a permanent settlement.[2] So it is possible that some of the cemeteries belong to nomadic or seminomadic tribes such as those of Sialk, Marlik, Khurvin, Dinkha Tepe, and Guilan in central and northwestern Iran. It has been established that the tradition of tribal cemeteries goes back to the beginning of the second millennium BC (Özfırat 1994, 1999, 2001). These are always located on the rich grazing grounds of the high plateaus to the west of the lake basin. As all of the graves found so far have, unfortunately, been robbed by treasure hunters, there is not a lot of information available on their types and the associated burial customs. But it is clear that stone cist graves and stone chambers covered by a stone or earthen barrow (kurgan) can be found at Sütey Yayla near Ahlat and especially at Malazgirt on the western shore of the Lake Van. In contrast, the Early Iron Age cemeteries we are considering here have descended as it were onto the alluvial plain of the lake shoreline. Yet there is some evidence that the early cemeteries of the plateaus were still in use at this period (Özfırat 1994, 1999, 2001).

The distinctive features of the Early Iron Age in the Van region are as follows: first, the transfer of the cemeteries from the high grazing lands to the alluvial plains; second, the disappearance of the painted ware of the Middle and Late Bronze Ages, its place being taken by a monochrome beige or cream-colored ware; and third, the appearance of the low carburized smelted iron weapons and ornaments. At the same time, we know very little about the period from the end of the painted pottery cultures of the second millennium to

Figure 9.2 Karagündüz cemetery, tomb K 2. *Courtesy of Karagündüz project, photograph by Mustafa Kalaycıoğlu.*

the beginning of the Early Iron Age nor about why or how this change occurred. In this obscure period between the end of the Middle Bronze Age and the beginning of the Early Iron Age, there is some weak evidence for a gradual sociopolitical development among the people of eastern Anatolia. Due to the lack of surveys and excavations, however, it is far from certain that some permanent settlements in the form of small fortresses with stone fortifications built atop hills start to occur at this time (Özfırat 1999, 2000: Fig. 1). In this work we will deal only with the evidence gained from the cemeteries of the Van region.

BURIALS

The graves of the Early Iron Age in the Van basin always contain multiple burials. Architecturally speaking there are several tomb types. First are stone cists of a rectangular plan measuring roughly five meters by two meters; the height, around one and a half meters. The walls are built into a false arch to support heavy roof slabs. The tombs were entered by raising one of the roof slabs. This type of tomb, which is known from

Ernis (Sevin 1987; 1996a), Hakkari (Sevin *et al.* 2001), and Avzini, 54 km south of Van (Sevin 1987:42 f., Fig. 7), are comparable in technique with Hasanlu V rather than with Geoy Tepe K (Rubinson 1991b). The large number of bodies found in these tombs were superimposed one upon another, separated by layers of earth. The method of carrying out the burial by opening up the roof makes these tombs comparable with that of Geoy Tepe K (Burton Brown 1951:142).

The second type of tomb can be seen as a transition between chamber tombs and stone cists. In these tombs the walls of the low chamber (approximately one meter in height) consist of vertical flagstones roofed over with heavy roof slabs. The main feature of these tombs, which are roughly rectangular in shape, is a low entrance in one of the short sides (figures 9.1, 9.2). The body is left in a flexed position; then when a new body is brought in, the previous one, along with earlier

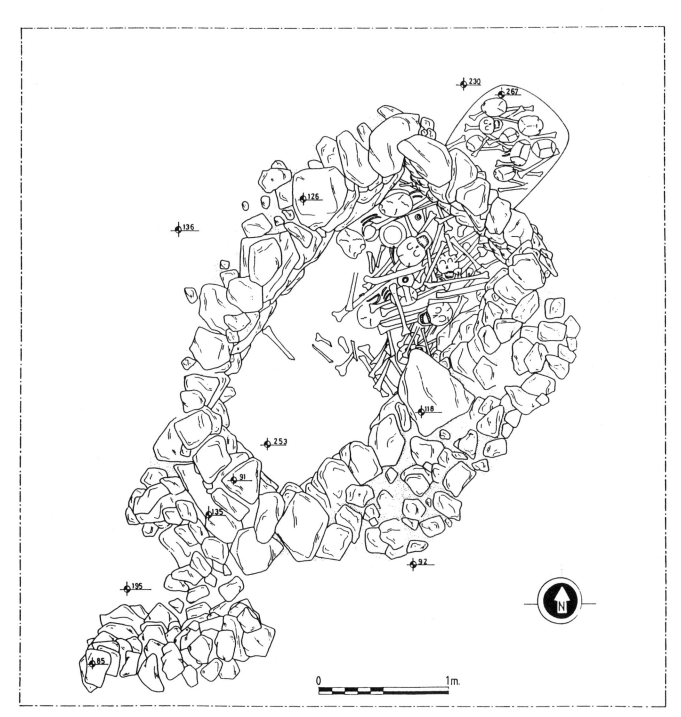

Figure 9.3 Karagündüz cemetery, tomb K 10. *Courtesy of Karagündüz project.*

remains, is pushed back to form a pile against the back wall of the tomb. This style of burial is seen again in the Middle Iron Age Urartian chamber tombs. The best examples are to be found at Dilkaya (Çilingiroğlu 1991: Fig. 3.1) and Karagündüz-K2 (Sevin 1999a; Sevin and Kavaklı 1996a, 1996b; Sevin and Özfırat 2000: Fig. 2).

The third type is fully developed chamber tombs. They are entered through a vertical entrance passage which is separated from the tomb chamber by a door

(figures 9.1, 9.3–9.7). The chamber is more or less rectangular and is lower than the entrance passage (figures 9.5, 9.6). The walls are constructed with false arches or corbelling and covered on top with roof slabs. At floor level the chamber is two by four m, and it is one and half to two and a half m high. The deceased were laid out in the flexed position; as new bodies were added, the remains of earlier occupants were pushed toward the back of the chamber (figures. 9.3, 9.8–9.10). These remains gradually accumulated into a pile against

Figure 9.4 Karagündüz cemetery, tomb K 8, entrance passage. *Courtesy of Karagündüz project, photograph by Mustafa Kalaycıoğlu.*

Figure 9.5 Karagündüz cemetery, tomb K 1 from inside. *Courtesy of Karagündüz project, photograph by Mustafa Kalaycıoğlu.*

Figure 9.6 Karagündüz cemetery, tomb K 8 from inside. *Courtesy of Karagündüz project, photograph by Veli Sevin.*

Figure 9.7 Karagündüz cemetery, tomb K 5. *Courtesy of Karagündüz project, photograph by Veli Sevin.*

the rear wall, and only the final burial in each tomb was found in its original position. One recourse taken to solve the problem of lack of space, seen only at Karagündüz so far, consists of making holes through the back wall and hollowing out the soil beyond to make additional space (figure 9.3; Sevin and Kavaklı 1996a:13, 22). The measure may be considered the forerunner of the multi-chambered Urartian tomb.

Figure 9.8 Karagündüz cemetery, tomb K 6. *Courtesy of Karagündüz project, photograph by Mustafa Kalaycıoğlu.*

As will be seen, the standard practice of the Early Iron Age is multiple burial in the Van region. Individual inhumation does not occur except in a few instances. The tradition of chamber tombs, which is foreign to the Lake Van basin during the Early Transcaucasian period—in fact to the whole of eastern Anatolia, northern Iran, and Transcaucasia—must have been brought to the region from the south, either from Assyria or more probably from Syria (Orthmann 1977:102 ff., Figs. 11–15; Sevin 1987:43ff.). Apart from the rockcut tombs of Shamseddin West, Tawi, and Halawa, in the Euphrates valley in Syria, chamber tombs with an entrance passage are found in the Titriş cemetery near Şanlıurfa, in southeastern Turkey, from the end of the Early Bronze Age onward (Algaze et al. 1995:26ff., Figs. 23–25, 29). It seems that this type of tomb chambers must have existed in the Van region at least from the tenth century BC onward.

POTTERY

One of the most obvious changes in the Early Iron Age of the Van region is in the pottery. The vessels, of which the vast majority are monochrome, are quite

Figure 9.9 Karagündüz cemetery, tomb K 8. *Courtesy of Karagündüz project, photograph by Mustafa Kalaycıoğlu.*

Figure 9.10 Karagündüz cemetery, tomb K 6. *Courtesy of Karagündüz project, photograph by Mustafa Kalaycıoğlu.*

different from the polychrome ware of the preceding Middle and Late Bronze Ages. They can be divided into two major groups according to technique, shape, and decoration. The first and larger group is pink in color and wheel made. The most popular forms are carinated bowls with horizontal grooves below the rim and small cups with S-shaped profiles usually nippled on their shoulders (figure 9.11–9.13). Vertically perforated triangular ledge handles occur quite often. Some vessels are decorated with incisions. The most popular motifs include wavy lines, triangles, and garlands (Sevin 1996a: Fig. 7). The technique and style put this

pottery in the same category with Iron Age pottery found from the Euphrates in the west to Lake Urmia in the east (Sevin and Kavaklı 1996a; Sevin 1996b).

The second group is rare compared to the first. Its most interesting characteristics are the carination, which suggests derivation from metal prototypes, and the thick reddish-brown slip. The most popular shapes are carinated flaring bowls and juglets with squat bodies. This group includes also trefoil pitchers (figures 9.14, 9.15; Sevin 1999a: Fig. 8), noticeable for their squat thick necks, globular squat bodies, and hollowed handles after the style of metal counterparts (Sevin and Kavaklı 1996b: Fig. 26). They can readily be compared with metal prototypes and reflect the characteristics known from the classical Urartian ware. Unlike the first group, which has a wide distribution, red polished ware seems to be limited to the Lake Van basin in the Early Iron Age (Sevin and Kavaklı 1996a; Sevin 1996a). Red polished ware is not found in the earliest graves of Karagündüz, suggesting that its introduction be dated later than that of the other group.

IRON

The most obvious feature of the Iron Age is the introduction into daily life of iron extracted from ore. It is thought that this important discovery was first made around this region (Pleiner 1967; Pigott 1980). It really does seem from the excavations in the cemeteries of Ernis, Dilkaya, and Karagündüz that iron was used in this region from a very early date. Just as with the

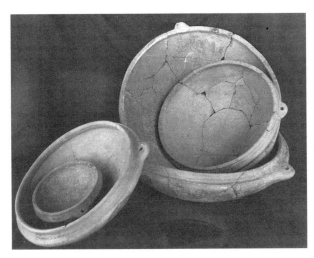

Figure 9.11 Pottery from Karagündüz. *Courtesy of Karagündüz project, photograph by Veli Sevin.*

Figure 9.12 A jar from Karagündüz. *Courtesy of Karagündüz project, photograph by Mustafa Kalaycioğlu.*

Figure 9.13 A jar with incised decoration. *Courtesy of Karagündüz project, photograph by Mustafa Kalaycioğlu.*

examples from the classical Urartian period, the Early Iron Age iron is usually of a low carbon content. All objects are in wrought iron. Most of the finds are ornaments or ceremonial weapons.

Bracelets are the most common iron objects. They are of two types, either having a round section (figure 9.16) or else are made of hammered sheet-metal bands (figure 9.17; Sevin 1987: Fig. 5/10, 14; Sevin and Kavaklı 1996a: Figs. 12-17). The first type was widespread and can be subdivided as to simple and overlapping ends. Similar examples were also found at Noratus in Armenia (Martirosian 1964:193ff.), at Talysh (Schaeffer 1948:433), at Dinkha Tepe II (Muscarella 1974: Figs. 36/417, 39/124, 47/412), at Haftavan Tepe

(Burney 1972: Plates III/a, V/a, Fig. 9), at Hasanlu IV (Pigott 1980:Table 12.3), at Kordlar Tepe (Lippert 1979:133, Figs. 15-16/a-b), and at Sialk B (Ghirshman 1939: Plate LIX/S.641/a-b, LXXVII/S.984/c). One example from Karagündüz may possibly have serpent head terminals (Sevin and Kavaklı 1996a: Fig. 13).

The second group, sheet-metal bracelets, can be divided into narrow and broad ones. It seems that this type was particular to Karagündüz and Ernis. Slightly similar examples in bronze can be seen at Hasanlu IV and Dinkha Tepe II (Lamberg-Karlovsky 1965: Plate IX/4, IV/9; Muscarella 1988:Nos. 14-15; 1974: Fig. 36/113).

Another popular type of iron ornament is rings. Again there are two types: plain loop rings and sheet-

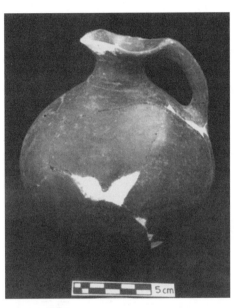

Figure 9.14 Red-polished trefoil pitcher. *Courtesy of Karagündüz project, photograph by Mustafa Kalaycıoğlu.*

Figure 9.15 Red-polished trefoil pitcher. *Courtesy of Karagündüz project, photograph by Mustafa Kalaycıoğlu.*

Figure 9.16 Iron bracelet with round section. *Courtesy of Karagündüz project, photograph by Selamet Taskin.*

Figure 9.17 Iron bracelet of sheet-metal band. *Courtesy of Karagündüz project, photograph by Selamet Taskin.*

metal rings. Those in the first group are sometimes a plain circle or sometimes a spiral of three turns. They can be found at Hasanlu IV (Lamberg-Karlovsky 1965: Plate IV/5; Muscarella 1988:No. 29), at Dinkha Tepe II (Muscarella 1974:60, Figs. 26/413,419, 36/426), at Sialk A (Pleiner 1967: Fig. 6/15) and also at Haftavan Tepe (Burney 1972: Plate Va). It is clear from in situ finds that multiple rings could be worn adjacently on many fingers at once.

Toggle pins are among the popular iron ornaments of the Van region in the Early Iron Age. These pins have a perforation on their upper parts. They are of three types. The first has a conical head (Sevin 1987: Fig. 5/5; Sevin and Kavaklı 1996a: Fig. 21 third and fourth rows); the second a small spherical head, where in one instance the pin was topped by a spherical carnelian bead (figure 9.18; Sevin and Kavaklı 1996a: Fig. 20); and the third always a quadrangular, prismatic head (Sevin and

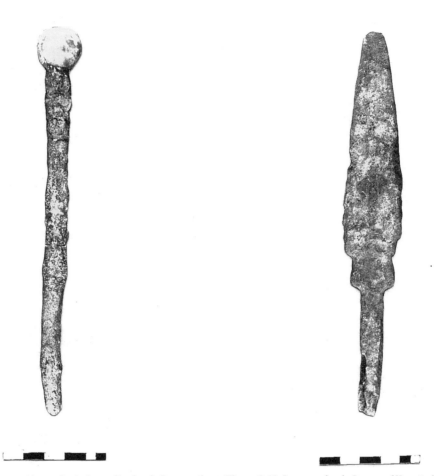

Figure 9.18 Iron pin topped by a spherical carnelian bead. *Courtesy of Karagündüz project, photograph by Selamet Taskin.*

Figure 9.19 Iron spearhead. *Courtesy of Karagündüz project, photograph by Selamet Taskin.*

Figure 9.20 Iron dagger. *Courtesy of Karagündüz project, photograph by Selamet Taskin.*

Figure 9.21 Carnelian, agate, frit, glass and bronze beads. *Courtesy of Karagündüz project, photograph by Selamet Taskin.*

Figure 9.22 Glass, carnelian and bone (in the middle) beads (original order not preserved). *Courtesy of Karagündüz project, photograph by Selamet Taskin.*

Figure 9.23 Carnelian and antimony beads (original order not preserved). *Courtesy of Karagündüz project, photograph by Selamet Taskin.*

Figure 9.24 Glass and carnelian beads (original order not preserved). *Courtesy of Karagündüz project, photograph by Selamet Taskin.*

Kavaklı 1996a: Fig. 21 second row). From the eye of one pin, a pendant of various beads and a *Conus* shell was suspended (Sevin and Kavaklı 1996a: Fig. 27).

Grave goods included ceremonial weapons such as mace heads, daggers, axes, and spearheads. The mace heads of Ernis have small but solid heavy heads of two types, shaft holed and socketed (Sevin 1987: Figs. 5/11-12). The small size of these objects may suggest that they are not maces but rather staff or scepter heads.

Daggers, all of which have a ribbed blade, are divided into two classes—those with tangs and those without tangs. The second type has two holes on their broad rounded shoulders, used in riveting the blade to the hilt (Sevin and Kavaklı 1996a: Fig. 23). Similar examples can be found in the Early Iron Age of the Guilan on the southwestern shores of the Caspian Sea in northern Iran (Härinck 1988: Figure 61/9) and in the Hittite levels (IIIa-b) at Alaca Hüyük in central Anatolia (Kosay and Akok 1966: Plates 47/h 192; 133/3; Maxwell-Hyslop 1946: type 16). In one example the wooden hilt is riveted on from below and above by two convex iron plates. The pommel of the hilt is crescent shaped. The tip of the blade is broken off (figure 9.20). Similar examples are seen at Hasanlu IV (Lamberg-Karlovsky 1965: Plate XXIV/1), and Dinkha Tepe II (Muscarella 1974: Fig. 45/1046) in northwestern Iran, and at Karmir-Blur in Armenia (Pleiner 1967: Fig. 2/10,16) but the dagger of Karagündüz is unique for its plated hilt. The only example of the tanged type comes from Ernis (Sevin 1987:39, Fig. 5/1). The complete tang is broken off. A strong midrib, rectangular in section, runs the length of the dagger.

The most interesting of the grave goods of the Early Iron Age are the axes. No examples of have yet been found at Karagündüz. One example from Ernis with its hammerlike head and tapering blade (Sevin 1987:39, Fig. 5/9) recalls those found in the cemeteries of Dinkha Tepe II (Muscarella 1974:67, Fig. 36/1033), Bard-i Bal and Tapa War Kabud in Luristan (Vanden Berghe 1973: Figs. 25, 13/4; 1968: Fig. 23/7, Plate 27/a). An iron spearhead was found at Karagündüz cemetery (figure 9.19; Sevin and Kavaklı 1996a: Fig. 25). It has a long tang and a flat blade with a raised narrow midrib; the shoulder is almost squared.

Whether the growth in the use of iron was rapid or gradual, at first metal was clearly highly prized and used for ornaments and other objects that probably had a symbolic value. As a matter of fact, all available iron evidence, together with some of the pottery, suggests that the earliest burials in the Early Iron Age cemeteries of the Van region could be contemporary with the beginnings of Hasanlu IV and Dinkha Tepe II or a little bit earlier. A calibrated C14 sample from one of the earlier chamber tombs (K6) of Karagündüz gives a date of 1250–1120 BC for the beginning of the cemetery.

BRONZE OBJECTS

Far less bronze has been found in the Early Iron Age tombs of the Lake Van basin than iron. It is mainly found in the developed tomb chambers with entrance passages and is always ornamental, usually in the form of toggle pins. These pins have a perforation on their upper parts and range in style from very plain to ones topped off with cockerels, eagles, poppies, and buds (Sevin and Kavaklı 1996a: Figs. 26-27). This kind of bronze toggle pin continued to be used among the classical Urartian artifacts with some minor alterations. Fibulae were not used in the Early Iron Age in the Van basin.

There are also a few examples of bronze rings. These are of two types, plain circles and those with knobbed decoration (Sevin and Kavaklı 1996a: Fig. 19). The second group can be compared to those found in Hasanlu IV (Muscarella 1988:No. 22), Iranian Talish (Schaeffer 1948: Fig. 232/18), and Khurvin (Van den Berghe 1964: Plate XL/287). Some of the earrings were made of bronze.

BEADS

Beads must have been very popular during the Early Iron Age in the Van region, since large quantities of beads were recovered from the tombs (figures 9.21–9.24; Sevin and Kavaklı 1996a: Figs. 30–35). They were used largely for necklaces, bracelets, and pin-pendants. As well as forming an important decorative function, it is very likely the beads also served as amulets for warding off evil. Most are made from semiprecious stones such as agate and carnelian or from glass or frit. They vary from biconical to cylindrical, elliptical, lentoid, disk, and barrel shaped. Examples in bronze, bone, antimony, rock crystal, and faience are less common, while those made from shells such as *Conus*, *Dentalium*, and *Cyprea* are rare. The most noteworthy of the popular types of bead are long thin tubes of white frit (Sevin and Kavaklı1996a: Fig. 307). These are also found in the levels of Haftavan Tepe which are contemporary with Hasanlu IV (Burney 1970: Plate Va). Small bronze wires coiled into a shuttle-shaped bead are rare. This type is to be found also at Hasanlu IV (Lamberg-Karlovsky 1965:244, Plate V/5; Muscarella 1988:No. 31), Haftavan Tepe (Burney 1970: Plate IVd), and Iranian Talish (Schaeffer 1948: Fig. 217/19, Plates LIX, LXI).

The burial customs, pottery, and iron workmanship imply a powerful cultural unity in the Lake Van region during the Early Iron Age. It is also evident that in the same period, in both the west and, in particular, in the southern Urmia region, the culture was different. One example is that, while in the Van region crowded multiple burials in chamber tombs were the normal practice, to the east around Lake Urmia simple inhumation prevailed. Pedestal goblets, worm bowls, bridged spouted vessels and the like (known in Iranian terminology as "Early Western Grey Ware" or "Iron I" and "Late Western Grey Ware" or "Iron II"), which are seen as characteristic of the Early Iron Age, particularly in the southern slopes of the Elburz mountains and in northwestern Iran, are not found in the Lake Van basin.[3] Haftavan Tepe, Kordlar Tepe, and Geoy Tepe on the western shores of Lake Urmia are the most westerly sites providing the diagnostic ware of so-called Iron I period, and it can be argued that these sites are the meeting point of eastern Anatolian and northwestern Iranian traditions of the Early Iron Age (Sevin 1996a).

While there are significant cultural differences between the Lake Van basin and the west and especially the south Urmia region in the early stages of the Iron Age, there is some evidence, though on a much smaller scale, of contact, especially in the ornamental iron and pottery types. A specific example would be the carinated ribbed bowls with lugs pierced for string.

The archaeological materials imply that there were different cultures between the Lake Van area and the western and southern Urmia regions and that two dif- ferent traditions were living together in the Van region during the Early Iron Age. It can be argued that Urartian culture was derived from the culture of red polished and metal inspired ware of the Van region (Sevin 1996a, 1996b).

The archaeological evidence from the Van region as a whole suggests that during the Early Iron Age a good portion of the ruling elite along with the tribal people did not have a settled lifestyle but lived in tents and migrated seasonally with their flocks and herds. The representations of tents on the Hakkari stelae found in 1998 seem to add confirmation (Sevin and Özfırat 1998; Sevin 1999b, 2000, 2001).

NOTES

1. For a study of the chronology of the Iron Age, see Sevin et al. 1997.

2. At the mound of Karagündüz, one very weak building level (level 5) was identified as contemporary with the cemetery. See Sevin et al. 2000.

3. The find spot of the grey pedestal goblet at Toprakkale near Van is open to some doubt (Lehmann-Haupt 1907:110, Fig. 83). There are no systematic records from Lehman-Haupt's excavation. Because no records were kept in the field, we are inclined to believe that this piece reached Berlin through private sale along with a torque (Wartke 1990: Figure 27/f., Plate XXXVII), a ring (Wartke 1990: Figure 27/e), and a toggle pin (Wartke 1990: Plate XXXIV/f), all in iron. It is a known fact that a major part of the metal objects published as being from Toprakkale were sold to the Berlin Königlischen Museum by antique sellers at the end of the nineteenth and the beginning of the twentieth century (Wartke 1990. 14 ff.).

CHAPTER 10

Recent Excavations at the Urartian Fortress of Ayanis

ALTAN ÇİLİNGİROĞLU

During excavations at Çavuştepe conducted by Dr. Afif Erzen, the team visited a site called Ayanis. At the time the writer thought that it would be an exciting place to excavate. After having excavated Ayanis since July 1989, I now know how right I was in thinking so some twenty years ago. The site has proven to be richer in material culture remains and historical information than any other Urartian site previously excavated.

Ayanis is 38 km north of the city of Van and very close to the village of Ağartı, known as Ayanis until recently. The ancient road leading to the north from the capital city of Urartu, Tushpa, heads toward Erciş and then follows the route alongside Lake Van, reaching Ayanis and Amik Kale before heading further north. The Ayanis fortress was constructed in the seventh century BC on a spur overlooking the lake, 250 m from the shore (figure 10.1). The hill was surrounded by mud-brick fortification walls that were raised on strong foundation walls built of stone blocks (figure 10.2). As was customary in Urartian military architecture, all the stone blocks were laid on bedding carved into the bedrock. The foundation stone blocks in the south are made of basalt (figure 10.3), while all others are of limestone. The height of the foundation is about two m and the surmounting mud-brick walls can still be seen atop many areas of the fortification walls.

The entrance to the fortress is in the southeast corner of the walls and consists of a threshold measuring 4 x 3 m and a monumental construction behind it (Çilingiroğlu 1996: 364). The gate is protected by two towers slightly projecting in the east and west (figure 10.4). Based on the position of the door socket, the door must have had two wooden panels that were not identical in size. The basalt inscription found in front of the door probably originally hung on the east tower. The inscription in Urartian sheds light on many issues concerning the fortress (Çilingiroğlu and Salvini 1995: 118–119; Salvini 2001:251–252):

Through the greatness of Haldi, Rusa, the son of Argishti, has built this fortress to perfection in front of the mountain Eiduru. Rusa says: the rock was

Figure 10.1 View of Ayanis citadel. *All photographs by Dr. Haluk Sağlamtimur.*

Figure 10.3 Stone foundation blocks, south side of fortress.

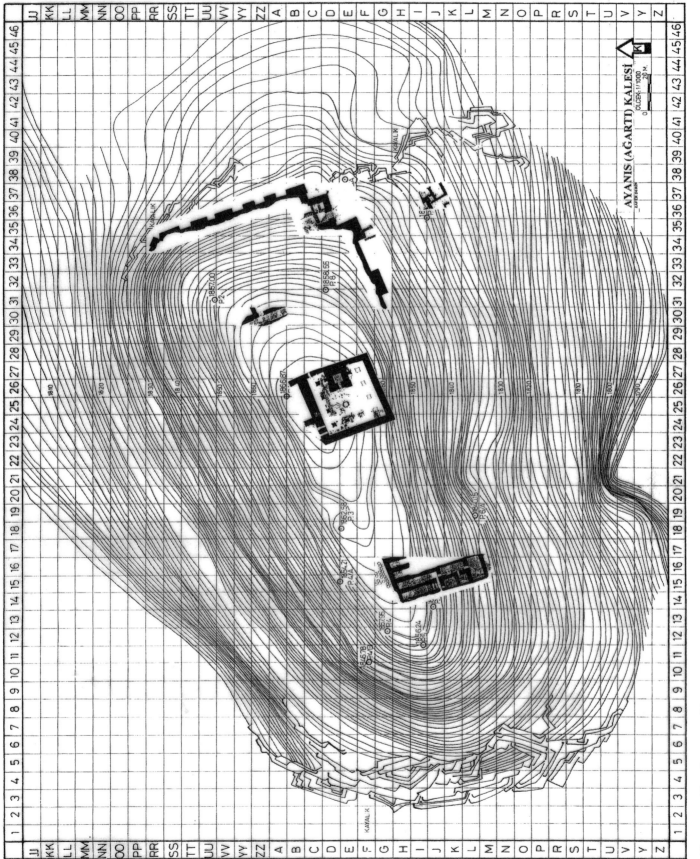

Figure 10.2 Plan of Ayanis citadel excavations. *Plan by Dr. Zafer Derin.*

Figure 10.4 Gate and towers.

untouched, nothing was built here before, I built a shrine as well as a fortress, perfectly. I set new vineyards and orchards and founded a new town (settlement) here. Mightily these accomplishments I made here. I imposed the Rushahinili. Through the greatness of Haldi (I am) Rusa, the son of Argishti, mighty king, great king, king of Biainili, lord of the Tushpa city. Rusa says: Whoever my name erases and puts his own name may Haldi and the Storm god and the Sun god annihilate him.

The Mt. Eiduru mentioned in the text seems to be Mt. Süphan, the second highest peak of Anatolia. The fortress of Ayanis is one of the great successes of Rusa II, following his building programs at Karmir-Blur, Toprakkale, Kef Kalesi, and Bastam. This fortress is even more important than the others Rusa founded, since it has an outer town built around it. The gateway inscription states that Rusa built an outer city; it has been proved, with the help of archaeological excavations, that Rusa II told the truth.

The excavations carried out for the last four years by our colleagues Elizabeth C. Stone and Paul Zimansky have revealed houses belonging to a planned city at Güney Tepe to the east of the fortress (Çilingiroğlu and Sağlamtimur 1999: 530–531; Stone and Zimanksy 2001:355–375; and

chapter 11). In addition, these excavations have revealed administrative buildings reaching 60 m in length, which have been unearthed in an area called Pınarbaşı. Such large buildings are usually found within Urartian fortresses; only rarely are they constructed outside the fortresses. We do see such large external buildings at Bastam, for example, but those at Ayanis are larger and more numerous. This was possibly one of the consequences of the reforms made by Rusa II. From the temple inscription, it is known that during his reign, Rusa II accommodated conquered peoples at Ayanis after having deported them from Muški, Hatti, Assyria, and Etiuni, among other places, where he had won military campaigns. Rusa said he had constructed dams, water channels, and vineyards and orchards for them, although the conquered peoples themselves may have supplied the labor for these improvements. We can now compare the extraordinary art found in the royal fortresses to the material culture of the common people who lived in the outer, planned city. It will be very interesting to see the cultural distinctions between the Urartian elite and the captured, nonelite population. With the help of findings from future excavations, it will be possible to talk more clearly about cultural and social life, economic activities, and urbanization in the Urartian Kingdom.

FORTRESS EXCAVATIONS

The fortress excavations, which began in 1989, have brought to light about 10% of the buildings situated within the fortification walls. The excavations have been carried out in two major areas within the fortress. In the west, a monumental building has been unearthed that had a basement used for storage (figure 10.5). The other area, excavated in the east of the fortress, has produced a temple complex that contained a *cella* (a small room or chamber containing a sacred image).

Within the western side of the fortress, storage buildings, constructed on either side of the wall 3 m in width and stretching in the east-west direction, were placed in a downward-sloping area. Although our knowledge about the plan of the building in the west is as yet uncertain, its basement clearly served as a magazine for hundreds of pithoi and other containers. Some of the rooms in the basement were connected to each other through doors or openings. Pithoi were buried up to their shoulders and many smaller pots were placed around them (figure 10.5). Almost all pithoi bear a measurement inscription on their shoulders in either Urartian hieroglyph or cuneiform, and many of them are associated with bullae covered with

Figure 10.5 Storage vessels *in situ.*

Figure 10.6 Inscription on pithos.

Figure 10.7 View of pillared hall and temple.

seal impressions with or without inscriptions (figure 10.6). The preliminary study of the bullae has shown that they declare the origins or shippers of the goods in the pithoi. According to the remains, it is clear that oil, wheat, barley, and millet were kept in the largest pithoi. Other vessels, smaller in size, must have been used for daily needs. Many geographical, personal, and material names are given in the inscriptions on bullae, which by 1999 totaled about 85 (Abay 2001:321–351; Salvini 2001:279–319). Further studies on the bullae will shed some light on how the needs of Urartian fortresses were met and what kind of distribution system they used.

West of the eastern fortification walls is a wide flat area covering the major area within the walls and the highest section of the fortress. The excavations carried out in trenches within the section called No. VI in the literature of the Ayanis excavations have revealed an east-west mud-brick wall that limits the north of the rooms in this area. The preserved height of the wall above the floor is 4.15 m. Many burned and unburned pieces of wooden construction beams and heavy fire traces can be seen on the floor formed by beaten clay. The bedrock has been flattened in some parts to make

a good floor and to form a foundation for the construction built on it. The plaster on the wall, as observed in many parts of the building, had blue paint up to 1.35 m from the floor. There are remnants to indicate that the rest of the walls had been painted white.

In section No. VI, within an area surrounded with mud-brick walls, are four free-standing pillars extending east-west near the north wall and another four (counting the corner pillar again) in a north-south direction. Recent excavations have revealed three more pillars south of the walled area, standing on mud-brick platforms instead of bedrock; thus the hall had ten free-standing pillars. The northern pillars are about 3.60 m from the north wall and lined up at intervals of 6.0 m. All pillars have shallow corner buttresses. The dimensions of the first and fourth pillars at the north side are 2.60 x 2.70 m, the second and third are 2.50 by 2.50 m. All pillars were built with mud-brick lying on a base composed of three courses of basalt-stone blocks (figures 10.7, 10.8).

Two alabaster bases have been found on either side of a door opening in the east wall. Since both have holes in the middle, they could be sockets for wooden and

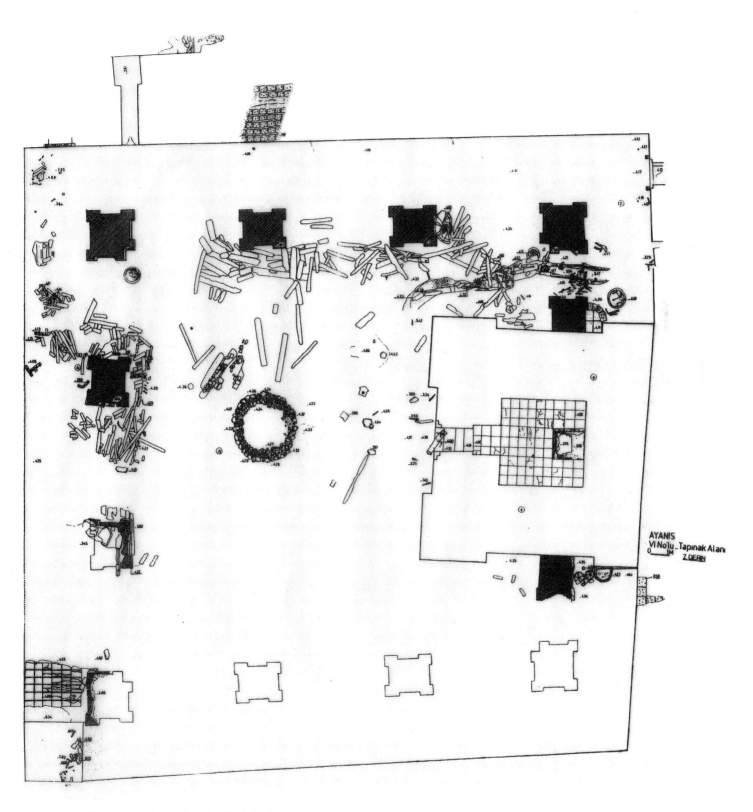

Figure 10.8 Plan of pillared hall and temple. *Plan by Dr. Zafer Derin.*

Figure 10.9 View of cella with ornamented platform.

Figure 10.10 Detail of ornamented platform decoration.

painted sacred trees on either side of the door, based on the trees seen on the relief from Adilcevaz now in the Ankara Museum. The inscriptions on two bronze discs (7.1 cm in diameter and 3.7 cm in height), uncovered just under the beaten floor in front of the alabaster bases, state that the pillared hall was constructed by Rusa, the son of Arghishti. The pillared hall is about 30 m long east-west and contains an Urartian temple in the standard plan (figures 10.7, 10.8). The east wall of the temple abuts the east wall of the hall. The Ayanis temple is 13.0 by 13.0 m, and the walls have been preserved to a height of 4.5 m, with a width of 3.5 m. However, due to the inclination of the east wall, the almost square measurement is a few centimeters shorter in the north and south. The *cella* is of 4.62 by 4.58 m. Although the buttresses of the temple in the front corners are complete, the rear corners have incomplete buttresses since they abut the east wall of the hall (figure 10.8).

Pillars connect to the south and north wall of the temple. This distinctive feature makes the Ayanis temple very special among all known Urartian temples (and brings the total number of pillars in the hall to 12). A half-round shaped hearth made of regular mud-bricks is connected to the north wall of the temple. The hearth is another point that makes Ayanis temple unique. Objects that have been dug out around the hearth—spearheads, weapons, and a bronze quiver filled with millet—suggest that some kind of ceremony was performed in this sacred area.

The entrance to the cella is through a corridor in the west facade of the temple. The corridor is 1.20 m wide and 2.10 m long. Four light green alabaster blocks 0.18 m thick form the threshold. The threshold is 0.15 m higher than the floor of the cella. The floor is paved with 90 tiles of alabaster stone measuring 0.48 by 0.52 m.

An ornamented platform connected to the east wall of the cella and just across from the entrance is another important characteristic of the Ayanis temple. The platform was built of wooden beams and mud-brick and the sides and top were completely covered with alabaster blocks (figure 10.9). The platform is 175 cm by 165 cm by 56 cm high decorated with various floral motifs and animal ornaments made of gold plates. Only a very small number of the golden plates have been preserved, since the temple was robbed in antiquity. Each animal figure had a drilled hole about 1 cm long and 0.2 cm wide which must have been used to connect the gold to the stone with gold nails, some of which have been found. Along the bottom of the sides

of the platform are many holes that were once filled with metal rosettes or stone mosaics. The upper alabaster blocks of the platform are decorated with winged lions and sirens in incised style (figure 10.10). All of the platform decorations are very skillfully made; the applied metal animal ornament is unknown at any other Urartian site. It is not certain what the platform was used for, but it may have served as an offering table, the base of a cult image, or a base for a throne. There are no traces on the platform to support the latter possibility, however, and no pieces of throne have so far come to light in the excavations at Ayanis. This is in contrast to the temple at Toprakkale, where pieces of a throne have been discovered associated with a temple.

The walls of the *cella* are decorated in a very unusual way, with ornamented courses of stone blocks: two courses on the north, east and south walls and three courses at the entrance and part of the west wall. The decoration is the first example in Urartian ornamental art made by carving out images in the basalt blocks. The technique can be called stone inlay (intaglio). The dark blocks were carved out in the shapes of gods, floral designs, animals, and rosettes; then white stone pieces, which were painted, were inlaid into the cutaway spaces and affixed by melted lead. The details of the inlays were emphasized with incised and painted lines. At the time of excavation, some of the inlays were still in place, but most were recovered from the *cella* floor (figures 10.11, 10.12) (Çilingiroğlu 2001:37–65).

Bronze bands were recovered, both on the *cella* floor and attached to the north wall. Thus we can assume that the walls of the *cella*, above the inlaid stone at the base, were decorated with horizontal bronze bands, fixed to the mudbrick wall with bronze nails. Similar bronze bands seem to be illustrated on the front façade of the Musasir temple depicted on the relief from Khorsabad, indicating that although the discovery at Ayanis is unparalleled, other Urartian temples may have had similar bronze decoration.

An inscription is carved on the front façade and entryway of the temple (figures 10.12, 10.13). It is not only the most complete Urartian temple inscription, it is the third longest extant Urartian inscription recovered to date. The other two are the Horhor inscription of Argishti I and the Anali-Kiz inscription of Sarduri II. The Ayanis inscription consists of eighty-eight lines covering the basalt stone blocks used at both sides of the cella entrance and in the passage into the cella. The inscription begins:

To Haldi, his lord, Rusa, the son of Argishti, has built this *susi*; also a gate of Haldi to perfection in Rusahinili Eiduru-kai (Rusahinili in front of Mount Eiduru) he has erected and consecrated (?) to Haldi. Rusa says: the rock was wild, the land was waste; nothing was built here before. (Çilingiroğlu and Salvini 1997:288–89; Salvini 2001:253–270)

It is clearly stated in the inscription that king Rusa II built a *susi* (that is, the standard square Urartian tower temple having a single inner room and heavily reinforced walls) for the fortress of Ayanis. Although the translation of the inscription has not been completed yet, it has already produced considerable important information about Urartian history and culture. According to the inscription, Rusa II deported peoples from the "enemy countries" of Hatti, Muški, Etiuni, and, significantly, Assyria, and built a city for them. The excavations carried out outside the fortress in recent years yielded architectural remains of administrative buildings and dwellings that seem to have been established for these peoples. The other important point that has already attracted attention in the inscription is that Mount Eiduru (Süphan Dağ), situated just across Lake Van from Ayanis fortress, was regarded as "God" and animals were sacrificed to him. Thus it is now understood why the fortress had been named after the god Eiduru although that god had not been included in the list of deities in the Meherkapısı inscription.

The eastern wall of the Ayanis *susi* temple, in a square pillared hall 30 m on a side, directly touches the east wall of the hall. The large area in front of the temple and inside the pillars must have been used as a courtyard to the temple. The limestone blocks with smooth surfaces unearthed in front of the temple entrance and in the courtyard were likely a floor pavement for the courtyard. Similar material found not in situ in previous years may support the idea. It should be noted that this kind of material was also used to cover the courtyard of the temple of Irmushini at Çavuştepe (Erzen 1978:10). Based on the archaeological evidence, the area in front of the temple must have had no roof. The two stone column bases uncovered in front of a pillar in the west indicate the existence of a portico around the courtyard, also indicated by the burned wooden pieces found around some of the pillars.

The only architectural remains found within the courtyard is a round platform, or perhaps the foundations of a round room, situated 7.5 m west of the threshold of the temple. The diameter of this round structure is 3.5 m; its masonry consisted of one line of medium-size stones around the outside with smaller stones forming the inner diameter. Pieces of red and white plaster found in and around this construction are assumed to have been used to decorate its walls. This construction might have had a similar function to those found in many other courtyards of Urartian temples (Erzen 1978; Özgüç 1966: Plate VI.).

To find a platform in the courtyard of the Ayanis temple should not be a surprise considering the precedents. However, based on information from other sites, the platform in the courtyard of Ayanis temple should have had a wall with a roof or other protection for the painted plaster, remains of which have not been found.

HISTORICAL DATA

An important question is in which years the fortress of Ayanis and the susi temple were built during the presumed forty-year reign of Rusa II. Although small objects, such as inscribed helmets, quivers, and inscribed building discs at Ayanis, make mention of dates, the long inscription does not. According to the temple inscription, the fortress was built following the successful campaigns against Hatti, Muški, Etiuni, and Assyria (Çilingiroğlu and Salvini 1995: 124). Consequently the fortress of Ayanis must have been built after the fortresses of Karmir-Blur, Bastam, Kef Kalesi, and Toprakkale. Dendrochronological studies carried out on the wooden pieces of the portico around the temple indicate that it might have been built between 656/655–651 BC. Other dendrochronological results obtained from other pieces collected from different parts of the fortress support the dating. However, if we take into account only the dendrochronological results and assume that the fortress of Ayanis was built in the same years that the wood suggests and also consider the presumed dates of Rusa's reign, we would have to say that the fortress was used for only five years. This assumption seems impossible when one considers the size of the fortress and the outer city. In addition, the excavations performed within the boundaries of the outer city show that those buildings were used for more than five years. It should be noted that most of the wooden pieces used for dendrochronology were collected from the portico around the temple. Some evidence gained from the pillared hall and other parts of the fortress indicate that the fortress was heavily damaged before the final destructive fire. Thus, it is possible that the wooden portico and some other parts of the fortress

Figure 10.11 Detail of lower cella wall ornament.

Figure 10.12 View of lower cella wall ornament.

Figure 10.13 View of temple inscription.

might have been renewed around 651 BC following a fire that devastated them.

However, new research on dendrochronology and radiocarbon dating has called this assumption into question. M. Newton and P. Kuniholm have suggested that the Ayanis dendrochronological dates (656–651 BC) should be taken back twenty years to 677–673 +4/-7 BC, based on new radiocarbon dates recently obtained (Manning et al. 2001:2534). If we accept the new dating, together with the archaeological evidence of a fire, then either Ayanis fortress had a fire around 675 BC and the fortress continued in use after a reconstruction, or the fortress was destroyed around 675 BC.

As we have suggested elsewhere, based on historical evidence (Çilingiroğlu and Salvini 2001:22–23), the fortress of Ayanis might have been built around 673/672 BC. In this case, taking the dendrochronological dates back twenty years does not create many problems, because the dendrochronlogical dates would coincide with the presumed initial construction. However, if we assume that 675 BC marks the destruction date of Ayanis, then we will definitely have many problems about the duration of the reign

of Argishti II and Rusa II, and even later kings of the Urartian kingdom. I believe that we need more archaeological and dendrochronological data to suggest anything new about the history of the later period of Urartu. The fact that no archaeological material or inscription has been found within the Ayanis fortress dating to any other Urartian ruler except Rusa II suggests that no settlement in the late period of the Urartian kingdom took place here. It is most likely that the fortress of Ayanis was not used after Rusa II due to the political situation that developed after his reign. Although four Urartian kings ruled after Rusa II until the end of the Urartian kingdom, the very limited written documents make it difficult to understand the history of the last fifty years of Urartu, which appears to be after the occupation of Ayanis.

BRONZES

Many metal objects have been found in the pillared hall and around the temple. The distribution of these objects on the floor leads us to assume that the walls of the temple and the pillars and even the north and east walls of the pillared hall itself had been decorated with various weapons. The most important objects are helmets, shields, spears or swords, spearheads and arrowheads, quivers, small or big nails (*siggatu*), and especially a shield that has a projecting lion's head in the center. Most of the objects mentioned here had inscriptions reading that the weapons were dedicated by Rusa II to the god Haldi.

A sword/spear found within the temple area during the excavation season of 1996, at a depth of 4.17 m in the corner of second pillar in the east, is a very important and unique find from the point of view of Urartian art. The sword/spear has a length of 73.8 m and was made of bronze (figure 10.14). The inscription on the weapon, in four lines of Urartian cuneiform, reads: "To Haldi, Lord, this *šuri* Rusa Argistehi (= son of Argisti) made [and] dedicated for his [long] life". The word "*šuri*" on the sword/spear is extremely important because it has ended the long-lasting discussion among scholars studying Urartian history and art about the meaning of "*šuri*". In the past, some scholars had suggested that "*šuri*" possibly meant "war chariot," others "sword" (König 1954: 33-35; Van Loon 1974:150). After this find at Ayanis, the argument about the meaning of *šuri* is certainly settled (Çilingiroğlu and Salvini 1999).

As we know from Urartian fortresses that had been excavated previously, such as Karmir Blur (Piotrovskii 1969: 159ff) and Toprakkale, the objects found in the courtyard of the temple are offerings to the "God Haldi" during weapons dedication ceremonies. Twelve quivers, which mostly bear an offering inscription, unearthed around the pillar located in the center of the western part of the temple entrance, probably are remains from such ceremonies. The inscribed and uninscribed nails with eagle or mushroom heads found on the floor, usually made of bronze, must have been used to hold the sacred weapons on the walls and pillars in the temple area (Sağlamtimur et al. 2001: 219-221). Hundreds of spearheads and arrowheads, which obviously could not be individually hung on the walls, have been discovered around the pillars located in the north of the pillared hall. A shield uncovered in reverse position in the northeast corner of the temple seems to have fallen from the north wall of the temple, heavily damaging the shield. The bronze shield, 1 m in diameter, has an inscription in two lines running along its whole edge. Unfortunately, the inscription is concealed by the folded part of the damaged shield. The surface of the shield has been separated decoratively by friezes that contain lion and bull motifs in procession (figure 10.15). The projecting

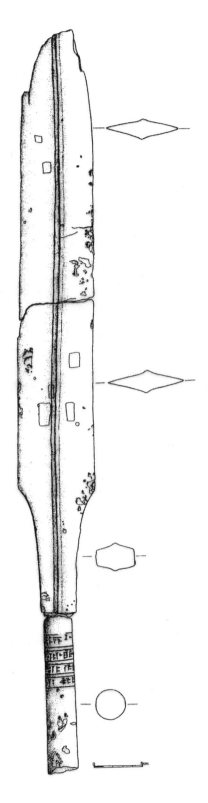

Figure 10.14 Inscribed sword/spear.

Figure 10.15 Shield with central projecting lion head (lion head figs. 10.16, 10.17).

Figure 10.16 Lion head from shield shown in fig. 10.15.

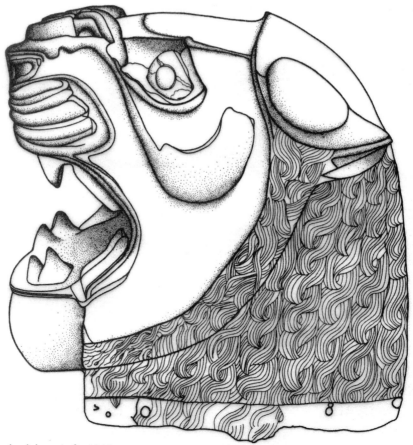

Figure 10.17 Drawing of lion head shown in fig. 10.16.
Drawing by Dilek Öztürk.

lion head in the center of the shield, weighing about 5.1 kgs, is the most significant element of this find (figure 10.16). The lion head was attached to the shield with the help of two holders on the reverse side of the shield and a riveted metal piece extended from the neck. The ears of the lion are separate pieces attached to the head and the eye holes had been filled with a soft material and inlaid stone. The mouth is open, the teeth are displayed clearly and the nose wrinkles are shown in detail. The mane of the lion has been depicted with incised lines (figure 10.17). This is the only recovered example of the type of shields described in the eighth campaign of Sargon II, the Assyrian (...."with the heads of snarling lions projecting from the hearts"....) (Luckenbill 1927:173). Some similar lion-headed shields can been seen on the walls of Musasir temple shown in the Khorsabad relief. The lion-headed shield of Ayanis must be regarded as solid proof that the written descriptions and the visual representations about Urartians in Assyrian written and visual sources reflect specific cultural elements.

URARTIAN TEMPLES

Many temples unearthed in Urartian excavations connected with the other buildings around the temple. Such buildings can be seen at the Irmushini temple of Çavuştepe, at Kayalıdere, Anzavurtepe, and Altıntepe. It is not certain whether the temple at Toprakkale, built on a massive rock, has any connection to any other building. However, the evidence shows that in general Urartian temples were not separate tower buildings with their square cellas erected to stand without having any connection to any other building or room, as has been suggested in the past. Although the cella of the Altıntepe temple has no building connected to it, some rooms were connected to the portico around that cella. It seems that most Urartian temples could not be noticed easily from outside the fortress because buildings at least two stories high surrounded them. The masonry of the walls surrounding the Ayanis temple courtyard had a width of at least 5 m, a thickness that indicates it was meant to support upper stories. When the monumental pillars of the courtyard are taken into account, it is reasonable to assume that the height of the second story would have been substantial. Thus, it is probable that the temple of Ayanis was built to be hardly detectable from inside most of the fortress or from outside the walls, since the temple was surrounded by a high building complex. However, there is no direct evidence of the total height of the cella walls, now preserved up to 4.5 m high. It is possible that the height of the temple should be equal to that of the pillared hall where the temple was built, since it seems unreasonable to think that the cella would have surpassed the height of the pillared hall, like a high tower. The full height of the temple might have been about 10 to 12 m, including the stone foundation, based on current evidence.

Future excavations at the fortress of Ayanis will definitely produce more evidence about Urartian temple architecture and very important information about the religious ceremonies performed in these architectural structures, in addition to other extraordinary results we are likely to obtain from such a well-preserved Urartian site.

CHAPTER 11

The Urartian Transformation in the Outer Town of Ayanis

ELIZABETH C. STONE & PAUL ZIMANSKY

THE STATE ASSEMBLAGE AND URARTIAN SETTLEMENT

One of the enigmas of Transcaucasian archaeology is the contrast between Urartu's striking impact on the material culture of its day and the scarcity of related materials in the archaeological record of the preceding period.[1] The Urartians are associated with radical innovations in most artifactual categories from majestic fortress architecture to lamps and cooking pots. They transformed the cultural landscape with a deliberate thoroughness rarely seen in the archaeology of empires, obliterating earlier manifestations of social sophistication at such sites as Hasanlu. In the two centuries they dominated eastern Anatolia and adjacent areas, Urartian rulers built prodigiously, erecting castles to defend and exploit widely-scattered areas of alluvium. These enclaves were furnished with magazines for food storage on a massive scale, enormous quantities of military hardware, and luxury goods displaying an extraordinary standard of craftsmanship.

The speed with which this new assemblage emerged suggests invention rather than evolution, and propagation through imposed decisions of a small controlling elite rather than changes in popular fashion. Indeed, most of the artifactual material that we can confidently identify as "Urartian" has been excavated from fortresses that were deliberate and artificial creations of royal authority and thus specifically associated with the government. Hundreds of the metal objects that constitute the basis for the study of Urartian art are personally linked to individual rulers by dedicatory inscriptions, and a non-royal example remains to be discovered. We have argued elsewhere that this type of "state assemblage" is analogous to what one sees in the Inca empire (Zimansky 1995: 110–111), where local populations performing corvée in administrative centers such as Huanuco Pampa created and used "Inca" materials, but left these behind when they completed their government obligations and returned to their villages (Morris 1988: 245). In the Urartian case, however, our ignorance of the character of the non-state assemblages is so profound that we cannot even be certain they existed at all. The description of the Urartian countryside provided by Sargon II in the narrative of his 8th Campaign indicates that there was indeed a significant rural population, but it has yet to be identified or investigated archaeologically.[2] A bias toward materials from citadels leaves open the question of how deeply "Urartian" elements penetrated the societies in eastern Anatolia at the time of the empire, and how completely various population groups were integrated into the whole.

A related issue is the question of where the human resources responsible for Urartu's outburst of focused creativity came from. Throughout history, the area that the Urartian kings controlled has been characterized by sparse and diffused populations of varied ethno-linguistic composition. Although earlier generations of scholars sought to link the state that coalesced under the leadership of Sarduri I, Išpuini, and Minua at the end of the 9th century BC with 14th century inhabitants of the land of Uruatri or Uratri (Goetze 1957: 191), there is little evidence to support this link beyond the fact that this geographical name was later applied to the Urartian kingdom. The strength of the putative association is not enhanced by the fact that the term was used only by outsiders, and never by the Urartians themselves. It would seem a more reasonable hypothesis that an Urartian-speaking group formed only the nucleus of the kingdom[3] and the general population was much more of an amalgam. At least some of it came to be where it was as a result of military actions, deportations, and resettlements. The two sets of royal annals we possess, both dating to the 8th century BC, were at pains to list human captives in various categories at the end of each campaign along with livestock, as if securing them were the primary objective of the enterprise. Other inscriptions, including the one recently discovered on the facade of the Ayanis temple (Çilingiroğlu, this volume) indicate these captives were settled in newly-created centers. Half a century ago, the issue of how much of the population was made up of prisoners and whether these people should be regarded as slaves was a contentious topic in Soviet scholarship (Diakonoff 1952; Sorkokin 1952; Melikishvili 1953), but discussed largely in theoretical terms.

Urartian settlements, however, are not entirely unknown and offer an opportunity for exploring, at least in some capacity, issues of the origins and integration of the population of the Urartian empire. The ones for which the best chronological control and historical context exist are those founded by the last significant king of Urartu, Rusa II, beside citadels at Karmir Blur, Bastam, and Ayanis. These cannot have been occupied for much more than a single generation since their primary *raison d'etre* was association with centers that were violently destroyed at the end of Urartu's history. In the following pages, we will summarize the current state of our findings in the settlement outside the walls of Ayanis with regard to this question of diversity and integration.

The Ayanis Outer Town Project was primarily designed to investigate the broad outlines of urban organization in Urartu as an example of a territorial state,[4] but its findings may also be of value in exploring the question of who actually resided in an Urartian city. In noting that captives from Assyria, Targu, Etiuni, Tabal, Qainaru, Hatti, Muški, and Siluquni were settled here, the temple inscription provides us with something of a gazetteer of Urartu's neighbors and suggests that at least some of the population originally stemmed from quite diverse cultures,[5] a few of which should be distinguishable by recognizable pottery and other artifacts. The archaeological record of Assyria in this period is of course well known, since Ayanis was founded only a few decades before the major Assyrian capitals suffered their final destruction. The artifactual associations of Hatti, which Urartian texts suggest lay beyond Malatya to the southwest and is probably to be construed as north Syria along and west of the Euphrates, are also well known from excavations at Carchemish, Til Barsip, Tell `Afis, `Ain Dara, and the `Amuq sites. Tabal, around modern Kayseri, and Muški, i.e. Phrygia, would have shared the assemblages unearthed at Gordion, Ališar, and Kültepe. Etiuni is a general term for areas north of Urartu, probably stretching to the Kura Valley. Siluquini can be firmly located south of Lake Sevan thanks to an Urartian rock inscription (Arutjunjan 1982). Targu and Qainaru cannot be identified. While it is highly unlikely that these people brought their pots with them when they were settled in Ayanis, one would not expect their cultural differences to be entirely expunged in the generation or two that separates the founding of Rusahinili Eidurukai and its abandonment at the end of Urartu's imperial existence. Thus an investigation of the settlement has the potential for showing the extent and nature of their integration.

CONFIGURATION AND SURVEY OF THE AYANIS SETTLEMENT

Systematic work in the outer town began in earnest in 1997 and has continued in annual summer seasons ever since.[6] Our basic strategy has been to establish the size of the settlement through shovel test survey and then to explore the character of several separate areas through magnetic field gradient survey and excavation.

The settlement was built on broken terrain at elevations ranging from roughly two hundred meters below the summit of the citadel on the level ground near the Lake, to at least thirty meters above it on the slopes of a ridge to the east known as Güney Tepe (fig. 11.1). Northeast of the citadel, at the foot of Güney Tepe, there is a spring and to the west of that an ancient terrace slopes gently downward for a few hundred meters before breaking sharply toward the lower ground by the Lake shore. This terrace, which is not under modern cultivation, we designated Pınarbaşı. The south face of the citadel descends precipitously into a gully and then the land rises again to another reasonably flat area, much of which is occupied by the modern village of Ağartı. For recording purposes, we designate the area between the citadel and Ağartı "Köy," although this term should not be construed as an indication of the character of the settlement there. It is within this varied landscape, consisting of a mixture of steep slopes, terraces, cultivated fields and orchards, that the Urartians built their settlement.

Shovel testing, as opposed to surface collection, was more or less dictated by the terrain. We wanted to compare sherd densities and proportions of various ware types from different areas, but the ground cover or lack of it skewed the numbers when one relied on visual observation alone. Some places were under cultivation, some plowed but uncultivated, and some almost denuded. By excavating and sifting forty liters of soil from points along a fifty by fifty meter grid over an area measuring 1000 x 1500 meters around the citadel, classifying and counting all the sherds we found, we were able to establish a degree of sampling uniformity for comparing areas. Using the criterion of five sherds per sample as the minimum for defining an inhabited square, and including the area within the citadel walls which we did not sample, the figure for the entire area of Urartian occupation comes out to be around eighty hectares. We have definitely reached the limits of the site in the north and east of our survey area, and appeared to be close to them in the west. We did not dig test pits in the village of Ağartı, which probably covers the southernmost part of the Urartian settlement.

Most of the sherds recovered were small body fragments and the numbers involved were not large. Almost

Figure 11.1 Ayanis citadel and surrounding area from the south. *Photo by Paul Zimansky.*

none were diagnostic in the sense of having distinctive shapes or decoration, but the ware categories were almost exclusively those seen in the Urartian excavations on the citadel. There was, however, considerable variation in the frequency of wares in different parts of the settlement. For example, red polished wares were relatively uncommon at lower elevations, and actually more abundant than they were in the fortress on the middle slopes of Güney Tepe (fig. 11.2).

To date some twenty hectares of the outer town have been subjected to a magnetic field gradient survey. Seven hectares were surveyed by Lewis Somers of Geoscan in 1997, both in Pınarbaşı and in Güney Tepe. More extensive work was conducted by the expedition in 1999, expanding the survey areas in both

Güney Tepe and Pınarbaşı, and conducting more limited survey both in the Köy area, immediately to the north of the modern village and in the low, flat area to the west of the citadel. Traces of sub-surface architecture were identified in all areas except for the flat lands to the west of the citadel, and we have now conducted soundings and excavations in seven different parts of the site. In the process we were able to sample both what we interpret as public buildings and the remains of houses (fig. 11.3).

Different sectors of the outer town seem to display different types of architecture. Pınarbaşı is dominated by large structures that appear to be public buildings of some sort, along with several very pronounced magnetic anomalies. On Güney Tepe there is a mixture of

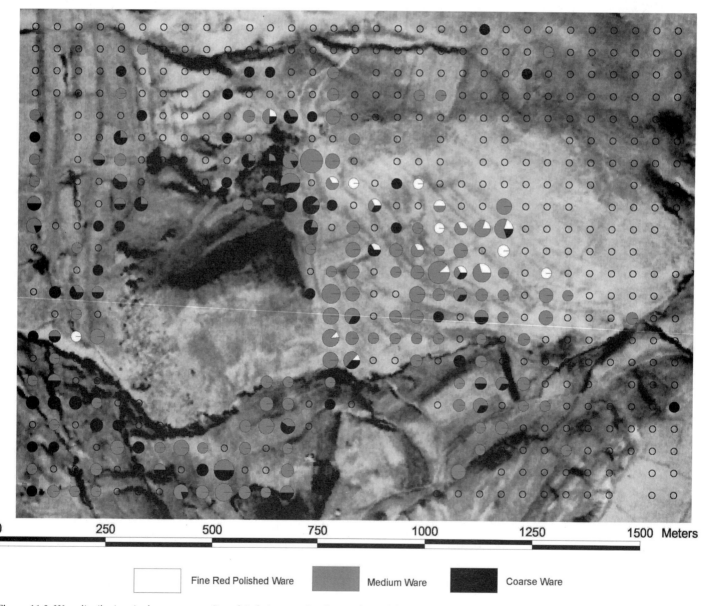

| 0 | 250 | 500 | 750 | 1000 | 1250 | 1500 Meters |

☐ Fine Red Polished Ware   ▨ Medium Ware   ■ Coarse Ware

Figure 11.2 Ware distributions in the outer town. Size of circle is proportional to numbers of sherds recovered in the 40 liter soil sample taken at each 50 meter interval. Samples were not taken on the citadel itself. *Figure by Elizabeth C. Stone.*

large and small structures, some apparently linked together almost as row houses following the contours of the slopes and others standing in isolation. There was at least one massive building in the Köy area. Almost nothing was found on the low ground between the citadel and the Lake.

EXCAVATIONS

Pınarbaşı

The one area in which the magnetic map suggests the presence of a complex of public buildings is Pınarbaşı (fig. 11.4) where we see the clear traces of five large buildings. The two easternmost of these are connected by a large, 60 meter long, courtyard. Between these buildings are a number of large magnetic anomalies, which we expect to be indicators of either kilns or furnaces, but so far we have failed in our attempts to pinpoint the sources of these anomalies.

Between 1998-1999, when less than one hectare of Pınarbaşı had been investigated using magnetometry, we focused our excavation on the westernmost of the structures in the area (fig. 11.5). Five 10 x 10 squares were excavated within this approximately 25 m. square building, with an additional two 10 x 2 trenches along the north side. This work showed the building to have been very well built and planned, with the walls set in foundation trenches cut into sterile soil. Where exca-

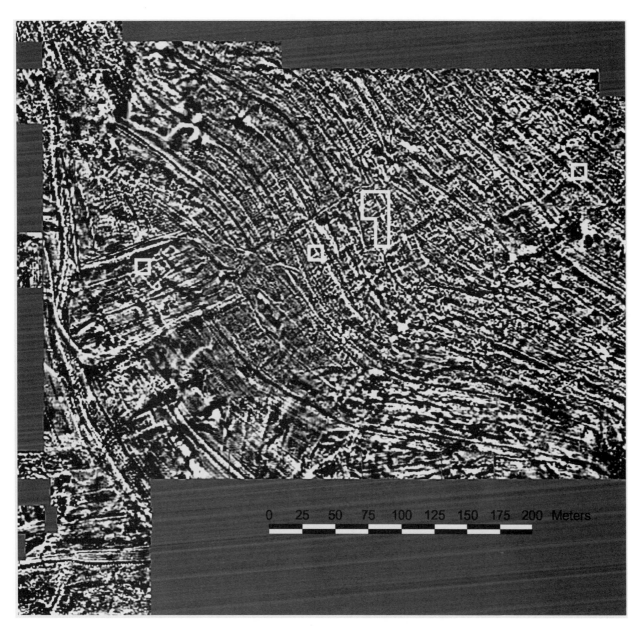

Figure 11.3 Areas of magnetic field gradient survey and traces of architecture detected. *Figure by Elizabeth C. Stone.*

Figure 11.4 Magnetic field gradients in Pınarbaşı. Area covered is 220 x 120 meters with north at the top. *Figure by Elizabeth C. Stone.*

Figure 11.5 Public building in Pınarbaşı. *Photo by Paul Zimansky.*

vated, the outer walls were found to be buttressed, and there was a paved area to the north of the building with traces of another wall by our northernmost baulk. Four rooms made up the northern portion of the structure, two with fire installations, one of which had a partially preserved sherd pavement. One of the other rooms contained large numbers of animal bones, among which those of sheep and goat were most in evidence. Only one doorway was well preserved, although slight gaps in the walls could be made out elsewhere which might indicate where other doorways may have been. The southern portion of the excavation area was dominated by two large spaces, although parts of rooms to the south and east were also found. A pair of stone column bases in the larger space to the west suggests that it may have been roofed in whole or in part. Pits were dug into both spaces, and the latter included the remains of a small hearth. Floor levels in this area were for the most part poorly preserved, but a small fragment of floor was found in the northeast corner of the smaller space, on which ceramics and a bulla with seal impressions were found *in situ* (fig. 11.6). The south and east sides of this building remain unexcavated.

Finds were generally sparse within this building, with less than 300 diagnostic sherds recovered from the entire excavation. To the extent that one can rely on so small a sample, the ceramics excavated here confirmed the impression gained from the shovel test survey. Only 2.5% of the sherds were of red polished ware, and the percentage of coarse wares was a high 56% with only 25% medium wares, most with quite simple forms.

In a second, much smaller, excavation in Pınarbaşı, a pair of 5 x 10 m trenches was designed to sample part of one of the structures in the easternmost building group and the large courtyard. As was the case with our more extensive excavations, the magnetic map proved an excellent predictor of subsurface features. The only feature not observed before excavation was the buttress on the inside of the courtyard—an indication, we think, that the courtyard should be seen as a space adjoining two separate buildings and not as a central space.

Here too, finds were very sparse in the interior of the building. Other than a badly worn unbaked clay bulla with a small stamp seal, they were restricted to a handful of sherds. We were more fortunate in the results of our excavations in the courtyard. There we were able to recover a sizable faunal assemblage, which has yet to be analyzed, as well as a significant number of sherds. Interestingly, this was dominated by fine red serving vessels, but unlike the typical Urartian highly polished red ware, these were almost without exception unpolished.

The buttresses, the scale, and the quality of the architecture in both our Pınarbaşı soundings suggest that the entire complex was built by the Urartian state. The bullae found in the two areas add testimony—admittedly limited—for administrative activities. The ceramics, however, were of much lower quality than those found in the citadel.

Köy

Pınarbaşı was not the only place where the magnetic map suggested there were public buildings. To the south of the citadel and separated from it by a gulley descending toward the lake is a large artificial terrace where our magnetometry revealed the presence of an extremely large structure, with massive walls encompassing spaces of some twenty-two by nine meters. There were, however, some traces within these larger spaces that hinted at smaller internal walls. We therefore positioned a 10-meter square for excavation across the large wall in an area where we could also establish whether partition walls were indeed present.

The architecture was as substantial as the magnetic survey suggested. The main wall was 2 meters thick, and faced with rows of massive stones (fig. 11.7). At its eastern end it was preserved slightly higher, with both the small stones that were used by the Urartian architects to connect the stone foundations with the mud-brick superstructure, and fragments of the mud-brick wall still preserved. Although this wall had foundations that continued more than 50 cm. below the lowest floor, the two floors that were preserved were very close to the top of the stones—a pattern which differs from all other structures excavated in the outer town.

The space northwest of the wall seems to have been an internal courtyard. The deposits there were quite unremarkable, save for a few small ash pits, and a larger area of burned trash. The southwestern space had a quite different character and must have been internal space. The lower level exhibited one continuous clay floor, which suggests that when it was first constructed, this building had massive rooms with no subdivisions, at least within the area excavated. The area above that floor was quite different—so different in fact that we suspect that we might be dealing with a quite separate occupation.

Here a series of very small and crudely-made walls were built of both stone and mud-brick, subdividing the large room into at least three spaces. This entire area appeared domestic, and was destroyed by fire. To the northwest it was dominated by a pair of large ovens, one dug into the other, within which a fine red polished ware trefoil pot was found, but with its neck broken off. Other smaller fire installations were found—generally built into broken pots—elsewhere in the structure. Numerous grinding stones, both large-scale querns and smaller handstones, were found throughout the area.

The space to the northeast appears to have been used as a storage area for cooking pots. These were found *in situ* in a room or bin, concentrated along the partition wall. Some were stacked within one another (fig. 11.8). Many of the pots were chipped in antiquity and one large jar contained the top half of a trefoil jug. The conclusion that is forced upon us by these data is

Figure 11.6 Bulla from Pınarbaşı. *Photo by Paul Zimansky.*

Figure 11.7 Large wall in Köy area. *Photo by Paul Zimansky.*

Figure 11.8 Late occupation pottery in Köy building. *Photo by Paul Zimansky.*

that the last occupants of this structure were using either second hand or at least broken and chipped vessels, presumably for cooking.

This domestic occupation within so very large a structure is perhaps best interpreted as the result of squatters moving into a building originally constructed by the state for a quite different purpose. Since the ceramics are all clearly Urartian—including trefoil jars with the typically Urartian markings on the handles—any later occupation must have taken place immediately after the destruction of the fortress, with the few remaining inhabitants scavenging what ceramics and other objects they could recover. Its destruction by fire is also something of a problem. To date none of our excavations in the outer town—or indeed in any Urartian outer town—evidence the massive destruction typical of Urartian fortresses. At present we are inclined to interpret the heavy traces of fire in this area as an accidental result of the cooking activities. Clearly more excavations are needed here.

Güney Tepe

The main Urartian town—and the place where we have done most of our excavation—was on Güney Tepe (fig. 11.9). Here the magnetometry identified an area of some 16 ha. with evidence for occupation, 10 ha. of which we believe represents an area of dense domestic housing. It is within the latter that our shovel tests found evidence for the highest percentages of fine red polished wares.

We dug one 10 meter square near the citadel where a large (at least 15 x 30 m.) structure visible in the magnetometry seemed to be both so well planned and so isolated that we thought that it, like the remains from Köy and Pınarbaşı might be another public structure. It proved to be the remains of a stable, with the typical long, paved room with a partition rather than a wall on one side (fig. 11.10). The walls were well built with exterior buttresses, features that we are inclined to associate with the hand of the Urartian state architects. Finds from within the structure were limited, but trash areas on the outside of the building yielded both

Figure 11.9 Excavation units on Güney Tepe seen from the citadel. *Photo by Paul Zimansky.*

a good sample of ceramics and animal bone, and a number of small finds.

The fine red wares and marked sherds typical of both the citadel and the domestic area higher up on Güney Tepe (see below) were either rare or absent, as they were in other public buildings outside the citadel, and the ceramic assemblage was dominated by medium wares, mostly in quite simple shapes. Apart from a few pieces of obsidian, grinding stones and bronze and iron fragments, the small finds consisted entirely of weapons. One socketed iron spearpoint and a trilobate bronze arrowhead were found in the external area. Socketed arrowheads like this one are known both from the citadel and from other Urartian fortresses, but this is only the second trilobate arrowhead to be found at Ayanis. Two other iron arrowheads were found here, one broken in antiquity, but both more closely resemble the iron arrowheads found on the citadel than the broad, flat arrowheads common in the residential areas (fig. 11.11). Although only 10% of the structure has been excavated, its form and content suggest an association with the military—and thus the state.

Between 1997 and 1999 we opened a 600 square meter excavation area approximately half way up the slope (fig. 11.12). In this were found two quite different

Figure 11.10 Stable building in Unit PP51 on Güney Tepe. *Photo by Paul Zimansky.*

Figure 11.11 Projectile points from Unit PP51, Güney Tepe. *Photo by Paul Zimansky.*

structures, each with a ground plan covering around 400 square meters. One (Building 1) was quite well built with large stones set on bedrock, sizable rooms and a comprehensible plan with clear doorways leading from one to another. Many of the rooms had fire installations, and one room had a bench on one side and an area of paving with a trough beside it—perhaps a stable area—on the other. The second building (Building 3) was much more haphazard in plan with smaller rooms. This house had intact floors in many places, with walls built of a mixture of stone and mudbrick—hence the difficulty of seeing them in the magnetometry. A number of grinding stones, fire installations and the *in situ* bases of pots were found, all of which suggest a domestic function. Although few doorways were preserved, the remains suggest a single structure (Building 3) some 20 meters long from north to south and more than 9 meters from east to west. We are inclined to see this as a separate house, rather than a subsidiary of Building 1.

The ceramics recovered from Building 3 had a higher percentage of medium wares and a lower percentage of coarse wares than Building 1. Both buildings had similarly high percentages (nearly 20%) of fine red wares, but whereas those from Building 1 were mostly polished in ways similar to those from the fortress, a majority of those from Building 3 were not and thus more closely resembled the red wares from Pınarbaşı. Nevertheless there were some striking similarities between the finds from Buildings 1 and 3. A significant number of the sherds from both were impressed or incised—as is the case with ceramics from the Ayanis citadel and from other Urartian fortresses. There were also similarities in the small finds. Building 1, Building 3 and the alleyway that separated them all yielded similar flat, iron arrowheads that are quite different from those from the citadel. Both buildings and the alleyway that separated them yielded a number of bronze pieces (fig. 11.13). Decorated bronzes were found in both Building 1 and the alleyway, but from Building 3 we recovered only a single undecorated piece of wire. In addition, pieces of Egyptian Blue pigment were found in both the alleyway and Building 3, but not Building 1. In sum, both Buildings and the intervening alleyway have yielded evidence for objects and ceramics normally associated with Urartian fortresses and therefore, we assume, with elites. There are, however, significant differences between the percentages of both coarse wares (more in Building 1)

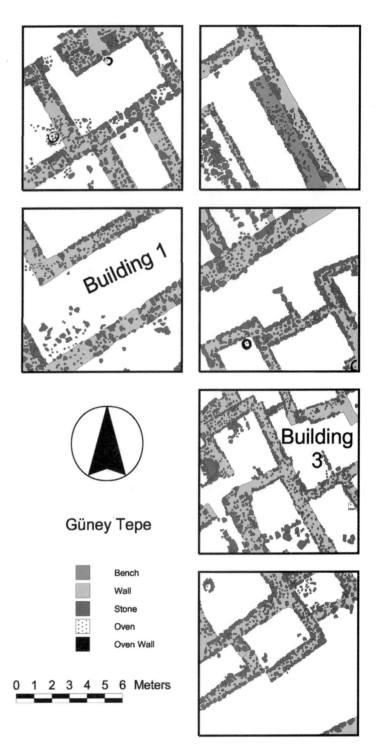

Figure 11.12 Plan of architecture in units LL-NN 68-69.
Illustration by Elizabeth C. Stone.

Figure 11.13 Fragment of bronze sculpture from building 1. *Photo by Paul Zimansky.*

and fine red polished wares (less in Building 3). These differences may be related to stratigraphic evidence collected in 1998 that indicates that Building 3 was built later than Building 1, with its walls partly founded on trash deposits generated by Building 1, or they may reflect differences in function or wealth.

Both alleyways were packed with ashy debris and animal bone. Preliminary examination suggests that both samples are dominated—at least in terms of mass—with the remains of cattle, but bones of ovi-caprids are also present in considerable numbers and both contain equid remains. The two alleyways differ with regard to dog and pig remains. No pig remains were found in the northern alley and dog bones were rare, whereas in the 1999 excavations of the southern alley, pig remains were certainly present, and both the skulls and post-cranial remains of large dogs were quite common, with at least one example suggesting that it had been butchered. We expect to have a much better understanding of the differences in the

economies of the two households when we have the results of the analysis of the faunal, phytolith and micromorphological data that are currently underway.

Also found in 1999 were two human burials, located immediately next to the wall of the substantial building in the southeastern corner of the excavated area. Both were covered with the ashy debris that characterized this area; both were contracted and devoid of grave goods, but both had what we believe to be red ochre on the underside of the bones. One was an infant and the other a small child.

We have also sampled two other areas within the approximately 10 hectares that we believe to have been residential, one higher up the slope from our main excavations and the other lower down the slope. The latter sampled one of a series of long, narrow buildings that stretched along one of the lower terraces and are quite different in plan from the larger, squarer buildings sampled at higher elevations. Here we located our excavation on one corner of the building, hoping to recover both internal architectural details and external trash areas. What we found was the remains of a building that had been progressively modified during its lifetime (fig. 11.14).

The original version of this structure had well-built walls with reinforced corners and at least one external buttress. It did not remain in this condition long, however. First a wall with a door was added to the outside of the building; then the door was blocked up and some flimsy walls were constructed on the outside. Inside another flimsy wall was added, dividing the large room in two. This had a central doorway with an *in situ* door socket.

The ceramics from this area differ significantly from those from the house areas already excavated further up the slope. Only 10% of the ceramics were fine red table wares, and few of these exhibited the typical Urartian polish. Other ceramics were dominated by open and closed medium wares, but none had the incised and impressed marks so typical of the ceramics from both houses excavated in previous seasons.

The small finds, however, were plentiful and do not suggest great poverty. Jewelry in the form of a bronze fibula (fig. 11.15) and earring was found, but most of the other objects were more mundane. Sickle blades, pestles, stone bowl or mortar fragments and various iron and bronze nails and other small pieces all testify to a domestic, agricultural economy. Only the arrowheads are similar to objects found in the other house area. Like those, they are of a thin, flat variety quite

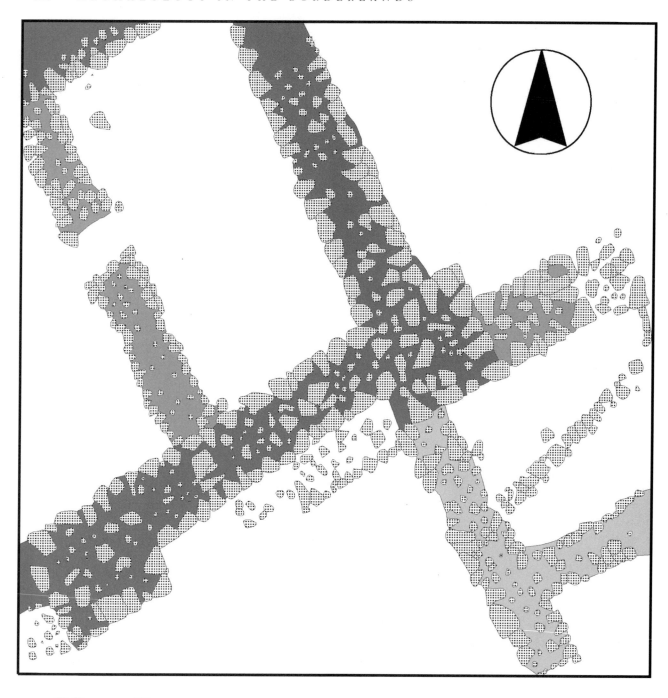

Güney Tepe
Square OO64

Figure 11.14 Building in unit 0064, Güney Tepe. *Illustration by Elizabeth C. Stone.*

different from those found in the citadel or the stable area near the base of the citadel. Our tentative interpretation of this structure is that it was probably built by the Urartian state for the inhabitants who then made significant alterations to it over time.

We also opened one square high on Güney Tepe, above the modern cultivation, in the hope of determining whether the terracing system that typifies this area was originally Urartian. We could not excavate any of the terraces in active use because of the damage this would do the fields, but we thought we might get away with looking at a square immediately above the highest field, where the magnetometry showed linear traces of what might once have been a terrace wall. As it turned out, erosion had removed almost all traces of architecture in this square. That it had been occupied in Urartian times is indubitable—although the ceramic inventory was necessarily small it was typically Urartian with about 10% fine but unpolished red wares, only one of which was incised. Small finds included the same thin iron arrowheads as had been found elsewhere on Güney Tepe, albeit either bent or broken, and a bone needle. Because of the paucity of the results from this area few conclusions can be drawn.

INFERENCES AND PROSPECTUS

The Outer Town project is still just beginning and the conclusions we can offer on this occasion about the relationship of the people who lived there to the controlling authorities are based on evidence that is quite literally superficial. Nevertheless, we are confident that the settlement was not uniform and that it grew and changed during the brief time that it was occupied. There is no evidence of urban occupation in the immediate vicinity before the founding of the citadel in the second quarter of the 7th century, BC[7] and thus the people who lived here appeared on the scene rather suddenly. If one accepts the premise that there probably were never very many Urartians, at least in the sense of those who spoke the language or were born to parents who regarded themselves as such, much of the population residing here must have consisted of groups who had been recently conquered and resettled from surrounding territories which were being assimilated.

While the artifacts that we see in the settlement are all indisputably of the "Urartian" material assemblage that is so well known from the fortresses of Rusa II and associated with the state, the preliminary work in the outer town shows that within a single Urartian enclave

Figure 11.15 Bronze fibula from unit 0064, Güney Tepe. *Photo by Paul Zimansky.*

different residential groups enjoyed different kinds of access to the products of Urartian state workshops and architects. The Güney Tepe architecture appears to have been laid out initially as substantial, isolated houses. These were then modified and the spaces between them filled by people using somewhat less refined and consistent building techniques. The faunal remains in every area we have excavated attest to different diets.

In short, what the Urartian government seems to have done was impose a superficial uniformity on a heterogeneous population. This lasted only as long as the government did, and when the Ayanis citadel was put to the torch, the settlement was soon abandoned. One does not know where the people went or what they did subsequently, but they certainly did not maintain the canons of Urartian art and architecture, or continue to produce Urartian weapons. Thus the Urartian interlude was more a question of wiping the slate clean for a new beginning than the establishment of a tradition in its own right.

To conclude on a cautionary note, it must be said that the picture of Urartian settlement at Ayanis may hardly be typical of Urartian settlements generally. The settlements beside Urartian fortresses that have so far received the attention of archaeologists—at Karmir Blur, Bastam, and Ayanis—were all created by Rusa II toward the end of the kingdom's history and may themselves be anomalies. Certainly the more rural component of the population remains unknown. The archaeology of settlement in the Urartian empire is in its infancy.

NOTES

1. The question of Urartian origins has been taken up most recently by Sevin 1999a.

2. For a discussion of the terminology and consideration of what types of settlement might be involved, see Zimansky 1985: 40–47.

3. There appears to be a consensus emerging in recent scholarship that the ruling dynasty of the kingdom of Biainili moved to the Van area from the vicinity of Rowanduz (Barnett 1973:332). Certainly the choice of the god Haldi, whose cult was originally centered around Musasir, for leadership of the state pantheon to unite diverse ideologies in the territory (Salvini 1995:40) would be explained if that were the ancestral area of the royal line.

4. The underlying theoretical position of our work is that the distinction between city states and territorial states made by Bruce Trigger (1993) should be reflected in urban layouts. In city states we would expect to see the rich living side by side with the poor and various controlling institutions scattered throughout the urban environment. With certain qualifications, we found this to be the case at Old Babylonian Mashkan-shapir in southern Mesopotamia, our previous field project (Stone and Zimansky 1995). Urartu shows the kind of centralization that is characteristic of territorial states and we were interested to see if the traits that Trigger notes—such as centralization of institutions, monopoly of craft specialties by the central government and segregation of elites—would be archaeologically manifest in one of its cities.

5. The claim is probably not to be taken literally, since the inscription (Salvini 2001: 251–270) is a more extensive version of one previously known from partially preserved exemplars from Karmir Blur, Armavir, and Adilcevaz. Still, it seems likely that at least some of these imported populations were settled here.

6. From 1997 through 1999 our work was supported by the National Geographic Society and a generous private donation; in 2000 we were awarded a grant from the National Science Foundation for two more seasons, most of which will be used for analysis of ceramic, metallurgical, and biological remains. The magnetometry of the 1999 season was made possible by the Glen Dash Foundation. The authors are also deeply grateful to Prof. Altan Çilingiroğlu for the hospitality and logistic support he has so warmly offered in allowing them to participate in the Outer Town project as members of the Turkish expedition. Our survey and excavations in the Outer Town have been conducted by Turkish and American students working together. Plans of the structures excavated there were made by Dr. Zafer Derin, to whom we owe a great debt.

7. For a discussion of the date of the founding of the citadel, see Çilingiroğlu and Salvini 1999: 55–56. The dendrochronological evidence presented there suggests that the wood was cut in 655 and 651 BC, which the authors regard as "unexpectedly late." We share their view that this may not be the final word. The fact that Rusa mentions neither the construction of Bastam (*Rusai.URU.TUR*) or Karmir Blur (*URU Teis̆ebaini*) in his lengthy list of projects in the inscription on the Ayanis temple suggests to us that these sites had not yet been built, and it is unlikely that he would have undertaken and completed all of these endeavors in the last years of his reign. [Wiggle-matching of radiocarbon dates and tree rings pushed these dates back to the 670s BC after this article was submitted. See Manning, et al. 2001.]

CHAPTER 12

The Culture of Ancient Georgia in the First Millennium BC and Greater Anatolia:

Diffusion or Migration?

GOCHA R. TSETSKHLADZE

Ancient Georgia, situated at the crossroads of East and West, from the earliest period of human activity was culturally connected to the civilizations of Mesopotamia, Anatolia, and the Aegean. Although there is nothing new in this statement, many difficulties are encountered in applying this generalization to the evidence. Usually, we are dealing with single artifacts or a group of objects that have passed from one cultural milieu to another through trade, as booty, by the exchange of artistic ideas, or by chance. The independent development of the same kinds of objects cannot be excluded. The end of the Bronze Age–Early Iron Age saw many political and cultural changes in the Caucasus, Anatolia, and throughout the Near East (Kuhrt 1995:473–622, esp. 547–572). The whole first millennium BC was a period of intensive cultural interaction, and many features spread from one culture to another (Boardman 1994:21–48; 2000; Curtis 1995; Dalley 1998; Tsetskhladze 1999:478–487; Pogrebova 1977:10–32, 141–173; 1984:10–46, 162–206). The mechanism of cultural exchange is frequently unclear and often a matter of speculation. It is difficult to establish why, how, and to what extent new elements appeared; sometimes it is impossible.

The main purpose of this chapter is to develop further the thoughts I have expressed in some of my earlier writings (Tsetskhladze 1999:469–497; 2001) about the interpretation of foreign elements in the culture of the ancient Caucasus and, at the same time, to present much stronger evidence for the possible expansion or migration of other ethnic groups into the territory of ancient Georgia.

Early Iron Age cultures in the territory of Georgia had very close links with the cultures of the central Caucasus. Colchian and Koban armor (daggers, axes, adzes, pickaxes, and so on) have close parallels with the same types of weapon from western Iran (Pogrebova 1977; Voronov 1980; Pantskhava 1986). Small bronze objects and decorations (pendants, pins, bracelets, and so on) have similarities to those of northwestern Iran. The same is also true of horse furnishings (Tsetskhladze 1999:478–479). The first Colchian goldsmiths were inspired by ancient Iranian craftsmen (Gagoshidze 1985; 1997). Even such characteristic features of Colchian and Koban cultures as axes have incised decoration stylistically close to Luristan (Tsetskhladze 1999:480). Terra-cotta figurines of two- and three-headed animals from Vani also demonstrate artistic ideas penetrating from northwestern Iran (Lordkipanidze 1995:41–49). One axe of the eighth/seventh centuries BC from Sulori, not far from Vani, Colchis, with the figures of horsemen in relief standing on the back of it (Lordkipanidze et al. 1987: Plate

CIV) has a close resemblance to a ceremonial axe from Sarkisla (Bittel 1976: Plates VII-12).

URARTU AND GEORGIA

The question of Urartian influence on the cultures of ancient Georgia has never received detailed scholarly examination. Several Urartian objects have been found in a destroyed grave in southern Georgia, including a cylindrical jar of ivory, beads, and other bronze and ivory objects (Chubinishvili 1965). They have very close

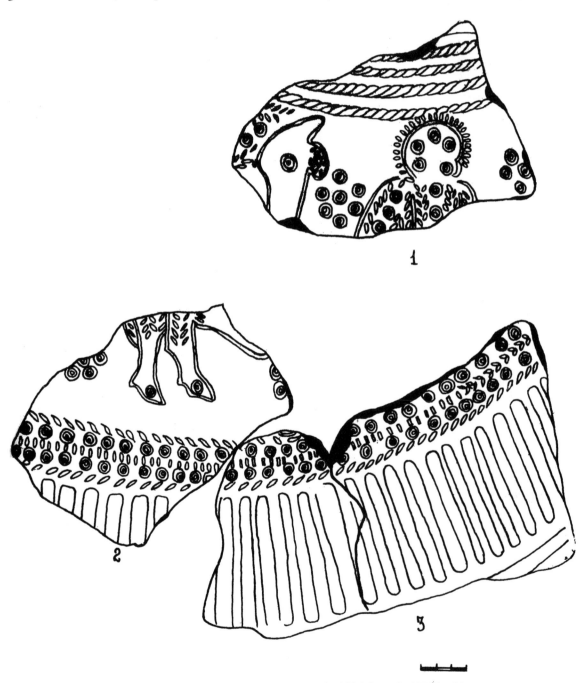

Figure 12.1 Fragments of pottery with incised decoration, from Namarnu. *After Mikeladze et al. 1997: Plate 20.*

parallels with material from Karmir-Blur (Piotrovskii 1967:60). Urartian belts and helmets are known from central and northern Caucasus (Tekhov 1981: Plates 94–96, 127–120; Galanina 1985:180); and a few bronze bowls have been found in Tli (Tekhov 1981: Plate 106,4; 1985: Plate 192,9; compare Merhav 1991:211). Urartian bronze weapons had a strong impact on the design of central Caucasian ones (Voronov 1980:216–217). Most probably the use of the chariot and horse fittings came from Urartu as well (compare Merhav 1991:53–113). In eastern Georgia a very well preserved bronze model of a chariot with horses of the ninth/eighth centuries BC has been found (Miron and Orthmann 1995:106).

Although the origin of Caucasian bronze belts is still a matter of debate, it is clear that the inspiration lay largely with Urartian prototypes (Khidasheli 1980; Pogrebova and Raevskii 1997:5–9, 58–71; Bouzek 1997:187; Yıldırım 1991). The distinctive incised decoration might well have been added by Caucasian artists. There is now much stronger evidence for this than previously. Only two finds of bronze belts from central Colchis have been made, both from Ergeta burial ground (Mikeladze 1990: Plate XXX,1; Papuashvili 1999: Plate IV,57). The most striking find is that at Namarnu settlement (not far from Ergeta): three fragments of local pottery have the same decoration as may often be seen on Caucasian belts (figure 12.1; Mikeladze et al. 1997:28–29, Plate 20).

All these Urartian features could have come to Georgia both directly and indirectly. Is there any evidence that could point either to Urartian expansion toward ancient Georgia or to some Urartian migration? The question is as important as it is difficult to answer. D. Muskhelishvili (1978:18–21), on the basis of a study of red burnished pottery from "Khovle III," proposed that the migration of Urartians or ethnic groups connected with Urartu. There is one kind of construction which, I think, might corroborate this: Early Iron Age shrine complexes from central Transcaucasia. As in Anatolia and the whole Near East, cultic centers had a very important part in religious life (Zimansky 1995:109; Joukowsky 1996:276–278, 348–349, 374–378; Van De Mieroop 1997:215–228). Like Anatolian and Mesopotamian cult centers, those of central Transcaucasia administered landholdings and were actively involved in animal husbandry. About seven such centers are known from eastern Georgia (Kikvidze 1976:197–209; Khidasheli 1988; Lordkipanidze 1989:178–181). They are large and consist not only of a place for cultic ceremonies but also of many other buildings. The shrine at Katnalis-Khevi was situated on two hills: on the smaller were storage and ancillary buildings; on the larger, the shrine itself. These shrines contained rooms with altars, hearths, ovens, smithies, etc., in which many objects have been found—most, it can be assumed, offerings to the gods. In Meli-Gele,

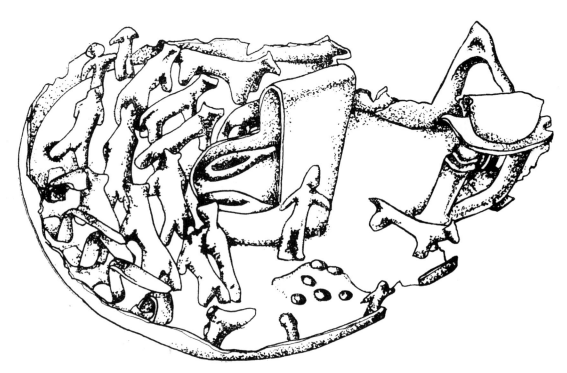

Figure 12.2 Bronze ritual object from Gamdlistskaro settlement. *After Khidasheli 1988:177.*

86,000 objects have been discovered; in Melaani, about 2,000; in Shilda, 3,457. The main ceremonial space was contained by dry stone walls, some with rubble infilling, and surrounded by a complex of buildings. One bronze ritual object of the eighth and seventh centuries BC, decorated with a three-dimensional scene and found in Gamdlistskaro settlement, is believed to give a general idea of the appearance of the venue and of the importance of animals in cultic ceremonies (figure 12.2; Khidasheli 1988).

Before making some suggestions, I would like to mention two architectural complexes found recently in the mountainous part of Colchis. Both demonstrate that cultic places like those mentioned above were widespread in western Georgia. In Svaneti, the Etsera settlement is situated on a high hill and surrounded by stone walls 1 m thick. There were rectangular towers at the corners of the fortification wall. Not only was domestic stone architecture discovered but also a cultic center, all dating to the middle of the first millennium BC. The cultic place,

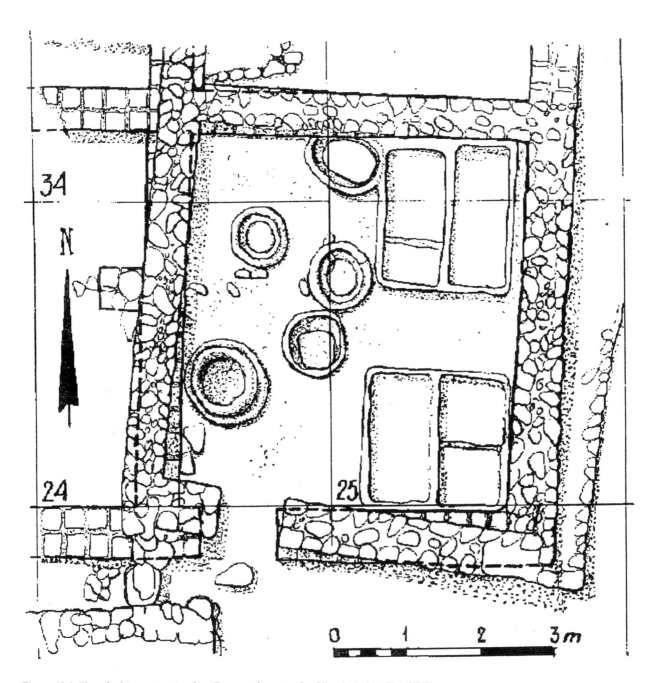

Figure 12.3 Plan of cultic construction from Etsera settlement. *After Chartolani 1996: Plate XLIXa.*

rectangular in shape and probably a tower, was incorporated into a dwelling and production complex. On its floor were two "baths" (in the terminology of the investigator), probably for animal blood, and five round altars (figure 12.3; Chartolani 1996:146–147). Unfortunately, little has been published about this settlement and cultic place. The remains of another cultic place were found at Ushguli settlement, situated on a hill 2,300 m above sea level (Chartolani 1996:147–149).

Rescue excavation at Goradziri in Sachkhere district, on the border between ancient Colchis and Iberia,

yielded another cultic center. It is poorly preserved. The cultic area is rectangular (10 x 8 m), surrounded by a stone wall (possibly two rows of wall) 50–70 cm thick whose surviving portion is about 1 m high. Above the stones were courses of mud brick topped off with a construction of clay-coated wooden poles and branches. One interesting detail is that in the north part and northeastern corner of the inner wall stucco fragments with a trace of white paint have been found, which could suggest that the walls were covered with murals. Below this complex another cultic place has been discovered: 100

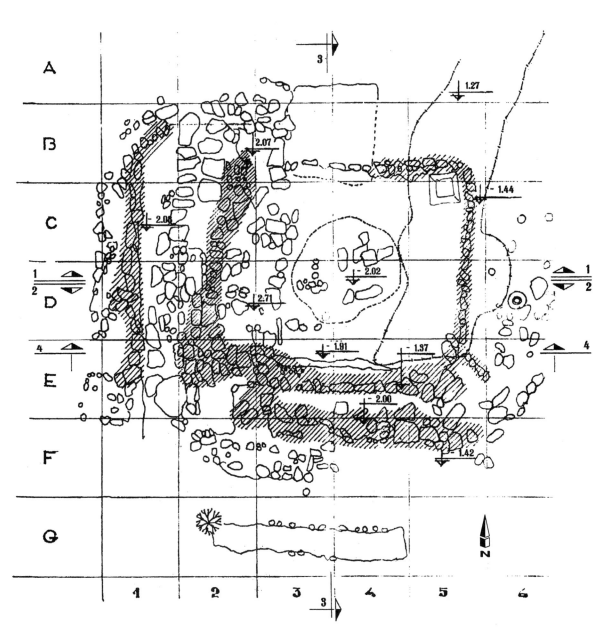

Figure 12.4 Plan of excavated trench with cultic construction, Goradziri. *After Meshveliani et al. 1999:72.*

m² of cobble pavement, a plastered floor with a pit in the middle. This was surrounded by the remains of other buildings (figure 12.4). Many pottery and metal objects were found here, as well as an exceptionally high number of charred animal and bird bones. The overall date of the two complexes is between the eighth and fourth centuries BC (Meshveliani et al. 1999).

As the abovementioned complexes show, the idea of a cultic center, situated within a settlement or, with its own production and agriculture, on a self-contained site, surely came from Anatolia. Comparing the architecture of these centers with Urartian temple architecture, many common features may be distinguished. According to D. Ussishkin:

> ...the available evidence indicates the existence of three different architectural types of Urartian standard square or rectangular temples. Nevertheless, all three types resemble one another and have many basic

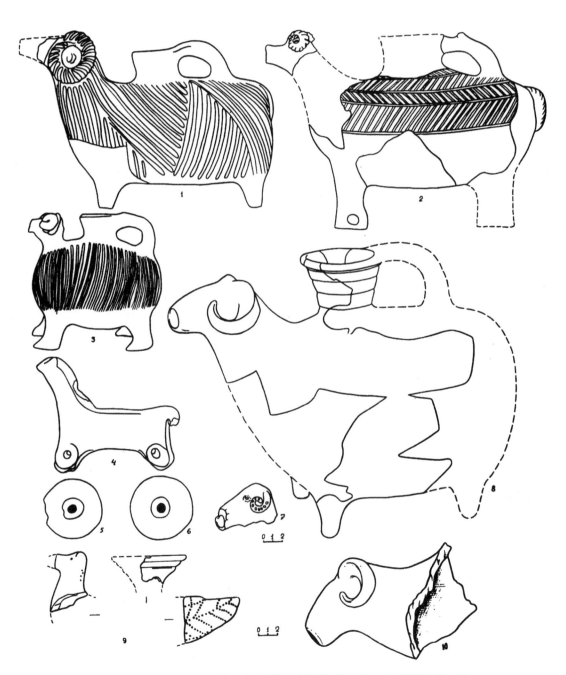

Figure 12.5 Pottery (*1-3, 7-10*) and terracotta (*4-6*) items from burial No. 16, Treli. *After Abramishvili 1995: Plate 11.*

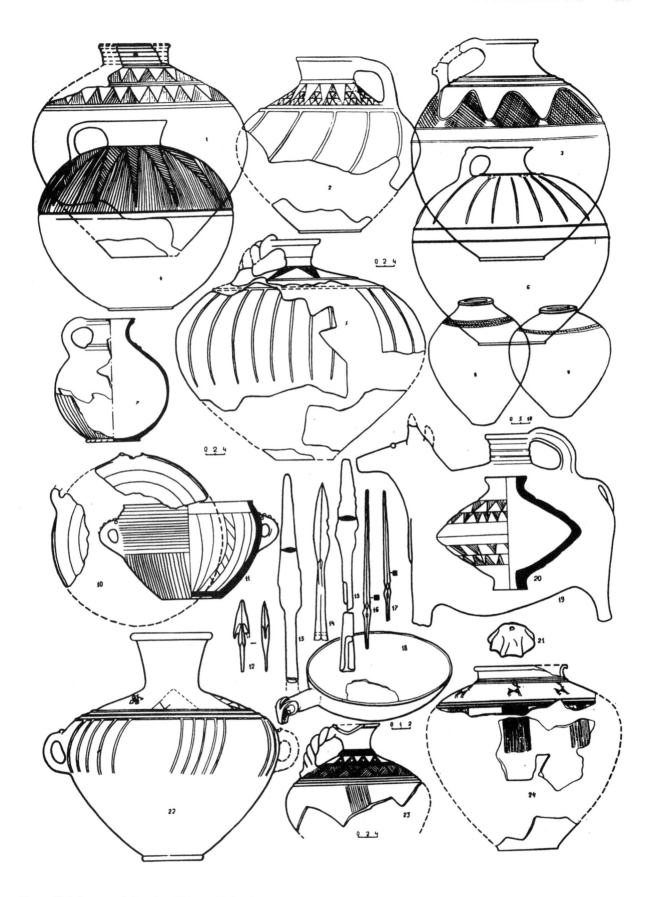

Figure 12.6 Grave goods from burial No. 24, Treli. *After Abramishvili 1995: Plate 12.*

features in common: (1) all the temples are either square or rectangular; (2) a large open area, a courtyard or piazza, extends in front of them; (3) cultic installations are placed in the courtyard in front of the entrance; (4) the sole entrance is located in the center of the building's facade; (5) there is a single cult room inside the temple; (6) the walls are thick, a possible indication of a high building; (7) one temple, possibly all temples, had a gabled or a pyramidal roof; (8) the lower part of the walls is faced with ashlar masonry and their upper part is built of bricks, plastered and in some cases decorated with murals. [1991:119]

I am not suggesting that eastern Georgia and the mountainous part of Colchis had been part of Urartu (although we are far from establishing the final limits of Urartian expansion; see, for example, Burney 1994; Parker 1999; Sevin 1991; Smith 1996:196–217, 274–285; 1999:45–57). However, it is obvious that we do not have just the exchange of artistic ideas or trade. Most probably, it is now time to accept that some kind of migration of Urartian ethnic groups took place from modern-day southern Georgia (Kvemo-Kartli) to central parts of eastern Georgia. The use of Urartian architects by the ancient Georgian nobility cannot be excluded. At this point it must be mentioned that Kvemo-Kartli, anciently bordering Urartu, has archaeological features that distinguish it from other parts of eastern Georgia: cyclopean and stone constructions, and the predominant burial custom uses stone cists. In other parts of eastern Georgia, fortification systems are usually made of earth, sometimes from stone and mud brick, and the predominant burial rite is inhumation (Gobedzhishvili and Pitskhelauri 1989:144, 146).

Thus, the idea of cultic centers as well as certain architectural features came most probably from Urartu. The origin of the Urartian fortress or tower temple with a single chamber goes back to the Levant in the Middle Bronze Age. It was adopted in Urartu as a standard type of temple; later, its plan and shape made their way to Iran to yield the Achaemenid tower temples (on the same type of temples in Georgia from the sixth/fifth centuries BC onward, see below) (Stronach 1967). In Urartu, this type of temple did not appear until the late ninth century BC (Ussiskhin 1991:121–122). The overall date for ancient Georgian temples of the same type is the eighth/seventh centuries BC (Khidasheli 1988). Furthermore, although Urartian burial rites are not well known (Derin 1994:49; Zimansky 1995:109–110), cremation in stone cists was widespread (Derin 1994:49).

Tombs Nos. 16 and 24 in Treli, Tbilisi, stand out not only because of their richness but also for the types of grave goods found in them. They date from the end of the eighth century/first half of the seventh century BC. Most of the goods are completely different from local objects but have close parallels with material from north-western Iran and Azerbaijan (figures 12.5, 12.6). R. Abramishvili (1995) in his publication discusses these objects, especially pottery, very fully and draws out the parallels. His interpretation is that the graves reflect the movement of Thraco-Cimmerian ethnic groups, and he links this to the establishment of the so-called Scythian Kingdom in Transcaucasia. It is very difficult to agree with him. All his conclusions are based on a convoluted tower of speculation. We know nothing about Cimmerian culture or of the existence of a Scythian kingdom in Transcaucasia. I will not discuss this here; I have already done so elsewhere, trying to demonstrate how scant is our current knowledge (Tsetskhladze 1999:482–486). As the richness and burial practices of these two tombs demonstrate, they probably belonged to members of the local nobility, although we cannot exclude that the deceased were of foreign origin. The wealth of foreign objects shows that some kind of change is taking place in this period. It would be much more plausible to connect this change to the migration of some ethnic group(s) from western Iran or from Urartu. There is a further possibility: if these graves belonged to local nobles, the foreign objects can be considered as gifts from representatives of ethnic groups connected with western Iran or Urartu. My interpretation is more realistic than Abramishvili's in view of the close links between eastern Georgia and Urartu (see above). In the Early Iron Age, the migration of some ethnic groups from western Iran throughout Transcaucasia seems very probable as well (Tsetskhladze 1999:481–482).

THE SCYTHIANS AND GEORGIA

To turn to the Scythians: their influence on the material culture of ancient Georgia was quite noticeable. First of all, there are about fifteen sites in eastern Georgia (Iberia) and some twenty sites in western Georgia (Colchis)—burial grounds (mostly) and settlements—which have yielded Scythian or Scythian-type objects: battle axes, akinakes, arrowheads, bits, chapes, bronze bridles, bone cheek-plates, scabbard chapes, ornaments of horse harness (Esaian and Pogrebova 1985; Pirtskhalava 1995). From Iberia even a Scythian balbal

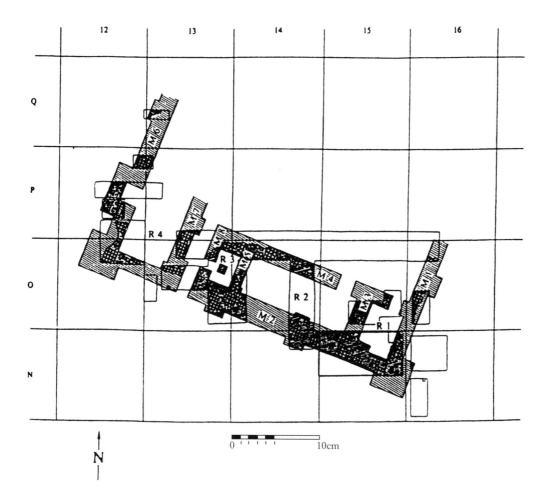

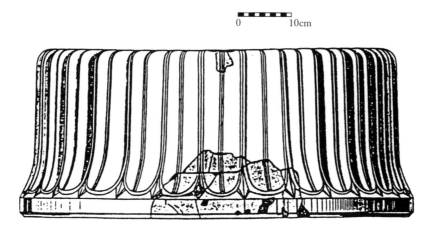

Figure 12.7 'Palace complex' from Gumbati: *1*, plan; *2*, bell-shaped column base. *After Knauß 1999: Plates 2 and 6.*

dated to the seventh/sixth centuries is known (Dashevskaya and Lordkipanidze 1995). There are so many sites and such a variety of objects that explanations such as trade or sporadic contacts between Scythians and the peoples of Colchis and Iberia are insufficient. The bulk of these Scythian or Scythian-type objects dates from the end of the seventh/beginning of the sixth century BC (although there is some debate), which is when the Scythians were returning from Asia Minor to the northern Black Sea littoral, after crushing Near Eastern empires (Pirtskhalava 1995:61–62).

Urartian culture had a quite strong influence on that of the early Scythians, and vice versa (Piotrovskii 1989). It is extremely likely that the Scythians did not simply pass through the territory of ancient Georgia but destroyed everything in their path. Everywhere in sites of eastern Georgia there are traces of destruction dating from the end of the seventh century BC. In the settlements and cultic centers, Scythian arrowheads are found in the destruction levels (Pirtskhalava 1995:61). Until the fifth/fourth centuries BC there is a lacuna in the archaeology of eastern Georgia. Life does not reemerge in full until the Hellenistic period (Lordkipanidze 1989:181–182, 312). The Scythians destroyed everything in Colchis as well: traces of fire can be identified in many of the settlements dated to the end of the seventh and through most of the sixth century BC (Tsetskhladze 1995:314–315).

The Scythians not only passed through present-day Georgia, especially Colchis, but some of them also settled there long term (particularly within the territory of modern Abkhazia, where the largest numbers of Scythian objects have been found). This is also demonstrated by the fact that virtually all weapons in Colchis between the fifth and first centuries BC were of Scythian type. It is likely that large scale production of iron objects in Colchis was connected with the Scythians (Tsetskhladze 1995:327).

THE ACHAEMENID EMPIRE AND GEORGIA

Both the creation of the Achaemenid Empire and its subsequent expansion had an impact on ancient Georgia (Briant 1996:80–81, 130–133; 1997:24–26). Recently, this subject has received a great deal of scholarly attention (Tsetskhladze 1993/94; 1994, 2001; Gagoshidze 1996; Knauss 1999; Furtwängler and Lordkipanidze 2000). It is frequently stated that the ancient written sources are very unclear as to whether eastern Georgia (Iberia) was part of the Achaemenid Empire or not

(Cook 1983:78–79; Boardman 1994:219; Gagoshidze 1996:125–126). At the same time, the material culture indicates that it was one of the satrapies. Excavation over the last twenty years, and especially the current efforts of a Georgian-German team, have indeed provided very strong evidence of the region's vassal status. I must mention immediately the discovery in Gumbati of an Achaemenid-type palace of the fifth/fourth centuries BC, which was very probably the residence of the local ruler (figure 12.7:1; Knauss 1999:85–92). It is built of mud brick and it yielded bell-shaped column bases (figure 12.7:2; Knauss 1999:90, 93, Plates 2, 6).

Before turning my attention to particular types of artifacts, it is essential that I discuss the architecture of Iberia, the strongest indicator of an Achaemenid presence. Most buildings of this period are built of mud brick. Although this technique was known in Georgia from the sixth to the fourth millennium BC, it was largely forgotten during the Bronze and Early Iron Ages. Its sudden revival is rightly connected by J. Gagoshidze (1996:130–131) to Achaemenid influence. Another distinctive feature is that all buildings, especially those of the Classical period, bear a very strong resemblance to the tower-type buildings of Urartu. This type of architecture was characteristic for the Achaemenids as well, and also came to them from Urartu (Stronach 1967; Gagoshidze 1996:130). In Tsikhiagora, for example, the temple complex has fortifications (Zkitischwili 1995:84) reminiscent of Urartian practice (figure 12.8; see, for example, Smith 1998: Fig. 3b; 1999: Figs. 7–8, 11–12).

From the fifth century BC all the temples so far known from eastern Georgia are fire temples (Kimsiasvili and Narimanisvili 1995/96). Most probably, the earliest example is that from Samadlo: a tower-type building (Gagoshidze 1996: Plate 3). These fire temples in Iberia formed part of complexes containing barns, a mill, bakery, winery, as in Tsikhiagora, for example, which is the best studied and very well preserved (Zkitischwili 1995). The temple there consists of a square cella, flanked by corridor-like spaces, fronted by a court enclosed by a high fence. The altar, built from rubble stones, is situated in the center of the court. It is likely that a wooden column with a bull double-protoma capital (Zkitischwili 1995: Figs. 5, 6) was set up in the center of the cella to carry the tie beam (Kimsiasvili and Narimanisvili 1995/96:312). The capital represents a clear example of provincial Achaemenid style (Gagoshidze 1996:132). The walls, coated with clay on both sides and built of rubble stones, above which is mud-brick masonry, are 1.5 m wide and

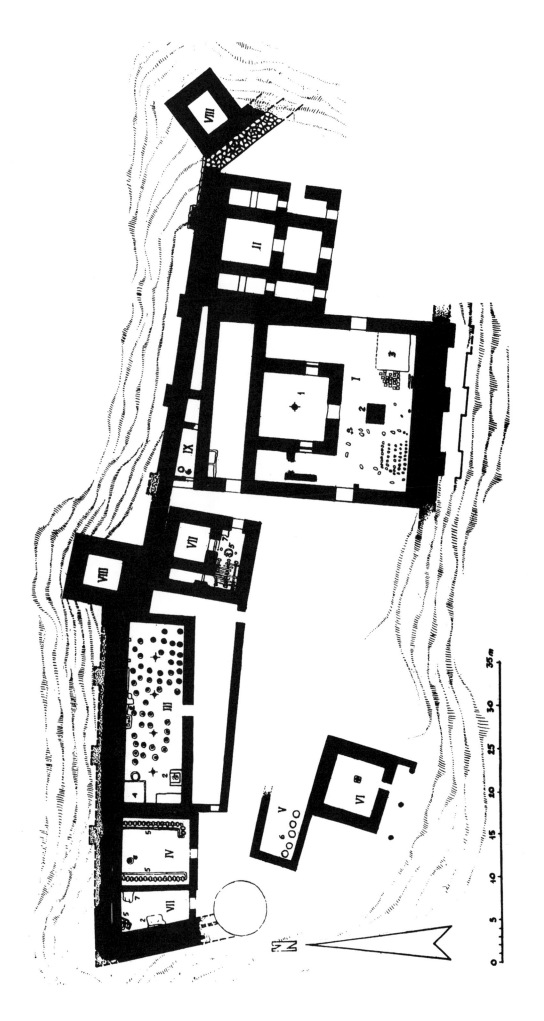

Figure 12.8 Plan of Tsikhiagora. *After Zkitischwili 1995: Plate 1.*

up to 2 m high. The roof was tiled; the floor made from wooden trunks covered by clay. The complex dates from the early Hellenistic period (figure 12.8; Kimsiasvili and Narimanisvili 1995/96:311–312). Other temples of the Hellenistic period, less well studied and less well preserved, have been excavated in Gharthiskari, Samadlosmidsebi, and Uphlistsikhe (so-called two column hall) (Kimsiasvili and Narimanisvili 1995/96). In Dedoplis Mindori a whole complex of temples from the late Hellenistic period has been studied (Gagoshidze 1992). An Achaemenid-type capital is also known from Shiomgvime (Gagoshidze 1996: Plate 8).

Ancient Iranian influences can be seen in other spheres of material culture. There are about two dozen precious metal phialai and rhyta from the Akhalgori and Kazbegi treasure and burials (Gagoshidze 1996:127). One fourth century BC glass phiale is known as well (Gagoshidze 1996:127). Golden jewelry bears clear Achaemenid features (Gagoshidze 1985; 1997). These luxury objects can be interpreted as gifts to the local nobility. It is supposed that one of the satrapal production centers for luxurious metal objects was situated in Iberia (Gagoshidze 1996:127). Most important, from the fourth century BC, production of ceramic imitations of Achaemenid phialai and rhyta began in Iberia (figures 12.9, 12.10; Gagoshidze 1979:81–84; Narimanishvili 1991:47–50). From the Hellenistic period, local pithoi are known, red-painted with animals and hunting scenes (figure 12.11:1; Gagoshidze 1981: Plates XIV–XVIII). The excavation at Samadlo has yielded fragments of early Hellenistic stone relief sculptures depicting a hunting scene and resembling Achaemenid sculpture (figure 12.11:2; Gagoshidze 1981: Plate XIX,236).

To summarize, the influence of Achaemenid culture had a strong impact on Iberia, which can be considered, with a great degree of certainty, a peripheral part of the Achaemenid Empire. One thing in particular is noticeable. Strong ancient Iranian traditions were displayed from the end of the fourth century BC. This is also the period when a completely new burial rite—burials in pithoi (known in Armenian territory and western Anatolia from an earlier date [Noneshvili 1992:3–10, 75–120 with bibliography])—appears in eastern Georgia, indicating the arrival of some new ethnic group(s) (Noneshvili 1992:12–55; Tolordava 1980:38–52) Maybe this new ethnic group is responsible for these essentially new cultural features as well (Achaemenid features in the Classical period were much weaker, which probably reflects the current lack of evidence.) This was the period of the collapse of the Achaemenid Empire after the march of Alexander the Great and, perhaps, as a result of its disintegration some of its former people migrated elsewhere, including to ancient eastern Georgia. Otherwise it would be very difficult to explain why there are features associated with Late Archaic-Classical Achaemenid culture preserved in Iberia in the Hellenistic period (if not, the chronology of Iberian antiquities must be revised).

COLCHIS AND FOREIGN ELEMENTS

Colchis (western Georgia) was not directly incorporated as one of the satrapies of the Persian Empire, but it was used as a buffer state between the Empire and the nomads of the southern Caucasus (Tsetskhladze 1993/94). The influence of Achaemenid culture is weaker here than in Iberia. Luxurious Achaemenid or Achaemenid-type gold, silver and glass items from rich local burials at Vani and Sairkhe, as well as Akhul-Abaa in Abkhazia, are well known and have been published and republished many times (Lordkipanidze 1981b:11–89; 1983; 1991a: Plates 3–7; Tsetskhladze 1993/94; Gigolashvili 1999; Makharadze and Siginashvili 1999; Nadiradze 1990:22–97; Kvirkvelia 1995: Fig. 4). There is no doubt that they represent diplomatic gifts to the local elite (Tsetskhladze 1993/94:24–31). From the Hellenistic period traces of the cult of Mithras can be found in Colchis (Tsetskhladze 1992). As in Iberia, Achaemenid jewelry had a strong influence on local designs (Gagoshidze 1985; 1997). The widespread appearance of torques is most probably connected with ancient Iranian tradition, although it could be linked to the Scythians (Gogiberidze 1989; Petrenko 1978:41–48). The same is true of burial rites used for the burial of local noblemen in Vani and Sairkhe (Lordkipanidze 1972a:66; Nadiradze 1990:22–97).

The architecture of Colchis displays Greek influence more strongly than Iranian (Tsetskhladze 1998:114–163). This is unsurprising in view of the Greek colonies along the Colchian Black Sea coast. To Achaemenid tradition can be linked the appearance of mud-brick architecture in Vani (Lordkipanidze 1972b:28). The discovery of a stone Doric capital decorated in relief with lotus leaves (Kipiani 1987:15–22; Shefton 1993) and, possibly, a bull protome capital in Sairkhe (Kipiani 1987:12–14), indicates the presence of some Achaemenid architects decorating buildings in the style of Persian court art for the local elite. Both sites, residences of local nobles, were situated in central Colchis, not far from

Figure 12.9 Iberian pottery of the 5th–1st centuries BC. *Adapted from Gagoshidze 1981 and Narimanishvili 1991.*

the Iberian border, and it is likely that both the ancient Iranian elements and the architects themselves came from there. As in Iberia, suddenly burials in pithoi appear in central Colchis from the early Hellenistic period—in the coastal zone they are, as yet, unknown (Noneshvili 1992:55–74; Tolordava 1980:6–37). Pottery from these burials, again as in eastern Georgia, represents new types for Colchian production. One kind is the flask decorated with sunlike slashes and circles, which has parallels from Anatolia

(Bilgi 1991: Fig. 02.7,1). The difference is that the Anatolian examples are asymmetrical and have one handle, the Colchian examples none (Tolordava 1980: Plate IV,9). In Iberia local asymmetrical flasks are known (Narimanishvili 1991:349). Thus, it is obvious that the appearance of this new burial tradition must be connected with the same migration process that occurred at exactly the same time in Iberia. Some of the migrants continued their journey and penetrated into central parts of Colchis.

Figure 12.10 Iberian pottery of 5th–1st centuries BC. *Adapted from Gagoshidze 1981 and Narimanishvili 1991.*

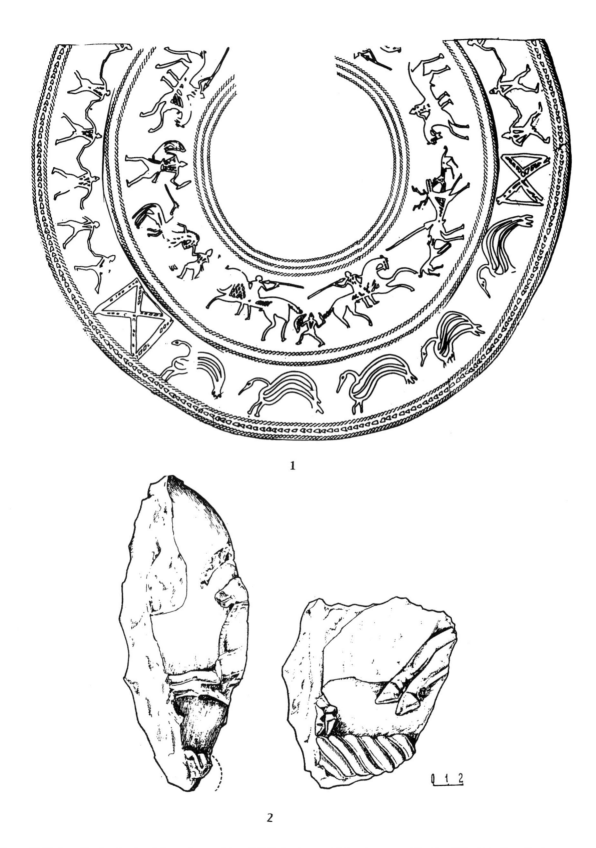

1

2

Figure 12.11 Samadlo: *1*, red-painted decoration on pithos; *2*, Relief sculpture with hunting scene. *After Gagoshidze 1981: Plates XVII and XIX, 236.*

Further evidence for the appearance of new features because of migration comes from Colchian pottery production. From the end of the seventh century BC jugs with so-called vertical tubular handles became widespread throughout Colchis; produced locally, they form a completely new type in Colchian culture (Mikeladze 1974:63). Jugs of the same type are known from ancient Iran, where they appeared at the beginning of the first millennium BC (Dyson 1965: Fig. 7; Seeher 1992: Figs. 3,9). Lugged pots with wave ornament came to Colchis from Iran as well (Carter 1994: Fig. 12,5).

A further group of pottery articles from central Colchis is of interest: one-handled, pear-shaped jugs made from pink clay. They have been found in Vani, both in burials and in the cultural levels (isolated fragments) (Lordkipanidze 1972b: Fig. 176; 1981b: Figs. 77, 4, 93). They are covered with yellow slip and bear red painted decoration, consisting of inverted isosceles triangles and sets of parallel lines around the neck and widest part of the body, between which chevrons are arranged. The jugs have been dated to the second or third quarter of the fourth century BC. The emergence of this painted pottery is linked with that (also with triangular decoration) widespread since early times on the Iranian plateau (see, for example, Muscarella 1994: Plate 12.1.1). So the appearance of painted jugs in Colchis should be linked to Iranian influence. As the number of such finds is quite small it is difficult to speak of direct trade relations. The jugs had probably come from neighboring Iberia, where they were widespread and where local production had started up in response (figures 12.9:top right, 12.10:2-3; Narimanishvili 1991:276–280).

Finally, let us pay attention to pottery marks. Colchian pottery provides much more evidence than Iberian (Tsetskhladze 1991). There are two kinds of mark: stamped and incised. Examples of the former are few: from Colchis, impressions of seals, four segmented rosettes on pots and pithoi (Tsetskhladze 1991: Plates 2 and 3); from Iberia, impressions of seals (figure 12.12:1; Zkitischwili 1995: Plates 12, 16). In two cases, the impressions of seals are on bullae (figure 12.12:2–3; Zkitischwili 1995: Plate 16; Meshveliani et al. 1999: Fig. 4). Incised marks are much more numerous, and all were made before the firing of the pot: cross or X-shapes, swastika motifs, tree motifs, pitchfork motifs, dot impressions, etc. (Shamba 1980: Plates XXI.8, XXIII–XXIV; Kiguradze 1976: Plate III.2; Lordkipanidze 1981a: Plate 74). All these marks are likely to be those of the potter. In fact, there are other

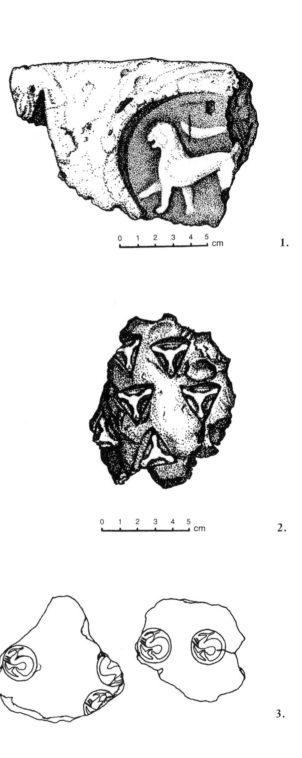

1.

2.

3.

Figure 12.12 *1*, Stamp on pithos, Tsikhiagora (*after Zkitischwili 1995: Plate 12*); *2*, bulla, Tsikhiagora (*after Zkitischwili 1995: Plate 16*); *3*, bulla, Goradziri (*after Meshveliani et al. 1999: Fig. 4*).

marks, such as Greek letters, which are probably numerical, as, for example, on tiles at Tsikhiagora (Khazaradze and Tskitishvili 1980; Zkitischwili 1995: Plate 17). These incised marks have striking similarities with the marks of Urartian potters (Derin 1999; see also Martirosian 1981; Khodzhash 1981). Close similarities can also be seen in the ornamentation of Colchian (Lordkipanidze 1981a: Plate 18) and, for example, Phrygian pottery (Sams 1994: Figs. 60 and 61). I would not, however, want to suggest that Urartians or Phrygians were responsible for introducing pottery production, either in Iberia or Colchis, especially when ancient Georgian marks date from the Classical and Hellenistic periods. This is, once again, a further example of how archaic traditions can reappear independently after several centuries. I consider this to be an indicator, albeit indirect, of links between ancient Georgian and Anatolian pottery production.

The aim of this chapter has been to demonstrate that the culture of ancient Georgia in the first millennium BC was influenced by its neighbors. Although the local culture was indigenous, the geographical location of Georgia is such that it has always been prone to external influences, thereby enriching its own culture. Some features came simply by way of the exchange of artistic ideas, but, as I have tried to demonstrate here, much more through the migration of new ethnic groups, which was often brought about by the quite frequent political changes in Anatolia and throughout the Near East. So much has been written about the strong influence of Greek culture in Colchis that I think it unnecessary to pay attention to this question here (Tsetskhladze 1998 with bibliography). It is obvious that some conclusions reached here may seem speculative. The nature of archaeological evidence is such that its interpretation can be difficult where other sources, for example, written, do not exist or survive. At best, we can establish, indicate, or illuminate. Even here, much depends on the extent to which the archaeological material has been published and studied—not to say the degree to which sites and whole areas have been excavated.

Bibliography

Abay, E.
2001   Seals and Sealings. In *Ayanis I*, edited by A. Çilingiroğlu and M. Salvini, pp. 321–351. Rome: Instituto Per Gli Studi Micenei Ed Egeo-Anatolici.

Abramishvili, R.
1995   Neue Angaben über die Existenz des Thrako-Kimmerischen ethnischen Elements und des Sog: Skythischen Reiches im Osten Transkaukasiens. *Archäologischer Anzeiger* 1:23–39.
1978   Delisis Namosakhlari. In *Tbilisi, Arqeologiuri Dzeglebi I* edited by R.M. Abramishvili, pp. 28–32. Tbilisi: Metsniereba.

Abramishvili, R. M. and D. Gotsiridze
1978   Trelis Mtkvar-araqsis Kulturis Namosakhlari, In *Tbilisi, Arqeologiuri Dzeglebi I* edited by R.M. Abramishvili, pp. 34–47. Tbilisi: Metsniereba.

Abramishvili, R. M., N. I. Giguashvili, and K. K. Kakhiani
1980   *Grmakhevistavis Arqeologiuri Dzeglebi*. Tbilisi: Metsniereba.

Adams, R. M.
1966   *The Evolution of Urban Society*. New York: Aldine.

Adzhan, A. A., L. T. Gyuzalian, and B. B. Piotrovskii
1932   Tsiklopichesckii Kreposti Zakavkaz'ya. *Soobshchenia Gosudarstvennoi Akademii Istorii Material'noi Kultury* 1/2:61—64.

Akurgal, E.
1968   *Urartäische und Altiranische Kunstzentren*. Ankara: Türk Tarih Kurumu Basımevi.

Akyurt, İ. M.
1998   *M.Ö. 2. Binde Anadolu'da Ölü Gömme Adetleri*. Ankara: Türk Tarih Kurumu Basımevi.

Alekseev, V. P., B. Arakelyan, A. R. Arutyunian, S. M. Ayvazian, L. A. Barseghian, A. A. Martirosian, K. A. Mkrtchian, and J. A. Ohanesian
1968   *Contributions to the Archaeology of Armenia*. Translated by A. Krimgold. Edited and with an introduction by H. Field. Russian Translation Series of the Peabody Museum of Archaeology and Ethnology, Harvard University III (3). Cambridge, MA: Peabody Museum.

Algaze, G.
1993   *The Uruk World System*. Chicago: University of Chicago Press.
1999   Trends in Archaeological Development of the Upper Euphrates Basin of Southeastern Anatolia during the Late Chalcolithic and Early Bronze Ages. In *Archaeology of the Upper Euphrates, the Tishrin Dam area*, edited by G. delOlm-Lete and J.L. Montero-Fenollós, pp. 535–572. Barcelona: Editorial Ausa.

Algaze, G., and P. Goldberg, D. Honça, T. Matney, A. Mısır, A. M. Rosen, D. Schlee, L. Somers
1995   Titriş Höyük. A Small EBA Urban Center in SE Anatolia. *Anatolica* XXI: 13–64.

Aliev, N. G.
1991   *Pozdne Eneolitichiskie Pamiatniki Azerbaidjana*. Abstract of PhD dissertation. Leningrad: Akademia Nauk SSSR, Institute of Archaeology.

Altınlı, E.
1963   *Türkiye Jeoloji Haritası Erzurum*. Ankara: Maden Tetkik Arama Enstitüsü.

Amiet, P.
1980   *Art of the Ancient Near East*. Translated by J. Shepley and Claude Choquet. New York: Harry N. Abrams.

Ammerman, A. and L. Cavalli-Sforza

1973   A Population Model for the Diffusion of Early Farming in Europe. In *The Explanation of Culture Change: Models in Prehistory*, edited by C. Renfrew, pp. 343–358. Pittsburgh: University of Pittsburgh Press.

Andreeva, M. V.

1977   K Voprosu o Yuzhnykh Svyazakh Maikopskoi Kultury. *Sovetskaya Arkheologiya* 1:39–56.

Anthony, D.

1990   Migration in Archaeology: The Baby and the Bathwater. *American Anthropologist* 92(4): 895–914.

1991   The Archaeology of Indo-European Origins. *Journal of Indo-European Studies*. 19 (3/4): 193–222.

1992   The Bath Refilled: Migration in Archaeology Again. *American Anthropologist* 94(1): 174–176.

1997   Prehistoric Migration as a Social Process. In *Migrations and Invasions in Archaeological Explanation*, edited by J. Chapman and H. Hamerow, pp. 21–32. Oxford: British Archaeological Reports.

Appadurai, A. (editor)

1986   *The Social Life of Things*. Cambridge: Cambridge University Press.

Appadurai, A.

1986   Introduction: Commodities and the Politics of Value. In *The Social Life of Things*, edited by A. Appadurai, pp. 3–63. Cambridge: Cambridge University Press.

Areshian, G. E.

1974   O Rannem Etape Osvoeniya Zheleza v Armenii i na Yuzhnom Kavkaze. *Istoriko-Filologicheskiy Zhurnal* 2:122–212.

1988   Éléments Indoeuropéens dans la Mythologie du Plateau Arménien et du Caucase du Sud au 11ᵉ mil. Av. J.-C. In *Šulmu: Papers on the Ancient Near East*, edited by P. Vavroušek and V. Soucek, 19–37. Prague: Charles University Press.

1990   Les Éleveurs non Sédentaires et les Civilisations Agricoles a l'Age du Bronze sur le Plateau Arménien et au Caucase Méridional. In *Nomades et Sédentaires en Asie Centrale: Apports de l'Archéologie et de l'ethnologie, Actes du Colloque Franco-soviétique, Alma Ata (Kazakhstan), 17–26 Octobre 1987*, edited by H.-P. Francfort, pp. 19–25. Paris: Editions du Centre national de la Recherche Scientifique.

Areshian, G. E., K. Kafadarian, A. Simonian, G. Tiratsian, and A. Kalantarian

1977   Arkheologicheskie Issledovaniya v Ashtarakskom i Nairiskom Raionakh Armyanskoi SSR. *Vestnik Obshchesvennikh Nauk* 4:77–93.

Areshian, G. E., V. E. Oganesyan, F. M. Muradyan, P. S. Avetisyan, and L. A. Petrosyan

1990   Konets Srednego Bronzovogo Veka v Mezhdurech'e Araksa i Kury. *Istoriko-Filologicheskij Zhurnal* 128(1):53–74.

Arsebük, G.

1979   Altınova'da (Elazığ Köyü Yüzlü Açıklı ve Karaz Türü Çanak Çömlek Araşındakı yıli kiler), VIII. *Türk Tarih Kongresi Kongreye Sunulan Bildiriler* I (1976), pp. 81–92. Ankara: Türk Tarih Kurumu.

Arutjunian, N. V.

1982   La Nouvelle Inscription Urartéene Découverte en Arménie Soviétique. In *Gesellschaft und Kultur im alten Vorderasien*, edited by Horst Klengel, pp. 89–93. Berlin: Akademie Verlag.

Avetisyan, P. and R. Badalyan

1996   On the Problems of Periodization and Chronology of Horom Mortuary Complexes. In *10th Scientific Session Devoted to the Results of Archaeological Investigations in the Republic of Armenia (1993–1995)*, edited by A. Kalantarian, pp. 6–8. Yerevan: Armenian National Academy of Sciences.

Avetisyan, P., R. Badalyan, S. Hmayakyan, and A. Piliposyan

1996   Regarding the Problem of Periodization and Chronology of Bronze and Iron Age Armenia. In *10th Scientific Session Devoted to the Results of Archaeological Investigations in the Republic of Armenia (1993–1995)*, edited by A. Kalantarian, pp. 8–10. Yerevan: Armenian National Academy of Sciences.

Avetisyan, P., R. Badalyan, and A. T. Smith

2000   Preliminary Report on the 1998 Archaeological investigations of Project ArAGATS in the Tsakahovit Plain, Armenia. *Studi Micenei ed Egeo-Anatolici*. 42(1): 19–59.

Badaljan, R. S., C. Edens, R. Gorny, P. L. Kohl, D. Stronach, A. V. Tonikijan, S. Hamayakjan, S. Mandrikjan, and M. Zardarjan

1993   Preliminary Report on the 1992 Excavations at Horom, Armenia. *Iran* :1–24.

Badaljan, R. S., C. Edens, P. Kohl, and A. Tonikijan

1992   Archaeological Investigations at Horom in the Shirak Plain of Northwestern Armenia. *Iran* 30:31–48.

Badaljan, R. S., P. L. Kohl, and S. E. Kroll

1997   Horom 1995. *Archäologische Mitteilungen aus Iran und Turan* 29:191–228.

Badaljan, R. S., P. Kohl, D. Stronach, and A. Tonikian

1994   Preliminary Report on the 1993 Excavations at Horom, Armenia. *Iran* 32:1–29.

Badler, V.

1995   The Archaological Evidence for Wine-making, Distribution, and Consumption at Proto-historic Godin Tepe, Iran. In *The Origins and Ancient History of Wine*, edited by J. Fleming and S. Katz, pp. 45–56. New York: Gordon and Breach.

1998   Gender and Archaeology of the Ancient Near East. Paper presented at the XLV Rencontre Assyriologique Internationale, Harvard University.

Bahşaliyev, V.

1997   *The Archaeology of Nakhichevan.* Istanbul: Arkeoloji ve Sanat Yayınları.

Bailey, D. (editor)

1998   *The Archaeology of Value.* BAR International Series 730. Oxford: British Archaeological Reports.

Barnett, R. D.

1950   The Excavations of the British Museum at Toprak Kale near Van. *Iraq* 12(1):1–43.

1956   Ancient Oriental Influences on Archaic Greece. In *The Aegean and the Near East: Studies Presented to Hetty Goldman*, edited by S. Weinberg, pp. 212–238. J.J. Augustin, Locust Valley, NY.

1973   Urartu. In *The Cambridge Ancient History*, edited by John Boardman et al., vol 3, pt. 1, 2nd ed., pp. 314–371. Cambridge: Cambridge University Press.

1982   Urartu. In *The Cambridge Ancient History*, edited by J. Boardman, I. E.S. Edwards, N.G.L. Hammond, and E. Sollberger, pp. 314–371., vol. 3. Cambridge: Cambridge University Press.

Barrelet, M.-T.

1984   Le Decor du Bol en or de Hasanlu et les Interpretations Proposées à Son Sujet. In *Problémes Concernant les Hurrites*, 2, edited by M.-T. Barrelet, 13–176. Editions Recherches sur les Civilisations, Mémoire no. 49. Paris: A.D.P.F.

Bashash Khanzaq, R.

1996   Qara'at- e Khatibeh-ye Sang-e Yadbud Tazeh Yab Rusta-ye Movana ya Sarzamin-e Arda va Asheh (Urumiyeh). *Mirathe-ye Farhangi*:15, 102–109.

Belgiorno M. R., Biscione R., Pecorella P. E.

1984a   Catalogo degli Insediamenti . In *Tra lo Zagros e l'Urmia. Ricerche Storiche ed Archeologiche nell'Azerbaigian Iraniano*, edited by Pecorella P. E., and M. Salvini, pp. 141–178. Edizioni dell'Ateneo, Roma.

1984b   I materiali della Ricognizione. In *Tra lo Zagros e l'Urmia. Ricerche Storiche ed Archeologiche nell'Azerbaigian Iraniano*, edited by Pecorella P. E., and M. Salvini, pp. 179–213. Edizioni dell'Ateneo, Roma.

Belgiorno M. R. and P. E. Pecorella

1984   L'Età del Ferro. In *Tra lo Zagros e l'Urmia. Ricerche Storiche ed Archeologiche nell'Azerbaigian Iraniano*, edited by Pecorella P. E., and M. Salvini, pp. 321–329. Edizioni dell'Ateneo, Roma.

Belli, O. and E. Konyar

2000   Van-Yoncatepe Kalesi ve Nekropolü Kazıları. In *Türkiye Arkeolojisi ve İstanbul Üniversitesi*, edited by O.Belli, pp.181–190. Istanbul: Istanbul Universitesi.

Benedict W. C.

1961   The Urartian-Assyrian Inscription of Kelishin. *Journal of the American Oriental Society* 81:359–385.

Berg, L. S.

1950   *Natural Regions of the U.S.S.R.* New York: MacMillan Co.

Bilgi, Ö.

1991   Iron Age Pottery from Köskerbaba Höyük. In *Anatolian Iron Ages, The Proceedings of the Second Anatolian Iron Ages Colloquium held at Izmir, 4–8 May 1987* (British Institute of Archaeology at Ankara Monograph 13), edited by A. Çilingiroğlu and D. H. French, pp. 11—28. Oxford: Oxbow books.

Billington, A.

1967   The American Frontier. In *Beyond the Frontier*, edited by P. Bohannon and F. Plog, pp. 3–86. New York: Natural History Press.

Binford, L.

1972   *An Archaeological Perspective.* New York: Seminar Press.

Biscione R.

2003   Iron Age Settlement Pattern in the Urmia Plain, Iran. *Studi Micenei ed Egeo-Anatolici* 45(1).

Biscione R., S. Hmayakyan, and N. Parmegiani (editors)

2002   *The North-Eastern Frontier. Urartians and non-Urartians in the Sevan Lake Basin I. The Southern Shores.* Rome: Istituto di Studi sulle Civiltà dell'Egeo e del Vicino Oriente.

Biscione R., S. Hmayakyan, N. Parmegiani, and Y. Sayadyan

2002   The Sites. In *The North-Eastern Frontier. Urartians and Non-Urartians in the Sevan Lake Basin I. The Southern Shores*, edited by Biscione R., S. Hmayakyan, and N. Parmegiani, 61–249. Rome: Istituto di Studi sulle Civiltà dell'Egeo e del Vicino Oriente.

Bittel, K.

1976   *Beitrag zur Kenntins Hethitischer Bildkunst.* Sitzunngsberichte der Heidelberger Akademie der Wissenschaften, Philosophisch-historische Klasse; Jg. 1976, Abh. 4. Heidelberg: Carl Winter Universitätsverlag.

Blackman, J., R. Badaljan, A. Kikodze and P. Kohl

1998   Chemical Characterization of Caucasian Obsidian Geological Sources. In *L'obsidienne au Proche et Moyen Orient*, edited by M.-C. Cauvin, A. Gourgaud, B. Gratuze, N. Arnaud, G. Poupeau, J.-L. Poidevin and C. Chataigner, 205–231. BAR International Series 738. Oxford: Archaeopress.

Boardman, J.

1994   *The Diffusion of Classical Art in Antiquity*. London: Thames and Hudson.

2000   *Persia and the West. An Archaeological Investigation of the Genesis of Achaemenid Art*. London: Thames and Hudson.

Boehmer, R. M. and G. Kossack

2000   Der figürlich verzierte Becher von Karašamb. In *Variatio Delectat: Iran und der Western: Gedenkschrift für Peter Calmeyer*, edited by R. Dittmann, 9–71. Alter Orient und Altes Testament 272. Münster: Ugarit-Verlag.

Bohannon, P.

1955   Some Principles of Exchange and Investment Among the Tiv. *American Anthropologist* 57:60–70.

Bokonyi, S.

1987   Horses and Sheep in East Europe in Copper and Bronze Ages. In *Proto-Indo-European: The Archaeology of a Linguistic Problem*, edited by S. Skomal and E. Polomé, pp. 136–44. Washington: Institute for the Study of Man.

Boroffka, N., J. Cierny, J. Lutz, H. Parzinger, E. Pernicka, and G. Weisberger

2000   Bronze Age Tin in Central Asia: Preliminary Notes. In *Late Prehistoric Exploitation of the Eurasian Steppe*, Volume 2, pp. 14–41. Cambridge: MacDonald Institute for Archaeological Research.

Bouzek, J.

1997   *The Aegean, Anatolia and Europe: Cultural Interrelations during the Early Iron Age*. Studies in Mediterranean Archaeology Vol. CXXII. Jonsered: Paul Åströms Förlag.

Bradley, R.

1988   Hoarding, Recycling and the Consumption of Prehistoric Metalwork: Technological Change in Prehistoric Europe. *World Archaeology* 20(2): 249–260.

Briant, P.

1996   *Histoire de l'Empire Perse. De Cyrus à Alexandre*. Paris: Fayard.

1997   Bulletin d'Histoire Achéménide I. *Topoi orient-occident*. Suppl. 1:5–127.

Bryce, J.

1896   *Transcaucasia and Ararat*. London: Macmillan.

Bryson, R. A. and R. U. Bryson

1999   Holocene Climates of Anatolia: As Simulated with Archaeoclimatic Models. *Tuba-Ar* II:1–13.

Burney, C. A.

1958   Eastern Anatolia in the Chalcolithic and Early Bronze Age. *Anatolian Studies* 8:157–209.

1970   Excavations at Haftavan Tepe 1968. *Iran* VIII: 157–171.

1972   Excavations at Haftavan Tepe 1969. *Iran* X: 127–142

1989   Hurrians and Proto-Indo-Europeans: The Ethnic Context of the Early Trans-Caucasian Culture. In *Anatolia and the Ancient Near East: Studies in Honor of Tahsin Özgüç*, edited by K. Emre, B. Hrouda, M. Mellink and N. Özgüç, pp. 45–51. Ankara: Türk Tarih Kurumu Basımevi.

1993   Arslantepe as a Gateway to the Highlands. In *Between the Rivers and Over the Mountains*, edited by M. Frangipane, H. Hauptmann, M. Liverani, P. Matthiae, and M. Mellinck, pp. 311–18. Rome: Universitá di Roma.

1994   Urartu and Iran: Some Problems and Answers. In *Anatolian Iron Ages 3, The Proceedings of the Third Anatolian Iron Ages Colloquium held at Van, 6–12 August 1990* (British Institute of Archaeology at Ankara Monograph No. 16), edited by A. Çilingiroğlu and D. H. French, pp. 31–35. Ankara: The British Institute of Archaeology.

1996   The Sheep are Sweeter. In *Cultural Interaction in the Ancient Near East*, edited by G. Bunnens. Abr Nahrain supplement series 5, pp. 1–15. Louven: Peters.

Burney, C. A. and D. M. Lang

1971   *The Peoples of the Hills: Ancient Ararat and Caucasus*. New York: Praeger Publishers.

Burton Brown, T.

1951   *Excavations in Azerbaijan 1948*. London: John Murray.

Byrne, W.

1978   An Archaeological Demonstration of Migration on the Northern Great Plains. In *Archaeological Essays in Honor of Irving Rouse*, edited by R. Dunnell and E. Hall, pp.247–274. Hague: Mouton.

Carneiro, R.

1970   A Theory of the Origin of the State. *Science* 169:733–739.

Carter, E.

1994   Bridging the Gap between the Elamites and the Persians in Southeastern Khuzistan. In *Achaemenid History VIII: Continuity and Change*, edited by H. Sancisi-Weerdenburg, A. Kuhrt and M.C. Root, pp. 65–95. Proceedings of the Last Achaemenid History Workshop, April 6–8, 1990, Ann Arbor, Michigan. Leiden: Brill.

Chapman J. and H. Hamerow

1997   Introduction: On the Move Again. Migrations and Invasions in Archaeological Explanation. In *Migrations and Invasions in Archaeological Explanation*, edited by J. Chapman and H. Hamerow, pp. 1–10. Oxford: British Archaeological Reports.

Chartolani, S.

1996   *Dzveli Svaneti*. Tbilisi: Kera-XXI.

Chataigner, C.

1995   *La Transcaucasie au Néolithique et au Chalcolithique*. Oxford: British Archaeological Reports.

Chernykh, E.N.

1992   *Ancient Metallurgy in the USSR*. Cambridge: Cambridge University Press.

Chikovani, G.

1999   *Shida Kartli dz. ts. V–IV Atastsleulebshi*. Abstract of Ph.D dissertation, University of Tbilisi.

Childe, V. G.

1929   *The Danube in Prehistory*. Oxford: Clarendon.

1950   The Urban Revolution. *Town Planning Review* 21:3–17.

1951   *Social Evolution*. New York: Schuman.

Chubinishvili, T. N.

1965   Novye Dannye o Proniknovenii Urartskoj Kul'tury v Yuzhnuyu Gruziyu. In *Novoe v Sovetskoj Arkheologii*, edited by E. I. Krupnov, pp. 198–201. Moscow: Nauka.

1971   *K Drevnei Istorii Yuzhnogo Kavkaza*. Tbilisi: Metsniereba.

Chubinishvili, T. N., G. Pkhakadze, G. Mirtskhulava, Z. Shatberashvili, D. Gogeliya, and K. Esakiya

1979   Otchet Kvemo-Kartliyskoy (Arukhlo) Arkheologicheskoy Ekspeditsii. In *Polveye Arkheologicheskiye Issledovaniya 1975 goda*, edited by O. Lordkipanidze, pp. 9–13. Tbilisi: Metsniereba.

Çilingiroğlu, A.

1987   Van-Dilkaya Höyüğü Kazıları, 1985. *VIII Kazı Sonuçları Toplantısı*:81–94. Ankara: Kültür Bakanlığı.

1988   Van-Dilkaya Höyüğü Kazıları, 1987. *IX Kazı Sonuçları Toplantısı*:229–248. Ankara: Kültür Bakanlığı.

1991   The Early Iron Age at Dilkaya. In *Anatolian Iron Ages II*, edited by A. Çilingiroğlu and D. H. French, British Institute of Archaeology at Ankara Monograph 13, pp. 29–38. Oxford: Oxbow Books.

1996   Van-Ayanis Kalesi Kazıları, 1993-1994. *XVII.I. Kazı Sonuçları Toplantısı*, Ankara, 363-377.

2001   Temple Area. In *Ayanis I*, edited by A. Çilingiroğlu and M. Salvini, pp. 37–65. Rome: Instituto Per Gli Studi Micenei Ed Egeo-Anatolici.

Çilingiroğlu, A. and H. Sağlamtimur

1999   Van-Ayanis Urartu Kalesi Kazıları, 1997. *XX. Kazı Sonuçları Toplantısı I*, 527–540.

Çilingiroğlu, A. and M. Salvini

1995   Rusahinili in front of Mount Eiduru: The Urartian fortress of Ayanis (7th century B.C.). *Studi Micenei ed Egeo-Anatolici* 35:111–129.

1996   Van-Ayanıs Kalesi Kazıları, 1993–1994, *XVII.I. Kazı Sonuçları Toplantısı I*, Ankara, 363–377.

1997   The 1997 Excavation Campaign at the Urartian Fortress of Ayanis. *Studi Micenei ed Egeo-Anatolici* 39:287–289.

1999   When was the Castle of Ayanis Built and What is the Meaning of the Word "Suri"? In *Anatolian Iron Ages 4. Proceedings of the Fourth Anatolian Iron Ages Colloquium held at Mersin, 19–23 May 1997*, edited by A. Çilingiroğlu and R. Matthews, 55–60. Ankara: British Institute of Archaeology.

2001   The Historical Background of Ayanis. In *Ayanis: Ten Year's Excavations at Rusahinili Eiduru-kai 1989–1998*, edited by A. Çilingiroğlu and M. Salvini,15–24. Rome: Instituto Per Gli Studi Micenei Ed Egeo-Anatolici.

Claessen, H.J.M.

1984   The Internal Dynamics of the Early State. *Current Anthropology* 25(4): 365–379.

Cleland, C.

1976   The Focal-Diffuse Model. *Midatlantic Journal of Archaeology* 1:59–76.

Cole, J.P. and F.C. German

1961   *A Geography of the USSR*. London: Buttersworths.

Collon, D.

1982a   Some Bucket Handles. *Iraq* 44(1): 95–101.

1982b   *The Alalakh Cylinder Seals: A New Catalogue of the Actual Seals Excavated by Sir Leonard Woolley at Tell Atchana, and from Neighbouring Sites on the Syrian-Turkish Border*. BAR international series 132. Oxford: British Archaeological Reports,.

1987   *First Impressions: Cylinder Seals in the Ancient Near East*. London: British Museum Publications.

Contenau, G.

1922   *La Glyptique Syro-Hittite*. Paris: P. Geuthner.

Conti, A. M. and C. Persiani

1993   When Worlds Collide: Cultural Developments in Eastern Anatolia in the Early Bronze Age. In *Between the Rivers and Over the Mountains*, edited by M. Frangipane, H. Hauptmann, M. Liverani, P.

Matthiae, and M. Mellinck, pp. 361–414. Rome: Universitá di Roma.

Cook, J. M.
1983 *The Persian Empire*. New York: Schocken Books.

Crawford, H.
1975 Geoy Tepe 1903. *Iranica Antiqua* 11, 1–28.

Cribb, R.
1991 *Nomads in Archaeology*. Cambridge: Cambridge University Press.

Curtis, J. (editor)
1995 *Later Mesopotamia and Iran: Tribes and Empires 1600–539 BC*. London: British Museum Press.

Curtis, J. E. and J. E. Reade (editors)
1995 *Art and Empire: Treasures from Assyria in the British Museum*. New York: Metropolitan Museum of Art.

Dalley, S. (editor)
1998 *The Legacy of Mesopotamia*. Oxford: Clarendon Press.

Dashevskaya, O. D. and G. A. Lordkipanidze
1995 Skifskoe Izviyanie iz Vostochnoj Gruzii. *Istoriko-Arkeologicheskij Al'manakh* 1:99–101.

Davis, D. E.
1983 Investigating the Diffusion of Stylistic Innovations. In *Advances in Archaeological Method and Theory*, 6, edited by M. B. Schiffer, pp. 53–89. New York: Academic Press.

de Jesus, P. S.
1980 *The Development of Prehistoric Mining and Metallurgy in Anatolia*. BAR International Series 74. Oxford: British Archaeological Reports.

de Morgan, J.
1889 *Mission Scientifique au Caucase*. Paris: Ernest Leroux.

de Tournefort, J. P. and H. H. Bartlett
1717 *Relation d'un Voyage du Levant*. Lyon: Chez Anisson et Posuel.

Dedabrishvili, Sh.
1977 *Alaznis velis Korganebi*. Tbilisi: Metsniereba.

Degens, E.T. and F. Kurtman (editors)
1978 *The Geology of Lake Van*. Ankara: Maden Tetkik Arama Enstitüsü.

Derin, Z.
1994 The Urartian Cremation Jars in Van and Elaziğ Museums. In *Anatolian Iron Ages 3, The Proceedings of the Third Anatolian Iron Ages Colloquium held at Van, 6–12 August 1990*, edited by A. Çilingiroğlu and D. H. French, pp. 49–62. Ankara: The British Institute of Archaeology.
1999 Potters' Marks of Ayanis Citadel, Van. *Anatolian Studies* 49:81–100.

Devedjyan, S. G.
1981 *Lori-Berd I*. Erevan: Izdatelstvo AN Armyanskoj SSR.
1986 Pogrebenie Zhretsa iz Lori-Berda. *Istoriko-Filologicheskiy Zhurnal* 3:108–124.

Dewdney, J. C.
1971 *Turkey, an Introductory Geography*. New York: Praeger.

Diakonoff, I. M.
1952 K Voprosu o Sud'be Plennych v Assirii i Urartu. *Vestnik Drevney Istorii* 1:90–100.
1984 *The Pre-history of the Armenian People*. Delmar, NY: Caravan Books.

Dietler, M., and I. Herbich
1998 *Habitus*, Techniques, Style: An Integrated Approach to the Social Understanding of Material Culture and Boundaries. In *The Archaeology of Social Boundaries*, edited by M. Stark, pp. 242–273. Washington DC: Smithsonian Institution Press.

Dinçol, A. M.
1994 Cultural and Political Contacts Between Assyria and Urartu. *Tel Aviv* 21(1): 6–21.

Dittman R.
1990 Eisenzeit I und II in West- und Nordwest-Iran Zeitgleich zur Karum-Zeit in Anatoliens? *Archäologische Mitteilungen aus Iran* 23:105–138.

Douglas, M., and B. Isherwood
1996 *The World of Goods*. Cambridge: Cambridge University Press.

Dumont, L.
1977 *From Mandeville to Marx*. Chicago: University of Chicago Press.
1980 On Value. *Proceedings of the British Academy* LXVI: 207–241.

Dyson, R. H.
1965 Problems of Protohistoric Iran as Seen from Hasanlu. *Journal of Near Eastern Studies* 24:193–217.

Dyson R. H., and O. W. Muscarella
1989 Constructing the Chronological and Historical Implications of Hasanlu IV. *Iran* 27:1–27.

Edens, C.
1995 Transcaucasia at the End of the Early Bronze Age. *Bulletin of the American Society of Oriental Research* 299/300:53–64.

Edwards, M.
1983 *Excavations in Azerbaijan (North-western Iran) 1: Haftavan, Period VI*. Oxford: British Archaeological Reports.

Eliade, M.
1978 *The Forge and the Crucible*. Chicago: University of Chicago Press.

Erzen, A.

1978   *Çavuştepe I*. Ankara: Türk Tarih Kurumu Basımevi.

Esaian, S. A.

1966   *Oruzhie i Voennoe Delo Drevnei Armenii*. Yerevan: Izdatelstvo AN Armyanskoj SSR.

1976   *Drevnyaya Kultura Plemen Severo-Vostochnoi Armenii*. Yerevan: Akademiya Nauk Armyanskoj SSR.

Esaian, S. A. and G. A. Oganesian

1969   *Katalog Arkheologicheskikh Predmetov Dilizhansckogo Muzeya*, Yerevan: Izdatelstvo AN Armyanskoj SSR.

Esaian, S. A. and M. N. Pogrebova

1985   *Skifskie pamyatniki Zakavkaz'ya*. Moscow: Nauka.

Esin, U.

1979   Tepecik ve Tülintepe Kazıları. *VIII Türk Tarih Kongresi*, 1:65–76. Ankara: Türk Tarih Kurumu Basımevi.

1982   Tepecik Excavations 1974. In *Keban Project Activities 1974–75*. pp. 95–118. Ankara: METU.

Fage, J.

1975   The Emergence of Bantu Africa. In *The Cambridge History of Africa*. Volume 2, pp. 342–409. Cambridge: Cambridge University Press.

Ferdinand, K.

1962   Nomadic Expansion and Commerce in Central Afghanistan." *Folk* 4:123–160.

Field, H.

1953   *Contributions to the Anthropology of the Caucasus*. Cambridge MA: Peabody Museum.

Flannery, K. V.

1972   The Cultural Evolution of Civilizations. *Annual Review of Ecology and Systematics* 3:399–426.

Frangipane, M.

1985   Early Developments of Metallurgy in the Near East. In *Studi di Paletnologia in Onore Salvatore M. Puglisi*, edited by M. Liverani, A. Palmieri, R. Peroni, pp. 215–228 Rome: Universitá di Roma.

1997a   Changes in Upper Mesopotamia/Anatolian Relations at the Beginning of the 3rd Millennium B.C. *Subartu* IV: 195–218.

1997b   Arslantepe 1996: the Finding of an EB I "Royal Tomb." XIX *Kazı Sonuçları Toplantısı* pp.291–309. Ankara: Kültür Bakanlı.

2000   The Late Chalcolithic/EB I Sequence at Arslantepe: Chronological and Cultural Remarks from a Frontier Site. In *Chronologies des Pays du Caucase et de l'Euphrate aux IVe–IIIe Millenaires: Actes du Colloque d'Istanbul, 16–19 Décembre 1998* (Acta Anatolica XI), edited by C. Marro and H. Hauptmann, pp. 439–471. Paris: Institut Francais d'Études Anatoliennes Georges Dumezil.

Frangipane, M. and A. Palmieri

1983   Cultural Developments at Arslantepe at the Beginning of the Third Millennium: The Settlements of Period VIB. *Origini* 12:523–574.

Frankfort, H.

1928   Sumerians, Semites, and the Origin of Copper-Working. *Antiquaries Journal* 8:217–235.

1963   *The Art and Architecture of the Ancient Orient*. Harmondsworth: Penguin Books.

Fried, M. H.

1967   *The Evolution of Political Society: An Essay in Political Anthropology*. New York: Random House.

Friedman, J., and M. J. Rowlands

1977   Notes Toward an Epigenetic Model of the Evolution of Civilisation. In *The Evolution of Social Systems*, edited by J. Friedman and M. J. Rowlands, pp. 201–276. London: Duckworth.

Furtwängler, A. and O. Lordkipanidze (editors)

2000   *Iberien (Königreich Kartli) und Seine Nachbarn in Achaimenidischer und Nachaimenidischer Zeit*. Archäologische Mitteilungen aus Iran und Turan 32. Berlin: Dietrich Reimer Verlag GmbH.

Gadzhiev, M. G.

1991   *Ranne Zemledelcheskaya Kultura Severo-Vostochnovo Kavkaza*. Moscow: Nauk.

Gadzhiev, M. G., P. Kohl, R. Magomedov, and D. Stronach

1995   The 1994 Excavations of the Daghestan-American Archaeological Expedition to Velikent in Southern Daghestan, Russia. *Iran* 33:139–147.

1997   The 1995 Daghestan-American Velikent Expedition: Excavations in Daghestan, Russia (with an appendix on the Velikent fauna by A. Morales and flora by A. Arnaz). *Eurasia Antiqua* 3:181–222.

Gadzhiev, M. G., and S. N. Korenevskii

1984   Metall Velikentskoi Katakomby. In *Drevnie Promysly, Remeslo i Torgovlya v Dagestane*, edited by M. M. Mammaev, pp. 7–27. Makhachkala: Nauk.

Gagoshidze, J.

1981   *Samadlo: Katalog Arkheologicheskogo Materiala*. Tbilisi: Metsniereba.

1985   Iz Istorii Yuvelirnogo Dela v Gruzii. In *Khudozhestvennye Pamyatniki i Problemy Kul'tury Vostoka*, edited by V. G. Lukonin, pp. 47—61. Leningrad: Iskusstvo.

1992   The Temples at Dedoplis Mindori. *East and West* 42 (1): 27–48.

1996   The Achaemenid Influence in Iberia. *Boreas* 19:125–136.

1997   Materialien zur Geschichte der Goldschmiedekunst im Alten Georgien. *Boreas* 20:123–136.

Galanina, L. K.
1985   Problemy Kubanskogo Tipa (Voprosy Khronologii i Proiskhozhdeniya). In *Kul'turnoe Nasledie Vostoka*, edited by Y. V. Bromlei, pp. 169–183. Leningrad: Nauka.

Ganji, M. H.
1968   Climate. In *The Land of Iran. Cambridge History of Iran I*, pp. 212–249. Cambridge: Cambridge University Press.

Gell, A.
1992   The Technology of Enchantment and the Enchantment of Technology. In *Anthropology, Art, and Aesthetics*, edited by J. Coote and A. Shelton. New York: Oxford University Press.

Ghirshman, R.
1939   *Fouilles de Sialk pres de Kashan 1933, 34, 37 II*, Paris: P. Geuthner.

Gigolashvili, N.
1999   The Silver Aryballos from Vani. In *Ancient Greeks West and East*, edited by G. R. Tsetskhladze, pp. 605–613. Mnemosyne, Bibliotheca Classica Batava, Suppl. 196. Leiden: Brill.

Glumac, P. and D. Anthony
1992   Culture and Environment in the Prehistoric Caucasus: The Neolithic through the Early Bronze Age. In *Chronologies in Old World Archaeology*, 3rd ed., edited by R. W. Ehrich, pp. 198–206. Chicago: University of Chicago Press.

Gobedzhishvili, G.
1980   *Bedenis Gorasamarkhebis Kultura*. Tbilisi: Metsniereba.

Gobedzhishvili, G. F. and K. N. Pitskhelauri
1989   Vostochnaya Gruziya v Epokhu Posdnej Bronzy i Rannego Zheleza. In *Ocherki istorii Gruzii*, edited by G.A. Melikishvili and O.D. Lordkipanidze, vol. 1, pp. 141–179. Tbilisi: Metsniereba.

Goetze, A.
1957   *Kleinasien*. 2nd ed. Handbuch der Orientalistik. 3. Abteilung, 1. Teil, 3. Band, 3. Abschnitt, 1. Unterabschnitt. Munich: C. H. Beck.

Gogadze, E.
1970   K Voprosu O Genezise i Periodizatsii Kurgannoy Kultury Trialeti. *Voprosy Drevney Istorii (Kavkasko-Blizhnevostchnyy Sbornik)* 3:221–251.

1972a   *Periodizatsiya i Genezis Kurgannoy Kultury Trialeti*. Tbilisi: Metsniereba.

1972b   *Trialetis Korganuli Kulturis Periodizatsia da Genezisi*. Tbilisi: Metsniereba.

Gogeliya, D. D.
1982   Kvemo-Kartiliyskaya Arkheologicheskaya Ekspeditsiya 1979–1980 gg. In *Polveye Arkheologicheskiye Issledovaniya 1980*, edited by O. Japaridze, pp. 13–17. Tbilisi: Metsniereba.

Gogeliya, D. D. and L. M. Chelidze
1992   Eneolith. In *Saqartvelos Arqeologia*, edited by N. Berdzenishvili, Vol. 2, pp. 17–70. Tbilisi: Metsniereba.

Gogiberidze, N.
1989   Adreantikuri da Elinisturi Khanis Gvergvebi Sakartvelos Arkeologiuri Masalebis Mikhedvit. *Sakartvelos Sakhelmtsipo Muzeumis Moambe* XL–B: 71–82.

Gould, S. J.
1996   *The Mismeasure of Man*. New York: Norton.

Graeber, D.
1996   Beads and Money: Notes Toward a Theory of Wealth and Power. *American Ethnologist* 23(1): 4–24.

2001   *Toward an Anthropological Theory of Value: The False Coin of Our Own Dreams*. New York: Palgrave.

Grayson, A. K.
1987   *Assyrian Rulers of the Third and Second Millennia B.C. (to 1115 B.C.)*. Toronto: University of Toronto Press.

Grigolia G. and T. Tatishvili
1960   Qvemo Qartlis Udzvelesi Dzeglebi. In *Saqartvelos Istoriuli Geographiis Krebuli*, Vol. 1. Tbilisi: Metsniereba.

Grossgeym, A. A.
1948   *Rastitelnyy Pokrov Kavkaza*. Moscow: Nauka.

Gudeman, S.
1985   Economic Anthropology. In *The Social Science Encyclopedia*, edited by A. Kuper and J. Kuper. London: Routledge and Kegan Paul.

Gvozdetskyi, N. A.
1954   *Fizicheskaya Geografiya Kavkaza*. Moscow: Nauka.

Haas, J.
1982   *The Evolution of the Prehistoric State*. New York: New York University Press.

Hall, M. E., and S. R. Steadman
1991   Tin and Anatolia: Another Look. *Journal of Mediterranean Archaeology* 4:217–234.

Hamilton, E.
1996   *Technology and Social Change in Belgic Gaul*. MASCA Research Papers in Science and Archaeology 13. Philadelphia: Museum Applied Science Center for Archaeology, University of Pennsylvania Museum of Archaeology and Anthropology.

Hançar, F.
1937   *Urgeschichte Kaukasiens von den Anfangen Seiner Besiedlung bis in die Zeit Seiner Frühen Metallurgie*. Vienna: A. Schroll.

Hannerz, U.

1989   Culture between Center and Periphery: Toward a Macroanthropology. *Ethnos* 54:200–216.

1992   *Cultural Complexity*. New York: Columbia University Press.

Härinck, E.

1988   The Iron Age in Guilan: Proposal for a Chronology. In *Bronzeworking Centers of Western Asia c. 1000–539 B.C.*, edited by J. Curtis, pp. 63–78. London: Kegan Paul.

Harper, P. O., E. Klengel-Brandt, J. Aruz, and K. Benzel (editors)

1995   *Assyrian Origins: Discoveries at Ashur on the Tigris*. New York: Metropolitan Museum of Art.

Harris, M.

1979   *Cultural Materialism*. New York: Random House.

Hauptmann, H.

1969   Norşun-tepe. *Istanbuler Mitteilungen* 19/20:21–78.

2000   Zur Chronologie des 3. Jht. v.Chr. In *Chronologie des pays du Caucase et de l'Euphrate aux IVe–IIIe millenaires*, edited by C. Marro and H. Hauptmann, pp. 419–438. Paris: Institut Francais d'Études Anatoliennes Georges Dumezil.

Haxthausen, B. von

1854   *Transcaucasia*. London: Chapman and Hall.

Hays, K.A.

1993   When is a Symbol Archaeologically Meaningful? Meaning, Function, and Prehistoric Visual Arts. In *Archaeological Theory: Who Sets the Agenda?*, edited by N. Yoffee and A. Sherratt, pp. 81–92. Cambridge: Cambridge University Press.

Helms, M. W.

1988   *Ulysses' Sail*. Princeton: Princeton University Press.

1993   *Craft and the Kingly Ideal*. Austin: University of Texas Press.

Hodder, I., and R. Preucel (editors)

1996   *Archaeology in Theory: A Reader*. Oxford: Blackwell.

Hoover, R.

1974   *The Origins and Initial Migrations of the Bantu*. Boulder: University of Northern Museum of Anthropology Colorado: Miscellaneous Series no. 34.

Howells-Meurs, S.

2001   *Early Bronze Age and Iron Age Animal Exploitation in Northeastern Anatolia: The Faunal Remains from Sos Höyük and Büyüktepe Höyük*. Oxford: British Archaeological Reports.

Japaridze, N. O.

1988   *Yuvelirnoye Iskusstvo Epokhi Bronzy v Gruzii*. Tbilisi: Isd. Tbilisskogo Universiteta.

Japaridze, O.

1961   *Qartveli Tomebis Istoriisatvis Litonis Tsarmoebis adreul Saphekhurze*. Tbilisi: Tbilisskogo Gosydarstvennogo Universiteta.

1969   *Arkeologicheskiye Raskopki v Trialeti v 1957–1958 gg.* Sabchota Sakartvelo, Tbilisi: Metsniereba.

1982   Iz Istorii Arkheologicheskogo Izuchenia Gruzii. *History of Archaeological Study in Georgia* XXXVI-B: 29–38.

1994   Trialetskaya Kultura. In *Rannyaya i Srednyaya Bronza Kavkaza*, edited by K. Kh. Kushnareva and V. I. Markovin, pp. 75–92. Moskow: Nauka.

1998   Kartveli Tomebis Etno-Kulturuli Istoriisatvis Dzveli Tseltaghritskhvis Mesame *Atastsleulshi*. In *Zur Ethnokulturellen Geschichte der Georgischem Stamme im 3. Jahrtausend V. CHR*, pp. 189–200. Tbilisi: Tbilisskogo Universiteta.

Japaridze, O., G. B. Avalishvili, and A. T. Tsereteli

1985   *Pamyatniki Meskheti Epokhi Sreney Bronzy*. Tbilisi: Metsniereba.

Javakhishvili, A.

1998   Ausgrabungen in Berikldeebi (Shida Kartli). *Georgica* 21:7–21.

Javakhishvili, G.

1966   Neolithuri Masala Lagodekhis Raionidan. In *Masalebi Saqartvelos Materialuri Kulturis Istoriisatvis*, edited by V. Japaridze. Tbilisi: Metsniereba.

1971   *K Istorii Rannezemledelcheskoi Kulturi Zapadnogo Zakavkazia*. Abstract of unpublished Ph.D. dissertation, University of Tbilisi.

Johnson, A. W. and T. Earle

1987   *The Evolution of Human Societies: From Foraging Group to Agrarian States*. Stanford: Stanford University Press.

Joukowsky, M. S.

1996   *Early Turkey. An Introduction to the Archaeology of Anatolia from Prehistory through the Lydian Period*. Dubuque: Kendall/Hunt.

Kafadarian, K.

1996   *History of Armenian Architecture*. Yerevan: Armenian Academy of Sciences.

Kafesoğlu, I.

1988   *A History of the Seljuks*. Carbondale: Southern Illinois University Press.

Kalantar, A.

1925   *Aragats in History*, Yerevan: Armenian Academy of Sciences.

1994   *Armenia: From the Stone Age to the Middle Ages*. Civilisations du Proche-Orient Serie 1 Archaeologie et Environnement 2. Paris:

Recherches et Publications.

Kaptan, E.
1983   The Significance of Tin in Turkish Mining History and its Origin. *MTA Bulletin* (95/96): 164–172.

Kavtaradze, G. L.
1981   *Khronologiya Arkheologicheskikh Kul'tur Gruzii Epokhi Eneolita i Bronzi v Svete Novykh Dannykh.* Tbilisi: Metsniereba.
1983   *K Khronologii Epokhi Eneolita i Bronzy Gruzii,* Tbilisi: Metsniereba.

Kelly-Buccellati, M.
1979   The Outer Fertile Crescent Culture: Northeastern Connections of Syria and Palestine in the Third Millennium B.C. *Ugarit-Forschungen*. Band 11:413–430.
1990   Trade in Metals in the Third Millennium: Northeast Syria and Eastern Anatolia. In *Resurrecting the Past*, edited by E. van Donzel, M. Mellinck, C. Nijland, J. J. Roodenberg, and K.R. Veenhof, pp. 117–131. Istanbul: Nederlands Instituut.

Kévorkian, R.H.
1996   *Arménie entre Orient et Occident*. Paris: Bibliothèque nationale de France.

Khachatryan, T. S.
1963   *Materialnaya Kultura Drevnogo Artika*. Yerevan: Izdatelstvo Yerevanskogo Universiteta.
1974   Iz Istorii Izuchenia Drevneyshikh Pamyatnikov Sklonov Gori Aragats. *Armenovedcheskie Issledovaniya* 1:109.
1975   *Drevnaya Kultura Shiraka*. Yerevan: Izdatelstvo Yerevansckogo Universiteta.
1979   *Artikskii Nekropol*. Yerevan: Izdatelstvo Yerevansckogo Universiteta.

Khanzadian, E.
1962   *Lchashenskii Kurgan 6. Kratkiye Soobshcheniya o Dokladakhi Polevykh Issledovannyakh Instituta Arkeologii ANSSR* 91. Monograph.
1967   *Kultura Armyanskogo Nagorya v III tys. do n.e.* Yerevan: Akademiya Nauk Armyanskoj SSR.
1979   *Elar-Darani*. Yerevan: Akademiya Nauk Armianskoe SSR.
1995   *Metsamor 2: La Necropole 1, Les Tombes du Bronze Moyen et Récent*. Neuchâtel: Recherches et Publications.

Khanzadian, E. V., K. A. Mkrtchian and E. S. Parsamian
1973   *Metsamor*. Yerevan: Akademiya Nauk Armyanskoj SSR.

Khanzadian, E. V. and B. B. Piotrovskii
1992   A Cylinder Seal with Ancient Egyptian Hieroglyphic Inscription from the Metsamor Gravesite. *Soviet Anthropology and Archaeology* 30(4): 67–76.

Khanzadian, E. V., G. K. Sarkisian and I. M. Diakonoff
1992   A Babylonian Weight from the Sixteenth Century B.C. with Cuneiform Inscription from the Metsamor Excavations. *Soviet Anthropology and Archeology* 30(4): 75–83.

Khatib-Shahidi, H.
1998   Narrazione Personale della Scoperta della Stele Urartea di Mergeh Karvan. *Studi Micenei ed Egeo-Anatolici* XL(1):131–142.

Khazaradze, N. and G. Tskitishvili
1980   Tsikhia-Goras Kramiti. *Kavkasiur-Akhloagmosavluri Krebuli* VI: 146–162.

Khidasheli, M.
1980   Tsentraluri da Agmosavletamierkavkasiuri Brinjaos Sartkelebis Mkhatvruli Stilis Sakitkhebi. *Kavkasiur-Akhloagmosavluri Krebuli* VI: 105–127.
1988   Model' Svyatilishcha Tsentral'nogo Zakavkaz'ya Epokhi Rannego Zheleza. *Kavkasiur-Akhloagmosavluri Krebuli* VIII: 173–180.

Khodzhash, S.
1981   Znaki na Urartskoj Keramike Erebuni. In *Drevnij Vostok i Mirovaya Kul'turi*, edited by I. M. Dyakonov, pp. 85–89. Moscow: Nauka.

Khorenats'i, M.
1978   *History of the Armenians*. Cambridge, MA: Harvard University Press.

Kiguradze, N.
1976   *Dapnarskij Mogil'nik*. Tbilisi: Metsniereba.

Kiguradze, T. B.
1976   *Agmosavlet Amierkavkasiis Adresamitsatmoqmedo Kulturis Periodizatsia*. Tbilisi: Metsniereba.
1986   *Die Neolithische Siedlungen von Kwemo Kartli Georgien*. München: Beck.
2000   The Chalcolithic-Early Bronze Age Transition in the Eastern Caucasus. In *Chronologies des Pays du Caucase et de l'Euphrate aux IVe –IIIe Millenaires: Actes du Colloque d'Istanbul, 16–19 Décembre 1998* (Acta Anatolica XI), edited by C. Marro and H. Hauptmann, pp. 312–328. Paris: Institut Francais d'Études Anatoliennes Georges Dumezil.

Kiguradze, T. B. and T. Segova
2000   On the Origins of Kova-Arakes Complex. In *Chronologies des Pays du Caucase et de l'Euphrate aux IVe –IIIe Millenaires: Actes du Colloque d'Istanbul, 16–19 Décembre 1998* (Acta Anatolica XI), edited by C. Marro and H. Hauptmann. Paris: Institut Francais d'Études Anatoliennes Georges Dumezil.

Kikvidze, I. A.
1972   *Khizanaantgoris Adrebrinjaos Khanis Namosakhlari*. Tbilisi: Metsniereba.

1976   *Mitsadmokmedeba da Samitsadmokmedo Kulti Dzvel Sakartveloshi (arkeologiuri masalebis mikhedvit).* Tbilisi: Metsniereba.

Kimsiasvili, K. and G. Narimanisvili

1995/96 A Group of Iberian Fire Temples (4th Cent. BC–2nd Cent. AD). *Archäologische Mitteilungen aus Iran* 28:309–318.

King, L. W.

1915   *Bronze Reliefs from the Gates of Shalmaneser, King of Assyria, B.C. 860–825.* London: Trustees of the British Museum.

Kipiani, G.

1987   *Sakartvelos Antikuri Khanis Arkitektura. Kapitelebi.* Tbilisi: Khelovneba.

1997   *Berikldeebi: Galavani da Tadzari. Saqartvelos Sakhelmtsipo Muzeumis Moambe,* 42–B: 13–57.

Kleiss W.

1970   Bericht über Erkundsfahrten in Nordwest Iran im Jahre 1969. *Archäologische Mitteilungen aus Iran* 3:107–132.

1971   Bericht über Erkundsfahrten in Iran im Jahre 1970. *Archäologische Mitteilungen aus Iran* 4:51–111.

1972   Bericht über Erkundsfahrten in Iran im Jahre 1971. *Archäologische Mitteilungen aus Iran* 5:7–68.

1973   Bericht über Erkundsfahrten in Iran im Jahre 1972. *Archäologische Mitteilungen aus Iran* 6:7–80.

1974   Planaufnahmen Urartäische Burgen und Neufunde Urartäischer Anlagen in Iranisch-Azerbaidjan im Jahre 1973. *Archäologische Mitteilungen aus Iran* 7:79–106.

1975a   Siedlungen und Burgen Azarbaidjan. *Archäologische Mitteilungen aus Iran* 8:27–42.

1975b   Planaufnahmen Urartäische Burgen und Neufunde Urartäischer Anlagen in Iranisch-Azerbaidjan im Jahre 1974. *Archäologische Mitteilungen aus Iran* 8:51–70.

1976   Urartäische Plätze in Iran (Stand der Forschung Herbst 1975). *Archäologische Mitteilungen aus Iran* 9:19–44.

1978   Hügelgräber in Nordwest-Azerbaidjan. *Archäologische Mitteilungen aus Iran* 11:13–26.

1983   Grössenvergleiche Urartäischer Burgen und Siedlungen. In *Beiträge zur Altertumskunde Kleinasiens. Festschrift für Kurt Bittel* edited by R. M. Boehmer, and H. Hauptmann, vol. I, pp. 283–290. Mainz: Philipp von Zabern Verlag.

1988   *Bastam II: Ausgrabungen in den Urartäischen Analagen 1977–1978.* Berlin: Gebr. Mann Verlag.

Kleiss W. and S. Kroll

1977   Urartäische Plätze in Iran: A, Architektur; B, Die Oberflächenfunde des Urartu-Surveys 1976. *Archäologische Mitteilungen aus Iran* 10:53–118.

1978   Urartäische Plätze. A. Architektur. B. Die Oberflächenfunde. *Archäologische Mitteilungen aus Iran* 11:25–71.

1979   Vermessene Urartäische Plätze in Iran (West-Azerbaidjan) und Neufunde (Stand der Forschung 1978): A, Architektur; B, die Oberflächenfunde. *Archäologische Mitteilungen aus Iran* 12:183–243.

Knauss, F. S.

1999   Achämeniden in Transkaukasien. In *Fenster zur Forschung,* edited by S. Lausberg and K. Oekentorp, pp. 81–114. Worte-Werke-Utopien. Thesen und Texte Münsterscher Gelehrter, vol. 9. Münster: Lit Verlag.

Kohl, P. L.

1989   The Use and Abuse of World Systems Theory: The Case of the 'Pristine' West Asian State. In *Archaeological Thought in America,* edited by C.C. Lamberg-Karlovsky, Cambridge: Cambridge University Press.

1992a   The Kura-Araxes Chiefdom/State: The Problems of Evolutionary Labels and Imperfect Analogies. In *South Asian Archaeology Studies,* edited by G. Possehl, pp. 223–232. New Delhi: Oxford and IBH Publishing.

1992b   The Transcaucasian Periphery in the Bronze Age. In *Resource Power and Regional Interaction,* edited by P. A. Urban and E. M. Schortman, pp. 117–137. London: Plenum Press.

1995   Central Asia and the Caucasus in the Bronze Age. In *Civilizations of the Ancient Near East,* edited by J.M. Sasson, J. Baines, G. Beckman, and K.S. Rubinson, pp. 1051–1065. New York: Charles Scribner's Sons.

2003   Bronze Production and Utilization in Southeastern Daghestan, Russia: c. 3600–1900 B.C. (with an Appendix on Lead-Isotope Analyses of Selected Velikent Tin-Bronzes by L. Weeks). Papers given at *Die Anfänge der Metallurgie in der Alten Welt* conference in Freiberg, Germany, November 1999.

Kohl, P. L. and G. R. Tsetskhladze

1995   Nationalism, Politics, and the Practice of Archaeology in the Caucasus. In *Nationalism, Politics, and the Practice of Archaeology,* edited by P. L. Kohl and C. Fawcett, pp. 149–174. Cambridge: Cambridge University Press.

König, F.

1954   Gesellschaftliche Verhältnisse Armeniens zur Zeit der Chalder-Dynastie (9–7 Jarh. v Chr.). *Archiv für Völkerkunde* 9:21–65.

Kopytoff, I.
1986   The Cultural Biography of Things: Commoditiza-
        tion as Process. In *The Social Life of Things*, edited
        by A. Appadurai, pp. 64–91. Cambridge: Cam-
        bridge University Press.

Koridze, D. L.
1955   *Tbilisis Arqeologiuri Dzeglebi*. Tbilisi: Sakartvelos
        SSR mecnierebata akademia.

Koşay, H.Z. and M. Akok
1966   *Ausgrabungen von Alaca Höyük. Vorbericht über die
        Forschungen und Entdeckungen von 1940–1948*. An-
        kara: Türk Tarih Kurumu.

Koshelenko, G. A. (editor)
1985   *Drevneishie Gosudarstva Kavkaza i Srednei Azii*.
        Moscow: Nauka.

Kozbe, G.
1987   Van Diklaya Höyü 1984-6: Kazı Dönemlerinde Ele
        Geçen Erken Kafkasasya Çanak Çömlei. Izmir:
        unpublished M.A. thesis.
1990   Van-Dilkaya Höyüğü Erken Transkafkasya
        Keramiği, *VII. Araştırma Sonuçları Toplantısı (1989)*,
        pp. 533–554. Ankara: Kültür Bakanlığı.

Kramer, C.
1977   Pots and people. In *Mountains and Lowlands: Essays
        in the Archaeology of Greater Mesopotamia*, edited by
        L. D. Levine and T. C. Young, Jr., pp. 91–112.
        Malibu: Undena Publications.

Kristiansen, K.
1989   Prehistoric Migrations: The Case of Single Grave
        and Corded Ware Cultures. *Journal of Danish Ar-
        chaeology* 8:211–225.

Kroll S.
1984   Archäologische Fundplätze in Iranisch-Ost-
        Azerbaidjan. *Archäologische Mitteilungen aus Iran*
        17:13–134.

Krupnov, E. I
1960   *Drevnyaya Istoriya Severnogo Kavkaza*. Moscow: Izd.
        Akademii Nauk SSSR.

Kuftin, B. A.
1940   K Voprosu o Rannykh Stadiyakh Bronzovoy
        Kultury na Territorii Kavkaza. *Kratkiye
        Soobshcheniya O Dokladakh i Polevykh Issledovaniyakh
        Instituta Istorii* 8:5–35.
1941   *Arkheologicheskie Raskopki v Trialeti*. Tbilisi:
        Akademii Nauk Gruzinskoj SSR.
1946   Prehistoric Culture Sequence in Transcaucasia.
        Southwestern Journal of Anthropology 2(3): 340–
        360.
1948   *Arkheologicheskie Raskopki 1947 g. v Tsalkinskom
        Rayone*. Tbilisi: Akademii Nauk Gruzinskoi SSR.

Kuftin, B. A. and H. N. Field
1946   Prehistoric Culture Sequence in Transcaucasia.
        Southwestern Journal of Anthropology 2(3):340–360.

Kuhrt, A.
1995   *The Ancient Near East c. 3000–330 BC*, vol. II. Lon-
        don: Routledge.

Kus, S.
1992   Toward an Archaeology of Body and Soul. In *Rep-
        resentations in Archaeology*, edited by J.-C. Gardin
        and C. S. Peebles, pp. 168–177. Bloomington: Uni-
        versity of Indiana Press.

Kushnareva, K.
1977   *Drevneshie Pamyatniki Dvina*. Yerevan: Academiya
        Nauk.
1985   Sevan-Uzerlikskaiya Kultura Epokhi Srednei
        Bronzi na Yuzhnom Kavkaze. In *Kul'turnoe nasledie
        vostoka*, pp. 89–l05. Leningrad: Nauka.
1993   *Yuzhnii Kavkaz v IX–II Tisiacheletii do Nashei eri*.
        Saint   Peterburg: Tsentr   Peterburgskoe
        Vostokovedenie.
1994a   Sevano-Uzerlikskaya Gruppa Pamyatnikov. In
        Rannyaya i Srednyaya Bronza Kavkaza, edited by K.
        Kh. Kushnareva and V. I. Markovin, pp. 118–128.
        Moscow: Nauka.
1994b   Karmirberdskaya (Tazakendskaya) Kul´turi. In
        Rannyaya i Srednyaya Bronza Kavkaza, edited by K.
        Kh. Kushnareva and V. I. Markovin, pp. 106–117.
        Moscow: Nauka.
1994c   Materialy k Probleme Vydeleniya Karmirvankskoj
        (Kyzilvankskoj) Kul'tury. In *Rannyaya i Srednyaya
        Bronza Kavkaza*, edited by K. Kh. Kushnareva and
        V. I.Markovin, pp. 128–132. Moscow: Nauka.
1997   *The Southern Caucasus in Prehistory: Stages of Cul-
        tural and Socioeconomic Development from the Eighth
        to the Second Millennium B.C.* Translated by H.N.
        Michael. Philadelphia: University of Pennsylvania
        Museum.
1999   Rannie Kompleksnie Obshestva na Yuzhnom
        Kavkaze. In *Drevnie Obshestva Kavkaza v Epokhu
        Paleometala*, pp. 11–43. Saint Petersburg: Nauka.

Kushnareva, K. and T. N. Chubinishvili
1970   *Drevnie Kulturi Iuzhnogo Kavkaza (V–III tys. do n.e.)*.
        Leningrad: Nauka.

Kushnareva, K. and V. I. Markovin
1994   Rannyaya i Srednyaya Bronza Kavkaza. Moscow:
        Nauka.

Kushnareva, K. and M. B. Rysin
2001   Novye Dannye k Probleme Datirovki Pamyatnikov
        "Tsvetushej pory" Trialetskoj Kul'tury. In *Caucasus:
        Essays on the Archaeology of the Neolithic-Bronze Age*

(Dedicated to the 80ᵗʰ Birthday of Prof. Otar Japaridze), edited by B. Maisuradze and R. Rusishvili, pp. 101–116. *Dziebani*, Supplement VI. Tbilisi: The Centre for Archaeological Studies of the Georgian Academy of Sciences.

Kvirkvelia, G.
1995   On the Early Hellenistic Burials of North-Western Colchis. *Archäologischer Anzeiger* 1:75–82.

Lamberg-Karlovsky, C.C.
1965   *Development of a Metallurgical Technology, Documented Early Finds of Metals in the Near East and the Evidence from Hasanlu, Iran*. Ph.D. dissertation, University Microfilms, Ann Arbor, Michigan.

Lechtman, H.
1984   Andean Value Systems and the Development of Prehistoric Metallurgy. *Technology and Culture* 25:1–36.
1999   The Production of Copper-Arsenic Alloys (Arsenic Bronze) by Cosmelting: Modern Experiment, Ancient Practice. *Journal of Archaeological Science* 26:497–526.

Lefferts, H. Jr.
1977   Frontier Demography: An Introduction. in *The Frontier, Comparative Studies*, edited by D. Miller and J. Steffen, pp. 33–55. Norman: University of Oklahoma Press.

Lehmann-Haupt, C. F.
1907   *Materialien zur Älteren Geschichte Armeniens und Mesopamiens*. Abhandlungen der Königlichen Gesellschaft der Wissenschaften zu Göttingen, Phil.-His.Klasse, NF IX, no. 3. Berlin. Weidmannsche Buchhandlung.
1910–31 *Armenien Einst und Jetzt*. Berlin: B. Behr.

Lemonnier, P.
1992   *Elements for an Anthropology of Technology*. Museum of Anthropology Anthropological Paper 8. Ann Arbor: University of Michigan.

Levine, L. D.
1976   East-West Trade in the Late Iron Age: A View from the Zagros. In *Le Plateau Iranien et l'Asie Centrale des Origines à la Conquéte Islamique*, pp. 171–186. Paris: Colloques Internationaux du Centre National de la Recherche Scientifique, no. 56.
1977   Sargon's Eighth Campaign. In *Mountains and lowlands: Essays in the Archaeology of Greater Mesopotamia*, edited by L. D. Levine and T. C. Young Jr., pp. 135–151. Malibu, CA: Undena.

Lippert, A.
1979   Die Österreichischen Ausgrabungen am Kordlar Tepe in Persisch-Westaserbaidschan (1971–1978). *Archäologische Mitteilungen aus Iran* 12:103–153.

Lisitsyna, G. and L. Prishchepenko
1977   *Paleoetnobotanicheskie Nakhodki Kavkaza i Blizhnego Vostoka*. Moscow: Nauka.

Litvinskii, B. A.
1950   K Istorii Dobychni Olova v Uzbekistane. *Trudi Sredniasiatskogo Gosudarstvenogo Universiteta* 11:51–67.

Longacre, W.
1968   Some Apects of Prehistoric Society in East-Central Arizona. In *New Perspectives in Archaeology*, edited by S. Binford and L. Binford, pp. 89–102. Chicago: Aldine.

Lordkipanidze, O.
1972a   Vanskoe Gorodishche (Raskopki. Istoriya. Problemy). In *Vani. Arkeologiuri Gatkhrebi 1947–1969*, vol. 1, edited by O. D. Lordkipanidze, pp. 43–80. Tbilisi: Metsniereba.
1989   *Nasledie Drevney Gruzii*. Tbilisi: Metsniereba.
1991a   Vani: An Ancient City of Colchis. *Greek Roman and Byzantine Studies* 32 (2): 151–195.
1991b   *Archaologie in Georgien: von der Altsteinzeit zum Mittelalter*. Weinheim: VCH, Acta Humaniora.
1995   Über zwei Dunde aus Vani. *Archäologischer Anzeiger* 1:41–52.

Lordkipanidze, O. (editor)
1972b   *Vani. Arkeologiuri Gatkhrebi 1947–1969*, vol. 1. Tbilisi: Metsniereba.
1981a   *Vani. Arkeologiuri Gatkhrebi*, vol. V. Tbilisi: Metsniereba.
1981b   *Vani. Arkeologiuri Gatkhrebi*, vol. VI. Tbilisi: Metsniereba.
1983   *Vani. Arkeologiuri Gatkhrebi*, vol. VII. Tbilisi: Metsniereba.

Lordkipanidze, O. D., R. V. Puturidze, D. D. Kacharava, V. A. Tolordava, M. N. Pirtskhalava, A. M. Chkoniya, N. N. Matiashvili, D. V. Akhvlediani, G. Sh. Naridze, and G. A. Inauri
1987   Raboty Vanskoj Ekspeditsii. *Polevye Arkheologicheskie Issledovaniya v 1984–1985 godakh (kratkie soobshcheniya)*, pp. 51–55. Tbilisi: Metsniereba.

Lucas, P.
1714   *Voyage du Sieur Paul Lucas : Fait en MDCCXIV, &c. par Ordre de Louis XIV, dans La Turquie, L'Asie, Sourie, Palestine, Haute et La Basse Egypte, &c.* Amsterdam: Steenhouwer & Uytwerf.

Luckenbill, D.
1927   *Ancient Records of Assyria and Babylonia*, vol 2. Chicago: University of Chicago Press.
1989   *Ancient Records of Assyria and Babylonia*. Reissue London: Histories & Mysteries of Man.

MAK
1888–1914 *Materialy po Arkheologii Kavkaza*. Moscow: Moskovskoe Arkheologischesiko Obshchestio.

Makharadze, G. and M. Saginashvili
1999 An Achaemenian Glass Bowl from Sairkhe, Georgia. *Journal of Glass Studies* 41:11–17.

Makharadze, Z.
1994 *Tsikhiagoris Mtkvar-Araksuli Namosakhlari*. Tbilisi: Metsniereba.

Makhmudov, F. and I. Narimanov
1972 Raskopki Alikemek-Tepesi. In *Archeologicheskie Otkritia 1971 goda*, pp 480–481. Moscow: Nauka.

Manning, S. W., B. Kromer, P. I. Kuniholm, and M. W. Newton
2001 Anatolian Tree Rings and a New Chronology for the East Mediterranean Bronze-Iron Ages. *Science* 294:2532–2535.

Mansfeld, G.
1996 Der Tqisbolo-Gora. *Antike Welt* 5:365–380.

Marcus, J. and G. Feinman
1998 Introduction. In *Archaic States*, edited by G. Feinman and J. Marcus, pp. 3–13. Santa Fe: School of American Research Press.

Marcus, M. I.
1996 *Emblems of Identity and Prestige: The Seals and Sealings from Hasanlu, Iran*. University Museum Monograph 84. Hasanlu Special Studies III. Philadelphia: University Museum, University of Pennsylvania.

Marr, N. I. and I. A. Orbelli
1922 *Arkheologicheskaya Expeditsiya 1916 goda v Van*. St. Petersburg: Akademicheskaya Topografia.

Marro, C. and H. Hauptmann (editors)
2000 *Chronologies des Pays du Caucase et de l'Euphrate aux IVe –IIIe millenaires: Actes du Colloque d'Istanbul, 16–19 Décembre 1998* (Acta Anatolica XI). Paris: Institut Francais d'Études Anatoliennes Georges Dumezil.

Martel, E.-A.
ND *La Cote d'Azur Russe*. Paris: Librarie Ch. Delagrane.

Martirosian, A. A.
1964 *Armenia v Epokhu Bronzi i Rannego Zheleza*. Yerevan: Akademiya Nauk Armyanskoj SSR.
1981 Pechati Masterov na Sosudakh iz Argishtihinili. In *Drevnij Vostok i Mirovaya Kul'turi*, edited by I. M. Dyakonov, pp. 80–84. Moscow: Nauka.

Marx, K.
1971 *Capital. A Critical Analysis of Capitalist Production*. Volume 1. Moscow: Progress Publishers.

Masson V. M.
1997 Kavkazskiy put' k Tsivilizatsii: Voprosy Sotsiokul'turnoy Interpretatsii. In *Drevnie Obshchestva Kavkaza v Epokhu Paleometalla (Rannie Kompleksnye Obshchestva i Voprosy Kul'turnoy Transformatsii)*, pp. 124–133. Sankt Petersburg: Institut Istorii Material'noy Kul'tury.

Mauss, M.
1990 *The Gift*. New York: W.W. Norton.

Maxwell-Hyslop, F.S.A.
1946 Daggers and Swords in Western Asia. *Iraq* VllI: 1–65.

McGovern, P.
1999 Georgia as Homeland of Winemaking and Viticulture. In *National Treasures of Georgia*, edited by O. Soltes, pp. 58–59. London: Philip Wilson Publishers Limited.

McGuire, R. H.
1983 Breaking Down Cultural Complexity: Inequality and Heterogeneity. *Advances in Archaeological Method and Theory* 6:91–142.

Melikishvili, G. A.
1953 K Voprosy o Carskich Chozjastvasch i Rabach-Plennikach v Urartu. *Vestnik Drevney Istorii* 1:22–29.
1954 *Nairi-Urartu: Drevnevostochnye Materialy po Istorii Narodov Zakavkaz'ia*. Tbilisi: Izdatelstvo Gruzinskaya SSR.
1965a Voznikoveniye Khettskogo Tsartsva i Problema Drevneyshego Naseleniya Zakavkazia i Maloy Azii. *Vestnik Drevney Istorii* 1:3–30.
1965b *Sakartvelos, Kavkasiis da Makhlobeli Aghmosavletis Udzvelesi Mosakhleobis Sakitkhisatvis*. Tbilisi: Metsniereba.
1999 Dziebani Sakartvelos, Kavkasiis da Akhlo Aghmosavletis Dzveli Istoriis Dargshi. In *Studies in the Ancient History of Georgia, Caucasus and Near East*, 103–305. Tbilisi: Metsniereba.

Menabde, M. and T. B. Kiguradze
1981 *Sionis Arqeologiuri Dzeglebi*. Tbilisi: Metsniereba.

Menabde, M., T. B. Kiguradze, and Z. Kikodze
1978 Qvemo Qartlis Arqeologiuri Eqspeditsiis 1976–1977 Tslebis Mushaobis Shedegebi. In *Saqartvelos Sakhelmtsipo Muzeumis Arqeologiuri Eqspeditsiebi*,VI. Tbilisi: Metsniereba.

Merhav, R. (editor)
1991 *Urartu: A Metelworking Center in the First Millennium BCE*. Jerusalem: Israel Museum.

Meshveliani, T., R. Papuashvili, E. Koridze and M. Dzalabadze
1999 Goradziris Arkeologiuri Gatkhrebi. In *Milsadenis Arkeologia*, vol. 1, edited by V. Licheli, pp. 71–81. Tbilisi: Centre for Archaeological Studies.

Metcalf, P. and R. Huntington
1991   *Celebrations of Death: The Anthropology of Mortuary Ritual.* Cambridge: Cambridge University Press.

Mikayelyan, G. A.
1968   *Tsiklopicheskie Kreposti Sevanskogo Bassena.* Yerevan: Akademiya Nauk.

Mikeladze, T. K.
1974   *Dziebani Kolkhetisa da Samkhret-Agmosavleti Shavizgvispiretis Udzvelesi Mosakhleobis Istoriidan.* Tbilisi: Metsniereba.
1990   *K Arkheologii Kolkhidy (Epokha Srednej i Pozdnej Bronzy-Rannego Zheleza).* Tbilisi: Metsniereba.

Mikeladze, T. K., N. P. Migdisova and P. I. Papuashvili
1997   Kolkhidskaya Arkheologicheskaya Ekspeditsiya. *Polevye Arkheologicheskie Issledovaniya v 1988 godu (kratkie soobshcheniya)* pp. 27–30. Tbilisi: Metsniereba.

Miller, D.
1995   Consumption Studies as the Transformation of Anthropology. In *Acknowledging Consumption*, pp. 264–295. London: Routledge and Kegan Paul.

Minns, E. H.
1942   Recent Archaeological Research in Transcaucasia. *Nature*, July 4, 28.
1943   Review of *Archaeological Excavations in Trialeti* by B.A. Kuftin. *Antiquity* 17:129–33.

Miron A. and W. Orthmann
1995   *Unterwegs zum Goldenen Vlies.* Saarbrüken: Museum für Vor- und Frühgeschichte Saarbrüken.

Miroschedji, P. de
2000   La Céramique de Khirbet Kerak en Syro-Palestine: État de la Question. In *Chronologies des Pays du Caucase et de l'Euphrate aux IVe–IIIe Millenaires: Actes du Colloque d'Istanbul, 16–19 Décembre 1998* (Acta Anatolica XI), edited by C. Marro and H. Hauptmann, pp. 255–278. Paris: Institut Francais d'Études Anatoliennes Georges Dumezil.

Mnatsakanyan, A. O.
1960   Drevnie Povozki iz Kurganov Bronzovogo Veka na Poberez'e oz. Sevan. *Sovetskaya Arkheologiya* 2:139–152.
1961   Lchashenskie Kurgany (Raskopki 1956 goda). *Kratkie Soobshcheniya Instituta Arkheologii* 85:65–72.
1965   Osnovnye Etapy Razvitiya Material'noy Kul'tury Lchashena. *Istoriko-Filologicheskiy Zhurnal* 2:95–114.

Moch, L.
1997   Dividing Time: An Analytical Framework for Migration History Periodization. In *Migration,* *Migration History, History: Old Paradigms and New Perspectives*, edited by J. Lucassen and L. Lucassen, pp.41–56. Bern: Peter Lang.

Moorey, P. R. S.
1985   *Materials and Manufacture in Ancient Mesopotamia: The Evidence of Archaeology and Art, Metals and Metalwork, Glazed Materials and Glass.* BAR International Series 237. Oxford: British Archaeological Reports.

Morris, Craig
1988   Progress and Prospect in the Archaeology of the Inca. In *Peruvian Prehistory*, edited by R. W. Keatinge, pp. 233–56. Cambridge: Cambridge University.

Morris, I.
1986   Gift and Commodity in Ancient Greece. *Man* 21:1–17.

MTA (Maden Tetkik ve Arama Genel Müdürlüğü)
1988   *Türkiye Jeoloji Haritalar Serisi.* Muş (H33, G33). Ankara: T.C. MTA.

Muhly, J. D.
1993   Early Bronze Age Tin and the Taurus. *American Journal of Archaeology* 97:239–257.

Müller-Karpe, M.
1991   Aspects of Early Metallurgy in Mesopotamia. In *Archaeometry 90*, edited by E. Pernicka and G. A. Wagner, pp. 105–116. Basel: Birkhuser Verlag.

Munchaev, R. M.
1975   *Kavkaz na Zare Bronzovogo Veka.* Moscow: Nauka.
1982   Eneolit Kavkaza. In *Eneolit SSSR*, edited by V. Masson and N. Merpert, pp. 100–164. Moscow: Nauka.
1994   Maikopskaya Kul'turi. In *Epokha Bronzy Kavkaza i Srednei Azii*, edited by K. Kh. Kushnareva and V.I. Markovin, pp. 158–225. Moscow: Nauk.

Munn, N.
1977   The Spatiotemporal Transformations of Gawa Canoes. *Journal de la Société des Océanistes* 33(54–55): 39–52.
1986   *The Fame of Gawa.* Cambridge: Cambridge University Press.

Muscarella, O.W.
1974   The Iron Age at Dinkha Tepe, Iran. *Metropolitan Museum Journal* 9:35–90.
1988   *Bronze and Iron. Ancient Near Eastern Artifacts in the Metropolitan Museum of Art*, New York: Metropolitan Museum of Art.
1994   North-western Iran: Bronze Age to Iron Age. In *Anatolian Iron Ages 3, The Proceedings of the Third Anatolian Iron Ages Colloquium held at Van, 6–12*

August 1990, edited by A. Çilingiroğlu and D. H. French, pp. 139–155. Ankara: The British Institute of Archaeology.

Muskhelishvili, D. L.

1978   K Voprosu o Svyazyakh Tsentral'nogo Zakavkaz'ya s Perednim Vostokom v Ranneantichnuyu Epokhu. In *Sakartvelos Arkeologiis Sakitkhebi*, vol. 1, edited by O. D. Lordkipanidze, pp. 17–30. Tbilisi: Metsniereba.

Nadiradze, D.

1990   *Sairkhe Sakartvelos Udzvelesi Kalaki*. Tbilisi: Sakartvelo.

Nagler, A.

1996   *Kurgane der Mozdok-Steppe in Nordkaucasien*. Archëologie in Eurasien 3. Berlin: Deutsches Archëologisches Institut, Eurasien-Abteilung.

Narimanishvili, G. K.

1991   *Keramika Kartli V–I vv do n. e*. Tbilisi: Metsniereba.

2000   Dzveli Tseltaghritskhvis Meore Atastsleulis Saritualo Gzebi Trialetshi. In *Dziebani*, vol.5, pp. 47–51. Tbilisi: Arkeologiuri   kvlevis   tsentris gamomtsemloba.

Narimanov, I.

1985   Obeidskoye Plemena Mesopotamii v Azerbaidzhane. *Abstracts of Papers Delivered at Vsesoyuznaya Arkheologicheskaya Konferentsiya "Dostizheniya Sovetskoi Arkheologii" v XI Pyatiletke*, pp. 271–272. Baku: Akademiia Nauk Azerbaidzhanskoi SSR.

1987   *Kultura   Drevneishego   Zemledelchesko-Skotovodcheskogo Naseleniia Azerbaijana*. Baku: Akademiia Nauk Azerbaidzhanskoi SSR.

Nechitailo, A.P.

1991   *Svyazi Naseleniya Stepnoi Ukraini i Severnogo Kavkaza v Epokhu Bronzy*. Kiev: Naukova Dumka.

Noneshvili, A. I.

1992   *Pogrebal'nye Obryady Narodov Zakavkaz'ya (Kuvshinnye Pogrebeniya VIII v. do n. e.—VIII v. n. e.)*. Tbilisi: Metsniereba.

Northover, P.

1989   Non-ferrous Metallurgy in Archaeology. In *Scientific Analysis in Archaeology*, edited by J. Henderson, pp. 213–236. UCLA Institute of Archaeological Research Tools 5. Los Angeles: University of California.

Oates, J. and D. Oates

1997   An Open Gate: Cities of the Fourth Millennium B.C. *Cambridge Archaeological Journal* 7(2): 287–307.

Oganesian, V.E.

1988   Serebryanyi Kubok iz Karashamba. *Istoriko-Filologicheskii Zhurnal* 4 (123): 145–161.

1990   *Kul'turi Pervoi Polovini Vtorogo Tisiacheletia do nashei eri v Srednem Techenii Reki Razdan*. Abstract of Ph.D. dissertation. Yerevan: Izd. Akademia Nauk Armenii.

1992a   A Silver Goblet from Karashamb. *Soviet Anthropology and Archaeology* 30 (4):84–102.

1992b   Raskopki Karashambskogo Mogil'nika v 1987g. *Arkheologischeskiye Raboty na Novostroikakh Armenii*, I: 26–36. Yerevan: Izd. Akademia Nauk Armenii.

Oliver, R.

1970   The Problem of Bantu Expansion. In *Papers in African Prehistory*, edited by J. Fage and R. Oliver, pp. 141–156. Cambridge: Cambridge University Press.

Orser, C. E., Jr.

1986   Beneath the Material Surface of Things: Commodities, Artifacts, and Slave Plantations. *Historical Archaeology* 26(3): 94–104.

Orthmann, W.

1977   Burial Customs of the 3rd Millennium B.C. in the Euphrates Valley. In *Le Moyen Euphrat: Zone de Contacts et d'échanges, Actes du Colloque de Strasbourg, 10–12 Mars 1977*, edited by J.Margueron, pp. 97–105. Leiden: Brill.

Özfırat, A.

1994   M. Ö. II. Binyıl Doğu Anadolu Boyalı Seramik Kültürleri. *XI. Araştırma Sonuçları Toplantısı*, Ankara, pp. 359–377.

1999   1997 Yılı Bitlis-Muş Yüzey Araştırması Tunç ve Demir Çağlari. *XVI. Araştırma Sonuçları Toplantısı*, Tarsus, pp. 1–22.

2000   Doğu Anadolu'da M.Ö. II. Binyıl Kültürlerinin Araştırılması. In *Türkiye Arkeolojisi ve İstanbul Üniversitesi*, edited by O. Belli, pp. 359–362. Istanbul: Istanbul University.

2001   *Doğu Anadolu Yayla Kültürleri*. Istanbul: Arkeoloji ve Sanat Yayınları.

Özgüç, N.

1965   *Kültepe Mühür Baskıların da Anadolu Grubu*. TTKY Series V, 22. Ankara: Türk Tarih Kurumu.

Özgüç, T.

1966   *Altıntepe, vol. I*. Ankara: Türk Tarih Kurumu Basımevi.

1986   *Kültepe-Kaniş II*. Ankara: Türk Tarih Kurumu Basımevi.

Palmieri, A.

1985   Eastern Anatolia and Early Mesopotamian Urbanization: Remarks Changing Relations. In *Studi di Paletnologia in Onore Salvatore M. Puglisi*, edited by M. Liverani, A. Palmieri, R. Peroni, pp. 191–214 Rome: Universitá di Roma.

Palmieri, A., K. Sertok, and E. Chernykh

1993   From Arslantepe Metalwork to Arsenical Copper Technology in Eastern Anatolia. In *Between the Rivers and Over the Mountains*, edited by M. Frangipane, H. Hauptmann, M. Liverani, P. Matthiae and M. Mellink, pp. 573–599. Rome: Gruppo Editoriale Internazionale.

Pantskhava, L.

1986   Nekotorye Voprosy Kolkhidskoj i Kobanskoj Kul'tur (po Materialam Chabarukhskogo i Pasanaurskogo Kladov). *Sakartvelos Sakhelmtsipo Muzeumis Moambe* XXXVIII–B: 23–34.

Papuashvili, R.

1999   Ergetis II Samarovani (samarkhi ormo No. 4). *Dzeglis Megobari* 106(3): 3–9.

Parker, A.

1999   Northeastern Anatolia: On the Periphery of Empires. *Anatolian Studies* 49:133–142.

Parker Pearson, M.

1984   Economic and Ideological Change: Cyclical Growth in the Pre-State Societies of Jutland. In *Ideology, Power, and Prehistory*, edited by D. Miller and C. Tilley, pp. 69–92. Cambridge: Cambridge University Press.

Peake, H.J.E. and H. J. Fleure

1928   *The Steppe and the Sown*. London: Clarendon Press.

Pecorella, P. E., and M. Salvini (editors)

1984   *Tra lo Zagros e l'Urmia. Ricerche Storiche ed Archeologiche nell'Azerbaigian Iraniano*, Roma: Edizioni dell'Ateneo.

Peirce, C. S.

1955   *Philosophical Writings of Peirce*. New York: Dover.

Pernicka, E., G. A. Wagner, J. D. Muhly, and O. Oztunali

1992   Comment on the Discussion of Ancient Tin Sources in Anatolia. *Journal of Mediterranean Archaeology* 5:91–98.

Petrenko, V. G.

1978   *Ukrasheniya Skifii VII—III vv. do n. e.* Moscow: Nauka.

Petrosyan, L. A.

1989   *Raskopki Pamyatnikov Keti i Voskeaska*. Yerevan: Akademiya Nauk.

Philip, G. and A. R. Millard

2000   Khirbet Kerak Ware in the Levant: The Implications of Radiocarbon Chronology and Spatial Distribution. In *Chronologies des Pays du Caucase et de l'Euphrate aux IVe –IIIe Millenaires: Actes du Colloque d'Istanbul, 16–19 Décembre 1998*, edited by C. Marro and H. Hauptmann, pp. 279–296. Paris: Institut Francais d'Études Anatoliennes Georges Dumezil.

Piggott, S.

1968   The Earliest Wheeled Vehicles and the Caucasian Evidence. *Proceedings of the Prehistoric Society* 34:266–318.

Pigott, V.C.

1977   Question of the Presence of Iron in the Iron I Period in Western Iran. In *Mountains and Lowlands: Essays in the Archaeology of Greater Mesopotamia*, edited by L.D. Levine and T. C. Young Jr., pp. 209–234, Malibu, CA: Undena.

1980   The Iron Age in the Western Iran. In *The Coming of the Age of Iron*, edited by T. A. Wertime and J. D. Muhly, pp. 417–461, New Haven, CT: Yale University Press.

Piotrovskii, B. B.

1949   *Arkheologiya Zakavkaz'ia*. Leningrad: Leningrad University Press.

1967   *Urartu. The Kingdom of Van and its Art*. London: Evelyn Adams and Mackay.

1969   *Urartu*. Geneva: Nagel.

1989   Skify i Urartu. *Vestnik Drevnej Istorii* 4 : 3–10.

Piotrovskii B. B. and L. T. Gyuzal'yan

1933   Kreposti Armenii Dourartskogo i Urartskogo Vremeni. *Problemy Istorii Material'noy Kul'tury* 5–6:51–59.

Pirtskhalava, M.

1995   Monuments of Scythian Culture in Georgia. *Archäologischer Anzeiger* 1:53–62.

Pitskhelauri, K. N.

1979   *Vostochnaia Gruzia v Kontse Bronzovogo Veka*. Tbilisi: Metsniereba.

1984   The Principles of Topography of Kakheti Bronze Age Settlements. *Proceedings of the Kakheti Archaeological Expedition*, VI:8–20. Tbilisi: Metsniereba.

Plashchev, A. and V. Chekmarev

1978   *Gidrografiya SSSR*. Leningrad: Gidrometeoizdat.

Pleiner, R.

1967   The Beginnings of the Iron Age in Ancient Persia. *Annals of the Naprstek Museum* 6:9–72.

Plutarch

1914   *Lives*. Translated by B. Perrin. Cambridge, MA: Harvard University Press.

Pogrebova, M. N.

1977   *Iran i Zakavkaz'e v Rannem Zheleznom Veke*. Moscow: Nauka.

1984   *Zakavkaz'e i Ego Svyazi s Perednej Aziej v Skifskoe Vremya*. Moscow: Nauka.

Pogrebova, M. N. and D. S. Raevskii

1997   *Zakavkazskie Bronzovye Poyasa s Gravirovannymi Izobrazheniyami*. Moscow: Vostochnaya Literatura.

Polanyi, K.

1971   *Primitive, Archaic, and Modern Economies: Essays of Karl Polanyi*. Boston: Beacon Press.

Porada, E.

1959   The Hasanlu Bowl. *Expedition* 1 (3): 19–22.

Puturidze, M.

1983a   *Kul'turi Epokhi Drevnei Bronzi Tsentralnogo i Vostochnogo Zakavkaz'ia i eo Lokalnie Varianti (Trialetskaya Kultura)*. Ph.D. dissertation, Tbilisi.

1983b   The Middle Bronze Age Burial from Gumbati. In *Dzeglis Megobari* 63:55–58.

1991   Traditsii i Innivatsii Srednego Bronzovogo Veka Trialetskoj Kul'turi. In *Kavkaz v Sisteme Paleometalicheskikh Kultur Evrazii*, pp. 208–220. Tbilisi: Metsniereba.

Ramsey, C. B.

2000   OxCAL. 3.5 ed. University of Oxford Radiocarbon Accelerator Unit, Oxford.

Rapp, G., Jr., J. Zhychun, and R. Rothe

1996   Using Instrumental Neutron Activation Analysis (INAA) to Source Ancient Tin (Cassiterite). *Abstracts of the International Symposium on Archaeometry, May 20–24, 1996*, 87. Urbana: University of Illinois.

Rassamakin, Y.

1999   The Eneolithic of the Black Sea Steppe: Dynamics of Cultural and Economic Development 4500–2300 BC. In *Late Prehistoric Exploitation of the Eurasian Steppe*, edited by M. Levine, Y. Rassamakin, A. Kislenko, and N. Tatarintseva, pp. 59–182. Cambridge: McDonald Institute Monographs.

Renfrew, C.

1975   Trade as Action at a Distance: Questions of Integration and Communication. In *Ancient Civilization and Trade*, edited by J. A. Sabloff and C. C. Lamberg-Karlovsky, pp. 3–59. Albuquerque: University of New Mexico Press.

1986   Varna and the Emergence of Wealth in Prehistoric Europe. In *The Social Life of Things*, edited by A. Appadurai, pp. 141–168. Cambridge: Cambridge University Press.

1987   *Archaeology and Language*. Cambridge: Cambridge University Press.

Rezepkin, A. D.

1991   Kul'turno-Khronologicheskie Aspekty Proiskhozhdeniya i Razvitiya Maikopskoi Kul'turi. In *Maikopskii Phenomenon v Drevney Istorii Kavkaza i Vostochnoi Evropy*. Leningrad: Nauka.

Rice, T.

1961   *The Seljuks in Asia Minor*. London: Thames and Hudson.

Rothman M. S.

1987   Graph Theory and the Interpretation of Regional survey Data. *Paléorient* 13/2:73–92.

1992   Preliminary Report on the Archaeological Survey in the Alpaslan Dam Reservoir Area and Muş Plain. *Araştırma Sonuçları Toplantısı* X, pp. 269–278. Ankara: TC Kültür Bakanlığı.

1993   Another Look at the 'Uruk Expansion' from the Tigris Piedmont. In *Between the Rivers and Over the Mountains*, edited by M. Frangipane, H. Hauptmann, M. Liverani, P. Matthiae, and M. Mellink, pp. 163–177. Rome: Universita di Roma.

1994a   The Pottery of the Muş Plain and the Evolving Place of a High Border Land, X *Araştırma Sonuçları Toplantısı*, pp. 281–294. Ankara: TC Kültür Bakanlığı.

1994b   The View from the Highland Border Lands. Paper delivered at the Society for American Archaeology Annual Meeting, Anaheim, CA.

2000   Environmental and Cultural Factors in the Development of Settlement in a Marginal, Highland Zone in *The Archaeology of Jordan and Beyond: Essays in Honor of James A. Sauer*, edited by L.E. Stager, J.A. Greene, and M.D. Coogan, pp. 429–43. Winona Lake, IN: Eisenbrauns.

2003   Style Zones and Adaptations along the Turkish-Iranian Borderland. In *Yeki Bud, Yeki Nabud: Essays on the Archaeology of Iran in Honor of William M. Sumner*, edited by N. Miller and K. Abdi, pp. 207–216. Los Angeles: Cotsen Institute of Archaeology Press.

Rothman, M. S. (editor)

2001   *Uruk Mesopotamia and its Neighbors: Cross-cultural Interactions in the Era of State Formation*. Santa Fe: SAR Press.

Rothman, M. S., R. Ergeç, N. Miller, J. Weber, G. Kozbe

1998   *Yarim Höyük and the Uruk Expansion*. Part I. Anatolica XXIV:65–99.

Rothman, M. S. and G. Fueusanta

in press   The Early Bronze I/II Period in Southeastern Turkey and North Syria. In *Esiu Festschrift*, edited by M. Özdoğan.

Rothman, M. S. and G. Kozbe

1997   Muş in the Early Bronze Age. *Anatolian Studies* XLVII: 105–126.

Rouse, I.

1986   *Migrations in Prehistory*. New Haven: Yale University Press.

Rowton, M. B.

1967   The Woodlands of Ancient Western Asia. *Journal of Near East Studies* 26:261–277.

Rubinson, K .S.

1976   The Trialeti Culture, Ph.D dissertation, Department of Art History and Archaeology, Columbia University. Ann Arbor, MI: University Microfilms.

1977   The Chronology of the Trialeti Culture. In *Mountains and Lowlands: Essays in The Archaeology of Greater Mesopotamia*, edited by L. D. Levine and T. C. Young, Jr., 235–249. Bibliotheca Mesopotamica, 7. Malibu: Undena Publications.

1991a   Mid-Second Millennium Pontic-Aegean Connections: A Note. In *Ancient Economy in Mythology*, edited by M. Silver, 283–286. Totowa, NJ: Rowman & Littlefield Publishers, Inc.

1991b   A Mid-Second Millennium Tomb at Dinkha Tepe. *American Journal of Archaeology* 95/3:373–394.

1994   Eastern Anatolia Before the Iron Age: A View from Iran. In *Anatolian Iron Ages 3, The Proceedings of the Third Anatolian Iron Ages Colloquium held at Van, 6–12 August 1990*, edited by A. Çilingiroğlu and D.H. French, pp. 199–203. Ankara: The British Institute of Archaeology.

1999   A Note on the Trialeti Goblet. In *National Treasures of Georgia*, edited by O. Z. Soltes, 66. London: Philip Wilson Publishers and The Foundation for International Arts and Education.

2001   Metal Vessels with Basket Handles at Trialeti. In *Caucasus: Essays on the Archaeology of the Neolithic-Bronze Age (Dedicated to the 80ᵗʰ Birthday of Prof. Otar Japaridze)*, edited by B. Maisuradze and R. Rusishvili, pp. 123–124. *Dziebani*, Supplement VI. Tbilisi: The Centre for Archaeological Studies of the Georgian Academy of Sciences.

in press   Over the Mountains and Through the Grass: Visual Information as "Text" for the "Textless," edited by D. Peterson, L. Popova, and A. T. Smith. In *Beyond the Steppe and the Sown: Proceedings of the 2002 University of Chicago Conference of Eurasian Archaeology*. Colloquia Pontica. Leiden: Brill.

Saggs, H.F.W.

1962   *The Greatness that was Babylon*. New York: Mentor Books.

Sağlamtimur, H, G. Kozbe, and Ö. Çevik

2001   Small Finds. In *Ayanis I*, edited by A. Çilingiroğlu and M. Salvini, 219–250. Rome: Instituto Per Gli Studi Micenei Ed Egeo-Anatolici.

Sagona, A.

1984   *The Caucasian Region in the Early Bronze Age*. Oxford: BAR International Series 214.

1992   Bayburt Survey 1991. *Araştırma Sonuçları Toplantısı X*. pp. 261–268. Ankara: TC Kültür Bakanlığı.

1994   *The Aşvan Sites 3. Early Bronze Age Rescue Excavations, Eastern Anatolia*, BIAA Monograph18, Ankara: British Institute of Archaeology at Ankara.

1998   Social Identity and Religious Ritual in the Kura-Araxes Cultural Complex: Some Observations from Sos Höyük. *Mediterranean Archaeology* 11:13–25.

2000   Sos Höyük and the Erzurum Region in Late Prehistory: A Provisional Chronology for Northeast Anatolia. In *Chronologies des Pays du Caucase et de l'Euphrate aux IVe–IIIe Millenaires: Actes du Colloque d'Istanbul, 16–19 Décembre 1998*, edited by C. Marro and H. Hauptmann, pp. 329–373. Paris: Institut Francais d'Études Anatoliennes Georges Dumezil.

Sagona, A. G., M. Erkmen, C. Sagona, and S. Howells

1997   Excavations at Sos Höyük, 1996: Third Preliminary Report. *Anatolica* 23:181–226.

Sagona, A. G., M. Erkmen, C. Sagona, I. McNiven, and S. Howells

1998   Excavations at Sos Höyük, 1997: Fourth Preliminary Report. *Anatolica* 24:31–64.

Sagona, A. G., M. Erkmen, C. Sagona, and I. Thomas

1996   Excavations at Sos Höyük 1995: Second Preliminary Report. *Anatolian Studies* 46:27–52.

Sagona, A. G., E. Pemberton, and I. McPhee

1992   Excavations at Böyük Höyük, 1992. *Anatolian Studies* 43:70–83.

Sagona, A. G. and C. Sagona

forthcoming   *Archaeology at the North-East Anatolia Frontier*, vol 1. Louvain: Peeters.

Sagona, C.

1999   A Survey of the Erzurum Province, 1999: The Region of Pasinler. *Ancient Near Eastern Studies* 36:108–31.

Sahlins, M. D.

1972   *Stone Age Economics*. New York: Aldine de Gruyter.

Sahlins, M. D. and E. Service

1960   *Evolution and Culture*. Ann Arbor: University of Michigan Press.

Salvini, M.

1967   Nairi e Ur(u)atri. *Incunabula Graeca* 16.

1977   Eine Neue Urartäische Inschrift aus Mahmud Abad (West Azerbaidjan). *Archäologische Mitteilungen aus Iran* 10:125–136.

1984a   La Storia della Regione in Epoca Urartea. In *Tra lo Zagros e l'Urmia. Ricerche Storiche ed Archeologiche nell'Azerbaigian Iraniano*, edited by Pecorella P. E., and M. Salvini, pp. 9–51. Roma: Edizioni dell'Ateneo.

1984b   I documenti. In *Tra lo Zagros e l'Urmia. Ricerche Storiche ed Archeologiche nell'Azerbaigian Iraniano*, edited by P. E. Pecorella and M. Salvini, pp. 55–96. Edizioni dell'Ateneo, Roma.

1995   *Geschichte und Kultur der Urartäer*. Darmstadt: Wissenschaftliche Buchgesellschaft.

2001   The Inscriptions of Ayanis. Cuneiform and Hieroglyphic. In *Ayanis I*, edited by A. Çilingiroğlu and M. Salvini, pp. 251–319. Rome: Instituto Per Gli Studi Micenei Ed Egeo-Anatolici.

Sams, G. K.

1994   *The Early Phrygian Pottery*. University Museum Monograph 79. The Gordion Excavations, 1950–1983: Final Reports Volume IV Illustrations. Philadelphia: The University Museum, University of Philadelphia.

Sanamyah H.

2002   The Fortresses of Tsovinar (Obzaberd), "The City of God Teisheba." In *The North-Eastern Frontier. Urartians and non-Urartians in the Sevan Lake Basin I. The Southern Shores*, edited by Biscione R., S. Hmayakyan, and N. Parmegiani, pp. 319–324. Rome: Instituto di Studi sulle Civilta dell'Egeo e del Vicino Oriente.

Santrot, J.

1996   *Arménie*. Paris: Somogy Editions d'Art and Nantes: Musée Dobrée-Conseil Général de Loire-Atlantique.

Sardarian, S. A.

1967   *Pervobytnoe Obshchestvo v Armenii*. Yerevan: Akademii Nauk Armianskoi SSR.

Schaeffer, C.F.A.

1943   La Date des Kourganes de Trialeti. *Antiquity XVII*: 183–187.

1944a   Archaeological Discoveries in Trialeti-Caucasus. *Journal of the Royal Asiatic Society*: 25–29.

1944b   In the Wake of the "Argo." *Man XLIV*: 43–45.

1948   *Stratigraphie Comparée et Chronologie de l'Asie Occidentale*. London: Oxford University Press.

Scott, D.

1991   *Metallography and Microstructures of Ancient and Historic Metals*. Malibu: J. Paul Getty Museum.

Seeher, J.

1992   Die Nekropole von Demircihuyuk-Sariket. *Istanbuler Mitteilungen* 42:5–19.

Selimkhanov, I.R.

1978   Ancient Tin Objects of the Caucasus and the Results of their Analyses. In *The Search for Ancient Tin*, edited by Franklin, J. S. Olin, and T. Wertime, 53–58. Washington DC: Smithsonian Institution Press.

Service, E. R.

1962   *Primitive Social Organization*. New York: Random House.

1975   *Origins of the State and Civilization*. New York: Norton.

Sevin, V.

1987   Urartu Oda-Mezar Mimarisinin Kökeni Üzerine Bazi Gözlemler. In *Anatolian Iron Ages* I, edited by A. Çilingiroğlu, pp. 35–55. Izmir: Ege Üniversitesi Edebiyat Fakültesi.

1991   The Southwestward Expansion of Urartu: New Observations. In *Anatolian Iron Ages, The Proceedings of the Second Anatolian Iron Ages Colloquium held at Izmir, 4–8 May 1987*, edited by A. Çilingiroğlu and D. H. French, pp. 97–112. Oxford: Oxbow.

1996a   Van/Ernis (Ünseli) Nekropolü Erken Demir Çağ Çanak Çömlekleri. *Jaahrbuch für Kleinasiatische Forschung XIV*: 439–467.

1996b   La Céramique de l'âge du Fer Ancien dans la Région de Van (Turquie de l'est). *Orient Express* 3:89–91.

1999a   The Origins of the Urartians in the Light of the Van/Karagündüz Excavations. *Anatolian Studies* 49:159–164.

1999b   Hakkari'nin Çiplak Krallari. *Atlas* 79:70–86.

2000   Mystery Stelae. *Archaeology* 53(4): 47–51.

2001   The Hakkari Stelae: A Nomadic Impact on the River Zap. *TÜBA-AR Turkish Academy of Sciences Journal of Archaeology* 4:79–88.

Sevin, V. and E. Kavaklı

1996a   *Van/Karagündüz. An Early Iron Age Cemetery*. Arkeoloji ve Sanat Yayınları.

1996b   Van/Karagündüz Erken Demir Çağı Nekropolü. *Belleten* 227:1–20.

Sevin, V., E. Kavaklı, and A. Özfırat

1997   Karagündüz Höyügü ve Nekropol, 1995–1996 Yili Kurtarma Kazılari. *XIX. Kazı Sonuçları Toplantısı* I, Ankara, pp. 571–589.

Sevin, V. and A. Özfırat

1998   Anadolu'da Yeni Bir Uygarlik/Hakkari Stelleri: Hubuskia Prensleri. *Arkeoloji ve Sanat* 87:6–9.

2000   Van-Karagündüz Kazıları. In *Türkiye Arkeolojisi ve İstanbul Üniversitesi*, edited by O. Belli, pp. 168–174. Ankara: Arkeoloji ve Sanat Yayınları.

Sevin,V., A. Özfırat, and E.Kavaklı

2000 Karagündüz Höyügü Kazılari (1997 Yili Calismalari). *Belleten* 238:847–867.

2001 1997–1999 Hakkari Kazılari. *22. Kazı Sonuçları Toplantısı* I: 355–368.

Shamba, G. K.

1980 *Esherskoe Gorodishche.* Tbilisi: Metsniereba.

Shefton, B. B.

1993 The White Lotus, Rogozen and Colchis: The Fate of a Motif. In *Cultural Transformations and Interactions in Eastern Europe*, edited by J. Chapman and P. Dolukhanov, pp. 178–209. Worldwide Archaeology Series 6. Alershot: Ashgate Publishing Company.

Shennan, S.

1993 After Social Evolution: A New Archaeological Agenda? In *Archaeological Theory: Who Sets the Agenda?*, edited by N. Yoffee and A. Sherrat, pp. 53–59. Cambridge: Cambridge University Press.

Sherratt, A.

1993 "Who are You Calling Peripheral?" Dependence and Independence in European Prehistory. In *Trade and Exchange in Prehistoric Europe*, edited by C. Scarre and F. Healy, pp. 245–255. Oxford: Oxbow Books.

Simmel, G.

1978 *The Philosophy of Money.* London: Routledge.

Smith, A.

1937 *An Inquiry into the Nature and Causes of the Wealth of Nations.* New York: Random House.

Smith, A. T.

1996 *Imperial Archipelago: The Making of the Urartian Landscape in Southern Transcaucasia.* Ph.D. Dissertation, University of Arizona. Ann Arbor: University Microfilms.

1998 Late Bronze/Early Iron Age Fortresses of the Ararat and Shirak Plains, Armenia: Typological Considerations. *Ancient Civilizations from Scythia to Siberia* 5 (2): 73–97.

1999 The Making of an Urartian Landscape in Southern Transcaucasia: A Study of Political Architectonics. *American Journal of Archaeology* 103(1): 45–71

2000 Rendering the Political Aesthetic: Ideology and Legitimacy in Urartian Representations of the Built Environment. *Journal of Anthropological Archaeology* 19:131–163.

2001 The Limitations of Doxa: Agency and Subjectivity from an Archaeological Point of View. *Journal of Social Archaeology* 1(2): 155–171.

Smith, A. T., R. Badalyan, and P. Avetisyan

1999 The Crucible of Complexity. *Discovering Archaeology* 1(2): 48–55.

Soltes, O. Z. (editor)

1999 *National Treasures of Georgia.* London: Philip Wilson Publishers Limited.

Sorokin, V. S.

1952 Archeologičeskie Dannye Dlja Characteristiki Social'no-Ëkonomičeskogo Stroja Urartu. *Vestnik Drevnej Istorii* 2:127–132.

Southall, A.

1965 A Critique of the Typology of States and Political Systems. In *Political Systems and the Distribution of Power*, pp. 113–140. A.S.A. Monographs 2. New York: Frederick A. Praeger.

1991 The Segmentary State: From the Imaginary to the Material Means of Production. In *Early State Economics*, edited by H. Claessen and P. van de Velde, pp. 75–96. New Brunswick: Transaction Publishers.

Stark, M. T. (editor)

1998 *The Archaeology of Social Boundaries.* Washington D.C.: Smithsonian Institution Press.

Stech, T., and V. Piggott

1986 The Metals Trade in Southwest Asia in the Third Millennium B.C. *Iraq* 48:39–64.

Stein, A.

1940 *Old Routes of Western Iran.* New York: Macmillan.

Stein, G.

1998a World Systems Theory and Alternative Models of Interaction in the Archaeology of Culture Contact. In *Studies in Culture Contact: Interaction, Culture Change, and Archaeology*, edited by J. G. Cusick, pp. 220–255. Occasional Paper 25. Carbondale, IL: Center for Archaeological Investigations.

1998b Discussion, *Mesopotamia in the Era of State Formation.* Santa Fe: SAR Advanced Seminar.

1999a The Uruk Expansion: Northern Perspectives from Hacınebi, Hassek Höyük, and Gawra. *Paléorient* 25:1.

1999b *Rethinking World Systems.* Tucson: University of Arizona Press.

2001 Indigenous Social Complexity at Hacınebi (Turkey) and the Organization of Colonial Contact in the Uruk Expansion. In *Uruk Mesopotamia and its Neighbors: Cross-Cultural Interactions in the Era of State Formation* edited by M. Rothman, pp. 265–306. Santa Fe: SAR Press.

Stein, G. J., R. Bernbeck, C. Coursey, A. McMahon, N. F. Miller, A. Misir, J. Nicola, H. Pittman, S. Pollock, and H. Wright

1996 Uruk colonies and Anatolian Communities: An Interim Report on the 1992–1993 Excavations at Hacınebi, Turkey. *American Journal of Archaeology* 100 (2): 205–260.

Stone, E. and P. Zimansky

1995 The Tapestry of Power in a Mesopotamian City: The Mashkan-shapir Project, *Scientific American* 272/4:92–97.

2001 Survey and Excavations in the Outer Town of Ayanis 1996–1998. In *Ayanis I: Ten Year's Excavations at Rusahinili Eiduru-kai 1989–1998*, edited by A. Çilingiroğlu and M. Salvini, pp. 355–375. Rome: Istituto per Gli Studi Mecenei ed Egeo-Anatolici.

Stos-Gale, Z. A.

1989 Lead Isotope Studies of Metal and the Metals Trade in the Bronze Age Mediterranean. In *Scientific Analysis in Archaeology*, edited by J. Henderson, pp. 213–236. Oxford: Oxford University Committee for Archaeology Monograph 19.

Stos-Gale, Z. A., N. H. Gale, and G. R. Gilmore

1984 Early Bronze Age Trojan Metal Sources and Anatolians in the Cyclades. *Oxford Journal of Archaeology* 3(3): 23–37.

Stronach, D.

1967 Urartian and Achaemenian Tower Temples. *Journal of Near Eastern Studies* 26:278–288.

Stuiver, M., P. J. Reimer and T. F. Braziunas

1998 High-Precision Radiocarbon Age Calibration for Terrestrial and Marine Samples. *Radiocarbon* 40(3): 1127–1151.

Summers, G.

1982 *A Study of the Architecture, Pottery, and Other Material from Yanık Tepe, Haftavan Tepe VIII and Related Sites*. Dissertation. University of Manchester.

Tainter, J. A.

1988 *The Collapse of Complex Societies*. Cambridge: Cambridge University Press.

Teissier, B.

1984 *Ancient Near Eastern Cylinder Seals from the Marcopoli Collection*. Berkeley: University of California Press.

Tekhov, B. V.

1981 *Tlijskij Mogil'nik (Kompleksy IX—pervoj poloviny VII v. do n.e.) vol. 2*. Tbilisi: Metsniereba.

1985 *Tliskij Mogil'nik (Kompleksy vtoroj poloviny VII–VI v. do n.e.), vol. 3*. Tbilisi: Metsniereba.

Thureau-Dangin, F.

1912 Tablette de Samarra. *Revue d'Assyriologie* 9:1–4.

Tite, M. S.

1996 In Defence of Lead Isotope Analysis. *Antiquity* 70(4): 959–962.

Tolordava, V.

1980 *Dakrdzalvis Tsesebi Elinisturi Khanis Sakartveloshi (Kvevrsamarkhebi)*. Tbilisi: Metsniereba.

Toramanyan, T.

1942 *Nyuter Haykakan Chartarapetutyan Patmutyan*. Yerevan: Haykakan SSR Gitowtyownneri Akademiayi.

Torosian, R.M.

1976 *Teghuti Vagh Erkragortsakan Bnakavairs*. Yerevan: Akademii Nauk Armyanskoj SSR.

Trifonov, V.A.

1994 The Caucasus and the Near East in the Early Bronze Age (Fourth and Third Millennia BC). *Oxford Journal of Archaeology* 13 (3): 157–160.

Trigger, B.

1993 *Early Civilizations: Ancient Egypt in Context*. Cairo: American University in Cairo Press.

Tsetskhladze, G. R.

1991 Die Kolchischen Stempel. *Klio* 73:361–381.

1992 The Cult of Mithras in Ancient Colchis. *Revue de l'Histoire des Religions* CCIX: 115–124.

1993/94 Colchis and the Persian Empire: The Problems of Their Relationship. *Silk Road Art and Archaeology* 3:11–49.

1994 Colchians, Greeks and Achaemenids in the 7th-5th Centuries BC: A Critical Look. *Klio* 76:78–102.

1995 Did the Greeks Go to Colchis for Metals? *Oxford Journal of Archaeology* 14:307–332.

1998 *Die Griechen in der Kolchis (Historisch-archäologischer Abriß)*. Schwarzmeer-Studien 3. Amsterdam: Verlag Adolf M. Hakkert.

1999 Between West and East: Anatolian Roots of Local Cultures of the Pontus. In *Ancient Greeks West and East*, edited by G. R. Tsetskhladze, pp. 469–496. Mnemosyne, bibliotheca classica Batava, Suppl. 196. Leiden: Brill.

2001 Iranian Elements in Georgian Art and Archaeology. *Encyclopaedia Iranica*. X.5:470–480.

Ussishkin, D.

1991 On the Architectural Origin of the Urartian Standard Temples. In *Anatolian Iron Ages, The Proceedings of the Second Anatolian Iron Ages Colloquium held at Izmir, 4–8 May 1987*, edited by A. Çilingiroğlu and D. H. French, pp. 117–130. Oxford: Oxbow.

Uvarova, G.

1900 Mogil'niki Severnago Kavkaza. *Materialy po Arkhologii Kavkaza* 8.

Van De Mieroop, M.

1997 *The Ancient Mesopotamian City*. Oxford: Oxford University Press.

Van den Berghe, L.

1964   *La Nécropole de Khurvin*, Istanbul: Nederlands Historisch-Archaeologisch Instituut in het Nabije Oosten.

1968   *Archeologisch Onderzoek naar de War Kabud (1965 en 1966)*. Brussels: Paleis der Academiën.

1973   Recherches Archeologiques dans le Luristan. Sixtieme campagne: 1970. *Iranica Antiqua* 10:1–79.

van Loon, M.

1974   The Euphrates Mentioned by Sarduri II of Urartu. In *Anatolian Studies Presented to Hans Gustav Güterbock on the Occasion of his 65th Birthday*, edited by K. Bittel, H. J. Hauwink, and E. Reiner, 187–194. Istanbul: Nederlands Historisch-Archaeologisch Instituut in het Nabije Oosten.

1975a   The Inscription of Ishpuini and Menua from Qalatgah, Iran. *Journal of Near Eastern Studies* 34:201–207.

1975b   Die Kunst von Urartu. In *Der Alte Orient*, edited by W. Orthmann, pp. 453–456. Frankfurt: Propylaen.

van Wijngaarden, G.-J.

1999   An Archaeological Approach to the Concept of Value. *Archaeological Dialogues* 6(1): 2–46.

van Zeist, W. and Bottema, S.

1982   Vegetational History of the Eastern Mediterranean and the Near East During the Last 20,000 Years. In *Palaeoclimates, Palaeoenvironments, and Human Communities in the Eastern Mediterranean Region in Later Prehistory*, edited by J. L. Bintliff and W. van Zeist, pp. 277–321. Oxford: British Archaeological Review, International Series 133.

Varazashvili, V. L.

1992   *Rannezemledel'cheskaia Kul'turi Ioro-Alazanskogo Basseina*. Tbilisi: Metsniereba.

Videjko, M.Y.

1995   Grosssiedlungen der Tripol'e Kultur in der Ukraine. *Eurasia Antiqua* I: 45–80.

Voronov, Y. N.

1980   O Khronologicheskikh Svyazyakh Kimmerijsko-Skifskoj i Kolkhidskoj Kul'tur. In *Skifiya i Kavkaz*, pp. 200–218. Kiev: Naukova Dumka.

Wallerstein, I.

1974   *The Modern World System: Capitalist Agriculture and the Origins of the European World-Economy in the Sixteenth Century*. New York: Academic Press.

Wartke, R-B.

1990   *Toprakkale. Untersuchungen zu den Metallobjekten im Vorderasiatischen Museum zu Berlin*. Berlin: Akademie Verlag.

1993   *Urartu: Das Reich am Ararat*. Mainz: Verlag Philipp von Zabern.

Weeks, L.

1999   Lead Isotope Analysis from Tell Abraq, United Arab Emirates: New Data Regarding the Tin Problem in Western Asia. *Antiquity* 73(1): 49–64.

Weiss, H., M. A. Courty, W. Wetterstrom, F. Guichard, L. Senior, R. Meadow, and A. Curnow

1993   The Genesis and Collapse of 3rd Millennium North Mesopotamian Civilization. *Science* 261:995–1004.

Whallon, R.

1979   *An Archaeological Survey of the Early Bronze Agean Reservoir Area of East-Central Turkey*. Memoir 11. Museum of Anthropology. Ann Arbor: University of Michigan.

Wilson, J. V. K.

1962   The Kurba'il Statue of Shalmaneser III. *Iraq* 24:90–115.

Winter, I. J.

1980   *A Decorated Breastplate from Hasanlu, Iran: Type, Style, and the Context of an Equestrian Ornament*. University Museum Monograph 39. Hasanlu Special Studies I. Philadelphia: The University Museum, University of Pennsylvania.

1989   The "Hasanlu Gold Bowl": Thirty Years Later. *Expedition* 31 (2–3): 87–106.

Wittfogel, K. A.

1957   *Oriental Despotism: A Comparative Study of Total Power*. New Haven: Yale University Press.

Wolff, J.

1984   *The Social Production of Art*. New York: New York University Press.

Wright, H.

1977   Recent Research on the Origin of the State. *Annual Review of Anthropology* 6:379–397.

1978   Toward an Explanation of the Origin of the State. In *Origins of the State: The Anthropology of Political Evolution*, edited by R. Cohen and E. R. Service, pp. 49–68. Philadelphia: Institute for the Study of Human Issues.

Xenophon

1972   *The Persian Expedition*. Harmondsworth: Penguin Books.

Yakar, Jak

1985   *The Later Prehistory of Anatolia: The Late Chalcolithic and Early Bronze Age*. Oxford: BAR International Series 268 (ii).

Yener, K. A.

2000   *The Domestication of Metals: The Rise of Complex Metal Industries in Anatolia*. Leiden: Brill.

Yener, K. A., H. Özbal, E. Kaptan, A. N. Pehlivan, and M. Goodway

1989   Kestel: An Early Bronze Age Source of Tin Ore in the Taurus Mountains, Turkey. *Science* 244:200-203.

Yener, K. A. and P. Vandiver

1993   Tin Processing at Göltepe, An Early Bronze Age Site in Anatolia. *American Journal of Archaeology* 97(2): 207–238.

Yıldırım, R.

1991   Urartian Belt Fragments from Burmageçit, Now on Display in Elazığ Museum. In *Anatolian Iron Ages, The Proceedings of the Second Anatolian Iron Ages Colloquium held at Izmir, 4–8 May 1987,* edited by A. Çilingiroğlu and D. H. French, pp. 131–148. Oxford: Oxbow.

Young, J.

1978   *Classical Theories of Value from Smith to Sraffa.* Boulder: Westview Press.

Zimansky, P.

1985   *Ecology and Empire: The Structure of the Urartian State.* Chicago: Oriental Institute Press.

1990   Urartian Geography and Sargon's Eighth Campaign. *Journal of Near Eastern Studies* 49(1):1–21.

1995   Urartian Material Culture as State Assemblage: An Anomaly in the Archaeology of Empire. *Bulletin of the American Schools of Oriental Research* 299/ 300:103–115.

2001   Archaeological Inquiries into Ethno-Linguistic Diversity in Urartu. In *Greater Anatolia and the Indo-Hittite Language Family: Papers Presented at a Colloquium Hosted by the University of Richmond: March 18–19, 2000,* edited by Robert Drews, 14-27. Washington, D.C: Institute for the Study of Man.

Zkitischwili, G.

1995   Der Frühhellenistische Feuertempel von Kawtiskhewi. *Archäologischer Anzeiger* 1:83–98.

Zograbyan, L. N.

1979   *Orografia Armyanskogo Nagor'ya.* Yerevan: Akademii Nauk Armyanskoj SSR.

Zucconi A.

1993   Un'applicazione dell'Informatica alla Ricerca Archeologica: Ricostruzione dello Schema di Amministrazione Territoriale nella Piana di Urmia (Azerbaijan Iraniano) in Periodo Urarteo Mediante il Sistema Informativo Geografico (G.I.S.). Unpublished *Diploma* dissertation, Scuola Speciale di Informatica. Roma: Università di Roma I 'La Sapienza.'

Contributors

PAVEL S. AVETISYAN
Institute of Archaeology and Ethnography
Academy of Sciences
Yerevan, Armenia

RUBEN S. BADALYAN
Institute of Archaeology and Ethnography
Academy of Sciences
Yerevan, Armenia

RAFFAELE BISCIONE
Instituto di Studi sulle Città dell`Egeo e del
Vicino Oriente
Consiglio Nazionale Delle Richerche
Rome, Italy

ALTAN ÇİLİNGİROĞLU
Department of Protohistory and
Near Eastern Archaeology
Ege University
Izmir, Turkey

TAMAZ KIGURADZE (deceased)
Georgia State Museum
Tbilisi, Georgia

PHILIP L. KOHL
Department of Anthropology
Wellesley College
Wellesley, Massachusetts

DAVID L. PETERSON
Department of Anthropology
University of Chicago
Chicago, Illinois

MARINA PUTURIDZE
Centre For Archaeological Studies
Georgian Academy of Sciences
Tbilisi, Georgia

MITCHELL S. ROTHMAN
Department of Anthropology and Archaeology
Widener University
Chester, Pennsylvania

KAREN S. RUBINSON
Department of Anthropology
Barnard College
New York City, New York

ANTONIO SAGONA
Centre for Classics and Archaeology
University of Melbourne
Melbourne, Australia

VELİ SEVİN
Yüzüncü Yıl Universitesi
Fen-Edebiyat Fakültesi
Arkeoloji Bölümü
Van, Turkey

ADAM T. SMITH
Department of Anthropology
University of Chicago
Chicago, Illinois

ELIZABETH C. STONE
Department of Anthropology
SUNY–Stony Brook
Stony Brook, New York

GOCHA R. TSETSKHLADZE
Centre for Classics and Archaeology
University of Melbourne
Melbourne, Australia

PAUL ZIMANSKY
Department of Archaeology
Boston University
Boston, Massachusetts